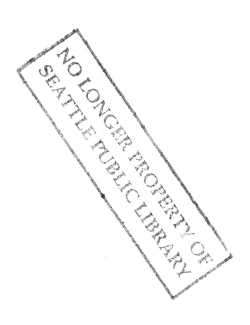

THE DISASTER RECOVERY HANDBOOK

SECOND EDITION

THE DISASTER RECOVERY HANDBOOK

SECOND EDITION

*A Step-by-Step Plan to
Ensure Business Continuity
and Protect Vital Operations,
Facilities, and Assets*

MICHAEL WALLACE
LAWRENCE WEBBER

AMACOM American Management Association
New York • Atlanta • Brussels • Chicago • Mexico City • San Francisco
Shanghai • Tokyo • Toronto • Washington, D.C.

Bulk discounts available. For details visit:
www.amacombooks.org/go/specialsales
Or contact special sales:
Phone: 800-250-5308
Email: specialsls@amanet.org
View all the AMACOM titles at:
www.amacombooks.org

Library of Congress Cataloging-in-Publication Data

Wallace, Michael
The disaster recovery handbook : a step-by-step plan to ensure business
    continuity and protect vital operations, facilities, and assets /
    Michael Wallace, Lawrence Webber. — 2nd ed.

    p. cm.
    Includes bibliographical references and index.
    ISBN-13: 978-0-8144-1613-6
    ISBN-10: 0-8144-1613-6
1. Emergency management—Handbooks, manuals, etc.   2. Crisis
management—Handbooks, manuals, etc.   3. Computer security—Handbooks,
manuals, etc.   4. Data protection—Handbooks, manuals, etc.   5. Data
recovery (Computer science)—Planning—Handbooks, manuals, etc.   6.
Business planning—Handbooks, manuals, etc. I. Webber, Larry.
II. Title.

    HD49.W36 2010
    658.4'77—dc22

        2010010633

About AMA
American Management Association (www.amanet.org) is a world leader in talent development, advancing the skills of individuals to drive business success. Our mission is to support the goals of individuals and organizations through a complete range of products and services, including classroom and virtual seminars, webcasts, webinars, podcasts, conferences, corporate and government solutions, business books and research. AMA's approach to improving performance combines experiential learning—learning through doing—with opportunities for ongoing professional growth at every step of one's career journey.

Printing number

10 9 8 7 6 5 4 3 2 1

CONTENTS

CHAPTER 1   Getting Started: Overview of the Project   1

CHAPTER 2   Building the Business Case: Measuring the Impact on the Business   23

CHAPTER 3   Evaluating Risk: Understanding What Can Go Wrong   35

CHAPTER 4   Selecting a Strategy: Setting the Direction   71

CHAPTER 5   Build an Interim Plan: Don't Just Sit There, Do Something   85

CHAPTER 6   Writing the Plan: Getting It Down on Paper   101

CHAPTER 7   Administrative Plan: Orchestrating the Recovery   115

CHAPTER 8   Crisis Management Plan: Minimizing the Damage   133

CHAPTER 9   Technical Recovery Plan: Putting Humpty Dumpty Back Together Again   149

CHAPTER 10   Work Area Recovery Plan: Getting the Office Up and Running   165

CHAPTER 11   Pandemic Plan   179

CHAPTER 12   Emergency Operations Center: Take Control of the Situation   199

CHAPTER 13   Testing Your Plans: Test, Test, Test   221

CHAPTER 14   Electrical Service: Keeping the Juice Flowing   249

CHAPTER 15   Telecommunications and Networking: Your Connection to the World   267

CHAPTER 16 **Vital Records Recovery: Covering Your Assets**   **291**

CHAPTER 17 **Data: Your Most Irreplaceable Asset**   **315**

CHAPTER 18 **Workstations: The Weakest Link**   **335**

CHAPTER 19 **Customers: Other People to Worry About**   **349**

CHAPTER 20 **Suppliers: Collateral Damage**   **355**

CHAPTER 21 **Fire: Burning Down the House**   **365**

CHAPTER 22 **Human Resources: Your Most Valuable Asset**   **381**

CHAPTER 23 **Health and Safety: Keeping Everyone Healthy**   **399**

CHAPTER 24 **Terrorism: The Wrath of Man**   **413**

Index   **423**

About the Authors   **439**

CHAPTER 1

GETTING STARTED
Overview of the Project

Nothing is impossible for the man
who doesn't have to do it himself.
—A.H. Weiler

INTRODUCTION

The job of a business executive requires coordination of the many activities necessary to create a successful business. Markets must be analyzed, potential customers identified, strategies for creating and delivering products and services must be developed, financial goals established and reported, legislative mandates followed, and many different stakeholders satisfied. To ensure that all of these objectives are met, businesses eventually develop a series of processes designed to produce the desired result. But the world is a dangerous place. Earthquakes, floods, tornadoes, pandemics, snow storms, fire, and other natural disasters can strike at any time and interrupt these important processes. Terrorism, riots, arson, sabotage, and other human-created disasters can also damage your business. Accidents and equipment failures are guaranteed to happen. As an executive responsible for the well-being of your organization, it is critical that you have a plan in place to ensure that your business can continue its operations after such a disaster and to protect vital operations, facilities, and assets.

You do this just like you do any other important task; you analyze the situation and create a plan. A disaster recovery plan keeps you in business after a disaster by helping to minimize the damage and allowing your organization to recover as quickly as possible. While you can't prevent every disaster, you can with proper planning mitigate the damage and get back to work quickly and efficiently. The key is having a well thought out and up-to-date disaster recovery plan. This chapter will lead you through the creation and implementation of a project plan for creating an effective disaster recovery plan.

THE DISASTER RECOVERY PLAN PROJECT

Building a disaster recovery or business continuity plan is much like any other business project. A formal project management process is necessary to coordinate the various players and company disciplines required to successfully deliver the desired results of the project. This chapter will give you a high-level roadmap of what you should expect as you prepare to lead or manage a disaster recovery project. A sample project plan is included on the CD-ROM accompanying this book. Adapt this chapter and the project plan to fit your business goals, company timeline, and scope of project.

Most projects tend to run in a well-defined sequence. For example, to build a new house, first you clear the land, then build the foundation, then build a floor, and so on. Many things cannot begin until the previous step is completed. A business continuity plan (BCP) project is a bit different. In its early stages, most actions logically follow each other. However, once the basic elements are in place, the project bursts out on to parallel tracks, as each department documents its own area. How you proceed in your company is, of course, determined by your corporate culture, the resources you have to work with to complete the process, and the level of visible support from the project's sponsor. Most business continuity projects follow these steps:

1. An executive within the organization decides that a business continuity plan is needed. This might be due to an auditor's report or the result of a business disruption that was more painful than it would have been if a plan had been in place. Or it could be that an alert employee realized that a good plan did not exist and brought this to the executive's attention. This executive normally becomes the *sponsor* for the project.

2. The first (and most important) step that the sponsor takes is to select someone to lead the project. This person is most often called the *Business Continuity Manager* and is responsible for the successful completion of the project.

3. The project sponsor and the Business Continuity Manager meet to clearly define the scope of the project, the project timeline, and expectations. The Business Continuity Manager must be comfortable that the resources available are adequate to meet all the objectives of the project.

4. The Business Continuity Manager selects the team that will work together to complete the project. Both technical and political considerations are important in selecting a team that can successfully develop a workable business continuity plan.

5. The Business Continuity Manager together with the team now develops the project plan to be used in managing the project. Tasks are identified and assigned, task durations calculated, and activities are sequenced as the project plans are developed.

6. The project plans are executed. The Business Continuity Manager oversees the project as the plan unfolds, keeping everyone focused on completing their

tasks, and ensuring that milestones are met and that important stakeholders are kept informed as to the project's progress. It is here where the actual continuity plans for the organization are created.

7. Once the business continuity plans have been developed and tested, the Business Continuity Manager closes the project by making sure that everything was documented properly and handing the project results over to the individual(s) responsible for keeping the plan up to date. Each affected department will normally have someone responsible for keeping their portion of the plan current. A report is also generated for the sponsor recapping the project and documenting lessons learned.

In many organizations, the job of Business Continuity Manager is not taken as seriously as it should be. Management in these organizations only wants you to write *something,* anything to make the auditors go away. That's OK because as you build the plan, and as they begin to see the benefits, their interest and support will grow.

A project plan organizes the team so members focus their skills on specific actions to get the job done. This respects their time and brings the project to a prompt, but successful, solution.

INITIATING THE PROJECT

Every project starts with a *sponsor.* A sponsor should be a person with enough organizational influence to give the project credibility, financing, and strategic direction. The sponsor should also be in a position to ensure the willing cooperation of other departments and to ensure that the project is adequately funded. Building a business continuity plan in many cases involves changing people's attitudes and some of their tried-and-true business processes. Business continuity planning is a logical step toward mistake-proofing a business. So, to suppress the reluctance to change or even participate in the project, it is important for the sponsor to be of sufficient stature as to overcome objections before they are raised.

Ideally, the sponsor is the company's CEO, or the Vice President in charge of the local facility. However, sometimes it is a department manager who realizes that something must be done. Whoever assumes this role must remain involved with the project throughout its lifetime. *As the sponsor's interest fades, so will the interest of your team.* Find out why they want to sponsor the project. It will tell you how much support to expect.

In some cases, the sponsor honestly believes the project is a good idea and is personally interested in seeing it is completed. In other cases, the sponsor may have been required to start this project due to an auditor's citation of a poor business practice. In this situation, the sponsor may only want the minimum recovery plan to satisfy the audit citation. Spend some time early in the project digging out what is motivating support for this project. By understanding what motivates the sponsor, you can gauge how much time and money will be available to you. It is also possible for you to educate the sponsor on the many advantages in having a well-written company-wide plan.

The sponsor's first task is the selection of the Business Continuity Manager, who will act as the project manager. In most companies, the cynics say that if you raised the issue, then the job is yours! This isn't a bad way to assign projects because only the people who believe in something would raise the issues. Still, the selection of the right Business Continuity Manager will help make this project a success and the wrong one will make success much more difficult to attain.

The sponsor has the additional duties of approving the plan's objectives, scope, and assumptions. The sponsor must also obtain approval for funding.

THE BUSINESS CONTINUITY MANAGER

The selection of the person to spearhead this project is the single most important part of building a plan. The Business Continuity Manager should be someone who can gain the willing cooperation of team members and their supervisors. To help ensure the support of everyone in the organization, the Business Continuity Manager should be publicly assigned to this task with the sponsor's unqualified support. This is essential to overcome internal politics and to let everyone know that their assistance is important and required. As the project moves forward, regular public displays of support are required if the project is to result in a complete and usable plan. Form 1-1 on the CD-ROM is an example of a letter appointing the Business Continuity Manager.

Some sponsors begin a business continuity project by hiring an outside consultant to build the plan. This can be a good way to get the project started and to mentor someone in the organization to assume the Business Continuity Manager position. Generally speaking, it takes more effort and expertise to organize and develop the plan than it does to administer it. As the plan is built, the consultant can teach the Business Continuity Manager the ropes.

Understand that even though the consultant is guiding the project, the consultant should not assume the role of Business Continuity Manager. Every company, every facility, every computer site is unique. The actions necessary to promptly restore service are the result of the key people at each site writing down what to do and how to do it. Outside consultants can provide considerable insight into the basic services (electrical, telephone, water, data processing), but lack in-depth experience at your company. They don't know your business processes. They don't understand the pulse of your business and what its key elements are.

Building a solid plan will take a lot of time. An experienced consultant working with an internal Business Continuity Manager can help move the project along quicker. The Business Continuity Manager is also the logical candidate to become the plan's ongoing administrator once the initial project is completed. This person will be responsible for keeping the plan relevant and current. Writing a plan and then filing it away is a waste of money. Whoever builds the plan will be intimately familiar with it. That person can easily continue responsibility for maintaining it and teaching others how to keep their portion of it current. Using an outside consultant as a Business Continuity Manager raises the possibility that no one has internal ownership to ensure it is updated and tested periodically. The plan must be kept up to date if it is to be useful when it is needed most.

As the plan administrator, the Business Continuity Manager will ensure that as new equipment enters the building, as new products are rolled out, and as new business processes are implemented, they are reflected in the business continuity plan. The Business Continuity Manager also schedules and evaluates the ongoing testing of the plan by department, or by a specific threat, such as the loss of electrical power, to ensure it works. Once the plan is written, the Business Continuity Manager's role will evolve into ensuring the plan is an integral part of the company's ongoing operations. No new company process or piece of equipment should begin operation until the mitigation and recovery plans have been tested and approved.

SCOPE OF THE PROJECT

One of the first tasks the Business Continuity Manager must perform is to come to an agreement with the project sponsor as to the scope of the project. The scope of the project defines its boundaries. It identifies what is included in the project and what is not. If the project is too vast, it will probably fail. If it is too small, then it would be best assigned to a single person like any other office detail. The scope of the project must be given a lot of thought. If in doubt, start with a narrow focus on a specific department or function to demonstrate the plan's value and build up from there. One guideline commonly used is any event that would cost (in lost wages, sales, etc.) more than 5% of your quarterly revenues merits its own plan. So if a temporary outage of a critical machine stops the entire factory, then it needs a plan. If the same machine stoppage means that three extra workers must drill holes with hand tools until the machine is repaired, then it probably does not need a plan.

A good way to approach the plan is to address areas that everyone uses, such as security, data processing, electrical, etc. Don't try to tackle too much, too fast. Start with building services, then security and safety, then data processing, etc. In this way, if the project is killed, you still have some useful documents.

If your recovery plans will encompass many sites, or a large complex, then start with a pilot project for a single building, a business function, or even for your Data Processing department. This will build your team's expertise and confidence, resulting in a very useful document, and demonstrate real value to top management. The scope of the project will drive the resource requirements for the project in terms of how many people it will involve, how long it will take, and the budget required to complete it.

The project scope must be a written statement. Here are three examples with gradually narrowing requirements. As you read these scope statements, imagine what sort of implied tasks these statements carry (or as they say, "The devil is in the details!"). Follow up on the scope statement by clarifying the timelines, criteria for success, and overall expectations for this project. Otherwise, you would be digging up information and writing forever.

Example #1

If you were in a factory's Data Processing department, your scope statement might be:

"Develop, implement, and provide ongoing testing for a business continuity plan for the factory's automated systems to include the computer rooms, the internal and external telephone system, the shop floor control systems, and data connections to both internal and external sites. This plan will provide specific action steps to be taken up to and including emergency replacement of the entire computer and telecommunications rooms."

Note that this statement does not include the factory machines (drill presses, mills, conveyors, etc.) or the front offices. It is focused on the telephone system and the internal data processing processes.

Example #2

If you were the Director for Building Security, your scope might be:

"Write an emergency contingency plan to address the possibility of fire, personal injury, toxic material spill, and structural collapse. Include escalation procedures, emergency telephone numbers, employee education, and specific emergency actions. Make recommendations concerning potential mitigation actions to take before a disaster strikes. Ensure the plan conforms to all legal, regulatory, and insurance requirements."

The project scope described in this statement does not include flood controls, security actions, etc. Although some security tasks may be implied, very little is called for.

Example #3

An even narrower approach might be:

"Document all the payroll procedures and recovery processes to ensure that paychecks are always on time and that the automated vacation balance tracking system is available even during an electrical outage."

Note that this scope statement does not include time clocks, exception reporting, or interfaces with your accounting system.

Most people do not have any idea of what a disaster plan would look like. They imagine some large book just sitting on the shelf. In this situation, you could demonstrate the usefulness of the plan by building it a piece at a time. You might build the part that covers the core utilities for a facility (electricity, gas, telecommunications, water, and heating and air conditioning). As you review with the sponsor how these essential services will be recovered after a disaster, the sponsor will begin to see the usefulness of your work. If your company has multiple sites, it might work better for you to build the plan one site at a time.

Timelines, Major Milestones, and Expectations

The output of a scope statement is to build a list of goals for the project. These are specific results against which the success of the project will be judged. Detail any expectations as to a completion date or major milestone dates. If this project is in response to an internal audit item, then the due date might be when the auditor is scheduled to return. If the Board of Directors required this to be done, then progress reports might be due at every directors meeting. Ensure all key dates are identified and explain why they were selected.

The term "expectations" can also be described as the criteria for success. Be clear in what you are asking for. A business continuity plan should only include critical processes. A critical process is usually defined as a process whose interruption would cause a material financial and operational impact over some period of time that you define (5% or greater of quarterly revenues is standard). You can't plan for what to do down to the front door being stuck open. That level of detail would be too difficult to maintain. Focus on the critical business functions and the processes that support them. Your long-run goal is that the business continuity planning process will become an integral part of how business will be conducted in the future.

Some example criteria for success include:

➤ Every department's continuity plan must provide for employee and visitor safety by detailing to them any dangers associated with this device or type of technology.

➤ Each department's continuity plan must be understandable to anyone familiar with that type of equipment or technology.

➤ A business continuity plan will be submitted for every critical piece of equipment or critical process in the facility.

➤ At the end of the project, the Business Continuity Manager will submit a list of known weaknesses in the processes or equipment along with long-term recommendations to address them.

➤ All continuity plans will be tested by someone other than the plan's author and certified by the department manager as suitable for the purpose.

➤ This project shall commence on June 1 and be completed by December 31. By that time, all plans must be complete, tested and approved by the department managers.

In terms of a timeline, the length of your project will depend on how supportive the team members are of this effort, how complex your operations are, and how detailed your plan must be. Generally, these projects have an initiation phase and then the various departments break off and work in parallel to write their respective plans. During this phase, they also perform initial testing of the plan. At the end, all the plans are compared and modified so as to avoid duplicate mitigation actions and to ensure one person's mitigation step doesn't cause problems for someone else. The capstone event is the system-wide disaster test.

As a general guideline, most plans can be completed in about 6 months, depending on the project's scope, the degree of management support, the number of locations to be included in the plan, and the amount of resources available. One month is spent on the start-up administration and training. About 3 months are needed to draft and test the departmental plans. Be sure to stay on top of these people so they don't forget about their plans! The final synchronization and testing should take an additional 2 months. However, as your team members are probably assigned to this project part time, their level of participation will vary according to their availability. The Business Continuity Manager must be flexible but, in the end, is responsible for driving the project to its completion.

ADEQUATE FUNDING

One of the indicators of the seriousness of a project is the presence of a separate budget item to support its activities. It is the Business Continuity Manager's responsibility to track the funds spent on the project and to demonstrate the benefit they provided. If a separate budget is not available, then clear guidelines on a spending ceiling for the project must be set.

Some of the items to include in the project budget are:

➤ The Business Continuity Manager and key team members should attend formal business continuity planning training to obtain a thorough grounding in its principles. This speeds the project along and removes some of the guesswork of building a plan.

➤ You may need to pay a consultant to advise the project and mentor the Business Continuity Manager as the plan is being developed.

➤ Sometimes the folks with the most knowledge about your processes are not available during normal working hours. For these people, you may need to schedule meetings on weekends or offsite to gain their full attention. This may incur overtime expense or the cost of a consultant to backfill the person while they work on the plan.

➤ Temporary help might be needed for administrative assistance, such as documenting the wiring of your data networks, transcribing notes for those without the time or inclination to type, conducting an asset inventory, etc.

➤ It is amazing what a few pastries brought into a meeting can do for attendance.

➤ It is a good practice to build team spirit for the project to carry you over the rough times. This might be shirts, hats, special dinners, performance bonuses, and many other things to build team cohesion. Visible recognition helps to maintain the team's enthusiasm.

Visible Ongoing Support

If the goal of this project was to determine which employees deserved to have their pay doubled, you would be inundated with folks clamoring to join your team. Unfortunately, an assignment to a business continuity planning team may not be considered a high-profile assignment. This could discourage the enthusiastic support of the very people you need to make this project a success. To minimize this possibility, the visible, vocal, and ongoing support of the sponsor is very important.

Once the sponsor and the Business Continuity Manager have agreed on the scope, the sponsor should issue a formal memo appointing the Business Continuity Manager in a letter to the entire organization. This letter should inform all departments of the initiation of the project and who has been appointed to lead it. It should also describe the project's scope, its budget or budget guidelines, and major milestones and timelines, as well as alert the other departments that they may be called upon to join the project and build their own recovery plans. This memo will detail who, what, where, when, why, and how the project will unfold. The closing paragraph should include a call for their assistance in ensuring the project will be a success.

The sponsor should provide periodic updates to senior management on the progress of this project, which should include milestones met and problems that need to be overcome. Regular visibility to senior management can go a long way toward the continued support of each department with which you'll be working.

SELECTING A TEAM

Once the sponsor and the coordinator have defined the scope of the project, the next step is to create a team. As you begin the project and start selecting your team, be ready for a chorus of resistance. Some departments will be indignant about being forced to join this project since they already have a plan (it's just no one can find it). Even if they have a plan, it does not mean that it is a good plan, or it may have interdependences with other areas and needs to be linked to other plans. Some will already have a plan being developed, but under scrutiny you see it has been under development for the last 10 years.

So, with the naysayers in tow, prepare to select your team. In the case of existing, workable plans, ask that a liaison be appointed. For the plans under development, ask that you be able to enfranchise these hard-working people. As for any parsimonious financial people trying to kill your project's training request, ask the sponsor to override objections and allow the team to attend training on the latest business continuity best practices.

Identify the Stakeholders

As you form your team, take time to identify the project's stakeholders. A stakeholder is anyone who has a direct or indirect interest in the project. Most stakeholders just want to know what is going on with the project. Stakeholders need to be kept regularly informed about the project's progress or problems with which they need to assist.

For all stakeholders, identify their goals and motivation for this project. Based on this list, you will determine what to communicate to them, how often, and by which medium. Some stakeholders' interests are satisfied by a monthly recap report. Some will want to hear about every minor detail. Form 1-2 (see CD) is a Stakeholder Assessment Map. Use it to keep track of what the key stakeholders are after in this project so you do not lose sight of their goals. The strategy is an acknowledgment that you may need to apply some sort of specific attention to a particular person to keep them supporting this important project.

Form the Team

The size and makeup of your team depends on how you will roll out the project. In the very beginning, it is best to start with a small team. Always respect people's time. Don't bring anyone into the project before they are needed. The initial team lays the groundwork for the project by arranging for instructors, coordinating training on building disaster plans, helping to sharpen the focus of what each plan should contain, etc.

The core team should consist of the sponsor, the Business Continuity Manager, an Assistant Business Continuity Manager, and an administrative assistant. This group will prepare standards, training, and processes to make the project flow smoother.

Several other key people will eventually need to join the team. You may want to bring them in early or as they are needed. This may include people such as:

➤ **Building maintenance or facilities manager.** They can answer what mitigation steps are already in place for the structure, fire suppression, electrical service, environmental controls, and other essential services.

➤ **Facility safety and security.** They should already have parts of a disaster plan in terms of fire, safety, limited building and room access, theft prevention, and a host of other issues. If these plans are adequate, this may save you from writing this part of the plan. Be sure to verify that these plans are up to date and of an acceptable quality.

➤ **Labor union representative.** In union shops, the support of the union makes everyone's job easier. Show leadership how a carefully created plan will help keep their members working and they will be very helpful.

➤ **Human resources.** The HR people have ready access to up-to-date information about the individuals who are important to the plan.

➤ **Line management.** These individuals tend to know the most about what is critical for getting the work done in their areas of responsibility.

➤ **Community relations.** A disaster may affect more than just your operations. You may need help from the surrounding community while recovering from a disaster.

➤ **Public information officer.** This is your voice to the outside world. The role is critical in getting accurate information out to customers and vendors when dealing with a disaster.

➤ **Sales and marketing.** These people know your customers the best and can provide insight on what level of service is required before customers begin to fade away.

➤ **Finance and purchasing.** These people know your vendors the best and can provide insight on what kind of support you can expect from vendors while recovering from a disaster.

➤ **Legal.** You need more than just common sense when taking action during an emergency. Your legal team can provide important insight on the legal ramifications of activities performed in response to an emergency.

The next step is to make a few tool standardization decisions. The company's technical support staff usually makes these for you. Announce to the group the standard word processing program, spreadsheet, and, most importantly, the project management software everyone will need on their workstations. Most people have the first two, but few will have the project management software already loaded. Be sure that as people join the team, copies of the software are loaded onto their workstations and training is made available on how to use this tool.

You will get the best results by investing some time training team members on how to write their portion of the plan and providing administrative help if they have a lot of paperwork to write up (such as network wiring plans). Every person reacts differently to a new situation and being assigned to this team is no exception. If you will take the time to assemble a standard format for the plan and a process to follow to write it, then people will be a lot more comfortable being on the team.

A project of this type will generate a lot of paper. If possible, the accumulation of the various plans, wiring diagrams, manuals, etc. should be shifted from the Business Continuity Manager to an administrative assistant. An administrative assistant will also free the Business Continuity Manager from coordinating team meetings, tracking the project costs, etc. Although these tasks are clerical in nature, this person may also be the Assistant Business Continuity Manager. Another value of appointing an Assistant Business Continuity Manager is that it provides a contingency back-up person in case something happens to the Business Continuity Manager, as they will quickly learn about all aspects of the plan.

Once you are ready to roll out the project plan to the world, you will need to pull in representatives from the various departments involved. When tasking the department managers to assign someone, ensure they understand that they are still responsible for having a good plan so that they send the proper person to work on the team. This person need not know every aspect of their department, but they should understand its organization, its critical hardware and software tools, and its major workflows.

Depending on the project's scope, you might end up with someone from every department in the company. This would result in too many people to motivate and keep focused at one time. Break the project down into manageable units. Start with an area you are most familiar with or that needs the most work. Involving too many people in the beginning will result in chaos. Plan on inviting in departments as you begin to review their area. An example is fire safety. Although it touches all departments, it is primarily a Safety/Security department function.

Given all this, just what skills make someone a good team member? An essential skill is knowledge of the department's processes. This allows the team member to write from personal knowledge and experience instead of spending a lot of time researching every point in the plan. Members should also know where to find the details about their departments that they don't personally know. Another useful skill is experience with previous disasters. Even the normal problems that arise in business are useful in pointing out problem areas or documenting what has fixed a problem in the past. And of course, if they are to write a plan, they need good communications skills.

Department managers should appoint a representative to the business continuity planning project team by way of a formal announcement. However, the Business Continuity Manager must approve all team members. If someone with unsuitable qualifications is sent to represent a department, they should be sent back to that manager with a request to appoint someone who is more knowledgeable about that department's processes. When rejecting someone from the team, be sure to inform your sponsor and the originating manager as to why that person is unsuitable.

The people on the initial project team are the logical ones to spread the good word of business continuity planning back to their departments. Time spent educating them on the continuity planning principles and benefits will pay off for the company in the long run. They can also learn more about the company by proofreading the plans submitted by the other departments. This has an additional benefit of broadening the company perspective of a number of employees. Use Form 1-3 (see CD) to map out the responsibilities of each member of the team.

Rolling Out the Project to the Team

Team meetings are an opportunity to bring everyone together so they all hear the same thing at the same time. This is when you make announcements of general interest to everyone. It is also a good time to hear the problems that the team has been encountering and, if time permits, to solicit advice from the other team members on how to approach the issue. A properly managed meeting will keep the team members focused on the project and the project moving forward.

In the beginning, conduct a project rollout meeting with an overview of why this project is important and an explanation of what you are looking for. This is your most critical team-building meeting (you never get a second chance to make a good first impression). In most meetings, you will work to bring out from the people their thoughts and impressions on the project. But at the first meeting, be prepared to do most of the talking. Lay out the roles of each player and set their expectations about participation in the project. Information makes the situation less uncertain and the people can begin to relax. This is your first big chance to teach, cheerlead, and inspire your team! Sell your project to them!

The team members should leave the meeting with a clear idea that this project is of manageable size—not a never-ending spiral of work. Use this meeting and every meeting to informally teach them a bit about business continuity planning.

As the project progresses, you will be surprised how hard it is to get business continuity information out of people. Some people are worried that others will use it to dabble with their systems. Some folks just don't know what they would do in a disaster and intend to ad lib when something happens, just like they always have. Have patience, ask leading questions, and get them to talk. When they have declared their plan complete (and you know it is only a partial plan), conduct a meeting with the team member, their manager, and the sponsor to review the plan. Step through it item by item. By the time that meeting is over, team members will realize that they will be accountable for the quality of their plans.

PLANNING THE PROJECT

Refer to the sample plans included on the CD-ROM for ideas to include in your plan. Any plan that you use must be tailored to your site and management climate. Always keep your plan in a software tool like Microsoft Project. Such programs will recalculate the project's estimated completion date as you note which tasks are complete. It can also be used to identify overallocated resources.

OK, now it is time to build the project plan. This is best done with input from your team. There are four basic processes to building your plan: identifying the activities, estimating how long each task will take, deciding who should do what (or what skills this person should have), and then sequencing the tasks into a logical flow of work. The general term for this is a work breakdown schedule, which describes it quite nicely.

Identifying the Activities

What must be done? Your core project team members can be a great help here by identifying the steps they see as necessary to complete this project. Although some tasks will logically seem to follow others, the focus here is to identify what needs to be done. How deeply you "slice and dice" each task is up to you. Unless it is a critical activity, you should rarely list any task that requires less than 8 hours of work (1 day). The times in the sample plan are calendar time, not how long the task will actually take. This is because your team members may only work on this project part time.

Write a brief paragraph describing each task. This will be very useful in estimating the time required to complete it. It also keeps the task's scope from spiraling out of control. You may understand what you mean for a task, but remember, someone else will probably execute the task, so an explanation will be very useful.

Always document your planning assumptions. When discussing the plan with others later, this explanation of what you were thinking at the time the plan was drafted will be very useful. By listing your assumptions, you can discuss them point by point with the team and your sponsor to avoid areas that the plan should not address and to identify why a specific course of action was followed.

Along with the assumptions, list all the known constraints for the project. This might be a specific due date to meet a business or legal obligation; it might be project funding issues or even a limit on the number of people available to be on the team. A major benefit of listing your project constraints is that upon examination they may be less than you think or can be used to prevent the scope of the project from expanding.

Determining Activity Durations

Once the tasks are laid out, estimate how much time should be set aside for each task to be completed. Creating reasonable time estimates for someone else is tough. You may think you know what needs to be done, but you could underestimate the true work required. Also, not everyone has your strengths—or weaknesses. Therefore, the estimates you assign at this stage are a starting point.

When a task is assigned to a team member, take the time to discuss with them what each task involves and see how long they think it will require. Be sure that they understand what each task entails so they can estimate accordingly. Update the plan with their estimated task durations and start dates. It is unfair to the team members to drop a task on them and demand a date without any further explanation.

Once you negotiate the duration of a task with someone, encourage them to stick with it. Other people further along in the project may be depending on this task to be completed before they can start.

Who Should Do It?

Some tasks are easy to assign. If the task is to validate the key locker security, it will go to the security manager. If that person chooses to delegate it to someone else, then it is still his or her responsibility to ensure the task is properly completed on time. Some tasks will be more general in nature and need to be spread around the team fairly. If a task is not needed, don't hesitate to delete it. If it is necessary, don't hesitate to assign it!

This is a good time to identify any gaps in your available labor. If you see a large time commitment for the Data Network Manager and little likelihood that team members will be available to do the assigned work, you might generate a task to bring in some temporary help to assist them. Other time issues may be on the horizon. For example, if you need to involve the Accounting Controller, and the project will run over the calendar time for closing the fiscal year accounts, then you would schedule their project participation to avoid this time period.

Sequencing the Activities

Now, put all the tasks in some sort of order. In this type of project, the beginning of the project is somewhat sequential. Later, many tasks will run in parallel when the various groups break off to write their respective plans. Select an estimated start date, and place some dates on your plan. With the plan held up against a calendar, check to see if any tasks need to be resequenced or if they conflict with some other critical company activity.

If your task contingencies are in place, the project management software will fill in the plan dates for you. If when you save the plan you select the option to save without a baseline, you can easily change the start date later.

Next, you should level your resources so one person isn't asked to complete more than 8 hours of work in 1 day. This occurs when people are assigned too many tasks that are running simultaneously.

Plan Risk Assessment

So now that you have a rough plan, with time estimates and in some sort of a logical flow, it is time to scrutinize the plan for problems. Are there any labor resources overobligated? Look at each task area. What is the risk that an item won't be completed on time? Yes, there is always a risk that a key person won't be available. List any other underlying issues.

Most projects share the same basic risks to their success. In addition, each project has its own risks unique to what you are trying to accomplish and to your environment. Common project plan risks include:

➤ The amount of experience the Business Continuity Manager has in leading this type of project. Less experience adds risk to the project. Extensive experience makes for lower risk.

➤ The level of management support for the project. If you have low management support, you will have high project risk, and vice versa.

➤ Adequate funding to complete the project with a top-quality result. Don't let needed training, support activities, or mitigation actions be cut from the budget.

➤ How many locations will this project involve at one time? The more locations that are involved, the greater the project's risk of failure. If possible, run a separate project for each site and do not attempt to do them all at the same time.

➤ The number of departments involved with the project at one time. Like trying to work across too many sites, trying to handle too many departments will fragment the Business Continuity Manager's time and increases the likelihood of failure. Consider tackling fewer departments at one time.

➤ The frequency and length of business interruptions to the project. This could be an upcoming ISO audit, it could be a quarterly wall-to-wall inventory, it might even be the end of the fiscal year, etc. The more interruptions to the project's flow you can foresee, the higher the risk of failure.

➤ The time required to complete your business continuity plans will depend on the knowledge and quality of the people assigned by the various departments. Typically, the Data Processing department has the most to write and will take the longest.

➤ A mandated completion date may not be realistic.

EXECUTING AND CONTROLLING

Now you have your sponsor, your budget, your plan, and a core team assigned. It is time to get your project underway! A Business Continuity Manager must be the inspiring force behind the project. At those times when everyone is piling work on your team members' desks, you must be the driving force in keeping this job as a priority project until it is finished.

As the project progresses, you will make decisions as to what is included in your project charter and what is not. This "scope verification" may mean that as the project progresses, you discover that it must involve specific actions that were not foreseen when the project was started. It may also involve the "nice-to-have" things that pop up as a project moves on. In either case, recognize these things as they occur and make a conscious decision to accept or reject them. Do not let anyone else add tasks to the plan without your approval or your tightly planned project will turn into an untamed monster!

Communications Plan

Every person within your organization has different information needs and preferred channels for receiving that information. The sponsor shouldn't be burdened with minute details; the department managers should be responsible for tracking what their people are doing. To provide the right level of information to the right person at the appropriate time, you need to build a communications plan. The more people involved with your project, the greater your need for communication.

A communications plan details who needs to report about what, and when. For example, who should receive project status reports? Who needs copies of the team meeting minutes? Who needs to know about minor project delays, etc.? To manage this, build a matrix that accounts for the information needs of all stakeholders. Your communications plan will address a wide range of audiences. Be sure to identify the person responsible for generating the communication and its major focus.

Evaluate every report and every meeting in your communications plan as to whether it will be worth the effort to prepare for it. Some reports may require more effort than they are worth. Some meetings are just a waste of time. Effective communication is important for focusing a team to a goal, but you must strike a balance between enough communication and the time wasted generating too much. Use Form 1-4 (see CD) to plan who is responsible for what communications.

The communications plan will encompass more than memos floating around the office. It should include meetings with your team, meetings with your sponsor, and presentations to the various departments. Another important communications task is to raise the awareness of the employees of your project and how it impacts them. Posters, newsletter articles, and open meetings all serve to answer their questions and are useful for instilling a business continuity culture in your company.

The information that you need to communicate falls into three main categories:

1. Mandatory communications are things that must be done, such as status reports to the sponsor, meeting minutes to the team members, etc. Skipping a mandatory communication may affect your project's support or credibility.

2. Informational communications include reports to the interested and curious. Many people will see the plan under development and believe that it directly or indirectly will involve them. Your informational communications will pass on project accomplishments, testing schedules, and things that may not directly affect them, but they would want to know about. Informational communications can help to shape expectations, so interested people can better understand what is next instead of being surprised or disappointed.

3. Similar to informational communications is marketing communications. Here you are out to build a positive image of your project to the rest of the company. Your marketing communications will help to educate the company as a whole on the business continuity planning principles (risk analysis, mitigation, documentation, etc.) and how they can relate to their own work processes. One effective method is to give a presentation on business recovery

planning to each of the various department staffs. The more they understand it, the greater your support is across the company.

Form 1-5 (see CD) is a sample stakeholder reporting matrix. Modify it to reflect your project team and business requirements. In this matrix, you will identify which persons might only want to see monthly status reports with summary comments, such as the sponsor. Who might need a weekly status report with specific accomplishments, such as the department managers? Who might want short stories on accomplishments, such as the facility's employee newsletter? The stakeholder reporting matrix also indicates the best way to deliver these reports. Do some of your executives ignore their e-mail? Do some require face-to-face reports? Indicate the method of delivery to which they would be most receptive.

Reporting Using the Communications Plan

As the project progresses, you should occasionally revisit the project's risk assessment. Things change; people come and go on a project; and what was once a looming challenge may at closer glance appear to be nothing at all. In addition, business conditions are in constant flux and that must also be figured into the update of your risk analysis.

Controlling is the process used to identify variation from the plan in the areas of:

➤ Change control.

➤ Scope control.

➤ Cost control.

➤ Quality control.

➤ Performance reporting.

➤ Risk response.

Your best tool for focusing the team on its goals will be a weekly team meeting. There are many fine books dealing with the proper way to conduct a meeting, but a few basics follow:

➤ First, always publish an agenda before the meeting. It acts as an anchor to keep people from drifting too far off the subject.

➤ Second, keep the meeting pertinent. Focus on recent achievements over the past 2 weeks and upcoming events of the next 2 weeks.

➤ Third, keep it under an hour. People lose focus the longer a meeting drones on. Side conversations should be stopped and taken outside the meeting. If you are finished in a half hour, cut it off! People will respect the meeting time limit as much as you do, so set a good example.

➤ Have your meeting at the same place and time every week, even if not much is happening. Try to make it a habit for them.

➤ When planning your team meetings, involve a bit of showmanship to keep people involved. If they sit there passively, ask specific people questions, but never to embarrass them if they are late. If the discussions seem tedious, jump in once in a while to keep them focused and interesting.

➤ Use slack time in the agendas to fill in with short training topics and visits by the sponsor or department managers.

➤ Publish a meeting recap as soon after the meeting as possible. Detailed meeting minutes may become too burdensome but a recap of the high points gives you a document to talk from at the beginning of the next meeting.

➤ Always include a copy of the updated project plan.

Test "Completed" Plans

The quickest way to snap people out of lethargy is to publicly test the first plans submitted. You don't need to pull the plug on a computer to do this. An easy test is to verbally walk through it. If the plan authors know that it is really going to be read and see how you test it, they will be more thorough.

Do the first desktop walk-through with the plan's author. You will uncover glossed-over steps where they clearly knew what to do but where, based on the plan, you had no clue as to what was next. After updating that version, do the same walk-through with the author's manager (who may very well be called on to execute this plan) and look for gaps.

Reward those contributors who complete their plans on time. This is where your sponsor comes in. Everyone likes to be appreciated, and some liberal rewards for the first few completed plans will go a long way toward motivating the rest of the team. You'd be surprised how fast this kind of word spreads throughout a company.

Set Up and Enforce a Testing Schedule

As the departmental plans roll in, update the project plan's testing schedule. Testing will uncover gaps and inconsistencies in the current draft. Normally, this is a multiple step process:

➤ The team member and the manager initially check completed plans by using a desktop walk-through.

➤ The next level is to walk through the plan with someone familiar with the area, but not involved with the plan development.

➤ Run a departmental test.

➤ Once enough plans are ready, it is time to schedule a simulated major disaster. This might be over a holiday period or whenever the systems are lightly used. Testing will teach people some of what to expect in a disaster. It will also make them more familiar with the procedures of other functions.

Always follow testing or a disaster event with an "after-action" meeting and report detailing the lessons learned and updates made to the plan. Be sure to praise its high points and to privately express what it is lacking. Depending on how well your group members know one another, you can use team members for a peer evaluation. People must feel free to speak at these meetings without fear of retaliation or their full value will not be realized.

After-action reviews are a very powerful learning tool. They require a moderator to keep them focused and moving through the following five questions. An after-action discussion follows a simple format:

➤ What happened?

➤ What should have happened?

➤ What went well?

➤ What went poorly?

➤ What will we do differently in the future?

Appoint someone to take notes on these lessons learned. Send a copy to each participant, and the Business Continuity Manager should maintain a file of these reports. Refer to this file when updating the plan.

CLOSING THE PROJECT

Once you have your plan written and the initial tests are completed, it is time to close the project. All good things come to an end, as when the plan is transformed from a project to an ongoing business process. The transition involves reporting the project results to management, closing out the project's budget, identifying known exposures for future action, and thanking your team members for their efforts. Closing the project involves the following steps:

➤ Turn all files over to the Plan Administrator. What was once your project may become someone else's regular responsibility. If the Business Continuity Manager is not to be the Plan Administrator, accumulate all files pertaining to this project and hand them over to the Plan Administrator. It is now the administrator's job to ensure the ongoing test plan is enforced, that plan updates are issued in a timely fashion, etc.

Make a final update to the project plan. It may be useful if sister companies want to use it for building their own business continuity plans. You can also refer to it when estimating task duration for future projects.

➤ Report results to management. To wrap up your project, draft a recap of the progression of the project to management. In this, point out any major successes that occurred during the project, such as low-cost solutions found to important problems, materials found stashed away in closets that could be put to good use, and so on. In the report, be sure to point out the benefit of the cross-functional training received by the project team as they worked with each other during plan development and testing.

You should provide a final account of the funds spent on the project, broken down as to what part of the project they supported. This will assist in estimating the funds required for similar projects in the future.

➤ Identify known exposures. A business reality is that not every worthwhile activity can be funded. During your risk analysis and mitigation efforts, you very likely uncovered a number of areas where there were single points of failure that called for redundant solutions, unmasked obsolete equipment that must be replaced, or other mitigation actions that would make your business processes more stable.

Roll up these exposures into a report to management. List each item separately along with a narrative explanation of why it is important. Detail the advantages and disadvantages of this course of action along with estimated (or known) costs. These narratives may not be reviewed again for many months, so the clearer the business reasons behind funding this action, the better. When your capital budgeting cycle rolls around, use this list as input to the budget.

➤ Thank the team. Hopefully, careful notes were kept during the course of the project so that team members could be recognized for their contributions to the project. In particular, those team members who overcame major obstacles to complete their plan and thoroughly test them are due special recognition. Acknowledgment of a job well done should be made as soon as possible after the fact. At the end of the project, it is time to again acknowledge these well-done jobs to remind everyone and management of the individual accomplishments during the project.

CONCLUSION

After reading this chapter, you should now have a good idea as to the overall strategy for developing a useful business continuity plan. Your odds for a successful project increase dramatically when you have a well-thought-out plan. The major steps for getting your project off to a good start are these:

1. Make sure the scope of the project is clearly defined. You need adequate time, funding, and support to be successful.

2. Carefully select the right team members. They must have a good understanding of the important processes within their departments and be able to clearly communicate the importance of the project back to their coworkers.

3. Identify the activities required, their durations, and who should do the work.

4. Communicate not only within the team but with the entire organization, as what you are doing is important for everyone's survival.

5. Test, test, test. If a plan isn't tested, you won't know whether it will work until it's too late.

CHAPTER 2

BUILDING THE BUSINESS CASE
Measuring the Impact
on the Business

If you don't know where you are going, any road will get you there.
—Lewis Carroll

INTRODUCTION

Once your team is in place and the scope of your disaster recovery planning is determined, the next step is to determine exactly what vital functions need to be included in the plan. Can you easily identify the most vital functions? What happens to the business if one or more functions are suddenly unavailable due to a system failure or other disaster? What is the cost if a function is unavailable? Intuitively, some functions must be more valuable than others, but what is that value? How can this value be measured? In a time of scarce resources, which functions need to be heavily protected and which if any can be safely ignored? In a major disaster affecting many functions, which functions are essential for the company's survival?

All of these questions are pertinent. Often, decisions are based on the perceived value of a particular function when comparing two functions and the resources for only one of them is available. Capital spending, major improvement projects, and, of course, support staff training often are decided by the perceived value that a function provides the company. But what is this value based on? Where are the data that support this value? How old are the data? Has the value provided by a function changed over time?

The problem with the business-as-usual approach is that it is based on a limited understanding or personal whim—not on the facts. A long-time manager might be acting on "rules-of-thumb" or assumptions that were valid at one time, but may not be any longer. A new manager lacks the "institutional knowledge" about which previous failures have caused the greatest damage. Another caveat is that the business impact of a function changes over time. Companies compete in an ever-shifting business environment. Yesterday's cash cow may be today's cash drain. Yesterday's cash drain may be today's regulatory compliance requirement and must be working smoothly to keep the government at arm's length!

Unfortunately, few executives fully appreciate which of their functions are truly critical. They draw on personal experience, but that is limited to the areas with which they are familiar. They can ask their peers, but each person sees the world through the narrow view of his or her own situation. The accounting department will identify all of its functions as critical since it handles the money. The materials management team will identify its functions as critical since the company's assets are reflected in a fragile collection of materials. The engineering department will think it is the most critical since its technology holds the company's valuable intellectual property. To some extent, all of these are right!

To determine where the true benefits lie, conduct a detailed Business Impact Analysis that breaks the business down by its major functions, and assigns value to each function in terms of cash flow and regulatory obligations. Then the systems that support these functions are identified and the functions rolled up. Based on this data—based on these facts—an executive can more efficiently assign resources for the greater benefit of the organization.

BUSINESS IMPACT ANALYSIS

A Business Impact Analysis (BIA) is an exploratory review of the important functions that are essential for the operation of the business. This review is used to quantify the value of each function to the business and to identify any risks to the most valuable functions. It also suggests mitigation actions to reduce the likelihood or impact of these risks. In the event of a disaster, the BIA indicates how much is lost per hour or per day for the length of the outage. Many of these functions are linked to an IT system that supports them (lose the IT system, and that function can no longer continue).

A BIA is a snapshot of vital business functions at a given point in time. Any major changes in the operation of the business will require an update to the BIA.

An organization's critical functions depend on its primary mission. For a call center, a BIA would focus on the key telecommunication services required to service the callers. For a manufacturing firm, this might be the functions required to make the end product. A bank might identify the various financial services offered to its customers. An online store would value availability of its Web page, speed of processing, and security of customer data. And of course each department within the organization will have its own list of critical functions.

A BIA provides many benefits to an organization, many of which are valuable beyond the scope of a business continuity project. These include:

➤ Quantifying the tangible and qualifying the intangible costs of the loss of a critical function.

➤ Identifying the most critical functions to protect.

➤ Pinpointing the critical resources necessary for each function to operate, such as people, equipment, software, etc.

➤ Determining the recovery time objective (RTO) of critical functions. The RTO is the length of time that the organization can operate with a function disabled before the effect of the loss of the function affects other functions.

➤ Identifying vital records and the impact of their loss.

➤ Prioritizing the use of scarce resources if multiple functions are affected at the same time.

There are numerous ways that the loss of a function can have a negative financial impact on the organization. The tangible financial costs of a disaster can include:

➤ Direct loss of revenue because products cannot be shipped or services not delivered.

➤ Increased waste from the spoilage of materials or finished goods.

➤ Penalties levied by customers for late shipments or lost services.

➤ Legal penalties for not conforming to government regulations or reporting requirements.

Intangible costs due to the loss of a vital business function can be harder to quantify, but are no less damaging. Intangible losses can include:

➤ Loss of customer goodwill.

➤ Reduced confidence in the marketplace that your organization is a reliable supplier.

➤ Employee turnover caused by concern for the viability of the organization.

➤ Damaged image in the community if your disaster harms the local community.

➤ Loss of confidence in the organization's executive management by key stakeholders.

A well-executed BIA can provide much valuable information to executive management about the organization's vulnerabilities. This includes:

➤ The maximum acceptable outage (MAO) that the organization can suffer before the organization will have difficulty meeting its objectives.

➤ The recovery time objective (RTO)—the amount of time that a function can be unavailable before the organization is negatively impacted—for each vital function. The cost of the recovery or mitigation solution selected will typically rise as the RTO decreases. This is a major driver of your disaster recovery plan.

➤ The recovery point objective (RPO) for each function that relies on data. The RPO is the amount of data that can be lost without causing serious damage to a function. The cost of the recovery or mitigation solution selected will typically rise as the RPO decreases.

Managing a BIA Project

To be successful, a BIA must be run as its own project within your overall disaster recovery project. The project must be supported financially and politically from the highest levels of the organization. Every part of the organization will be touched by a BIA; it is therefore important to appoint a senior executive as the sponsor of the project. Many department heads may be reluctant to share sensitive information about their department due to legitimate concerns about the use of the information or because they are concerned that the information could be used for political purposes. The sponsor's role is to:

➤ Work with the Business Continuity Manager to select the project manager (who could be the Business Continuity Manager).

➤ Approve the project budget.

➤ Communicate to every department the importance of its participation in the BIA.

➤ Address any objections or questions raised about the BIA.

➤ Approve the BIA report for submission to the executive team.

A well-run BIA will build credibility for the overall disaster recovery planning project; a poorly run BIA will make a disaster of your disaster recovery project. The key to a successful BIA (as with any other project) is the selection of the right project manager. For a BIA it is especially important, as the BIA will expose every part of the organization to the light of day. The BIA project manager must be able to moderate discussions among department heads about the true value of internal functions. In many cases, there has been no formal examination of the functions performed within each department, which may cause heated discussions about the value of each department. In choosing a project manager, the executive sponsor has two options:

1. Internal—An employee of the organization is appointed as the project manager. The advantages of this approach are that this person already understands the corporate structure, is familiar with the personalities involved, knows where to find people, etc. This approach also builds internal expertise. A possible disadvantage is that the project manager could be caught in the middle of any political battles over the BIA, which could negatively impact the manager's career at the organization.

2. External—A person from outside the organization is brought in to lead the project. The possible advantages are that this person does not have any internal ties and loyalty is to the executive paying the bill. A potential problem is that the organization's business functions, finances, and problems will be exposed to this third party.

The BIA project manager is responsible for developing a formal project plan, which is critical for the success of the project. In a large organization, many people have to be interviewed, many meetings need to be held, interim reports must be prepared, and deliverables have to be created. A formal project plan is vital for managing this process. The project plan will be used to manage the activities of the BIA team, which typically consists of several business analysts.

BIA Data Collection

Once the BIA team is created, the next step is to begin the data collection process. The goal of the BIA is to identify the most vital functions in the organization; just what is vital will vary depending on whom you ask. An effective data collection process will help quantify the value of each function in terms of its financial and legal impacts. The level of success of the BIA is directly related to the quality of the information collected. You cannot have a high-quality disaster recovery plan without a foundation of accurate data about your vital business functions.

Your data collection plan must address what data to collect and from whom it is to be collected. It may also be important to consider when to collect the data. As this process takes people away from the important business of their departments, it is critical that the data be collected only once. Time spent in careful development of the questionnaire will save time later by only having to collect the data one time. A data collection plan consists of the following steps:

1. Identify who will receive the questionnaire using an up-to-date organization chart.

2. Develop the questionnaire to be used to collect the data from each department. Many organizations will begin with a standard form which is then modified for use.

3. Provide training to small groups (usually a department at a time) on how to respond to the questionnaire.

4. Follow up with each department to ensure timely completion of the questionnaire.

5. Review responses with respondents if the responses are not clear or are incomplete.

6. Conduct review meetings with each department to discuss responses.

7. Compile and summarize the BIA data for review by the various levels of the organization.

IDENTIFY RESPONDENTS

The first step in identifying who should receive the BIA questionnaire is to obtain a current organizational chart. The organizational chart should identify the different departments or business units within the organization and who their leaders are. These leaders are made responsible for the completion of the questionnaire(s) for their areas. Your executive sponsor must provide you with support in ensuring their cooperation.

Each department first needs to identify the vital functions performed in its area. A form such as Form 2-1, Department Function Identification Form (see the CD-ROM), can be used to develop this list. A separate function is typically identified if it has different resource requirements (e.g., IT systems or machines), staffing roles, or service providers who perform other functions in the department. Each department can have many business functions to report. Therefore, each department numbers its forms according to how many functions it is reporting. This reduces the chance of missing a questionnaire.

Consider including suppliers where their activities are critical to your business.

DEVELOP THE QUESTIONNAIRE

At this time, you should select a single department or business unit as a test case for your questionnaire. This might be a department under the sponsor's direct control or one where the department head has voiced support for the project. This test department can provide valuable feedback on the questionnaire, including its instructions, the clarity of the questions, or if something is missing. Often what is clear to the BIA team is obscure or has a different meaning to someone who is not familiar with the subject.

Next, develop the questionnaire. Because the end result of the data collection process is the creation of an aggregated report, it is important that everyone responding to the questionnaire use important terms consistently. To ensure consistency, create a glossary of terms as part of the questionnaire. A glossary not only improves reporting consistency, but also speeds up responses and makes it obvious when something new or unexpected is encountered. The use of consistent terminology can also be enforced by using an electronic form for the questionnaire (such as an Excel spreadsheet) with checklists or dropdown lists that confine the answers to a predefined set of answers or range of numbers. If you choose this approach, have an "Other" option available for unexpected situations. Otherwise, the respondent may stop filling out the questionnaire if such a question is encountered. By allowing the choice of "Other," you can go back later for clarification rather than have the respondent hold the questionnaire until informed about how to respond to a particular question.

A question can be answered in two ways: qualitatively and quantitatively. Qualitative data represent attributes for which you cannot assign a numerical value, such as color or gender. Quantitative data are represented by a numerical value, such as length of time or dollars. Quantitative data can be aggregated, averaged, etc., which makes it easier to analyze a series of responses. As much as possible, make the answers to the BIA questions quantitative; some questions are naturally quantitative, but others may need to be framed in such a way as to require a quantitative response.

The BIA questionnaire begins with an identification block that indicates the department and function to which the questionnaire applies (see Form 2-2, Business Impact Analysis Questionnaire, as an example). The business function name must be the one that it is most commonly known by within the organization. When the final report is reviewed, executives will question high values for functions that no one can recognize, so be sure to use the function's common name. The name in the function manager field will be used by the BIA team as the contact person if there are any questions. The form should also include the name of the person who completed the form and the date the form was completed.

The next series of questions on the example questionnaire are designed to get a sense of the time sensitive nature of the function: Does the function have to be performed at a certain time? Can it operate at a reduced level for some period of time? How long can it be unavailable before other functions are affected? It is also important to know if this function depends on things outside the control of this department, including a dependency on any particular technology. If yes, this helps the IT department in developing its specific plans and for financial justification to purchase redundant equipment to reduce the likelihood or duration of an outage. To ensure consistency among the answers, the IT department provides a list of all applications on all platforms (desktop, server, mainframe, online). The list is included in the instructions accompanying the form. Be sure to include both the official name and the commonly used name (if one is better known). Respondents can select from this list to minimize variation of system names. This section also documents whether the function depends on outside suppliers.

The next section in the example questionnaire is a matrix that is used to quantify important categories of impact (across the top) with a time scale (along the vertical axis). It is the heart of the analysis and must be tuned to the local requirements. Categories used in the example questionnaire are:

1. Cumulative Financial Loss (revenue lost plus costs incurred)—measured in dollars. This might include:

    a. lost revenues.

    b. lost sales.

    c. financial penalties.

    d. wages paid for no work.

    e. overtime wages paid to catch up.

    f. spoiled materials and finished goods.

2. Legal Compliance Impact—Yes or No. For this and the following items, space is provided later for an explanation.

3. Impact on Customer Confidence—Answers can be Low, Medium, or High.

4. Loss of Supplier Confidence—Answers can be Low, Medium, or High.

5. Damaged Public Image—Answers can be Low, Medium, or High.

Rate each of the impact categories according to its impact over time. For example, what is the Cumulative Financial Loss for one hour of outage? Some examples include:

Example #1

If the function is a busy online catalog, then a one-hour outage might have a significant financial impact because buyers may look elsewhere for goods. Loss of customer confidence and a damaged public image would also come into play.

Example #2

If the function is the shipping department for a factory, then a one-hour outage would mean that shipments would leave the dock late that day. A four-hour outage might involve shipments arriving late to the customer. Beyond four hours, late shipments would be widespread and, depending on the purchasing stipulations, may be refused by the customer. There may even be penalties for late deliveries. Also, at some point, the rest of the factory is shut down since finished goods are piled up with nowhere to go.

Example #3

If the payroll department was down for an hour, then the clerks can tidy up around the office or even leave early for lunch, and the cost is minimal. However, if the same payroll department was inoperable for a week, the company may not have lost revenue but the employees definitely would be angry. If the employees belonged to a union, they might walk off the job.

Other categories to consider adding to the questionnaire include:

➤ Shareholder Confidence.

➤ Loss of Financial Control.

➤ Employee Morale.

➤ Customer Service.

➤ Employee Resignations.

➤ Vendor Relations.

➤ Potential Liability.

➤ Competitive Advantage.

➤ Health Hazard.

➤ Additional Cost of Credit.

➤ Additional Cost of Advertising to Rebuild Company Image and Reliability.

➤ Cost to Acquire New Software and to Re-Create Databases.

➤ Damage to Brand Image.

➤ Potential Reduction in Value of Company Stock Shares.

The next section on the sample questionnaire is used to document any documents or other vital records that are critical for the success of the function. Departments that originate, use, or store vital business records must be identified. This information can be used to develop protection plans for this data. It can also identify documents that should be properly destroyed instead of stored on-site.

Next on the sample questionnaire is a section in which to document critical non-IT devices that may be difficult or impossible to replace. This can spawn a project to modify the function to eliminate these unique devices (and thereby reduce the chance of a business function outage due to the failure of a special machine).

The last question on the sample questionnaire offers the department an opportunity to give a subjective rating of the importance of a specific function to the overall functioning of the department. This information will be used in conjunction with the financial impact data to help prioritize the functions to be restored in the event of a disaster.

Once the questions have all been determined, develop a set of written instructions to be distributed with the questionnaire. The instructions should explain how every field on the form will be used and what the respondent should fill in for each field. Ideally, include a telephone number for someone on the BIA project team to quickly answer questions; the quicker you can resolve questions the more likely the questionnaire will be completed.

COLLECT THE DATA

Once the questionnaire has been developed, you need to distribute it to the various departments. An important first step is to meet with each of the department leaders and help them to draft the list of vital business functions within their domains. Use this list to provide a numbered stack of questionnaires. Assign a number to each person the department leaders indicate should receive one. An important management tool is a log of which form number went to which person. This is used to verify that all of the forms are returned.

Next, coordinate a series of meetings with the various departments to review the questionnaire and give people a chance to ask questions. While this will be time consuming, it will speed up the process by helping to prevent the completion of the questionnaire from getting sidetracked. Try to keep the groups smaller than 20 people. This provides opportunities to ask questions. During these meetings:

➤ Explain the purpose of the BIA and how it will help the company and their department—*sell the concept to them!*

➤ Provide copies of the letter from the executive sponsor that supports this project; this serves to reinforce the importance of this project.

➤ If possible, ask the executive sponsor to drop by the meetings for a brief word of "encouragement."

➤ Provide copies of the questionnaires, along with a printed explanation of what each item means.

➤ Walk through every item in the questionnaire and provide examples of how they might be filled in.

➤ Set a deadline (typically one week) for the questionnaire to be completed and returned.

Check vacation and travel schedules to ensure that all respondents will be available to complete the questionnaire. If not, make sure that an appropriate substitute is identified.

For collecting data from departments with a limited number of functions and highly paid employees (such as the legal department), it may be more time and cost effective to have the BIA team interview critical members of the department and fill out the questionnaires for them.

As questionnaires are returned to the BIA team, carefully track which teams have returned their questionnaires. Visit any department you think might be less than diligent in filling out the questionnaires. Make the visit a friendly reminder of the deadline and use it as an opportunity to answer any questions or respond to any problems with the questionnaire. As the deadline for each department passes, visit each department that has not returned the questionnaires to see if help is needed and to encourage them to complete the form. As the forms are returned, be sure to check them for:

➤ **Clarity.** Ensure that you understand the answers.

➤ **Completeness.** Return any incomplete forms and ask if department members need help in completing the questionnaire. If only a few items are missing, it is likely that they simply did not understand them.

➤ **Other.** Review any items answered "Other" to see if one of the existing categories may have been a fit or if a new category is needed.

Reporting the Results

Once all of the questionnaires have been returned, it is time to compile the reports. The reports are organized into a hierarchy of reports, starting with each business function. Depending on the size of the organization, you might have several layers between each function and the overall organization. A typical organization will use the following levels for the BIA report:

1. Function

2. Workgroup

3. Department

4. Business Unit

5. Overall Organization

The example below shows a workgroup report for the A/R function within the Accounting department. Each business function is listed along the left side, with the time ranges used in the questionnaire across the top. Each column then shows the impact if that function is unavailable for that amount of time.

Workgroup Report						
Workgroup:	Accounts Receivable					
	Cumulative Impact					
Business Function	**1 hour**	**4 hours**	**1 day**	**2 days**	**1 week**	**2 weeks**
Generate invoices	$0	$5,000	$10,000	$20,000	$100,000	$250,000
Daily cash balance	$0	$0	$5,000	$15,000	$75,000	$200,000
Process checks	$0	$0	$0	$0	$10,000	$30,000

Once the workgroup report is completed, you should meet with everyone who responded to the questionnaire and their next level manager. A copy of the report is provided to all participants, which is then reviewed with the group one line at a time. The entire group then must reach a consensus about each line item. The BIA analyst's job is to remain nonjudgmental and to only guide the discussion. During this process, the collective knowledge of the group is used to correct any errors, point out any missing functions, and discuss options that may be available to reduce potential losses.

The amount of time a vital business function can tolerate downtime and at what cost determines the disaster recovery strategy. The less tolerant a business function is to an outage, the more expensive the disaster recovery strategy must be and the more urgent it becomes that business continuity mitigation is implemented.

Every line in the report should either be validated or updated. In this way, the BIA report is the product of both the team and that workgroup's management. The entire discussion is important, because the workgroup's management must defend the workgroup's consensus at the next level of data validation.

This process is then repeated at the next level. If the next level is a department, then the impact of the loss of each workgroup that makes up the department is reviewed by each workgroup manager along with the manager of the department. As each team reviews its report, expect vigorous discussion about what is important and the impact on the organization. For many managers this process is very educational. Many are often surprised at the impact some functions really have and how vulnerable they are to a loss of that function.

An important consequence of performing a BIA is to get the different departments at least thinking about how their functions fit within the mission of the organization, which makes improvements easier to identify.

CONCLUSION

After reading this chapter, you should now be able to determine which functions are vital to the success of your organization, as well as the priority in which these functions should be restored. Performing a BIA can be a tricky process politically, as each department within an organization will naturally believe that its functions are the most critical and may be hesitant to share details with someone outside of the department. A successful BIA requires the following:

➤ Strong and vocal support from senior management.

➤ A capable project leader.

➤ A well-crafted questionnaire.

➤ Complete and honest answers from each department.

With a complete and accurate BIA in hand, you are now ready to begin evaluating the actual risks to your organization's vital functions and develop a strategy for dealing with them.

CHAPTER 3

EVALUATING RISK
Understanding What Can Go Wrong

Luck: 1a, a force that brings good fortune or adversity;
1b, the events or circumstances that operate for
or against an individual; 2, favoring chance.

INTRODUCTION

The heart of building a business continuity plan is a thorough analysis of events from which you may need to recover. This is variously known as a *threat analysis* or *risk assessment*. The result is a list of events that could slow your company down or even shut it down. We will use this list to identify those risks your business continuity plan must address.

First, let's define the terminology we'll use when discussing risk:

➤ The potential of a disaster occurring is called its **risk**. Risk is measured by how likely this is to happen and how badly it will hurt.

➤ A **disaster** is any event that disrupts a critical business function. This can be just about anything.

➤ A **business interruption** is something that disrupts the normal flow of business operations.

Whether an event is a business interruption or a disaster sometimes depends on your point of view. An interruption could seem like a disaster to the people to whom it happens, but the company keeps rolling along. An example might be a purchasing department that has lost all telephone communication with its suppliers. It is a disaster to the employees because they use telephones and fax machines to issue purchase orders. The facility keeps running because their mitigation plan is to generate POs on paper and use cell phones to issue verbal material orders to suppliers.

Risk is defined as the *potential* for something to occur. It could involve the possibility of personal injury or death. For example, insurance actuaries work to quantify the likelihood of an event occurring in order to set insurance rates. A risk could be an unexpected failing in the performance of duties by someone you had judged as reliable. It could be a machine failure or a spilled container of toxic material.

Not all risks become realities. There is much potential in our world that does not occur. Driving to work today, I saw clouds that indicate the potential of rain. Dark clouds don't indicate a certainty of precipitation, but they do indicate a greater potential than a clear sky. I perceive an increased risk that I will get wet on the long walk across the company parking lot, so I carry an umbrella with me. The odds are that it will not rain. The weatherman says the clouds will pass. I can even see patches of blue sky between the massive dark clouds. Still, to reduce my risk of being drenched, I carry an umbrella.

Some risks can be reduced almost to the point of elimination. A hospital can install a backup generator system with the goal of ensuring 100% electrical availability. This will protect patients and staff against the risk of electrical blackout and brownouts. However, it also introduces new risks, such as the generator failing to start automatically when the electricity fails. It also does not protect the hospital against a massive electrical failure internal to the building.

Some risks are unavoidable and steps can only be taken to reduce their impact. If your facility is located on the ocean with a lovely view of the sea, defenses can be built up against a tidal surge or hurricane, but you cannot prevent them. You can only minimize their damage.

Some risks are localized, such as a failure of a key office PC. This event directly affects at most a few people. This is a more common risk that should not be directly addressed in the facility-wide business continuity plan. Rather, localized plans should be developed and maintained at the department level, with a copy in the company-wide master plan. These will be used mainly within a department, whose members address these challenges as they arise. If a problem is more widespread, such as a fire that burns out just those offices, all the combined small reaction plans for that office can be used to more quickly return that department to normal.

Other risks can affect your entire company. An example is a blizzard that blocks the roads and keeps employees and material from your door. We all appreciate how this can slow things down, but if you are a just-in-time supplier to a company in a sunnier climate, you still must meet your daily production schedule or close your customer down!

In building the list, we try to be methodical. We will examine elements in your business environment that you take for granted. Roads on which you drive. Hallways through which you walk. Even the air you breathe. In building the plan, a touch of paranoia is useful. As we go along, we will assign a score to each threat and eventually build a plan that deals with the most likely or most damaging events (see Figure 3-1).

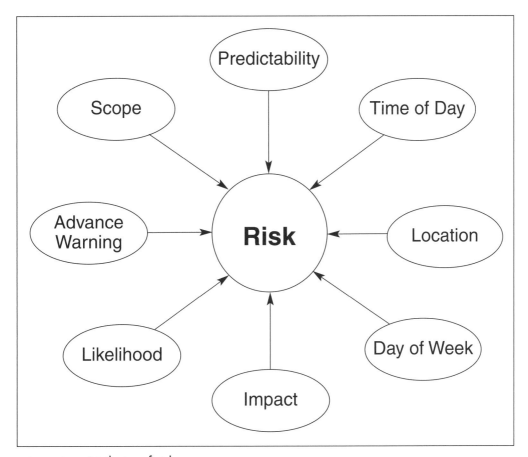

FIGURE 3-1: Attributes of risk.

BUILDING A RISK ANALYSIS

At this point we can differentiate among several common terms. We will begin with a *risk analysis.* A risk analysis is a process that identifies the probable threats to your business. As we progress, this will be used as the basis for a *risk assessment.* A risk assessment compares the risk analysis to the controls you have in place today to identify areas of vulnerability.

The recommended approach is to assemble your business continuity planning team and perform the layers 1, 2, and 3 risk analyses (see the section below on The Five Layers of Risk) together. Your collective knowledge will make these reviews move quickly. Such things as the frequency of power or telephone outages in the past, how quickly these were resolved, and types of severe weather and its impact are all locked in the memories of the team members.

What Is Important to You?

A risk analysis begins with a written statement of the essential functions of your business that will be used to set priorities for addressing these risks. Essential functions could be business activities, such as the availability of telephone service. It could be the flow of information, such as up-to-the-second currency exchange rates. It is anything whose absence would significantly damage the operation of your business.

Most functions of a business are nonessential. You may think of your company as being tightly staffed and the work tuned to drive out waste. But think about the functions whose short-term loss would not stop your essential business from running. One example is payroll. Losing your payroll function for a few days would be inconvenient, but should not shut your business down. Most people can't delay paying their bills for long, so over a longer period of time, this rises to the level of critical. This illustrates how a short-term noncritical function can rise to be a critical function if it is not resolved in a timely manner.

Another example is a manufacturing site that states its essential functions as building, shipping, and invoicing its products. Anything that disturbs those functions is a critical problem that must be promptly addressed. All other functions that support this are noncritical to the company, although the people involved may consider them critical. On a more local scale, there may be critical functions for a department or a particular person's job. These are also important to resolve quickly. The difference is one of magnitude. Company-wide problems have company-wide impact and must be resolved immediately.

Another aspect to consider is the loss of irreplaceable assets. Imagine the loss or severe damage to vital records that must be retained for legal, regulatory, or operational reasons. Safeguarding these records must be added to your list of critical functions. Included in this category are all records whose loss would materially damage your company's ability to conduct business. All other records are those that can be reproduced (although possibly with great effort) or whose loss does not materially affect your business.

With all of this in mind, it is time to identify those few critical functions of your facility. These functions will be broad statements and are the primary purposes toward which this site works. The easiest way to start is for the top management team to identify them. Often the company's Operations Manager has some idea of what these should be. They would have been identified so that business continuity insurance could be purchased.

Another way to identify critical functions is for your team to select them. Based on your collective knowledge of the company, just what are they expecting you to provide? Another way to think of this is what is the essence of your site's function?

Some examples to get you thinking:

➤ **A factory.** To build, ship, and invoice products. This implies that the continuous flow of products down the assembly line is critical, along with prompt shipment and invoicing (to maintain cash flow).

➤ **A national motel chain call center.** To promptly respond to customer calls, make accurate reservations, and address customer concerns in a timely manner. This implies that telephone system availability and speed of switching are critical, along with accurate databases to reserve rooms.

➤ **A public utility.** To provide electrical service to all the customers, all of the time. This implies that no matter what other crises within the company are under way, the delivery of this product is critical.

SCOPE OF RISK

The scope of risk is determined by the potential damage, cost of downtime, or cost of lost opportunity. In general, the wider the disaster, the more costly it is. A stoppage to a manufacturing assembly line can idle hundreds of workers, so of course this is a company-wide critical event. Even a 15-minute stoppage can cost many thousands of dollars in idled labor. Consequently, a problem of this nature takes priority on the company's resources in all departments to resolve the issue.

On a smaller scale, there may be a spreadsheet in the accounting department that is used to generate reports for top management. If this PC stops working, work has ceased on this one function, but the plant keeps building products for sale. The Accounting Manager can request immediate PC repair support. The problem and support are local issues peripheral to the company's main function of building, shipping, and invoicing material.

When evaluating the likelihood of risks, keep your planning horizon to 5 years. The longer the planning horizon is, the greater the chance that "something" will happen. Since the purpose of the analysis is to identify areas of concentration for your business continuity plan, 5 years is about as far out as you can plan for building mitigation steps. If the risk analysis is updated annually, then 5 years is a sufficient planning horizon.

Cost of Downtime

Calculating the cost of downtime is critical to determining the appropriate investments to be made for disaster recovery. But calculating the costs due to the loss of a critical function is not a simple process. The cost of downtime includes tangible costs, such as lost productivity, lost revenue, legal costs, late fees and penalties, and many others. Intangible costs include things such as a possibly damaged reputation, lost opportunities, and possible employee turnover.

TANGIBLE COSTS The most obvious costs incurred due to a business interruption are lost revenue and lost productivity. If customers cannot purchase and receive your product, they may purchase from a competitor. Electronic commerce is especially vulnerable, because if your system is down, customers can in many cases simply click on a competitor's Web site. The easiest method to calculate lost sales is to determine your average hourly sales and multiple that value by the number of hours you are down. While this can be a significant value, it is simply the starting point for calculating the total cost of downtime.

Lost productivity is also a major portion of the total cost of downtime. It is usually not possible to stop paying wages to employees simply because a critical process is unavailable, so their salaries and benefits continue to be paid. Many employees may be idle while the process is unavailable, while others may continue to work at a much-diminished level of productivity. The most common method to calculate employee downtime costs is to multiply the number of employees by their hourly loaded cost by the number of hours of downtime. You may need to do this separately for each department, as their loaded cost and their level of productivity during the outage may vary. You will also need to include the employee cost for those who are assisting with any recovery or remediation processes once the process is back up. These employees may be doing double duty once the system is back up, doing their regular jobs and also entering data that were missed or lost during the downtime.

Other employee-related costs may include the cost of hiring temporary labor, overtime costs, and travel expenses. You may also incur expenses for equipment rental for cleanup or for temporary replacement of critical machinery and extra costs to expedite late shipments to customers.

If the business interruption was due to damages, such as fire or flood, the direct loss of equipment and inventory must of course be added in. Other tangible costs may include late fees and penalties if the downtime causes you to miss critical shipments to customers. You may also incur penalties if the downtime causes you to miss deadlines for government-mandated filings. Stockholders may sue the company if a business interruption causes a significant drop in share price and they believe that management was negligent in protecting their assets.

INTANGIBLE COSTS Intangible costs include lost opportunities as some customers purchase from your competition while you're down and may not return as customers. You don't just lose the immediate sale, but possibly any future business from that customer. You need to calculate the net present value of that customer's business over the life of the business relationship. If you have repeated problems with systems or processes being unavailable, some employees may become frustrated and leave the company. The cost to replace them and to train new employees should be considered. Employee exit interviews can help determine if this is at least a factor in employee turnover.

Other intangible costs can include a damaged reputation with customers, business partners, suppliers, banks, and others who may be less inclined to do business with you. Your marketing costs may increase if customers defect to the competition during an outage and you need to work harder to win back their business. Calculating the true total cost of an outage is not easy, but it is important to know when determining the investment necessary to prevent and/or recover from a disaster.

THE FIVE LAYERS OF RISK

The impact of risks varies widely according to what happens to whom and when. Your reaction to a disaster that shuts down the entire company will be quite different from that which inconveniences a single office or person. When considering risks, it is very helpful to separate them into broad categories (or layers) to properly prioritize their solutions. When evaluating risk, we look at five distinct layers. The layers range from what affects everyone (including your customers) in Layer 1 down to the processes performed by each individual in Layer 5.

The first layer concerns external risks that can close your business both directly and indirectly. These are risks from nature, such as flooding, hurricanes, severe snowstorms, etc. It can also include risks from manufactured objects, such as railroads or airplanes. Risks of this type usually disrupt our customers and suppliers as well as our own employees.

The second layer examines risks to your local facility. This might involve one or more buildings—everything at this site. Some of these risks are due to the way your offices were constructed; some risks are a result of severe weather, etc. Second-layer risks include those to basic services, such as electrical power and telephone access to your building. We will also look into issues such as bomb threats, hazardous material spills, and medical emergencies.

The third layer is your data systems organization. Everywhere throughout your organization computers are talking through a data network, sharing information, and performing other functions. In addition to operational issues, loss of data can lead to severe legal problems. Most data can be re-created, but the expense of doing so can be quite high. Data systems deserves its own layer, as its disasters can reach across your company. In most companies, if the computers stop working, so do the people.

The fourth layer is the individual department. This will drive the main part of your plan. Level four risks are the periodic crises we all confront on a weekly basis. Each department has critical functions to perform to meet its production goals and weekly assignments. These processes depend on specific tools. Each department needs to identify the risk that might prevent its members from performing their assigned work. These risks may not threaten the company's primary functions, but over time can degrade the facilities' overall performance.

The fifth and final layer is your own desk or work area. If you can't do your job in a timely manner, it may not stop the company from shipping its products, but it sure adds a lot of unnecessary stress to your life. Typically the risk assessment you perform on your own job will be more detailed (because you know more about it), making it easier for you to take time off (as you will be more organized), and making bouncing back from the crisis of the week look so very easy.

LAYER 1: EXTERNAL RISKS

Many natural disasters are wide-area risks. That means they not only affect your facilities, but also the surrounding area. Consider, for example, a hurricane. The damaging winds can affect hundreds of square miles before slowly moving up the seacoast. These winds can bring on tidal surges and torrential downpours, spawn tornadoes, and result in downed power lines and other calamities all at the same time.

Now consider your business in the midst of this. All companies are affected by this disaster, including your customers, your suppliers, and your emergency services support. Damage can be widespread. Technicians and machinery you had counted on for prompt support are tied up elsewhere. Bridges may be out, your workers may be unable to leave the facilities, and fresh workers may be unable to come to work. Employees critical to your recovery may not be available due to damage to their homes or injuries to their families. The list of problems could go on and on.

Don't forget to consider how the disaster may affect your employees' ability to respond to the disaster. After the terrorist attacks on the World Trade Center, many disaster recovery plans called for surviving employees to be at the recovery site the next day. After watching their friends and coworkers dying around them, getting to the recovery site was not at the top of their priority list!

Don't live in a hurricane zone? How different is this from a major snow storm? Power lines snap, which cuts off the electrical heat to your building, which causes sprinkler pipes to freeze and burst, etc. Impassable roads mean that help is slow to move around the area. Extreme temperatures reduce the productivity of power line technicians.

The risk to your site from natural disasters is determined by its topographic, hydrologic, and geologic conditions. This can be determined from maps provided by the United States Geologic Survey. The maps show elevations and drainage patterns.

The same goes for critical highways or railroads. Depending on where you live, a blocked highway may be easily bypassed. In some places, it may be the only practical route for tourists to reach your hotel. A damaged bridge on a key road could shut you down for days. A railroad derailment that spills toxic material may force an evacuation of your offices, even if it is quite a distance away.

With all of this "doom and gloom" in mind, let's break external risks into four categories: natural disasters, manufactured risks, civil risks, and supplier risks.

WHAT TO DO?

Use Form 3-1, the "Risk Assessment Tool for Layer 1." It is on the CD-ROM included with this book.

Evaluate the risk to your site in each of the categories over the next 5 years.

The columns of the tool are:

LIKELIHOOD is how likely this risk is to happen.

IMPACT is how bad you believe the damage would be.

RESTORATION is the length of time to get your critical functions back into service, not the amount of time for a complete recovery.

See section "Making the Assessment" at the end of this chapter for details on how to score each risk.

The risks listed in Form 3-1 are just a starting point. Add any other risks that you see for your site.

Natural Disasters

Natural disasters are the first events that come to mind when writing a disaster plan and are risks that we all live with. They vary greatly according to the part of the country in which you live. The damage from natural disasters usually covers a wide area. This not only affects your building, but also your employees, suppliers, customers, and the time required for a full recovery.

A major problem with wide-area disasters is that the help you are depending on for recovery may not be available or able to reach you. If major electrical lines are down, then your power company may take a long time to rerun the wire from the downed power pole to your building.

How much warning will you typically receive of an impending disaster? For a hurricane, you should know days before it arrives. In the case of an earthquake, you may not know until it is upon you.

TORNADOES Tornadoes are the most violent type of storm and can occur at any time of the year. They can appear with little or no warning anywhere at any time. Where you live has a great deal to do with the likelihood of a tornado occurring, with the greatest risk per square mile in Florida and Oklahoma. Tornadoes can do significant damage to facilities as well as to the homes of your employees.

You can obtain information about the likelihood of tornadoes in your area from the Severe Thunderstorm Climatology Web page of the National Severe Storms Laboratory of the National Oceanic and Atmospheric Administration at http://www.nssl.noaa.gov/hazard/hazardmap.html. This U.S. map displays the probability of tornadoes, wind, or hail for broad sections of the country. You can use this map, together with your team's collective memory, to determine the likelihood of these events happening to you.

PANDEMICS A pandemic is an outbreak of disease that affects a large area. Pandemics in modern times are most often associated with outbreaks of an influenza virus for which there is little or no immunity in the affected population. In recent times severe acute respiratory syndrome (SARS) and H1N1 (the so-called swine flu) have impacted the ability of organizations to do business. A pandemic can have a major impact on the availability of your employees, as they or members of their family are sick from the disease. Many governments are requiring important industries, such as finance, energy, government, banking and transportation, to prepare plans for continuing operations during a pandemic.

EARTHQUAKES Earthquakes occur in all 50 states. They can affect both your facilities and the homes of your employees (see Figure 3-2). Forty-one of these states are in the moderate- or high-risk category. To see if your area has an earthquake risk, check out http://earthquake.usgs.gov/research/hazmaps/.

THUNDERSTORMS Information about the typical annual threat of severe thunderstorms in the United States can be found at http://www.nssl.noaa.gov/

FIGURE 3-2: Seattle, WA, March 2001. Businesses in and around Seattle were damaged by a February 2001 earthquake in Washington State. (FEMA News Photo.)

hazard/totalthreat.html. Severe thunderstorms include winds in excess of 58 mph and hailstones greater than .75 inches in diameter. These storms can include:

➤ High winds that may rip off parts of your roof, exposing your equipment to damaging rain. High winds may also pick up objects and smash them into your windows, or even tip over semitrailers and close mountain passes.

➤ Hail that can be smaller than a pea or larger than a softball. It can destroy field crops, put a massive number of dents in a car, damage unprotected material you have stored outside, and can be extremely annoying if you own a car lot.

➤ Deluge and flash flooding that can cause roads to close, which slows the flow of customers, employees, and material in and out of your facility. Your building may change from a hilltop with a view to an island in a sea of muddy water.

➤ Lightning that can damage electronic equipment without striking it. The charge can run up telecommunication wires to a PC and toast it easily. It can also damage electronics in your office without leaving a mark. Lightning is a danger to your employees, and steps should be taken to protect them from the danger of being struck and from lightning igniting flammable gases.

SNOW Heavy snow or blizzards can close access roads leading into and out of your building, keeping employees in and the next shift at home. Even if your local weather is manageable, you may still close if trucks full of materials cannot drive over snow-blocked roads. Snow storms should be monitored for wind speed and the distribution of snow. Snow piled high against buildings or on roofs can lead to structural problems or failure (see Figure 3-3).

EXTREME TEMPERATURES Extreme temperatures, whether hot or cold, can wreak havoc on your facility, your materials, and your employees. These are also peak energy demand times, which will further throw off your operating budget. Like snow and other risks, your team can decide what an extreme temperature is and the risk it will occur within the next 5 years.

HURRICANES Hurricanes are severe storms that form in tropical waters anywhere in the world. Their occurrences can be predicted by the weather service, but they cannot accurately predict where they will strike landfall and at what strength. Organizations located in or near coastal areas must have an evacuation plan in place for when hurricanes threaten. Hurricanes can spawn tornadoes, create tidal surges, and cause flooding. Evaluate the risk of just a hurricane occurring. Then evaluate the risk to each of the other categories separately.

FLOODS Floods or tidal surges are usually detected by the weather service. Thus, you have some warning that trouble is coming. The Federal Emergency Management Agency (FEMA) reports that more than 90% of natural disasters involve flooding. The tidal surge may be the result of a hurricane or severe storm

FIGURE 3-3: Little Rock, AR, December 29, 2000. Downed power cables were among the damage after an ice storm. (Photo by John Shea/FEMA News Photo.)

at sea. Floods can result from melting snow, severe downpours in the areas upriver from your location, and other natural causes. Usually, there will be some warning, but there may not be enough time to evacuate all your vital records and machinery.

Floods damage your property in many ways (see Figure 3-4):

➤ A flood will damage just about everything by soaking it in water. Office materials, computers, and manufacturing materials all can be seriously damaged by water. When the water finally moves out, mold can move in.

➤ The flood waters themselves may contain raw sewage or chemicals that will end up inside your building.

➤ Debris of all sizes is carried in the flood waters and can batter your walls, smash in windows, and be left strewn about when the waters subside.

➤ Flood waters typically contain mud and sand that will coat the floors and walls as the waters recede. This material will also be contaminated with whatever was in the flood waters.

FIGURE 3-4: Mullens, WV, July 17, 2001. An office supply store was in shambles after flood waters up to 9 feet hit earlier in the month. (Photo by Leif Skoogfors/FEMA News Photo.)

OTHER NATURAL DISASTERS Forest fires or large brush fires may threaten your facility or the access roads to it. Landslides can close roads and damage facilities, depending on your topography. This is more common if your facility is located on or near a hill or your main roads pass along hillsides. Mudslides can result from heavy rainfall. Sinkholes (subsidence) are the result of surface collapse from a lack of support underneath, as might be caused by groundwater dissolving a soft material such as limestone, or from abandoned mine tunnels. Sandstorms resulting from high winds can damage vehicles, seep dust and grit into machine shops, and close access roads.

Manufactured Risks

All around you are potential human-created risks. If you are in a city, this is an even greater problem. These risks are the result of someone else's disaster or actions that affect your daily operations. Stand outside for a moment and look around. Drive around the nearby roads and make notes of what you see. Look for large outside storage tanks, semitrailers with gas, or hazardous warning signs.

HOW TO IDENTIFY MANUFACTURED RISKS:

Get a map of your area from FEMA. It will show the routes taken by hazardous material carriers. It will have similar information on railroad usage and pipelines. Determine if a problem with these would block your only decent road access or if a toxic gas leak were blown your way, how close must it be to cause your facility to be evacuated.

Get a good local road map. Mark any obstacles that would hinder or prevent access to your facility if routes were inaccessible, such as major bridges and primary highways. Now mark those things whose operation would stop or hinder access, such as drawbridges or surface-level railroad tracks. This map will be further used when studying Layer 2 risks.

INDUSTRIAL SITES Note any industrial sites with large outdoor storage tanks. What is in them? Do they contain distilled water or industrial chemicals? A major chemical release could cause a wide area to be evacuated. Your facility or access to your facility could be affected while the chemical spill is being contained.

TRANSPORTATION Major highways may be used to transport toxic materials through your area. If a truck flipped over and there was a major toxic spill, do you have another access road into your facility? (If this occurs close by, your building may need to be evacuated.) Bridges across large bodies of water or intercoastal waterways can be damaged by collisions with barges or boats. If you are on an island, do you have another suitable way in? If the bridge arches high into the air to allow seagoing vessels to pass underneath, is it often closed during high winds or ice storms? Railroads also transport toxic material. Does your building have a railroad siding next to it where someone else's railcars with potentially hazardous cargo could be temporarily stored? Is your facility located on or near a flight path? This includes small dirt strips as well.

PIPELINES Are there any underground pipelines in your area? These often carry fuels. A pipe rupture can force an evacuation lasting several days.

CHEMICAL USERS These are all around, often unknown to their neighbors. For example, many water treatment plants use chlorine to treat water. A chlorine gas leak can force an evacuation of a wide area.

DAMS Dams require regular maintenance. In extreme weather, they may overflow or become damaged; ask about soft spots.

Civil Risks

The risk from civil problems is a tough area that covers a lot of ground. Organizations are susceptible to civil disturbances because of some political agenda or they might simply be located in an affected area.

RIOTS What is the risk of a riot occurring in your area? Is it higher in an urban area (where the people are) than in a rural area? In general, it would be less likely in an affluent area than in an area with a concentration of less affluent people. It might be less likely in the middle of an industrial park than on a busy street corner.

LABOR DISPUTES Another risk is the potential of a labor dispute turning into a strike. The picket lines that usually accompany a strike might cause material and employee flow problems if truck drivers and employees refuse to or cannot cross the picket lines. Similar to a labor stoppage is the risk of secondary picketing. If your labor relations are sound, but one of your suppliers is in the midst of a labor dispute, their employees may choose to publicize their dispute by picketing companies that continue to use products made by their company. Even though these picket lines tend to be much smaller, you may have union truck drivers who will not drive across them.

TERRORISM The threat from terrorism is unfortunately a growing problem worldwide. It is typically defined as the calculated use or threat of violence against civilians for reasons that are political, religious, or ideological in nature. Acts of terrorism can include bombings, kidnappings, hijackings, hacking, or other forms of violence or intimidation. As the attacks on 9/11 demonstrated, terrorism can have an impact over a wide area both on physical facilities and the ability of employees to do their jobs.

BIOLOGICAL ATTACKS This is the intentional release of germs or other biological agents in an attempt to cause serious illness or death over a wide area. Some agents are contagious and can spread from person to person (e.g., smallpox) or are limited to individuals who come into direct contact with the agent (e.g., anthrax). As we have seen in the many anthrax scares recently the material does not have to be real to cause a disruption to your business.

Supplier Risks

Another category of risk is how well your suppliers can maintain their flow of goods into your facility. Make a list of your key suppliers and ask yourself, in every case, what is the risk that they cannot manufacture and deliver your required material to your dock on time in the event of any of the aforementioned disasters. This is critical for manufacturers who depend on just-in-time deliveries.

You need to consider the condition of the access roads or rail service between your facility and your key suppliers. This could be interrupted by area-wide disasters, such as blizzards or flooding.

SUPPLIER RISKS

What to Do?

1. Make up a list of key suppliers or service providers whose absence for more than 48 hours would shut you down. (You can change the 48 hours to whatever value you think is appropriate.)

2. Plot their location on a map (down to the road intersection if local, or to the town if distant). Pushpins work well for this.

3. Identify potential problems along their routes. For example, are they in St. Louis and need to cross the Mississippi River to reach your facility? If so, what is the risk they can't get across in the event of a major flood?

4. For local suppliers, check to see if they have multiple routes to reach you or have their own traffic flow bottlenecks.

Sources of Information for Layer 1 Risks:

Earthquakes: http://earthquake.usgs.gov/research/hazmaps/

Tornadoes: http://www.nssl.noaa.gov/hazard/hazardmap.html

Severe storms: http://www.nssl.noaa.gov/hazard/totalthreat.html

Manufactured hazards: Your local Federal Emergency Management Agency (FEMA) office can be found in the county or state sections of your local telephone book or at the FEMA Web site at http://www.fema.gov/about/contact/statedr.shtm. They will be an invaluable source of the risks and mitigation actions for Layer 1 risks in your locale.

Access hazards: A road map and a topographical map.

LAYER 2: FACILITY-WIDE RISK

A facility-wide risk is something that only impacts your local facility. Some companies span many locations and will need to make a separate risk assessment for each location. Each assessment can be for one building or a cluster of buildings. In either event, a facility-wide risk involves multiple departments and would slow or stop the flow of business.

An example might be a facility that takes toll-free calls from around the country for hotel reservations. The loss of their internal telephone switch could idle hundreds of workers. Customers who could not complete their calls would phone a different hotel chain. This costs the company in direct revenue and is compounded by the loss of valuable customer goodwill through the uncompleted calls.

Another example is the loss of electrical power. Unless you sit next to a window on a sunny day, the loss of electrical power will mean all work stops when the lights go out. In addition, all your desktop PCs will "crash" and lose any data in their memories. Just the labor time alone to reboot this equipment can be substantial.

We will begin with the essential utilities we all take for granted, and then move into the important areas of people risks. There are five basic office utilities that we all take for granted, but without them, the doors might close quickly. They are:

➤ Electricity
➤ Telephones
➤ Water
➤ Climate Control
➤ Data Network

WHAT TO DO?
Use the local map that was marked up in Layer 1 and indicate the location of the local fire department, ambulance service, hospital, and police station. Look for access problems.

Electricity

Electricity gives us lights. It powers our office and manufacturing machines. It is magically there every time we need it—just plug in! Stop and think of the complexity involved in generating electricity and then moving it hundreds of miles to where it is needed. This is truly an engineering marvel. And it is very reliable. So reliable that when it is stopped, people become very annoyed as if something they had a right to expect was taken from them.

To properly determine the risk of an electrical outage, begin with the team's own experiences with the frequency, timing, and length of outages in this area. Frequency is how many times it might occur within your 5-year planning window. Timing is what time of day or day of the week it usually happens. In some places, it seems most likely to occur during severe thunderstorms. In other locales, it might be most likely to stop during ice storms.

The second step is to consult your facilities maintenance department. Find out how many power feeds run into the building and if they enter from opposite ends of the building. It is not uncommon to only have one. If so, then you have just uncovered a potential single point of failure. It is better to have more than one power feed to your building.

One thing to understand is that even if electricity is unavailable across a wide area, the landline telephone system may still work. You might consider maintaining at least one landline connection if your organization moves to other technologies such as voice-over-IP (VoIP) or all cell phones, as a blackout could last longer than your UPS or cell phone batteries. You can use this to notify the power company of the outage, to see how widespread it is, and to ask when they expect to have it operational again.

Telephones

Telephones are your window to the world. In the blink of an eye, you communicate with customers and suppliers in any corner of the world. Telephones also provide a crucial lifeline to emergency services during a disaster. Loss of telephone service hurts some companies more than others, but few companies can function without it for an extended period of time.

A critical aspect of telephone communications is that your external company data network often runs over the same cables. So if a backhoe operator cuts the cable to your building, you could lose both the telephones and the external data lines at the same time.

When evaluating your telephone risk, check out your local telephone service architecture. If the local central office was inoperable, would your telephones still work? If you can reach multiple central offices, then the answer is yes. If you are only connected to one central office, then its loss is your loss.

Most companies have their own Private Branch Exchange (PBX) system. Damage to this room could very effectively shut down your internal telephone system. How do you rate the risk or likelihood of this happening?

Water

One thing we can look forward to every winter is the breaking of water mains. As the ground is saturated with fall or winter moisture and then freezes, it expands and contracts, stressing older water main lines. Eventually, one will give way and a section of the town will be without fresh water until it is fixed.

If you are operating a restaurant, you use a lot of water for sanitation and for customers. So, of course, if a water main broke you could be closed for several hours. If this occurred during a particularly profitable time of day or day of the week, you could lose a lot of money. If it happened very often, you could lose customer goodwill.

Office buildings are also major water users. Many computer and PBX rooms are cooled by "chilled water" systems. If these units lose water pressure, they can no longer cool the air and the central computer equipment could overheat. If this occurred on a weekend, you might find out when everyone streams in on Monday. By then, the heat has damaged expensive electronic components and your systems are useless.

Office buildings also use water for sanitation. If you have 500 people in a building, you have a lot of flushes in one day. If your neighborhood water main was broken, how long would your building be habitable?

Climate Control

Loss of heating or air conditioning might be an inconvenience depending on the time of the year. In the depth of winter or the height of summer, this could make for very uncomfortable working conditions and be very damaging to your manufacturing materials and electronic systems.

Loss of heat in the depths of winter:

➤ Can cause your building to cool to the point of freezing. This could lead to frozen sprinkler pipes that could rupture and leak upon melting.

➤ Can affect integrated circuits in electronic equipment that are not designed for extreme cold and may malfunction.

➤ Can, in a manufacturing environment, stop production as the viscosity of paint, lubricants, and fluids used in normal production is increased. Water-based products may be ruined if frozen.

Loss of air conditioning in the heat of summer:

➤ Can result in office closures because the high heat could lead to heat stroke or heat exhaustion. Remember to consult the heat index for your area, as humidity can make the air temperature feel much warmer and can impact people sooner.

➤ Can, in a factory, lead to the overheating of moving machinery much faster and potentially beyond its rated operating temperature.

➤ Requires that you monitor the temperatures of your computer and PBX rooms and shut down if it is in excess of the manufacturer's rated temperatures or risk losing warranty claims.

➤ Can result in a loss of humidity control that may add moisture to your vital records storage room, leading to the potential for mildew growth.

Data Network

Most companies depend heavily on their data communication network to conduct daily business. It is the tool that allows desktop workstations to share data, send e-mail confirmations, and receive faxed orders into e-mail, as well as providing a wealth of other benefits. In many companies, losing the data network is as severe a problem as losing electricity. We'll discuss data communications issues more thoroughly below in Level 3, Data Systems Risks.

Other facility-wide risks to review are those that endanger the people in the facility. These people risks include:

➤ Fire

➤ Structural Problems

➤ Security Issues

➤ Medical Concerns

FIRE What do you think the risk is of a fire occurring in your facility? This can be a fire of any size depending on what you see in place today to deal with it. There may be fire extinguishers in every corner, but that does not mean there is a low risk of fire. This risk should take into account the local conditions (does it get very dry in summer), the amount of combustibles stacked around the facility, and the construction of the building itself (wood, cement, etc.).

Another risk factor to add is the reaction time for fire crews to reach your site. If it is rural, it may take additional time to collect volunteer firefighters at the stationhouse before they can respond (see Figure 3-5).

STRUCTURAL PROBLEMS Structural problems may be caused by design flaws, poor materials, or even human mistakes. In any event, consider the risks of damage from the very building you are sitting in.

➤ Weather-related structural failure might arise from a heavy snowfall weighing on the roof or even from high winds.

FIGURE 3-5: NOAA news photo. (From Frankel et al., U.S. Geological Survey, 1997.)

➤ A fire on one floor of a building may be quickly contained, but the water used to extinguish it will seep through the floor and damage equipment and vital records stored below. Any large fire, no matter how quickly it is contained, has the capability to weaken an entire structure.

➤ Water pipe breakage can occur from a part of the building freezing from heat shut off over a holiday, or from a worker snapping off a sprinkler head with their ladder as they walk down a hall.

➤ Lightning does not have to hit your building to damage sensitive electronic components. However, if it does, you could lose valuable data and equipment in a very, very short time. Buildings must have proper grounding and lightning protection.

SECURITY ISSUES The quality of security surrounding a workplace has gained widespread attention in recent years. Historically, the facility's security force was used to prevent theft of company property and to keep the curious away from company secrets. In more recent years, the threat of workplace violence, often from outsiders, has led to a resurgence of interest in having someone screen anyone entering your facility. Issues that your security people must be trained to deal with include:

➤ **Workplace Violence.** What is the risk of someone in your facility losing his or her temper to the point of a violent confrontation with another person?

➤ **Bomb Threats.** Every occurrence of a bomb threat must be taken seriously. A bomb threat can disrupt critical processes while police investigators determine if there is a valid threat to public safety or if it is just a crank call. This risk can vary according to the public profile of your company, the type of products you produce, or even the level of labor tension in your offices.

➤ **Trespassing.** Employee and visitor entrance screening is critical. What is the likelihood of someone bypassing or walking through security screening at your entrance? You might wish to break this down further into the risk of a deranged nonemployee out to revenge some imagined wrong by an employee to a thief looking to rummage through unattended purses. These things can tragically occur anywhere, but you can set this risk according to the team's experience at this facility.

➤ **Physical Security of Property.** This involves theft, either by employees or outsiders. The thief can steal from employees or from the company. It is expensive for a company to have a laptop PC stolen. It is even more expensive if that PC has company confidential data in it. Physical security involves employee identification badges, a key control program, and electronic security access to sensitive areas.

➤ **Sabotage.** Sabotage is the intentional destruction of company property. This can be done by an employee or by an outsider. There are some parts of your facility that are only open to authorized people. Examples are the PBX room, the computer room, and the vital records storage. What is the risk that someone will bypass the security measures and tamper with or destroy something in a sensitive area? Another thing to think about is to determine if all your sensitive areas are secured from sabotage.

➤ **Intellectual Property or Theft of Confidential Company Information.** What is the risk that valuable company information will miss a shredder and end up in a dumpster outside? This could be customer lists, orders with credit card numbers, or even old employee records.

WHAT TO DO?

Obtain copies of your company policies for security and safety. The security team often has emergency procedures for fire and police support. Add them to your plan.

Examine your security policy for a date that it was last reviewed or published.

Compare the written policy to how security is actually implemented at your facility.

MEDICAL CONCERNS The standard answer you hear to evaluating medical risks usually involves calling for an ambulance. This is a good answer. But when evaluating the likelihood of these risks, you might add to your disaster plan equipment and personnel who could provide aid while waiting for the ambulance to arrive. Examples are hanging emergency medical kits or defibrillators around the facility. Some companies register all employees who are certified Emergency Medical Technicians (EMTs) and pay them extra to carry a pager. In the event of a medical emergency, they are dispatched to the location to assist until proper medical support arrives. It may even make sense to staff an industrial nurse during production hours. Medical issues might include these:

➤ **Sickness.** What is the risk of someone coming down with a serious sickness while at work? Some serious illnesses can come on suddenly.

➤ **Sudden Death.** What is the risk of someone falling over dead? This risk should factor in the age of the workforce and the types of materials used in your facility.

➤ **Serious Accident.** Do you use heavy machinery or high voltages in your processes? Are serious accidents a real risk in your line of business?

➤ **Fatal Accident.** Along the lines of the serious accident, is there a risk of a fatal accident at your site?

What other Layer 2 Risks can you or your team identify? Add them to Form 3-2 on the CD-ROM.

WHAT TO DO?

Find out about local fire/ambulance service. What hours is it staffed? Is it full time or run by volunteers?

What is the distance from the stationhouse to your door?

Are there obstacles that might delay an ambulance, such as a drawbridge or surface-level railroad tracks?

What is the distance to a hospital?

LAYER 3: DATA SYSTEMS RISKS

Data systems risks are important because one problem can adversely affect multiple departments. Data systems typically share expensive hardware, such as networks, central computer systems, file servers, and even Internet access. A complete study of data system risk would fill its own book, so this chapter examines these risks from an end-user perspective.

Your data systems architecture will to a great degree determine your overall risks. Its design will reflect the technology costs and benefits of centralized/decentralized software and data. A more common company-wide risk is a loss of the internal computer network. With a heavy dependence on shared applications and data files, many companies are at a standstill without this essential resource. Even a short interruption will lose valuable employee time as they reconnect to the central service.

A major goal in examining data systems risks is to locate your single points of failure. These are the bottlenecks where a problem would have wide-reaching impact. In later chapters, we will review our single points of failure for opportunities to install redundant devices.

Some of the hidden risks in data systems are processes that have always been there and have worked fine for a long period of time. It is possible that they are running on obsolete machines that could not be repaired if damaged in a disaster, and their software program likely could not be readily transferred quickly to another processor. Your only choice is to try to make your old program function on the new hardware. As anyone who has tried to use an old program while leaping generations of hardware technology can tell you, this can be a time-consuming process. Due to the sudden change to new equipment and operating software, your programs may require substantial fine-tuning to run. This "forced upgrade" will delay your full recovery.

Computer programs exist in two forms. The "English-like" source code is what the programmer writes. The computer executes a processed version of the program called "machine code." A typical data processing problem is finding the original source code. Without this, programs cannot be easily moved to a different computer. This leads to processes relying on obsolete languages or programs to work.

The risk analysis at this level is from the end-user perspective, as the data department should already have a current plan. If so, these items may be lifted from their plan.

WHAT TO DO?
Use the Critical Process Impact Matrix (Form 3-3) found on your CD. We will also use this matrix for Layers 4 and 5.

The Critical Process Impact Matrix will become a very valuable part of your disaster recovery plan. Whenever the IS department wants to restart the AS/400 over lunchtime to address an important error, you can sort the matrix by the platform column and see which systems will stop working during this time and thereby quickly see the impact of this action. You would also know which customer contacts to notify.

The matrix has the following columns:

➤ **System.** Enter the name commonly used to refer to this overall computer system, such as Accounts Payable, Materials Management System, Traffic Control System, etc. However, this does not have to be a computer-based system as it can apply to any important process.

➤ **Platform.** Enter the computer system this runs on, such as AS/400 #3, a VAX named Alvin, etc.

➤ **Normal Operating Days/Times.** What times and days do you normally need this? Use the first one or two letters for the days of the week and enter 24 hours if it must always be up.

➤ **Critical Operating Days/Times.** Use the same notation as for normal times and days. Some systems have critical times when it must be up for 24 hours, such as when Accounting closes the books at the end of the month, end of quarter, etc. Use as many critical days/time entries as you need.

➤ **Support Primary/Backup.** Who in the IS department writes changes or answers questions about this system? These must be someone's name and not a faceless entity like "Help Desk."

➤ **Customer Contacts Primary/Backup.** Who should the IS department call to inform them of current or upcoming system problems? Often this is a department manager.

Fill in the matrix. This will take quite a while. Every system on this list must have at least a basic disaster recovery plan written for it—but more on that later.

Now that we have identified the critical processes, we need to break each process down into its main components. Remember, this is only necessary for your critical processes. Use the Critical Process Breakdown matrix (Form 3-4 found on your CD). This matrix helps to identify the critical components for each system. By focusing on the critical components, we can keep this sheet manageable. If your facility is ISO compliant, then much of this is already in your process work instructions.

> **System.** This name ties the Breakdown matrix to the Critical Process Impact Matrix. Be sure to use the same system names on both matrixes.

> **Platform.** Enter the computer system this runs on, such as AS/400 #3, a VAX named Alvin, etc.

> **Key Components.** There may be more than one of each item per category for each critical process.

  ◆ **Hardware.** List specialized things here such as barcode printers, check printers, RF scanners, etc.

  ◆ **Software.** What major software components does this use? This is usually multiple items.

  ◆ **Materials.** List unique materials needed, such as preprinted forms or special labels.

  ◆ **Users.** If this is widely used, list the departments that use it. If its use is confined to a few key people, then list them by name or title.

  ◆ **Suppliers.** Who supplies the key material? If the materials required are highly specialized, then list supplier information. Ensure this is included on the key supplier list. If the material is commonly available, then we can skip this.

Data Communications Network

The data communications network is the glue that ties all the PCs to the shared servers and to shared printers. Without the data network, the Accounting department cannot exchange spreadsheets, the call center cannot check its databases, and the Shipping department cannot issue bills of lading.

A data network is a complex collection of components, so the loss of network functionality may be localized within a department due to the failure of a single hub card.

Based on the collective knowledge of your team, what do you believe is the likelihood of a failure of your data network? Ask the same question of your network manager. Based on these two answers, plug a value into the risk assessment for this category.

Telecommunications System

Modern Private Branch Exchanges (PBXs) are special-purpose computers, optimized for switching telephone calls. They may also include voice mail and long-distance call tracking.

Your facility's telephone system is your connection to the outside world. If your company deals directly with its customers, special care must be taken because a dead telephone system can make them very uneasy. Telephones are used constantly internally to coordinate between departments and, in an emergency, to call outside for help.

Based on the collective knowledge of your team, what do you believe the likelihood is of a failure of your company's telephone system? Ask the same question of your Telecommunications manager. Based on these two answers, plug a value into the risk assessment for this category.

Shared Computers and LANs

There are many types of shared computers used by companies. They usually are grouped under the old name of "mainframe" but refer to shared computers of all sizes. It also includes the common term of LAN (Local Area Network). These computers typically support a wide range of programs and data. When evaluating the risks here, you have two questions:

➤ What is the risk of losing a specific shared application (such as inventory control, payroll, etc.)? You should list each critical application separately.

➤ What is the risk of losing use of the machine itself? This could be due to damage to the machine or more likely through a hardware failure.

These risks should be based on the collective knowledge of your team. Ask the same question of your computer operations manager. Based on these two answers, plug a value into the risk assessment for this category. If desired, list each of the network servers individually.

Viruses

What do you think the likelihood is of a computer in your facility contracting a software "virus"? How severely would this interrupt business? What would your customers think of your company if, before it was detected, you passed the virus on to them? What if it struck a key machine at a critical time? What if its mischievous function was to e-mail out, to anyone in your address book, anything that had the words "budget," "payroll," or "plan" in the file name?

Most companies have an Internet firewall and virus scanning software installed. When evaluating this risk, ask your data manager's opinion of the quality of his software. Ask how often the catalog of known viruses is updated.

Viruses can also enter your company through many other sources. Often they come in through steps people take to bypass the firewall or virus scanning, both of which take place only on files coming into your facility from the outside over your external data network.

➤ Does your company allow employees to take their laptop computers out of the office, for example, to their homes? Are their children loading virus-laden programs? Are the employees downloading files from their home Internet connection that would be filtered out by their desk-side connection?

➤ Does your antivirus software automatically update its catalog of known viruses, or must each person request this periodically?

➤ Do consultants, vendors, or customers bring laptop PCs into your facility and plug into your network to retrieve e-mail or to communicate orders?

➤ Is there virus-checking software to validate the attachments to your e-mail?

Data Systems

Theft of hardware (with critical data) can be a double financial whammy. You must pay to replace the hardware and then try to recreate valuable data. This risk spans your local site (do PCs disappear over the weekend?) all the way through laptop PCs taken on business trips.

Theft of software can be a major issue if someone steals a PC program and then distributes illegal copies of it. You may find yourself assumed guilty and facing a large civil suit. This can also happen if well-meaning employees load illegal copies of software around the company.

Theft of data can occur, and you will never realize it. This could be engineering data, customer lists, payroll information, security access codes, and any number of things. What do you believe your risk is of this?

Data backups are the key to rapid systems recovery. But what if you reach for the backup tapes and they are not readable? What is the risk that these tapes are not written, handled, transported, and stored correctly?

Hacker Security Break-In

One aspect of connecting your internal network to the Internet is that it is a potential portal for uninvited guests to access your network. Even well-built defenses can be circumvented with careless setup or news of gaps in your security firewall software. In some cases, they invade your system only to mask their identity when they attack a different company. This way, all indications are that you originated the attack!

Hackers generally fall into several categories, none of them good for you:

➤ Curious hackers just want to see if they can do it. You never know when this person will advance to the malicious level, and they should not be in your system.

➤ Malicious or criminal hacking involves invading your site to steal or to damage something.

➤ In extreme cases, a hacker may conduct a denial of service attack and shut you down by bombarding you with network traffic, which overwhelms your network's ability to answer all the messages.

What other Layer 3 risks can you and your team identify? Add them to the list in Form 3-5, Risk Assessment Form Layer 3, on the CD-ROM.

LAYER 4: DEPARTMENTAL RISKS

Departmental risks are the disasters you deal with in your own department on a daily basis. They range from the absence of a key employee to the loss of an important computer file. Most of these obstacles are overcome through the collective knowledge of the people in the department who either have experienced this problem before or know of ways to work around it.

At this stage of the risk analysis, we are looking at disastrous local problems. Consider for a moment what would happen if a worker changing light bulbs were to knock the head off a fire sprinkler. You know the ones I mean. A fire sprinkler nozzle typically protrudes from the ceiling into your office.

Losing a sprinkler head will put a lot of water all over that office very quickly. Papers will be destroyed, PCs possibly sizzled, and all work stopped for hours. The carpets will be soaked, water seeps through the floor to the offices on the floor below—what a mess!

A small fire is another localized disaster. It may spread smoke over a large area, making an office difficult to work in. Depending on how it was started and the extent of the damage, that area might be inaccessible for several days, especially if the Fire Marshall declares an arson investigation and no one is allowed near the "crime scene"!

Departmental risks also include the situation referred to in the data systems section where a unique device is used that is not easily or economically repairable. If this device is also a single point of failure, then you had better treat it like gold.

To build a departmental risk assessment, assemble a department-wide team to identify your critical functions, risks unique to your department, and risks to other departments that will cause problems in your group. Draft a fresh list of the critical functions that apply to your department. You can omit those functions already listed in the first three layers unless you are particularly vulnerable to something.

If a risk from an earlier layer will cause you to take particular action in your department, then include it here also. For example, if the loss of telephone service for your facility can be charged back against your telephone bill (based on your service agreement), then the Accounting department would need to time the outage and make the proper adjustment to their monthly bill. Another example is if you run the company cafeteria and an electrical outage threatens the food in your refrigerators.

Some examples of critical functions might include:

➤ Payroll

◆ To provide correct pay to all employees on time.

◆ To maintain accurate payroll records for every employee.

◆ To deduct and report to the appropriate government agency all payroll taxes that apply to every employee.

➤ Materials

◆ To maintain an accurate accounting of all material and its location in all storage locations.

◆ To maintain an accurate accounting of all materials issued.

◆ To ensure that material constantly flows to the manufacturing floor with minimal stock-outs, and with minimal inventory on hand.

➤ Building Security

◆ To provide immediate first aid to stricken employees until proper medical assistance arrives.

◆ To maintain the integrity of the building security cordon at all times, even in the face of disaster.

◆ To detect and notify appropriate authorities of any emergencies observed by security personnel.

◆ To monitor all personnel on the premises after normal business hours and during weekends and holidays.

WHAT TO DO?

Make a list of critical processes for your department.

Take a copy of the Critical Process Impact list and pull off those processes unique to each department. Now expand it to include the critical processes in your department. Not all critical processes involve computers.

Break down the newly added critical processes into their components.

Key Operating Equipment

After identifying your department's critical functions, make a list of your processes and equipment. This list will drive your department's recovery plan. A process would be something like "Materials Management." That process requires (within the department) access to the materials database, materials receiving docks, order processing, etc.

Is there a piece of equipment in your department whose absence would hinder your ability to perform your critical tasks? Is there an important printer directly tied to a far-off office or company? Is your only fax machine busy all the time? Does your payroll department have a dedicated time clock data collection and reporting system whose absence might prevent accurate recording?

Make a list of all your critical equipment. Be sure to include unique items not readily borrowed from a nearby department.

Lack of Data Systems

Begin with a list of all the data systems you use in your department. Add a column of who uses each system and for what function (some people may perform updates, some people may only write reports from it). You will find this list very useful later.

Most data systems have a manual process to record data or work around when it is not available. But set that aside and examine the risk that each system on your list might not be available. Here is a good place where the team's collective experience can state how often a system seems to be unavailable.

Vital Records

What are the vital records originated, used, or stored by your department? List each category of records and where they are stored. Identify the risk (or damage) to the company if these records were lost or destroyed. Vital records are paper or electronic documents retained to meet business, regulatory, legal, or government requirements.

What other Layer 4 risks can you and your team identify? Add them to Form 3-6, Risk Assessment Form Layer 4, on the CD-ROM.

LAYER 5: YOUR DESK'S RISKS

This means more than avoiding paper cuts. You must examine every process (manual and automated), tool, piece of incoming information, and required output that makes up your job. Since you are so familiar with your daily work, this will be faster than you think. You are also familiar with your office priorities and can focus on the most critical functions.

Performing a Layer 5 risk analysis may seem to be a bit of overkill, but it closely resembles what was done at the department level. It is useful for ensuring that everything you need to do your job is accounted for in some manner, and may be in your department's disaster recovery plan as nice to have but not essential. Still, if you want to go on vacation sometime, this documentation will make slipping out of the office a bit easier.

Layer 5 risks are a bit different because it really includes all of the risks from Layers 1 through 4. You should be able to start figuring out your critical functions from your job description. Next, you add in what you actually do and then you will have your critical functions list.

Make a list of the tools and data systems that you use every day. All of these should be in the departmental risk assessment. What is the likelihood that one of these tools will be missing when you need them? This means that the tools are only missing from your desk. Everyone else in the department can do their job. Therefore, if your job is the same as the person's next to you, the risk at this layer is quite low that you could not complete your work since you could borrow the necessary equipment.

If you had confidential files on your PC and it crashed, that would be a risk. If you had a unique device that you used for your job, such as a specialized PC for credit card authorizations, then that is also a unique risk (but is probably in your departmental plan if it impacts one of their critical functions).

Another area to consider is vital records. Do you build or store vital records on or around your desk? Could there be a localized fire, water pipe breakage, etc., in your area that would soak these papers? This could be backed-up personal computer files, engineering specifications of old parts, employee evaluations, etc.

What other Layer 5 risks can you or your team identify? Add them to Form 3-7, Risk Assessment Form Layer 5, on the CD-ROM.

WHAT TO DO?

Make a list of critical processes for your department.

Take a copy of your department's Critical Process Impact list and pull off those processes unique to your job. Now expand it to include all the critical processes for your position. Not all critical processes involve computers.

Break down the newly added critical processes into their components.

SEVERITY OF A RISK

As you consider such things as fire, you quickly notice that except in the total loss of the structure, it all depends on where and when the fire occurs. In addition, it depends on the day of the week and the time of day.

Time of Day

Imagine a large factory. It's 7:00 AM and the assembly line has begun moving. Off to one side of the assembly line is a 300-gallon "tote" of paint, waiting for a forklift to carry it to another part of the facility. When the forklift approaches, the operator is distracted and hits the tote at a high rate of speed, puncturing it near the bottom with both of his forks. The punctured tote begins spewing hundreds of gallons of potentially toxic paint across the floor, into the assembly line area, etc. Of course, the assembly operation is shut down while a long and thorough cleanup process begins.

If this same forklift and the same operator were to hit the same tote after normal working hours, we would have the same mess and the same cleanup expense, but we could possibly have avoided shutting down the assembly line. With hard work, the assembly line could be ready for use by the next day. Therefore, the time of day that a disaster event occurs can have a major impact on its severity.

Day of Week

Along the same lines as the time of day, the day of the week (or for that matter, the day of the year) also determines the severity of a problem. If this same factory were working at its peak level with many temporary workers in an effort to deliver toys to stores in time for the Christmas season, this situation would be much worse than if it occurred during their low-demand season. If it happened on a Saturday instead of on a Monday, the severity would also be less as you have the remainder of the weekend to address it.

Location of the Risk

In terms of where this theoretical toxic material spill occurred, you can also quickly see that its location, near the assembly line, had an impact on how damaging it was. Some risks, like paint containers, float around a manufacturing facility. In an office, a similar situation exists. A small fire in an outside trash dumpster might singe the building and be promptly extinguished. The damage would be annoying, but your office productivity would not miss a beat.

The same small fire in your vital records storage room would be a disaster. Water damage to the cartons of paper would cause papers to stick together, cartons to weaken and collapse, and a general smoky smell that will linger for a long time. There is also a potential long-term problem with mold damaging the records.

SOURCES OF RISK ASSESSMENT INFORMATION

The Federal Emergency Management Agency (formerly known as Civil Defense) can provide you with a wealth of local information about your Layer 1 risks. It has already mapped the approved hazardous materials routes and know what the local natural disaster likelihood is. FEMA is listed in your telephone directory and can also be found at http://www.fema.gov. Figure 3-6 shows a sample of the type of maps available from the government that show the likelihood of various hazards; this map shows the probability of an earthquake occurring.

Local fire and police departments are also likely sources for information on anticipated arrival times for help. If you have a volunteer fire department, you would like to know their average response time for your area and what you might expect for timely ambulance support. The longer the delay in responding, the more mitigation steps that your company should plan for. Some volunteer departments staff a few full-time members to provide an immediate response and the rest of the volunteers join them at the accident site.

The local law enforcement authorities can also provide insight into crime activity patterns for determining your risk of theft or civil disorder.

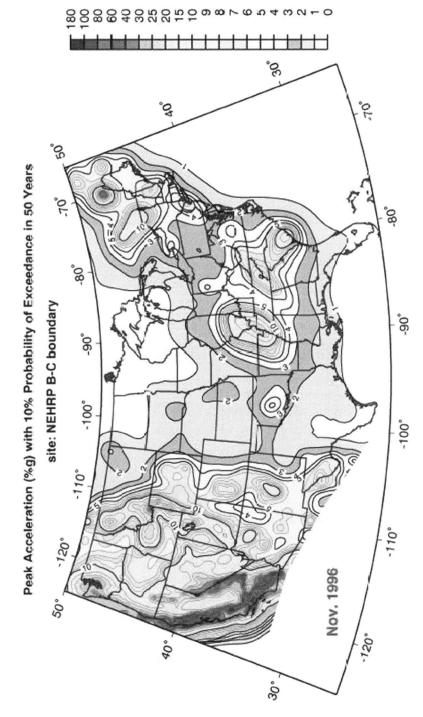

Peak Acceleration (%g) with 10% Probability of Exceedance in 50 Years site: NEHRP B-C boundary

Nov. 1996

FIGURE 3-6: U.S. Geological Survey National Seismic Hazard Mapping Project.

MAKING THE ASSESSMENT

Wow! Now that we see that risks are all around us, that they vary in time, magnitude, and business impact, let's make some sense of all of this. This is a good time to bring your Disaster Planning Project team together. The more "institutional knowledge" you can tap for this list, the better tool it becomes.

Scoring

OK, now the risk analysis sheets have been filled and the scores calculated. Now it is time to identify the more likely risks and build plans for them.

Scoring the list involves your judgment of several factors. First, how likely is it that this will occur? If you think about, given an infinite amount of time, you could predict that about everything will occur at least once. So for this scoring exercise, let's use a 5-year horizon. Of course, you can use any timeframe you wish. Just be consistent.

We will use the electrical power outage as an example as we examine the column headings:

➤ **Grouping.** These are the overall categories provided to keep similar issues together.

➤ **Risk.** This is where you list the various risks to your business.

➤ **Likelihood.** 0 through 10, with 0 being no likelihood at all, 1 to 3 if there is little chance of this type of disaster occurring, 4 to 6 if there is a nominal chance of occurrence, 7 to 9 if the disaster is very likely to occur, and 10 if it is a sure thing that the disaster will occur. Remember your planning horizon. If it is 5 years, be sure to keep that in the forefront of everyone's mind. So over the next 5 years, what is the likelihood that the facility will lose electrical power at any time of the day, or any day of the week?

➤ **Impact.** 0 through 10, with 0 being no impact at all, 1 to 3 if there is an inconvenience to some people or departments, 4 to 6 if there is a significant loss of service to some people or departments, 7 to 9 if there is a loss of a mission critical service, and 10 as a death sentence for the company. How badly would this disaster hurt us? To judge this, consider the problem occurring at the busiest time of the day, on the busiest day of the year.

➤ **Cost of Mitigation.** 1 through 10, with 10 being there is little to no cost to mitigate the risk, 7 to 9 if the cost to mitigate can be approved by a supervisor, 4 to 6 if the cost to mitigate requires a department head to approve, and 1 to 3 if senior management approval is required to cover the cost of mitigation. This scale runs the opposite of the other two columns, as we assign high values to risks that are easier to mitigate. Carrying forward the electrical service example, what would it cost to mitigate the risk of losing power (which would probably require the installation of a standby generator)?

Sorting

The spreadsheet multiplies the Likelihood times the Impact times the Cost of Mitigation to get a rough risk analysis score. As you can see, a zero value in the Likelihood or Impact columns makes the risk score a zero.

You should sort the spreadsheet on the "score" column in descending order. This will bring your biggest risks to the top. These will be the risks that are the most likely, have the biggest impact on your operations, and are the easiest to mitigate. As you start your disaster recovery and mitigation plans, these risks deserve the most attention.

Setting Aside the Low Scores

It is true that there is a risk that the sun may quit shining within the next 5 years, but it is very low. So along with the risk of being run over by an iceberg, we will discard any of the extremely low likelihood risks. We will be fully occupied addressing the more likely ones.

Pick a point on each list and draw a line across it. All critical systems above the line will have plans written for them and plans for all below the line will come at some later time.

CONCLUSION

Your assessment of the risks faced by your operation is a critical piece of the business continuity puzzle. The steps in identifying the major risks to your operation as discussed in this chapter are:

1. First, determine the cost of downtime. This is critical when evaluating the potential avoidance and mitigation options.

2. Identify the potential risks at each of the five levels. Use a 5-year time horizon to keep things manageable.

3. For each risk, determine the impact based on the time of day, the day of the week, and the location where the disaster occurred. Each of these factors has an impact on the severity of the risk.

4. Identify and use outside sources of risk information, such as emergency response operations at the local and state level.

5. Prioritize the risks based on the severity of the possible damage, the probability of the risk occurring, and the difficulty of available avoidance and mitigation options. You'll want to start with the risks that do the most damage, are the most likely, and are the easiest to avoid or mitigate.

Now that you've identified the risks that can affect your business, you are much better prepared to recover from any disaster. The steps required to identify risks are time consuming but are critical in building a foundation for your business continuity plans.

CHAPTER 4

SELECTING A STRATEGY
Setting the Direction

However beautiful the strategy,
you should occasionally look at the results.
— Sir Winston Churchill

INTRODUCTION

With the results of the Business Impact Analysis and risk assessment in hand, it is time to select a recovery strategy. The recovery strategy is the overall direction for planning your recovery. It provides the "what" of your recovery plan. Individual plans are the "how" it will be done. An approved strategy keeps the company's recovery plans in sync and avoids working at cross purposes.

A recovery strategy is not for restoring things to the way they were before. It is for restoring vital business functions to a minimally acceptable level of service. This minimal level of service enables the company to provide a flow of goods and services to its customers and buys time for planning a permanent recovery. There will be a separate recovery strategy for different parts of the company.

Disaster recovery planning is all defensive. Like insurance, you pay year after year so that if something did occur, you are covered. If nothing happens, then the money is spent with nothing tangible to show for it. The business benefit of disaster recovery planning (a subset of business continuity planning) is that it reduces the risk that a major company catastrophe will close the doors forever.

Another strategy deals with business continuity for operating a company that overcomes "in-process disasters" and keeps operating. Facility-destroying disasters are rare. More common are the many local disasters that occur in a process. Business continuity returns value to the company by developing contingency plans in case of a vital business function interruption. It also forces the company to examine its critical processes and to simplify them for easy recovery. Simpler processes are cheaper to operate, more efficient and more reliable. The business continuity strategy is in addition to and complementary to the disaster recovery strategy.

SELECTING A RECOVERY STRATEGY

Your recovery strategy determines the future costs and capability of your overall program. All subsequent plans will be written to fulfill the recovery time required, and solution selected. A poorly selected strategy will require all plans to be rewritten when it is replaced.

Companies have long struggled with how much money to spend on a quick recovery that may never be used. A recovery strategy is a tradeoff between time and money. The faster the ability to recover (up to near instantaneous), the higher the expense. The maximum recovery time that a company can tolerate an outage is its recovery time objective (RTO). This was identified by its Business Impact Analysis (BIA). Rapid recoveries are often favored until the initial and ongoing costs are detailed. However, a rapid recovery may also become a marketplace advantage by providing a more reliable product delivery.

The RTO is measured from the time when the incident occurs. Hours lost dithering around whether to declare a disaster or not is time lost toward your recovery time goal.

The classic error is to recover the data center which then sits idle because the various departments that use the IT systems were not recovered. Companies must craft a separate recovery strategy for each significant area:

➤ **Information Technology.** Recovering a data center, internal and external network connections, and telecommunications.

➤ **Work Area Recovery.** Recovering a place for office workers along with a personal computer, telephone, printer access, etc., all securely connected to the recovered data center.

➤ **Pandemic.** Maintaining business during a public health emergency that may run for 18 months or more.

➤ **Business Continuity.** Keeping the flow of products and services to customers despite significant failures in company processes.

➤ **Manufacturing.** Recovering the flow of products after a crisis.

➤ **Call Centers.** Maintaining customer contact throughout the crisis.

Whatever is decided, the recovery strategy must be communicated throughout the recovery project. All team members must understand the company's timeframe for recovering and the budgeted way to achieve it. It is the starting point for each recovery plan.

Recovery Point Objective

Another important factor is your recovery point objective (RPO). This is the amount of data that may be lost since your last backup. If your IT systems recover to the point of their last backup, perhaps from the night before, and the incident occurred at 3:00 PM the next day, then all of the data changes from the time of the last backup up to that 3:00 PM incident must be re-created after the data center is recovered. If not, the information is lost. Consider how many people take orders over the telephone and enter them directly into the order processing system. How many orders are shipped to customers with only online documentation? How many bank transfers are received in a day? In the past, this data might be reentered from paper documents. However, most of the paper products have been discontinued. Where will this data come from?

Time

We live in a "right now" world. Will the company's customers wait a week while someone cobbles together a data center to restore the data or for someone to answer customer service questions? The amount of time required to recovery a company's vital business functions is the first question. Can your company survive if it loses a day's worth of data? The BIA identified your RTO. The recovery strategy for all plans must meet this time goal. The RTO typically drives the cost of the entire program.

Distance

The distance between the primary and backup recovery sites depends on the risk assessment. Wherever you go, the recovery site must be far enough away so that the same catastrophe does not strike both sites. Wide-area disasters, such as floods, earthquakes, and hurricanes, can impact hundreds of square miles. Use your personal experience and that of the BCP team to identify areas that are not likely to be affected by the same risks.

The farther away your recovery site is, the more likely that the team must stay there overnight. This requires additional expense for hotel rooms, catered food, etc. However, there is a point where a recovery site is too far away. It is not unusual for a company to depend on a critical employee who is also a single parent. These people cannot stay away from home for extended periods.

In many cases, the distance is determined by the type of local threats from nature. If your company is located on a seacoast that is susceptible to hurricanes, then the recover site may be hundreds of miles inland to avoid the same storm disabling both sites. The same would be true in a floodplain such as along the Mississippi River. However, if you are located in the Midwest, then a one hour distance for a recovery site may suffice.

You cannot foresee everything that might go wrong. After the terrorist attack of September 11, 2001, many New York companies activated their disaster recovery plans. Since their recovery sites were hundreds of miles away, they had planned to fly to them. Who would have predicted that all of the country's civil air fleet would be ordered to remain grounded for so many days? In the end, driving was the only way to get there, delaying most recoveries by at least a day.

Recovery Options

Recovering a data center is different from recovering a warehouse is different from recovering a call center. In the end, all strategies come together to restoring a minimal level of service to the company within the RTO.

The primary recovery strategies are to:

➤ **Recover in a Different Company Site.** This provides maximum control of the recovery, of testing, and of employees. Some companies split operations so that each facility can cover the essential functions of the other in a crisis. The enemy of this approach is an executive's desire to consolidate everything into one large building to eliminate redundancies.

➤ **Subscribe to a Recovery Site.** This leaves all of the work of building and maintaining the recovery site to others. However, in a wide-area disaster (such as a hurricane), the nearest available recovery site may be hundreds of miles away since other subscribers may have already occupied the nearest recovery sites.

➤ **Wait Until the Disaster Strikes and Then Find Some Empty Space.** This approach requires lots of empty office and warehouse space that is already wired, etc. All we need to do is to keep tabs on availability and when needed, take out a lease on short notice. This approach results in a long recovery time but is the least expensive.

IT RECOVERY STRATEGY

IT systems were early adapters of disaster recovery planning. However, as technology has evolved, so have expectations for how quickly they must recover. Today's companies keep almost all of their data in their computer systems. Without this information, they stop working altogether. The time and expense to completely re-create it is unacceptable. Companies examining their alternatives must face up to the high cost of immediate recovery versus the lower cost of slowly rebuilding in a new site. IT recovery steps (even for a temporary facility) include rebuilding:

➤ **Environmental.** IT equipment must stay within a specific temperature and humidity range.

➤ **Infrastructure.** External network connection into the data center of the local service provider, and throughout the recovered data center; critical servers used by application servers such as a domain controller, DNS, DHCP, etc.

➤ **Applications.** Company specific software used by the business to address customer and internal administrative requirements.

➤ **Data.** The information needed by the company's business departments to support the flow of products and services.

In the past, the issue was to have a standby recovery site ready to go when needed. This model is based on reloading software and data from backup media (typically magnetic tape). However, this recovery strategy takes days. At best, when company data is loaded onto backup media, vital data is separated from nonvital data. Few companies bother to do this. The result is shuffling media in and out of a loader to load critical files while the company waits for a recovery. Refer to Figure 4-1 for a list of IT disaster recovery solutions; these fall into several general categories from slowest to fastest.

How much can these solutions cost? A hot-site contract will cost about as much per month as leasing your existing data center equipment. In a crisis, you must pay the monthly fee for each day of use. So, if you use a hot site in a disaster for 12 days, you might pay the same as you would for a year of disaster recovery coverage.

Recovery solutions, such as hot sites, are expensive. A popular solution is for a company to establish a second company data center about one hour's drive from the main data center. This location should use a different power grid and telecommunications company link than the main facility. A one-hour drive enables workers to sleep at home every night. (Remember that some of the employees will live in the opposite direction from the recovery site and the drive might be two hours each way.) This is especially important for single parents. Hopefully this is far enough away that the same wide-area disaster cannot strike both.

To prepare the recovery site, move to the second data center all of the test servers for the critical IT systems. Also move servers for the noncritical systems. Include adequate disk and network support. This provides equipment that is ready in a disaster, but not sitting idle. To save more time on recovery, mirror the critical data between the data center and the recovery site. Data replication requires a high-speed data connection with replication equipment at each end. The costs include data replication controllers at each end and a significant set of disk drives at the recovery site.

Let someone else do it. Application Service Providers (ASPs) provide data processing equipment, software licenses, and services to companies. Instead of operating your own data center, you run on their equipment at their site. Require that they maintain a Business Continuity Program. If this is your strategy, you must witness and audit their tests to ensure they provide the level of protection that you expect. The advantage is that this is their line of business and they will be more efficient at writing these plans and recovering at a different site. Ensure that

	Pros	Cons	Good for
Cold Site - an empty computer room without equipment	Inexpensive	Long recovery time (weeks) All data lost since last backup	Good for companies with a low reliance on data center through dispersed processing
Hot Site - adequate equipment installed and loaded with an operating system; internal and external network is active	Recovery in days (infrastructure is in place)	As expensive as a second data center All data lost since last backup	Good for companies that can wait days to recover
Hot Site with Data Replication	Recovery in hours as everything is already on disk Little data loss	Very expensive	Good for a quick recovery where a 1/2 day outage is tolerable
Failover - mirrors data and CPU operation; when the primary fails, the secondary site automatically takes over with minimal data loss	Outage measured in minutes or less	Very, very expensive to purchase and maintain Duplicate hardware to become obsolete Duplicate software licenses and hardware to pay maintenance fees	Online companies, hospitals, banks, and any company with a low tolerance to IT outages
Application Service Provider (ASP)	The ASP provides for disaster recovery planning and testing	Expensive Lack of control - Must ensure ASP regularly tests plans at their recovery site	Companies that do not manage their own applications recovery

FIGURE 4-1: IT disaster recovery solutions.

the ASP is contractually required to meet your RTO irrespective of its commitments to other customers.

Recommended IT Recovery Strategy

Establish a second company site at least a one-hour drive away in a place that is on a different power grid and data network. In this site, operate the company's primary production data center. Ensure this satellite office has telecommunications and network capacity to provide for a 25% surge in employees. Place the "Test" IT systems and noncritical IT equipment in the company headquarters building. The reasons for recommending this option include:

➤ If the headquarters offices are destroyed, the data center is safe, or vice versa. Then we only have to recover from one disaster at a time.

➤ We can continue telephone contact with our customers if either office fails and our customers will see only a slight drop in service.

➤ Using test servers as a backup data center avoids expensive "just-in-case" machines sitting idle. In an emergency, the test servers become the production machines for the applications they already support. Noncritical servers are repurposed for critical systems support.

➤ The company's application software is already on disk; we only need to load the current version.

➤ We know the alternate data center is connected to a live network because we use it daily.

➤ The company controls security access and facility maintenance of both sites.

➤ Backup media can be maintained in the headquarters facility (except for archive copies), which means savings on third-party storage for short periods.

➤ Potential to add data replication to avoid time lost loading data from tape and to minimize data losses.

➤ Recovery tests can be scheduled whenever we wish.

Example IT Recovery Strategy

The myCompany Data Center Disaster Recovery Strategy provides general guidance for critical system recovery after an incident renders the myCompany Data Center unusable. A recovery site has been prepared at our Shangrila data center that is about a one-hour commute from the existing work site. This recovery site is on a separate power grid and telecommunication connection. This site is also furnished and equipped to accommodate 75 office workers.

To facilitate this recovery, myCompany has located all test servers (and adequate disk storage) at the backup Data Center and keep production IT equipment at myCompany. The underlying assumption is that the test system hardware is an adequate substitute for the critical systems (CPU & RAM), and that each critical system has a corresponding set of test servers. In this way, myCompany has an operational hot site that is proven to work (idle sites tend to develop unnoticed problems).

Under this approach, servers in the backup Data Center are already loaded with the necessary version and patch level of the operating system. During a disaster, the test system is offloaded to tape or removable media. The equipment is then loaded with the current production version of the application (which should be present on their local disk drives).

All critical data is mirrored between the operational data center and the backup site. The estimated recovery time is in seconds with minimal data loss.

Reasons for this selection are:

➤ Quick recovery at the lowest cost.

➤ The recovery site is under myCompany control.

➤ Segregating test servers facilitates testing of DR plans.

➤ Keeps production data in myCompany for easier backups.

WORK AREA RECOVERY STRATEGY

The general term for recovering damaged offices is "work area recovery." A common disaster recovery error is to focus solely on the IT recovery without providing a place from which to access it.

On September 14, 2008, the remnants of Hurricane Ike swept through the Ohio Valley with sustained winds equal to a Category 1 hurricane. This resulted in widespread power outages that lasted for many days. The author worked for an organization whose generator promptly roared to life and kept the data center in operation even though none of the offices were wired for backup power. The people arrived at work to hear the generator running but no lights inside or power for desktop PCs. No one had any place to work, so they were all sent home. After several (expensive) days of running the generator, power was restored to that portion of the city.

Just like your IT recovery strategy, the work area recovery strategy must execute in a prepared site. It does not take that long to run electrical connections down the middle of a conference center, string some network wiring, and erect work tables and chairs. The longest delay is the time required to add adequate bandwidth to the outside world (which includes the data center recovery site). Without this external connection of adequate size, the recovery is hobbled or delayed. If the disaster covers a wide area, it may be weeks before the telecom connection is ready.

In a crisis, only the personnel essential to operating the critical IT systems, required to answer customer calls, or necessary to fulfill legal requirements must be recovered immediately. The rest of the offices can be recovered over time. Employees equipped with Virtual Private Network (VPN) authentication may connect to the data center through secure connections. Scarce work area can be maximized by adding a second shift for staff who do not directly work with customers (such as the Accounting department).

One option for recovering offices is through the use of specially equipped office trailers. These units come with work surfaces, chairs, generators for creating their own electrical power, a telephone switch, and a satellite connection to bypass downed lines. When on site, these trailers are typically parked in the company parking lot to use any surviving services—and then provide the rest.

Beware of counting on hotels as large-scale work area recovery sites for offices. Like everyone else, they watch their costs and do not want a monthly bill for data capabilities far in excess of what is normally used. A T-1 provides sufficient bandwidth for a hotel and its guests but not enough to support 100 office workers filling the conference rooms. Also the hotel switchboard will lack capacity for busy offices.

Setting up a recovery site requires:

➤ A location far enough away that it is not affected by the same disaster.

➤ Chairs to sit on and tables for work surfaces.

➤ Locating together any business teams that frequently interact or exchange documents during business. Otherwise, there may be multiple work area recovery locations.

➤ Desktop equipment, such as a computers and telephones. Loading the company software image on PCs takes time. Also, people will miss their personal data.

➤ Alternative communications, such as fax and modem.

➤ Historical documents that must be checked during the course of business.

➤ Preprinted forms required for legal or other business reasons.

Refer to Figure 4-2 for a list of work are a disaster recovery solutions; these fall into several general categories from slowest to fastest.

Example Work Area Recovery Strategy

myCompany's Work Area Recovery strategy is to use the company's IT training rooms adjacent to the backup data center as temporary offices in an emergency.

These classrooms are equipped with workstations on every table. A telephone switch is online and wires are run to each workstation. In an emergency, telephones can be quickly installed.

This recovery site, approximately 60 minutes of travel from the main office, is used as an off-site conference center and IT training facility. It can accommodate enough of the critical office workers to keep the company operating until permanent facilities have been prepared.

IT staff not involved with the IT recovery plan will work from home via VPN.

Executive staff is to meet in the Sleepy-Head motel conference center until a local office is ready.

The Work Area Recovery Manager is also responsible for the ongoing maintenance of the office recovery site. The recovery site must be tested semi-annually to ensure that the network and telecom connections are functional and available when needed.

	Pros	Cons	Good for
Cold Site	Inexpensive. This can be an empty warehouse. Hotel conference rooms may also be booked.	Long recovery time (a week or more)	Low data speed and limited telecom capabilities will hinder operations
Hot Site	Recovery in a day.	As expensive as a second call center Pay on declaration Nearest available site may be hundreds of miles away	Companies with a single office site and a short recovery time
Hot Site - Trailers in your company parking lot	Recovery in a day. Everyone sleeps at home.	Expensive, local units may be taken in a regional disaster This is a subscription service	Companies with a strong desire to recover as close to home as possible

FIGURE 4-2: Work area disaster recovery solutions.

PANDEMIC STRATEGY

The goal of the Pandemic Emergency Plan is for the company to continue operations at a level that permits it to remain in business. This requires steps to prevent the spread of disease into and within the organization. Actions to minimize the spread of infection represent an additional cost for the company which must be borne until the danger passes. Unlike other contingency plans, a Pandemic Recovery Plan will be in operation from 18 to 24 months.

In 2003, in response to a local outbreak of severe acute respiratory syndrome (SARS), the World Health Organization urged postponement of nonessential travel to Toronto. Some conferences scheduled for the city were canceled and hotel occupancy rate sank to half of normal. Although reported SARS cases were few, the financial impact was significant.

Pandemic emergency steps require different strategies for major stakeholders:

➤ Employees

    a. Employees who can work from home should use a VPN connection to minimize the amount of time that they spend in the office.

    b. The company sick policy must be relaxed so that sick people are not forced to come into the workplace. Anyone who is sick is encouraged to stay home. They should also stay home if they have a sick family member.

    c. Areas used by company workers must be periodically cleaned thoroughly to address any infection brought in from the outside.

    d. Employees who travel into areas with a high rate of pandemic infection should work from home for the first week of their return.

➤ Customers

    a. Areas where customers enter the facility must be cleaned thoroughly to address any infection brought in from the outside.

    b. Provide complimentary hand sanitation at all store entrances.

    c. It may be necessary to bring in individual sanitation supplies for an extended period of time.

    d. All returned products should be sanitized before examination.

➤ Vendors

    a. Use video conferencing and other electronic tools to meet with vendors.

    b. Carefully select meeting places with a low incidence of pandemic.

Example Pandemic Strategy

myCompany's Pandemic Emergency Plan is designed to contain the potential spread of illness within the company. It is initiated when the state public health authorities in the headquarters building's state declare a pandemic. Limitations on the number of sick days provided to each employee in the company's sick leave policy are suspended. Employees are encouraged to stay home with sick family members.

All company areas where employees are in close physical contact with customers or vendors must be thoroughly sanitized every day. Each employee is provided with personal sanitation gloves and face masks.

Any employee returning from a business trip will work from home via VPN for seven days before entering the office.

BUSINESS CONTINUITY STRATEGY

A successful business continuity strategy is when your customers never notice an interruption in service. It is a proactive plan to identify and prevent problems from occurring. To implement this in a company, begin with the list of critical processes identified by the BIA. Develop a process map for each vital process that shows each step along each. Identify areas of risk such as bottlenecks into a single person or device, limited resources or legal compliance issues. Mitigate each point of risk by implementing standby equipment, trained backup personnel, etc.

A severe blizzard in Minnesota is not visible to a customer in Arizona who is waiting on a rush order. An instant failover for IT systems is essential for online companies, banking, hospitals, vital government service offices, public utilities, etc. The dollar loss of customer impact is so high that it justifies the high cost. Other companies regret the interruption but are not so real-time with their customers. As a result, they have several days to recover with minimal customer interruption. An example might be a health spa where a one-week interruption in service is overshadowed by the strong customer relationship.

A business continuity strategy deals with your company's vital processes. It might be anything whose absence disrupts the normal flow of work. For example, many companies have eliminated their company telephone operator and replaced that person with an automated telephone directory. Key in the person's name, and you are connected. However, if that device fails, the rest of the company is still creating and shipping products to the customer, but no one canall into the facility. A Business Continuity Plan provides information on how to recover that device or quickly replace it.

The strategy is to begin with your list of critical processes. Assign someone to develop a process map of each to identify potential single points of failure or places where the flow of products and services are constrained. Then reduce the likelihood of failure by providing duplicate (or backup) equipment to single threaded devices, trained backup personnel, etc.

Therefore, a business continuity strategy deals with processes. It might include:

➤ Identification of vital processes (this list is updated quarterly).

➤ Drafting a process map to examine each step for single threading or weakness, such as unstable equipment or operators.

➤ Identification of steps to eliminate (simple processes are easiest to recover).

➤ Drafting a risk assessment for the process.

➤ Drafting an end-to-end recovery plan for each remaining step in the process.

CONCLUSION

Selecting a recovery strategy is an important step. Its boundaries are determined by how quickly the company must recover in order to survive. Another factor is the amount of data it can afford to lose. When the risk from natural is evaluated, a recovery strategy can be created.

The strategy selected will drive the cost of the company's recovery plans. Therefore it must be based on the data gathered by the Business Impact Analysis. This focuses efforts on the "vital few" processes. Each strategy selected must be approved by the project's executive sponsor. Otherwise, most work will be lost when a revised strategy is issued.

A separate strategy must be developed for each plan. The primary plan is for recovering the data center. Next, the strategy for the work area recovery must be based on when the data center will be ready for use. The pandemic plan is different in that the crisis comes on slowly, eventually hits a peak and then gradually fades away.

In the end it comes down to how much security the company can afford. Where possible, try to combine recovery capabilities with existing assets (such as using "test" IT servers to recover the data center) with disaster recovery requirements to reduce the program's ongoing cost.

CHAPTER 5

BUILD AN INTERIM PLAN
Don't Just Sit There, Do Something

Build it and they will come.
— *Field of Dreams*

INTRODUCTION

Building an effective business continuity plan can take a great deal of time and resources. By this point, you have identified the processes critical to your business in the Business Impact Analysis (Chapter 2), identified the risks to these processes in your risk assessment (Chapter 3), and determined your strategy for building a comprehensive plan (Chapter 4). Until the primary disaster plan begins coming together (Chapters 14 to 20), there are 11 steps you can take *right now* to provide some initial protection. The steps you follow in this chapter will be expanded in great detail in later chapters. Even if your disaster planning stops after this chapter, you will be noticeably better prepared.

Create an Interim Plan Notebook to organize your information. It should contain:

1. **Access to People.** Organization charts should be included to show who is assigned what areas of responsibilities and who their assistants are. Contact information for each key person—work phone, home phone, cell phone number, pager number, and home address—should be included.

2. **Access to the Facility.** A set of keys must be available to every door, cabinet, and closet that holds equipment you support, all maintained in a secure key locker. This includes copies of any special system passwords.

3. **Service Contracts.** Be sure you have the name, address, telephone number (day and night), contact name (day and night), serial numbers of equipment

on the contract, contract number, and expiration date. This section may also include a copy of the service agreement renewal calendar.

4. **Vendor List.** A list of companies where you have accounts set up for quickly buying emergency supplies. This includes contact information.

5. **Walk-Around Asset Inventory.** This is necessary to properly build a plan. A thorough asset inventory will come later. What assets might you need to recover or to restore to service right away?

6. **Software Asset List.** What software are you protecting, insuring against loss, and supporting?

7. **Critical Business Functions.** What are the business functions you are trying to protect, to keep running with minimal disruption?

8. **Operations Restoration Priorities.** What do you fix first, and in what order do you restore functions to service?

9. **Toxic Material Storage.** Locations of toxic material anywhere on the company grounds.

10. **Emergency Equipment List.** Where are the equipment and materials you need to help clean up a mess?

11. **Trained First Responders.** Do you have any volunteer firefighters or Emergency Medical Technicians (EMTs) on your staff? Does anyone have critical skills you can use in a crisis until emergency crews arrive?

In most emergencies, there are several keys to a successful recovery: key people, keys to the doors, and key support account information. For your interim plan, you will pull together basic contact information on the people you would call on in a disaster, the service contracts you would invoke, and keys/passwords necessary to gain entry into where you need to be.

A quick way to gauge your current state of disaster readiness is to make unannounced visits asking for critical support information. Watch the people as you ask for this information, and you will see how organized some are. See who can quickly provide a copy of their list and who has everything scattered about in a "sticky-note file." As you watch them fumbling through folders of documents, aren't you glad this isn't happening during a real crisis? How high would the quality of their hurriedly gathered information be? How quickly could they provide the correct answers? Rapid availability of this information is very useful even if the computer room is not on fire. Imagine the same people doing this during an emergency, and with the office illuminated only by emergency lighting.

As the information flows in, take time to carefully organize it. Label each item as to who sent it to you and the date you received it. If you later need an explanation about their information, you'll know who to call. The date indicates when you received it, not how old this information actually is. It never hurts to validate critical information like telephone numbers and contract agreements. Set up a tabbed three-ring binder to hold all the information. Later, you will consolidate this information into your own lists and they will take a lot less space.

Remember that what you collect for an interim plan must be useful to anyone involved in disaster recovery. Readability, accuracy, and clarity are important. The various documents must be accumulated in a single binder and presented to your various managers. Place a date on each document to show when it was created. This will also act as a built-in reminder to call for updated documents if you feel they are too old. Be sure to keep a copy of these documents at home; emergencies don't always happen during normal business hours.

Keep track of who has a copy of the binder. Then, as updates are created, you know whom to pass them on to. Ensure all binders are tabbed for quick reference and clearly marked as Company Confidential in accordance with your company's document guidelines (remember, you have home telephone numbers in here).

At a minimum, each of the following people should have an up-to-date copy of this interim plan.

➤ Business Continuity Manager (you—the person writing the plan).

➤ Disaster Recovery Manager (to be kept at home).

➤ Information Technology department's Help Desk (useful for providing support).

➤ Facility Security Manager (in a place the after-hours guard on duty can reach it).

ACCESS TO PEOPLE

Reaching key people is a two-step task. The first step is to know whom to notify. The second step is to know how to reach them. You should know not only how to reach your boss, but also the head of the purchasing department, the public relations manager, the custodians' office—many more than just the people in your department.

Start with an organization chart that shows who works in what department, from the top person down to the night-shift custodians. Current charts are often hard to come by. Organization charts reflect the formal lines of authority within an organization, not the actual day-to-day flow of authority.

The organization chart will help you identify who is responsible for what areas and who you might need to call if a disaster occurs. Think of the ways this will be useful. If the accounts payable system crashes over a weekend, you might need to call the accounting clerk who uses that system to test your fix before work starts on Monday. If there is a fire in the Quality Assurance office overnight, you need to know which manager to notify.

The second piece is a complete telephone list for all employees that includes home telephone numbers, cell phone numbers, pager numbers, etc. In most cases, you will only notify the department managers, but by having a complete list, you should always be able to call in the "resident expert."

A funny thing about a telephone recall list is that some people lie to the company about their home telephone number. Imagine that! Others "forget" to pick up their pager every night before they go home. We can't change all the bad habits of the world, but for those key people who are critical to your disaster recovery efforts, ensure their numbers are correct even if you have to call them yourself.

An easy way to check this list is whenever it is used to call someone off-hours, make a small notation of the date next to their name. If the call went through, that is validation enough. Once every several months, take time to make a call to any of the unchecked phone numbers just to verify them.

Try to never call people after hours unless it is necessary (like checking the list). Check with your human resources manager to see what the impact is on hourly and salary workers' compensation for calling people after hours.

If your company has multiple sites, you will also need the telephone numbers for their key technical, support, and management people. In an emergency, it is sometimes quicker to borrow material from a sister company than to buy it. Also, instead of hiring unknown consultants to assist in your recovery, it is far better to borrow skilled people from sister companies. They are already familiar with your company's procedures, and they should have already had a security screening (something your emergency consultants may not have). All around, it is preferable to call on your fellow employees to supplement your recovery staff than it is to hire someone on the spur of the moment.

ACCESS TO THE FACILITY

Limiting access to the company's assets is not an optional activity. It is something your auditors will be checking. All sensitive areas must be secured, such as computer rooms, telephone switch room, vital records storage, and personnel files. There may be other areas unique to your company that must also be safeguarded. If in doubt, ask the auditors. They are a valuable source of information for disaster planning.

Don't be shy about asking detailed questions of your company's security force concerning the arrangements protecting your area of responsibility. Do not take for granted that the force provides the proper protection for your equipment. Review their after-hours entry policy to ensure it meets your emergency needs.

Physical Keys

Murphy's law says that problems will happen in the worst possible places. Wherever the problem occurs, you will need to get into the location. Imagine a network problem. You may need keys to access a number of equipment closets checking data hubs until you find the defective equipment, another key to gain entry to the hub's cabinet, and still a third key to enter the secure area where spare hub cards are maintained.

In most facilities, the security force maintains copies of the physical keys to all doors and locks. If this is the case in your company, then you should review their key management policies and key locker procedure. Things to look for and for you to do if they are missing:

➤ There should be a formal request form for requesting a key. Each request should be properly authorized before a key is issued. People who feel accountable for a key will treat it more like a valued object. If someone keeps losing their keys, then they should not be given any more of them. Note how often their car keys turn up missing and you'll see that it is only your key that they don't care about.

➤ There should be a "Key Log" of who has what keys. Verify that people who work for you only have what is needed. Use this list to recover keys when people leave the company. If a theft of company property is detected, this list will be a valuable starting point for the investigation. If locks must be changed, this will tell you how many keys are needed for the new setting. Review this list at least quarterly to recover keys from people who no longer need them.

➤ There should be a locked cabinet where copies of all keys are maintained.

Sometimes paranoid people attach their own locks to cabinets to keep others away from their equipment. You may not even be aware there is an unauthorized lock on this door or know whom to even ask for a combination. Personal locks on company doors and cabinets must be vigorously discouraged as it will hinder your recovery at a time when you can ill afford it.

Even if your facility security force has a "Key Locker," you might want to have one just for your department in a place that you can get to quickly. For your own department, you might establish a key locker to hold a copy of every key to every door and cabinet in your facility. Then no matter who is on-site during a disaster can quickly enter the room or cabinet and begin containing the damage until the expert support team arrives.

For security reasons, only a few people should have access to this cabinet. Otherwise, you would be surprised how fast these keys will disappear. A sign-out sheet in the cabinet can be used to track what has been loaned out, to whom, when, and by whom it was authorized.

Note the phone numbers of local locksmiths who are available around the clock, every day of the week. If you are depending on the building security folks to provide this service, inspect their operation to ensure it includes all keys and that they are available 24/7. Whoever maintains the key locker should also have a large set of bolt cutters. This "master key" will open most locks by slicing through them. Use it liberally on all noncompany locks you encounter.

Master keys are keys that open more than one door. The way that door locks are keyed is such that security zones are created. This allows a master key to open all the doors in a given department and not in other departments. Master keys must be closely guarded and issued sparingly.

Electronic Keys

An excellent solution to the problem of propagating keys is electronic locks. Electronic locks are expensive to install but provide a wide range of benefits. An electronic lock not only opens the door but it tells you who tried to open a door, when they opened the door, and how long it was open.

You see electronic door locks in most modern hotels. Hotels had a problem. Customers often lost their keys or continued their journey without turning them in. The hotel had to assume that someone was walking around with the key to a room that they might use to break in later. This forced hotels into an expensive rekeying of the doors. Rekeying cost their customers money and was a constant problem for the innkeeper. Now, if someone checks out of a hotel with an electronic key, that key is disabled. Door locks no longer need changing and customers are no longer billed for rekeying.

Another problem with physical keys is that they get lost, get copied (with and without permission), and the people holding them may pass them on to less-trusted individuals. You can never be sure if a key is truly lost or has been intentionally stolen so that some miscreant can gain access to a particular area. This forces an expensive lock change. It also means that anyone else with one of these keys (those who are entitled to have one) must exchange their key for a current version.

There is no law against copying keys. Even the keys stamped with an admonition of "Do Not Copy" have no legal standing. Key makers will copy them as they please. So anytime a key is provided to someone, that person can easily make a copy. Once a key is surrendered, you cannot be sure that door is still safe. For all anyone knows, the employee made a copy of that key for a friend in another department.

An electronic lock uses the digital number on a key or a key code to determine who has access to what area. All information is kept in a master database. When you try to open a door, the badge's number is read or the key code used is recorded and sent to a database. The database checks to see if you are authorized to open that door. If you are, then the door latch releases. If not, then usually nothing happens and the lock ignores the key. At the database, a record is saved of the key number trying to open a door, where, when, and if the door was opened or not.

In this way, people can be given access or denied access via the database without issuing or recovering keys to each door. If a key is lost, it can be disabled at the database and be worthless to a thief. Anyone who finds it has a useless piece of plastic. This of course depends on the individual to report the lost key and have it promptly disabled. If an employee leaves the company, you can disable the key quickly.

Whether you are allowed in or not, each attempt is recorded with a date and time for tracking who went where. Denied access can be used to see who is testing your security system. If something is missing from an area, you can see who entered each room. This log must be reviewed daily to see which unauthorized cards are attempting to get through which doors.

An electronic lock can also track doors that are propped open. Depending on how your system is configured, this may trigger a security alarm to see if this is a legitimate activity or if someone wanted a door left ajar. Since the log also told you who opened the door, it could be a good time to find out why they did this. If you wanted the door left open, you would save money and remove the lock!

Electronic locks also allow for master keys and security zones. For example, this lets you set up the electronic key for the telephone systems technician to open all telephone room doors but none of the computer room doors. Electronic keys are nice because it is easy to enable various levels of security at any time.

Just as you would manually with physical keys, you should use the electronic lock software to generate a quarterly key access report to review which employees have access to what areas. This will catch those cases where someone's project once needed access to an area that is no longer required. It may also highlight more than one card issued to a person (they lost one, were issued a "temporary" replacement, and then kept it and the original). Usually this list is circulated among your managers to ensure people have the proper access. Keep in mind your after-hours support requirements or you'll be making some late-night trips to open doors!

System Passwords

A system password is like a master key. Usually keyed to the user ID or administrator, passwords provide unlimited security access to every feature on a computer system. In our case, we may need them to perform an emergency shutdown of main computer systems. For this reason only, we need them kept in the key locker. These passwords have an unlimited potential for mischief, so they must be closely guarded.

Establish a secure area to store system passwords. They can all fit on a sheet of paper and must include all administrator-level accounts. This is kept in a sealed envelope near your equipment in the event that a rapid system shutdown is required. Another place to store this is inside your key locker. Check the seal on the envelope from time to time to ensure it has not been tampered with.

You will need this information if you ever need to shut down or restart your computer system when the systems experts are not available. This might be due to a fire in an adjacent room where the loss of electrical power [and Uninterruptible Power Supply (UPS) power] is imminent.

SERVICE CONTRACTS

How could someone qualify the downtime on a piece of machinery as a disaster? You would if that was the only printer that could print paychecks and today is payday! These normally must be distributed at a given time, and you may not be able to wait another 4 hours for a staff member to come in just to look at it. It might be critical if your primary data communications hub began emitting blue smoke. It might be critical if . . . but I think you get the picture.

A service contract isn't much good to you if you can't call for help when you need it. Round-the-clock service coverage is very useful for maximizing system uptime. This is especially true for critical hardware and software. Unfortunately, 24/7 service can easily double the cost of a service contract. So if you are paying out this large premium every month, take steps to ensure it is available when needed. People cannot call for it if they don't know how.

Obtain a list of all service providers you have service agreements with. Cross-check this list with a walk-around to ensure that all your major equipment is accounted for on the list. We will need to include all these service provider names later when we build our vendor contact list.

There are four basic types of contracts with endless variations:

1. **24/7.** They provide unlimited around-the-clock coverage for time and materials. Pay one price per month and leave your worries behind. This is necessary for mission-critical equipment and is the most expensive approach.

2. **8 to 5.** They will work on equipment problems during the business day and usually supply any parts that are needed.

3. **Time and Materials.** They will work on the problem and charge you by the hour for the repair technician's time. The costs of any parts required are also included on the bill. This is good for nonessential equipment that rarely breaks.

4. **Exchange.** Send them your broken equipment and they will either send you a refurbished replacement or repair it and send it back. This is good for devices where you have on site spares, such as monitors, terminals, scanners, printers, etc.

Begin building your list of service agreements. This list will be very useful in many areas of your company—the help desk, the late-shift operators, the security guards, and many other places. Use Form 5-1 on the CD-ROM to develop your list. The essential information to gather from each of your service agreements includes:

➤ **Contact Names.** Whom do I call? There may be multiple people involved with your account. There may be a sales representative, a dedicated technician, and even an after-hours contact name and number. When time is short, you need to know whom to talk to for the fastest service.

➤ **Company Address.** Look at the city to see how far away they are. You can gauge an approximate response time for the technician. Any spare parts the technician may need will probably be that far away also. If the service company is too far away, make a note to look for someone closer to home. On the other hand, some companies use a work-from-home field workforce, so using the company's address is only a starting point for this inquiry.

➤ **Telephone Numbers.** This could be a rather long list. You may have a separate number for normal hours, their fax machine, the technicians' direct line, and an after-hours number. You need them all clearly identified. Like your recall list, when you use one, pencil in the date next to it so you know the last time that telephone number was validated.

➤ **E-mail Address.** Many companies use e-mail to pass noncritical information to their customers. This might also help if your sales representative was away from the office on a business trip and was checking for messages.

➤ **Customer Number.** The identification code number by which this contract is known to the vendor. You will need this when you call the problem in. Service centers normally will not budge until they verify that you are paid up and eligible for this service.

➤ **Hours of Support Under Contract.** This is VERY important. It will determine if you will be billed for the service call. If you are paying for 8:00 AM until 5:00 PM service and then demand a technician come out late at night, you will be billed for a hefty hourly fee. This may be acceptable, so long as you are aware of the potential costs. Paying for 8 to 5 service means that if the repair isn't finished at 5:00, the repair technician is going home and will be back tomorrow. Otherwise, you will again be paying a large overtime hourly fee.

➤ **When Does the Agreement Expire?** Some equipment inconveniently breaks on the wrong side of the deadline. All service contract expiration dates should be placed on a calendar so that you can see this coming and negotiate a new agreement before the old one expires. This information can also feed into your annual budget process.

➤ **Description of What You Buy from Them.** This could be a wide range of things. Some contacts provide everything for a fee to include materials and labor. Service companies you don't often need may be contracted under a time-and-materials scheme for all repairs. Whatever you buy from them, very briefly describe it here.

➤ **Your Internal Designated Contact Persons.** Many contracts require that several persons be designated as the company's representatives for contacting them to prevent their lines from being flooded by minor calls. Even though specific people are named in the contract, by declaring an emergency the service company should begin assistance until the named parties arrive.

Now that you have this list, assign someone to make up small cards for each machine covered by a service agreement. On this card, print all the essential information you have gathered. Firmly attach this information to the machine or inside of its cover. This is the ideal—information available at the point it is needed. Now if that device quakes, shakes, and begins to moan, the information on whom to call is immediately at hand.

When attaching these cards, check the machine over for advertising stickers. Some service companies attach them to whatever they repair. This is OK except when you change service companies and some well-meaning soul calls the number on the sticker to repair the machine. Without a service agreement, they may come out and send you an expensive bill. So when you see these stickers, remove them. People will get into the habit of depending on the cards you tape to the machines.

If you have a lot of equipment in the same room, make up an information station with a notebook attached to the wall that contains all the same information. Keep track of wherever you place this information for the times when you need to update your service providers or hours of coverage.

VENDOR LIST

Now that you know whom to call for a service call, make up a list of the other companies you routinely deal with using Form 5-2 (see CD). Since we have the major equipment covered, we can now focus in on the companies that provide your routine supplies. Why is that important?

Have you ever run out of something seemingly mundane like a special toner cartridge, and your usual purchasing agent is on vacation? The company kept moving along but there was someone out there who was very vocally upset. As you collect vendor contact information, you will quickly see how this can be very useful.

You want vendor contact information for the companies that supply your support materials such as custom cables, preprinted forms, backup tapes, any number of things you need to keep your operation flowing smoothly. Most suppliers don't list an after-hours number. They have one but it is not published. Try to get it from the salesperson. If they don't have it, get the salesperson's home number. Often when you really need something, a salesperson will go the extra mile to build customer loyalty.

Obtain a list of all support materials suppliers. This includes companies that provide off-site storage of your backup tapes, courier services, companies that provide preprinted forms, and companies that sell or lease you equipment as well as companies that repair it. Mandate that it be kept current. Essential data elements include:

➤ Contact names.

➤ Company address.

➤ Telephone numbers: normal hours, fax, and after-hours number.

➤ E-mail address.

➤ Your internal vendor number.

➤ Description of what you buy from them.

Public utilities are another set of vendors you need to know about. Loss of service from telephone, Internet, electric, gas, and water companies can shut down your operations in the blink of an eye. These companies all have 24-hour service support numbers. They may also have a special trouble reporting number for companies and major customers. For each utility, you will need:

➤ Contact names for sales, technical support, after-hours dispatch.

➤ Telephone numbers for each contact to include their normal hours number, fax number, and after-hours number.

➤ E-mail address for handling routine issues.

Public safety telephone numbers must also be prominent on your list. The ubiquitous 911 is always a good starting point, but you may find the normal telephone numbers for police, fire, ambulance, and the local hospital are all handy to have in a crisis. Use Form 5-3 (see CD) to start your list of whom to call in an emergency.

WALK-AROUND ASSET INVENTORY

Most companies have a lot of equipment to keep track of. We'll get to that later. Start by doing a walk-though of your areas of responsibility (do not trust this to memory). Draft a list with key information on all your major equipment. A major piece of equipment is one that costs a lot of money, or that takes a long time to replace, or your operation depends on it and it is the only one like it you have. This will usually be your larger or shared pieces of equipment.

As you walk around, be sure to open all closet doors and look into boxes. You would be surprised what you will find stashed away by people for emergencies. Note the location of any spare equipment. Arrange to have it picked up later. It should all be collected into one central point to cut down on the number of duplicate spares. Computers and computer component parts are like fresh fish; they lose value quickly with age. If everyone is hiding something like a spare printer in case they have system problems, you could be paying for many more spares than you need. Consolidate and lock up all your spares in one location to minimize costs and to ensure they will be available to whoever needs them. This may even free some equipment for use elsewhere.

When you examine each machine, look for indications of who sold or maintains the device. Sometimes repair services place large stickers with their telephone number on devices they service. Note these in case you cannot locate the service contract for this device.

Another sticker often found somewhere on the inside is a notice of the last time this device received preventative maintenance. Some equipment such as a network server may need as little as an occasional shakeout of the fan filter. Other devices, such as your UPS system, need their batteries checked every 6 months. The frequency that preventative maintenance is required can be found inside the manual that accompanies the equipment. Therefore, also begin locating the manuals you need. All preventative maintenance must be recorded in a log for that device. Note what was done and by whom. If the service was improperly done, and then the equipment fails, you may have a claim against the service company.

To continue with the thought on hardware manuals, the books should either be prominently displayed adjacent to the equipment or collected into a central place. This reduces the amount of time lost looking for answers. As you walk around, make a note next to each piece of equipment on your list as to whether the manual could be located.

In each room note the following information. Again, this is for critical systems, not a wall-to-wall inventory. Be sure to include all the equipment in your computer room, telephone switch room, and network closets (a chain is only as strong as its weakest link). The list should include:

➤ Manufacturer's Name.

➤ Model Number.

➤ Serial Number.

➤ Warranty Expiration Date. Tracking this will save on service costs and help you to know when to add that item to a service contract. Be sure to add it to your service contract renewal calendar.

➤ Location. You may need to work up your own notation for this if everything is not conveniently set up in an easily identifiable room.

➤ Serviced by. This may be a sticker right on the device.

➤ Connected to. This will take some asking around but will be very useful. Out of this, you may uncover the weak link in a chain.

➤ Feeds into What. Same benefits as connected to.

Think back to previous problems. Are there any other critical or unique devices around your facility that should be on the list? How about the UPS in your computer room? I bet there is another one on your telephone switch. Both rooms require climate control for the equipment to operate safely, so the HVAC repair number must be on there also.

Now that you have a list of your critical equipment, take time to cross-reference the equipment list to the vendor service agreement list. Are any of your critical devices lacking service coverage? Be sure to check the serial numbers because that is how service companies determine what is covered. Note the type of service agreement that each item has.

Consider each item on the asset list separately. Based on your experience, should any of the coverage be increased to include after-hours support? Should any of the items be reduced to 8:00 AM to 5:00 PM (or whatever they offer)?

With all this information at hand, draft a vendor list of whom to call and the normal billing method (time and materials, flat rate, etc.). Consider making a matrix that allows you to quickly check to see who supplies services or materials per device, such as every vendor that supports your AS/400. Use Form 5-4 (see CD) as a starting point for creating your list.

SOFTWARE ASSET LIST

If you lose a server, a critical PC, or a shop floor controller to a fire, you need to know what to replace it with. There is much more to a computer than what you see on its outside; there is all the very important software inside of it. Replacing the hardware without loading all the appropriate software (and data) will only result in a dark monitor staring back at you.

For each of the critical systems you have previously identified, you need to make a list of any software they require to drive them. This includes copies of custom software, any nonstandard driver programs, or operating system settings. (Cross-check this against your vendor list!)

This sometimes creates a problem if the machine that dies is old and only the latest hardware is available. You can reload the software from a data backup (you hope), but the hardware and existing operating system might create some conflicts.

In many cases, you can recover the software for that machine by reloading its full disk image backup. If you must reload the software from the original media, you need to be able to locate it. Once purchased software has been loaded onto a server, it should be stored along with your backup tapes at an off-site location.

CRITICAL BUSINESS FUNCTIONS

A key driver to your disaster planning is a clear identification of the critical business functions performed at your facility. You cannot protect everything equally, so you need to concentrate your recovery plans on the most important functions. Identifying this is a top management function.

Every company has a few essential things it does. Everything else can be delayed for a short time while the critical functions bring progress to a halt. Critical items must be recovered before all other areas. If you must draw up your own list, be sure to discuss them with your accounting manager or controller. Don't be surprised if they cannot rattle off a list to you. They probably never worked a list up either.

For each critical function you identify, explain why it is important. Does it involve cash flow? Does it fulfill a regulatory requirement? If you have a broad understanding of your business, your list may be quite long—too long. Try to narrow it down to 10 or fewer items. The longer list is still very useful, but what we are after is a guideline.

OPERATIONS RESTORATION PRIORITIES

If three things break at once, which one do you fix first? That is a restoration priority. Based on the critical business functions identified in the previous step, you now take your asset list and identify restoration priorities for every asset.

Some of these are easy. If there is a file server used by many departments across the company, it will have a high priority for service restoration. A telephone switch is the same high importance. But how important is your e-mail server? Is it more important than the Materials department's warehouse server? Probably not, unless it is the conduit for e-mailed and faxed orders from customers.

Consider this from another angle. If the electric company called and said they were shutting off two thirds of the power to your building, which equipment would you shut down, which would you ensure stayed up, and which would you stand by to start as soon as the outage was over?

TOXIC MATERIAL STORAGE

For the safety of all concerned, you should know if there is any toxic material stored on the premises and where it is. If there is a fire, building collapse, or flood, you will want to help warn people away from that area.

Use a map of the facility to indicate where this material is stored and what it is. If it is flammable, be sure to note that also. This is an important part of your plan so ensure everyone is aware of it.

Everyone on the recovery team must know where these dangerous materials are located and how to identify if they are leaking. They should know what to do if they encounter them.

EMERGENCY EQUIPMENT LIST

When a disaster occurs, you're going to want to know where things are to help reduce the amount of damage to equipment and the facility. This includes things such as electrical shutoff, water valves, gas shutoff, sprinkler system controls, etc. You also want to know where any special equipment such as portable pumps, wet/dry vacuums, and special fire extinguishers are kept so that damage can be kept to minimum.

Everyone on the recovery team must know where these items are located and how to use them in the event of an emergency. See Form 5-5 (on CD) to start your list of emergency equipment. And yes! Don't forget the keys to the doors!

TRAINED FIRST RESPONDERS

Many rural communities depend on volunteer fire departments and ambulance crews to support their towns. If any of your employees are EMT qualified, this is important to note. If anyone is a trained volunteer firefighter, this is important; a ham radio operator, a homebuilder, any number of things might show up. An additional question is if they have any hobbies or outside interests that would be of use in a crisis.

If you have any military Reserve or National Guard personnel, the training for their military job classification may be useful. They may be military police, hospital workers, or a wide range of things. It is not unusual to work in a military field that is entirely different from your civilian job. A possible downside to having these people on staff is that, in a wide-area emergency, these people may be called to government service and not be available to assist in your recovery.

Anyone that you identify with additional skills should be added to your recall roster. You need to indicate what skills each has, along with details on how to contact them during and after work hours. This list will have the same format (and be a continuation of) the emergency notification and recall list drawn up in the "Access to People" section of this chapter. You will need their work telephone number, home telephone numbers, cell phone numbers, pager number, home address, etc.

You should check this list with your Human Resources department to ensure you are not violating any company rules by calling on these people in an emergency.

CONCLUSION

Once you have finished the steps outlined in this chapter, you'll have created a basic interim plan that will drastically improve your ability to handle any disaster that occurs. This interim plan will provide the recovery team the critical information they need to:

1. Get access to key people who can get the recovery process started as soon as possible.

2. Get access to facilities and computer systems to get them back up and running.

3. Have the service contracts they'll need to get the vendors you've contracted with for outside support busy as quickly as possible.

4. Order emergency supplies quickly from critical vendors.

5. Document assets damaged using the walk-around asset list.

6. Order replacement copies of important software.

7. Identify the critical business functions that must continue during restoration.

8. Restore the operational functions in the best order.

9. Identify the location of toxic materials to cleanup crews for their protection.

10. Locate onsite emergency equipment and materials you need to help clean up the mess.

11. Ask for assistance from any volunteer firefighters or EMTs who are on staff.

If you have followed these steps and collected this information, you have the material for a basic business continuity plan. If your project stopped right now, your company is noticeably better prepared for a crisis than it was before. But don't stop now! There is much more important information to gather and mitigation actions to identify. What you have now is a good starting point. Continue reading to get the information you need to develop a complete plan.

CHAPTER 6

WRITING THE PLAN
Getting It Down on Paper

No one plans to fail; they just simply fail to plan.
— *Disaster Recovery Journal*

INTRODUCTION

Writing a plan is not difficult. It is as simple as telling a story to someone. It is the story of what to do. It addresses the basic concepts of *who, what, where, when, why,* and *how* of a process. Although you cannot predict exactly *what* will happen *where,* upon reflection, you can identify the basic steps that must be done in any emergency.

Throughout your plan writing process, keep in mind that emergencies affect people in different ways. Some will panic, others will sit and wait for the expert (but many are really waiting for someone else to take responsibility for any recovery errors), and some will make excuses and leave. The goal of your plan is to minimize this chaos by providing some direction to the people onsite so they can get started on containment and recovery. Once team members are in motion, the chaos lessens and their professional training will kick in.

It is impossible to write a specific recovery plan for every possible situation. Instead, the plans provide a set of guidelines to reduce the chaos at the point of incident and to position the company for a recovery once adequate facts become available. Whether you are rebuilding a data center due to a fire or due to a roof collapse, it is the same set of steps.

Business continuity plans come in many forms according to local requirements and the preferences of the person writing them. The CD contains four separate plans. Each plan is executed by a different team, based on the circumstances of the incident. They are:

➤ **Administrative Plan.** Contains reference information common to all plans, such as vendor call lists, recovery strategy, risk assessment, etc.

➤ **Technical Recovery Plans.** Many independent plans that contain the step-by-step actions to recovery of a specific process or IT system from scratch. These plans assume that the process must be rebuilt from nothing. These plans are often referred to when addressing local emergencies.

➤ **Work Area Recovery Plan.** The details for relocating the critical company office workers to another site.

➤ **Pandemic Management Plan.** Actions the company will take to minimize the impact of a pandemic. Unlike a data center disaster whose recovery can be completed in a few hours or days, a pandemic can easily run for 18 months or more.

The essential elements of a business continuity plan are that it is:

➤ Flexible to accommodate a variety of challenges.

➤ Understandable to whoever may read it (assuming they know the technology),

➤ Testable to ensure that it completely addresses interfaces to other processes (in and out).

Writing your plan is simply documenting before the fact what should be done when a disaster strikes. The basic steps to follow are:

1. **Lay the Groundwork.** Here the basic decisions are made about who will execute the plan, what processes need a plan, the format of the plan, etc.

2. **Develop Departmental Plans.** Departments are the basic structure around which organizations are built; they are a good place to start developing your plans.

3. **Combine your Departmental Plans into an Overall Corporate Plan.** Here you check to ensure that departmental recovery activities do not conflict with one another and that any interdependencies are considered.

LAY THE GROUNDWORK

Your first step in developing continuity plans is to establish a standard format. This will give at least the first few pages of each plan the same "look and feel." When drafting your plan, consider the following:

➤ Who will execute it? If you are the local expert on that process, then why do you need a plan? The odds are you don't. In a crisis, you would know what to do. But if you like to take days off, occasionally get sick, or even take a vacation, then whoever is on the spot when the emergency occurs must be able to stand in for you and address the problem. A plan must consider who may be called on in an emergency if the expert is not available. Another consideration is that if you are the manager over an area, and you want to be able to recover a process in case the "expert" is promoted, transferred, quits, or is discharged, a written plan is essential. You should especially look for highly stable processes that never break and no one has experience working on. They must have a plan on file since whoever worked on them may have already left the company.

➤ How obvious is the problem? Some problems, like magnetic damage to backup tapes, are invisible until you try to read them. Other problems, such as the entire building shaking in a massive earthquake, are easier to recognize. If a problem is hard to detect, then step-by-step troubleshooting instructions are necessary.

➤ How much warning will there be? Is a severe thunderstorm in your area often a prelude to a power outage? Will the weather forecast indicate a blizzard is imminent? However, if a local building contractor cuts your connection to the telephone company's central office, there is no warning of an impending problem at all. Emergencies that provide a warning, such as a weather bulletin, often trigger automatic containment actions. This might be to purchase extra flashlight batteries, install sandbags, or to have essential technical personnel pitch camp within the building in case they are needed.

➤ How long must they continue running with this plan before help arrives? Should they have enough information to contain the problem for 10 minutes or 2 hours?

➤ How soon must the process be restored before the company suffers serious damage? This is called the recovery time objective for this process.

➤ Are there any manual workaround actions that can be used until the process is restored? For example, if your payroll computer system dies at the very worst moment, can you write 40-hour paychecks for everyone? This makes a mess for the Accounting department to clean up later, but in an organized labor facility, the worker's contract may allow them to walk off the job if their paychecks are late.

What Needs Its Own Plan?

Is the answer anything that could break? Some processes are like links in a chain, where the failure of any single item brings the entire process to a stop, such as a data network. In this case, any number of items along a chain of equipment could be at fault. The plan would step you through the basic fault-location steps and tell you what to do to address the problem you find. Some problems are isolated to one or a few devices, such as a Web server failure. In this case, you would focus all efforts on the server and its connections to the network.

You must have a plan for every critical business function identified by the Business Impact Analysis (BIA). This includes manual processes and every piece of critical equipment that supports the facility. For each critical business function, explain the steps necessary to restore the minimal acceptable level of service. This level of service might be achieved by performing machine functions with manual labor. It might be achieved by shifting the work to another company site or even paying a competitor to machine parts for you. The goal is to keep your company going. Optional plans may be written to support those functions essential to your own department (and peace of mind), but that are not essential to the facility's critical business functions.

Consider how a plan will be used when you write it. Your goal is not a single large soups-to-nuts document. Usually a department has an overall plan for recovering its main processes or machinery and then specific action plans for individual problems. For example, Vital Records may have detailed plans for recovering documents based on the media on which they are stored. This information should be readily available to the department. But some specific action should be kept on laminated cards and provided to the security guards (for after-hours emergency action) and posted on the walls of the rooms it affects. Examples of these laminated pages might be immediate actions to take for a water leak, for an electrical outage, for a fire, etc. See Form 6-1, Sample Business Continuity Action Plan (on the CD), for an example.

Another example would be an electrical outage in the computer room. The overall plan will contain information on calling the power company and who to call for emergency generators, etc. But, a notice on the wall of the computer room will provide specific power shedding instructions and indicate immediate steps to take to monitor and potentially reduce the load on the UPS.

Word Processing Guidelines

Your company may have some specific guidelines in place for important documents like this. If not, consider these guidelines for the plans.

PAGE LAYOUT

➤ Set your word processor to default to 12 point, Arial font (don't make me search for a pair of glasses in the midst of a crisis!).

➤ Set the page footers to include a page number in the center and the current date in lower lefthand corner. This date will help to indicate which copy of the plan is the latest. The footers should also include the phrase "Company Confidential" on every page.

➤ Each document should read from major topic to minor topic—or broad view to narrow view. The beginning of the document deals with actions that would affect the entire process and, as you move further into the document, more specific issues would be addressed.

DOCUMENT FORMAT

➤ On the first page, include a brief narrative (one paragraph) of the business function of the equipment that this particular plan supports.

➤ The name of the primary support person.

> ➤ The name of the secondary support person.

> ➤ The name of the primary customer for this process (Accounting, Manufacturing, Sales, etc.). It is better that you tell them what is wrong than they find out there is a problem the hard way.

> ➤ Immediate action steps to contain the problem.

> ➤ Known manual workaround steps to maintain minimal service.

> ➤ In the case of telecommunications, data networks, or data processing services outages, include the names of other technical employees in sister companies with expertise in this area who can be called onsite in a crisis.

DEPARTMENTAL PLANS

A departmental recovery plan has several components. The main component is the plan itself, a narrative that explains the assets involved, the threats being addressed, the mitigation steps taken, and what to do in the event of a disaster. This sounds simple enough, but such a plan could easily fill notebooks. Instead, base your plans on a primary scenario with specific threats addressed in attached appendices. In addition, more abbreviated instructions for security guards, computer operators, etc., should be included as part of the departmental recovery plan.

The main part of the plan has three major components:

1. **Immediate Actions.** Steps that anyone can take to contain the damage (similar to applying first aid to an injured person). This involves simple tasks, such as shutting off the water main to stop a leak, evacuating people if there is a toxic spill, or opening the computer room doors if the air conditioning fails. Once people are safe, an early action in "Immediate Action" is to alert the appropriate people for help. It takes time for them to drive to the disaster, so the earlier you call, the sooner they will arrive.

2. **Detailed Containment Actions.** To reduce the spread or depth of damage. What else can be done until the "experts" get there? What actions should the "experts" take after they arrive to stop the damage from spreading?

3. **Recovery Actions.** To return the process to a minimal level of service is an important third component of every plan. This is the part that most people think about when considering disaster recovery planning.

There are four inputs into building your plan. First, begin with the Critical Process Impact Matrix you developed in your BIA (Form 3-3). This lists the critical processes and the time of day that they are essential. This list was further broken down in the Critical Process Breakdown matrix (Form 3-4). These two tools can provide the essential information for building your plans. Add to these lists your risk assessment and your process restoration priority list. With these items, you have everything necessary to write your plans. Write your primary plan for the worst case scenario—complete replacement of the process.

In many cases, the damage is caused by multiple threats, but their associated recovery steps are the same. Therefore, a plan that details what to do in one disaster situation is probably applicable to most other situations. For example, the loss of a critical computer server due to a fire, physical sabotage, or a broken water pipe would have essentially the same recovery steps. Separate plans are not necessary, although the mitigation steps for each threat in the example would be quite different.

Begin by drafting your plan to address this central situation. Add to the central plan an appendix for any other specific threats or recovery actions you think are appropriate. All together, this is your department's (or critical processes') disaster recovery plan and should be available in your office, with a printed copy at your home and your assistant's home. In addition, the plan administrator must maintain both a printed copy and an electronic copy. (Recovery plans contain information useful to people with bad intentions, so keep them in a secure location.)

Looking at your department's main plan, you still have a document that is too unwieldy to use in the first few moments of the crisis. Remember, emergencies are characterized by chaos. Some people are prone to act, and others are prone to run in circles. You need to have something quick and easy to follow in the hands of those who will act. These terse instructions must detail basic disaster steps to safeguard people and to contain the damage. They are usually laminated and posted on the wall. Include them as an appendix to your plan identified with their own tab.

As you write your plan, consider the following:

➤ **Who Will Execute This Plan?** A minimum of three people must be able to execute a plan: the primary support person, the backup support person, and the supervisor. Usually, the weak link is the supervisor. If that person cannot understand the plan, then it is not sufficiently detailed or it lacks clarity.

Most facilities operate during extended first-shift hours, from Monday through Friday. However, if this plan is for a major grocery store, it might be open 24 hours a day, 7 days a week. Problems occur in their own good time. If they occur during normal working hours, and your key people are already onsite, then the emergency plan is to summon these key people to resolve the problem. Referring to the written plan will also speed recovery, since time is not wasted identifying initial actions.

However, if the problem arises at 3:00 AM on a Sunday and is discovered by the security guard, he needs to know the few essential containment actions to take until help arrives. Because this is the worst case scenario—someone unfamiliar with an area tasked to contain a problem—this is the level of detail to which you must write. One of the first action steps is always to notify the appropriate person of the problem. This gets help in motion. Then, the person on the spot works on containment until that help arrives.

This approach works well with crises that are common knowledge or are basically understood by the general population, such as the sounding of fire alarms, burst water pipes, or power outages. But for some of the technical areas, such as data processing, writing such a level of detail would make a volume of instructions so thick that the computer room would have long since burned down while the containment team struggled through the text. In those cases, the level of detail should be sufficient for someone familiar with the technology, but unfamiliar with this particular piece of equipment, to work through the steps. In addition, specific containment actions should be posted on the wall so that the vital first few minutes are not wasted looking for a misfiled disaster plan book.

➤ **How Obvious Is the Problem?** Standing in an office with water lapping over your shoe tops is a sure sign of a problem. Smoke pouring out of a room is likewise a sign that immediate action is needed. When drafting your plan, consider how obvious the problem might be to the typical person. Obvious problems are usually of the on/off type, such as electrical service, air conditioning, machine-works-or-it-doesn't type of situations.

Problems that are difficult to pinpoint require step-by-step troubleshooting instructions. In these cases, something stops functioning, but the cause isn't obvious. In these instances, the call for help goes out first, but if there is anything that the person on the spot can do, then he or she should have detailed instructions on how to do it. For example, if a critical piece of shop floor machinery stops working, yet everything else in the factory is working fine, your immediate action troubleshooting steps would include tracing the data communications line back to the controller and back to the computer room to look for a break in the line. The plan should identify all the system interdependencies so they can be checked.

➤ **How Much Warning Will They Have Before the Problem Erupts?** Most weather-related problems are forecast by local news services. Flood warnings, severe thunderstorm warnings, and tornado watches are all forewarnings of problems. If your facility is susceptible to problems from these causes, then you can prepare for the problem before it strikes. However, the first indication of many problems does not appear until the problem hits, such as a vital machine that stops working or the loss of electrical power.

➤ **How Long Must They Continue Running with This Plan Before Help Arrives?** Begin with immediate actions steps, sort of like first-aid. There are always some basic actions that can be taken to contain the damage and prepare for the recovery once the "experts" appear. Detail these in your plan.

Some plans have a short duration. For example, in the case of a computer room power outage, only so much electrical power is available in the UPS before the batteries run dry. By turning off nonessential equipment, this battery time can be extended in the hopes that power will be restored soon. This assumes the person standing in the computer room knows which equipment is not essential or has a way to identify these devices. In this case, the time horizon for the containment plan is the maximum time that battery power remains available, or until the computer operations manager arrives to begin shutting down noncritical servers.

A different example is in the case of a broken water pipe. Shutting the water main to that portion of the building is the immediate action to stop the damage, at which time you switch over to containment efforts to prevent the water from spreading and the growth of mold. Your immediate actions steps would list the facility maintenance emergency telephone number or tell the person the location of the water shutoff valve.

In any case, if people in the affected room or adjacent rooms are in danger, the first step is always to notify and evacuate them. Safeguarding human life is always the number one immediate action step!

➤ **Manual Workaround.** Most automated processes have a manual workaround plan. Unfortunately, this plan is rarely written down. If you know that one exists, put it on paper immediately. If you don't know about this, ask the process owner. Manual workaround processes may not have the same quality, they may require many more workers, and they may require substantial overtime work just to keep up, but they may quickly restore your process to a minimal level of operation (the least that a disaster plan should provide). Manual workarounds may allow you to go directly to the recovery phase with minimal containment actions.

Some manual workaround processes for computer systems will require a data resynchronization action when the computer system returns to service. In those cases, work logs must be maintained of the items processed manually so that the data files can return to accuracy.

I Still Don't Know What to Write!

Write your plan in the same way as if you were explaining it to someone standing in front of you. Overall, you start with the overview and then drill down to the details. For example, if you were writing a plan to recover the e-mail server, you would state what the system does, its major components, and any information about them. Then you would have a section explaining each major component in detail.

Imagine that you are standing in a room when an emergency occurred. Also imagine several other people in the room who work for you and will follow your directions. Now imagine that you can speak, but cannot move or point. What would you tell them to do? Where are your emergency containment materials? Whom should they call, and what should they say? Write your plan in the same conversational tone that you use when telling someone what to do.

Include pictures and drawings in your plan (for example, floor plans showing the location of critical devices in a building). Digital cameras can be used to create pictures that can be easily imported into a word-processing program.

It is also very important to include references to the names of the service companies that have support contracts for your equipment. In the back of the notebook, include a copy of the vendor contact list, so they know whom to call with what information (such as the contract identification number).

So, the plan for your department will include:

1. Immediate Actions.

    a. Whom to call right away.

    b. Appendices: specific threats.

       ◆ Loss of electricity.

       ◆ Loss of telephone.

       ◆ Loss of heating, air conditioning, and humidity control.

       ◆ Severe weather and low employee attendance (perhaps due to a blizzard or flood; how can you maintain minimal production?).

2. Detailed Containment Actions.

    a. What to do to reduce further damage.

    b. First things the recovery team does once onsite.

3. Recovery Actions.

    a. Basic actions.

    b. Critical functions.

    c. Restoration priorities.

4. Foundation Documents.

    a. Asset List.

    b. Risk Assessment.

    c. Critical Process Impact Matrix.

    d. Critical Process Breakdown Matrix.

5. Employee Recall List.

6. Vendor List.

7. Manual Workaround Processes.

8. Relocating Operations.

How Do I Know When to Stop Writing?

Your primary plan only needs to contain enough explanation for someone to restore service to minimal acceptable levels. Once you have established that, your normal approach for handling projects can kick in. Some plans only cover the first 48 hours. As an alternative to setting a time guideline, link it to the function the plan is intended to protect and then it takes however long it takes.

Provide as much detail as necessary to explain to someone what they need to do. For the Immediate Action pages, assume they are unfamiliar with the details of the function and keep your instructions simple and to the point. For your primary plan, assume they are familiar with the function and understand basically how it works.

To be useful, your plan must be clear to others and include all pertinent details. The best way to know if your plan is sufficient is to ask someone to read it. Hand it to someone and then leave the room. See if they can understand and would be able to act on it. What is clear as day to you may be clear as mud to someone else. Then test it again without the involvement of your key staff members.

RECOVERY PLANNING CONSIDERATIONS

Prompt recovery is important to a company. It is also important to you because if the company has a hard time recovering, the owners may simply close your office and absorb the loss. For the sake of yourself and your fellow employees, include recovery considerations in your plan.

1. **Planning.** Each of these steps can provide valuable information for your plan development.

   ➤ Before an emergency arises, contact disaster recovery organizations that support your type of department. For example, if you are in charge of the company's Vital Records department, you might meet with and negotiate an on-demand contract for document preservation and recovery. Then you would know whom to contact and what to expect from them. They might offer some free advice for inclusion in your plan.

   ➤ Every department must have a plan for relocating its operations within the facility. A classic example of this is an office fire where the rest of the facility is intact. Your offices would be moved into another part of the facility until the damage is repaired, but the company's business can continue.

   ➤ Meet with your insurance carriers to discuss their requirements for damage documentation, their response time, and any limitations on your policies. This is a good time to review the company's business disruption insurance policy to see what it does and does not cover. Different parts of the facility may have different insurance specific to their type of work.

   ➤ Meet with vendors of your key equipment to understand how they can help in an emergency. Some equipment suppliers will, in the case of a serious emergency, provide you with the next device off of their assembly line. (Of course, you must pay full retail price and take it however it is configured.) If this is something you wish to take advantage of, then you must clearly understand any preconditions.

   ➤ Meet with the local fire, police, and ambulance services. Determine what sort of response time you should expect in an emergency from each. Identify any specific information they want to know from you in an emergency. Understanding how long it will take for the civil authorities to arrive may indicate how long the containment effort must allow for, such as for a fire or for first aid in a medical emergency.

➤ Consider shifting business functions to other sites in case of an emergency such as specific data processing systems, the sales call center, and customer billing. The effort is not trivial and may require considerable expense in travel and accommodations, but again, the goal is to promptly restore service.

2. **Continuity of Leadership.** When time is short, there is no time for introductions and turf battles. Plan for the worst case and hope for the best. Assume that many key people will not be available in the early hours of an emergency.

➤ Ensure that your employees know who their managers are, and who their manager's managers are. A good way to approach this is to schedule luncheons with the staff and these managers to discuss portions of the plan.

➤ If you plan to use employees from a different company site in your recovery operations, bring them around to tour the site and meet with the people. Although an introduction is a good start, the longer the visit the better the visual recognition later during an emergency.

➤ When exercising your plan, include scenarios where key people are not available.

3. **Insurance.** Cash to get back on your feet again. Evaluating your current insurance and selecting additional coverage should involve insurance professionals to sift through the details. In light of that, consider:

➤ What sort of documentation does the insurance company require to pay a claim? Does it need copies of receipts for major equipment? If I show a burned-out lump of metal, will the insurer believe me that it used to be an expensive server?

➤ If the structure is damaged, will the insurer pay to repair the damage? What about any additional expense (beyond the damage repair) required for mandatory structural upgrades to meet new building codes?

➤ In the event of a loss, exactly what do my policies require me to do?

➤ What do my policies cover? How does this compare to my risk assessment?

➤ Am I covered if my facility is closed by order of civil authority?

➤ If attacked by terrorists, does the company still have a claim or is that excluded under an "acts-of-war" clause?

➤ Can I begin salvage operations before an adjuster arrives? How long will it take them to get here? What about a wide-area emergency? How long must I wait for an adjuster then?

4. **Recovery Operations.**

➤ Establish and maintain security at the site at all times. Prevent looting and stop people from reentering the structure before it is declared to be safe.

➤ During recovery operations, keep detailed records of decisions, expenses, damage, areas of destruction, and where damaged materials were sent. Use video and still cameras to photograph major damage areas from multiple angles.

➤ Plan for a separate damage containment team and a disaster recovery team. The containment team focuses on limiting the damage and is very much "today" focused. The recovery team starts from the present and focuses on restarting operations. Its goal is to restore the minimal acceptable level of service.

➤ Keep employees informed about your recovery operations. They have a lot at stake in a recovery (their continuing employment) and are your staunchest allies.

➤ Protect undamaged materials from such things as water, smoke, or the weather by closing up building openings.

➤ Keep damaged materials onsite until the insurance adjuster releases them.

PREPARE A DOCUMENT REPOSITORY

A business continuity program generates a lot of documents. Recovery plans, Business Impact Analyses, risk assessment, and test results are just examples of the many things that must be kept handy. Further, many people contribute and maintain these documents. A central place is necessary to store everything so that it can be found when needed. There are several popular options:

➤ Establish a file share with subdirectories to separate the technical plans from the public areas. This is inexpensive and access permissions are controlled by the Business Continuity Manager.

➤ Use a document management product, such as Microsoft's Sharepoint™. This also tracks who has which document checked out for updates.

➤ Another alternative is to purchase a purpose-built product such as Strohl's™ LDRPS (Living Disaster Recovery Planning System) which can be used to build an automated DR plan.

The challenge is to control access to plans so that the Business Continuity Manager ensures the quality and accuracy of anything accepted for storage. Some people will write little and call it enough. They will want to store it and declare the job complete. Other well-meaning people may want to use their unique recovery plan format which will also cause confusion. Whatever tool you use, set aside a submissions area to receive proposed plans that will be reviewed

To be useful in a crisis, the repository must be available at the recovery site. This may mean that it runs on a server at a third-party site or at the recovery site. This introduces other issues such as ensuring the network connection to the server is secured.

CONCLUSION

Writing a business continuity plan seems like a big project. As with any big project, break it down into a series of smaller projects that are not quite so intimidating. Starting at the department level, work up the organization, combining department plans as you build toward an organization-wide business continuity plan.

Developing the plan is an iterative process, and you won't get everything right the first time. Testing the plan, discussed in a later chapter, will help to verify what you've written and point out gaps in the plan. Your plan should become a living document, never finally done, but changing as the organization grows and changes.

CHAPTER 7

ADMINISTRATIVE PLAN
Orchestrating the Recovery

All things are difficult before they are easy.
— Thomas Fuller

INTRODUCTION

Business continuity addresses continuing a company's business (the flow of goods and services to the customer) after an adverse event. This event might be the breakdown of a critical machine or the loss of the data center.

Historically, disaster recovery was the term for rebuilding the data center at another site after it had been rendered unusable. This solved the problem of a total data center loss, but the real issue is business processes, of which the automated systems are just one part. Disaster recovery planning is still important for both the data center and the offices. It resides inside of a business continuity plan, which deals with the overall issue of keeping the business running.

Most companies run their business continuity program as a series of projects. Each project has a defined start and stop resulting in a specific product, such as a plan test or the creation of a plan. Some of these activities require the same resources, such as a network technician to set up a test environment or to write a recovery plan. Running the program as a series of plans reduces the amount of resource conflict.

TYPES OF CONTINUITY PLANS

Business continuity plans come in many forms according to local requirements and the preferences of the person writing them. On the CD, you will find sample plans (Administrative, Technical, Work Area Recovery and Pandemic). Each plan is executed by a different team, based on the circumstances of the incident. Each sample plan must be modified to meet your company's specific situation.

The administrative plan describes how the company's business continuity program is conducted. It pulls together documents created during the initial program development, such as the BIA and the risk assessment, into a single document for future reference. The administrative plan also contains the company's long-term strategy for contingency planning. The initial phase is to write and test plans. Then, it moves into an ongoing maintenance phase to keep the plans current. The high-level details of these efforts are explained in the administrative plan. It also describes the expectations as to what each team member will be working on, such as the program sponsor and the Pandemic Administrator.

Another valuable resource in the plan is a series of reference information common to all plans, such as vendor call lists, service contract information, etc. In most companies, this information is held by the people who use it on a regular basis, which means it is scattered all around the department. During an emergency, it will be difficult to find all of this material.

Many people think that once there is a binder on the shelf, all is done. This is not true. The administrative plan details how the plans will be periodically tested in ever-increasing depth. It explains how the plans will keep pace with significant process changes and how to maintain an ongoing employee awareness campaign.

The administrative plan repeats some of the same information found in the overall business continuity plan (BCP). This is because the overall business continuity plan is the working document for the Business Continuity Manager, while the administrative plan is a reference document used by the entire recovery team. Repeating things such as the program scope and assumptions here sets the context for the rest of the plans.

Included on the CD included with this book is a sample Administrative Plan (Form 7-1). This sample plan is only a starting point. Customize it to meet your own company requirements. For instance, there are example risk assessments and restoration priority charts which you must replace with those based on your own information developed in other chapters.

ASSEMBLING AN ADMINISTRATIVE PLAN

Much of what is in the administrative plan was developed elsewhere. However, in an emergency no one has time to search everywhere for it. Consider that the audience for this material may not be involved with it on a regular basis. This makes the administrative plan a good place to insert copies that guide the company's business continuity program.

Over time, all programs tend to drift, as they are pulled this way and that by corporate forces. The BCP program materials in the administrative plan provide an anchor for the program's goals and create the strategy to achieve them. If the goals change, let it be an intentional change rather than the result of the program drifting through the company. Such drifting is sure to lead to program cancellation. The administrative plan consists of several sections which are described below.

Table of Contents

Few people will read this plan from cover to cover. It was never intended for that. Instead, they will want to quickly find whatever they need. A table of contents is a great tool for quickly finding the latest information. It is easily built using tools within the word processor. The table of contents in the example administrative plan is built and updated using Microsoft Word. An automated table of contents usually includes hyperlinks if viewing an electronic copy. This also speeds the location of information.

Demonstrated Executive Support

The BCP program charter is signed by the top company executives. Business continuity programs touch all parts of the company. Many departments will resent your intrusion into how they conduct business or initially refuse your requests for assistance. A signed statement of support will reduce this resistance. A good place for this document is at the beginning of the administrative plan.

Another item in the charter is if this program is intended to assist in achieving company compliance with legal requirements, such as the Sarbanes-Oxley Act, HIPAA, and other laws. If so, then the BCP program must list the legal requirements to ensure the appropriate steps are taken and documented. The program may also be justified as a Board of Directors mandate or in response to an audit finding.

Business Continuity Planning Charter

The goals of the business continuity planning process are often found in the program definition of the charter. The charter specifies the scope, responsibilities, and delegated authority to create and maintain the program. Some companies specify narrow authorities to the business continuity manager while others leave the question of specific authority wide open. This charter should have been provided to the Business Continuity Manager at the beginning of the project. However, if it was not, then as early in the program as possible, work with the business continuity program's executive sponsor to create one. This is your official company "marching orders" authorizing you to expend company resources and compel assistance from others.

Plan Scope

The program scope sets the boundaries for the administrative plan. The long-term goal may be a contingency plan for every company process and every site—but that can wait. The most important action is to cover all vital business functions and their supporting IT systems. After that is completed and tested, then the plan can expand to secondary sites and other processes.

Most companies have standard ways of describing the scope of an effort. You can also use the scope description of the program plan. Example scope dimensions might include:

➤ **Geography.** This might be for operations in certain cities, states, and countries.

➤ **Company Business Units.** Perhaps only domestic sales and services is in the scope, with international sales and services left for another time.

➤ **Specific Sites.** Perhaps only the company headquarters in Ohio is included and the warehouses in Arizona are not.

➤ **Business Processes.** The program is bounded by the business processes identified in the BIA and all others are excluded.

Out of scope are aspects of the company that are specifically to be excluded. It is easy to say that everything not in scope is "out of scope." However, by listing specific locations, business units, sites, etc., the program demonstrates that they were considered (and not forgotten), but were intentionally deferred to a later time. For the out-of-scope list, use the same dimensions that were used to describe what was in scope.

Plan Assumptions

Writing a plan that encompasses every possible incident to every company location would be impossible. Such a document would be so huge that it would be useless in a real disaster. To fill in gaps and to contain the planning effort to just the most critical company business processes, state a set of assumptions.

Use assumptions to define the program scope:

➤ This plan assumes that only one company site will be impacted by a disaster at a time. (No doomsday plans with many buildings inoperable, across the country.)

➤ This plan only addresses the vital business functions identified by the BIA.

Use assumptions to define the recovery plan scope:

➤ The recovery site is intact.

➤ Nothing (equipment, materials, etc.) from the original business process will be available to help with the recovery process.

➤ Key contract support firms (suppliers and vendors) have a knowledge of this plan and can follow instructions to recover critical applications.

➤ Staff members away from the office can be reached by telephone.

➤ Cross-functional teams have been developed and trained.

➤ Internal and external communication procedures have been defined and are in place which will provide quick access by the IT Disaster Recovery Team to other managers, employees, authorities, suppliers, distributors, and customers.

➤ Nothing in the data center can be used in the immediate recovery effort.

Use plan execution assumptions to define the recovery plan scope:

➤ Skilled people will be available to perform recovery work detailed in this plan.

➤ Each technical plan can be successfully executed by someone with expertise in that technology, but not necessarily familiar with that system.

Program Organization

People have an important part to play in your program. They may be experts at their day-to-day job, but lack a technical understanding of business continuity principles and techniques. Create a list of responsibilities to explain what is expected of each project role.

Thinking through the responsibilities of each position helps to share the workload and to identify additional expertise needed for the program. For example, the Business Continuity Manager might be tasked to conduct classes to train the various stakeholders. This might imply a role for the corporate trainers to assist or even take on this role.

Business continuity plans must be written by the people most familiar with a process. Processes cross departmental boundaries, and the responsibility for writing plans may be at odds with work team priorities. The Business Continuity Manager is provided direct access to the CEO to break down internal barriers that hinder plan development and testing. Subordinate managers may lead specific parts of the plan (Pandemic, Work Area Recovery, IT Systems).

Every company staffs their business continuity program based on its importance to the organization or their perceived level of risk. In most companies, the Business Continuity Manager works full time on planning, training and testing business continuity. For everyone else, their assistance to the program is part time. These roles include:

BUSINESS CONTINUITY PROGRAM SPONSOR To oversee this important program, an executive sponsor is assigned. The project sponsor audits plans and test results to ensure that the business continuity program fulfills regulatory requirements. The sponsor's involvement keeps the program synchronized with ever-changing company directions. The sponsor represents the program during business meetings, so that status reports and support requests are not sidetracked or filtered by intervening management layers.

An important role is to oversee the work of the Business Continuity Manager to ensure that person's performance meets company expectations. (It is a bad thing in the midst of a disaster to find out the Business Continuity Manager talked a good story but did not deliver workable plans.)

The program sponsor is involved with the program from beginning to end. During plan development, the program sponsor addresses reluctant departments and individuals who are less than enthusiastic about cooperating. The sponsor occasionally attends plan training and testing to gauge the level of participation.

During plan testing, the sponsor observes the test to ensure it is reasonably realistic given limitations of funds and resources. The results of the test are reviewed with everyone involved with the testing, and the sponsor submits his or her own report to executives on the results.

Over time, the program sponsor reviews existing plans to ensure that they remain current. As enhancements to new systems are proposed, the program sponsor helps to ensure that the expansion is reflected at the recovery site as well.

During an emergency, the BCP sponsor leads the Command Center. The sponsor focuses on the immediate damage containment and recovery within the recovery time objective. This frees the CEO to focus on long-term recovery and customer relations.

BUSINESS CONTINUITY MANAGER The Business Continuity Manager leads the company's planning and recovery efforts. This person's duties encompass the entire program from assisting in editing plans to providing strategic leadership and vision. The role of the Business Continuity Manager is to educate technical experts on the proper way to write a plan and to assist them in its creation. The Business Continuity Manager is typically a full-time position, with a part-time assistant.

Most employees focus on day-to-day issues and are not interested in writing plans for something that they think is unlikely to happen. Therefore, the Business Continuity Manager needs to drive the program forward. At every opportunity, he educates people, encourages them in their planning efforts, and assists with testing. Reluctant team members are persuaded, pushed, begged, and cajoled into completing their plans on time.

Once a year, the three-year program strategy is updated. The plan for the upcoming year is created. Once the sponsor approves the plan, then a budget is drafted to support the plan.

The Business Continuity Manager must be knowledgeable in company processes and work well with people. This person does not write the recovery plans. The department experts must do that. Instead, the Business Continuity Manager provides assistance and encouragement to ensure they are completed on schedule. This person also ensures that the plans are complete and of a consistently high quality. On the CD, you will find Form 7-2, Business Continuity Manager Job Description.

IT BUSINESS CONTINUITY MANAGER The IT Business Continuity Manager is an IT technical expert who provides overall control and coordination of the IT recovery effort, removing obstacles from the path of the recovery teams and providing information to other disaster teams. This person must understand the interdependencies of modern technologies to ensure they are included within the appropriate recovery plans.

The best people are always fully booked with work. Yet they may also be the most knowledgeable people about processes and the best candidates to write plans that are succinct and right the first time. The IT Business Continuity Manager ensures that the least qualified employees are not delegated to write the plans.

The IT Business Continuity Manager verifies that technical mitigation actions take place. Examples of this are to ensure that all vital data is backed up and that the backups are readable at the recovery site. It might also include verifying that the data center humidity, fire, and security alarms are regularly tested and that the Uninterruptible Power Supply batteries are regularly maintained.

TECHNICAL RECOVERY TEAM Technical plans for vital business processes must be written in such as way that someone knowledgeable about that technology (but not necessarily that process or IT system) could successfully follow it. The people who provide day-to-day support for an IT system or a business process know how it works; they know its quirks and linkages that have caused problems in the past. If an emergency occurred during a normal work day, they would pitch in and fix it. These plans are written for use by someone else where the primary support is not available.

Obtaining a slice of this valuable worker's time is the issue. This is where the authority provided by the CEO comes in handy. Keep in mind that you will be working with this person and their department for many years to come so allow time for them to fit this requirement into their work schedule.

WORK AREA RECOVERY MANAGER The Work Area Recovery Manager leads the recovery of critical office functions at the office recovery site. This person is familiar with steps for analyzing and building office processes.

A successful work area recovery requires an understanding of workflows and layouts. Some teams exchange documents frequently or need to consult each other regularly. These teams should be collocated. Some teams, such as human resources or the legal team, need privacy. To the extent possible, this must be accommodated.

The Work Area Recovery Manager must know enough about the organization to keep pace with reorganizations and shifts in business focus. He or she must ensure that the work area recovery plan remains current.

Just as the IT Business Continuity Manager coordinates the IT system support team that is writing plans for the processes its members know so well, the Work Area Recovery Manager works with the various business departments to write their plans. This requires some understanding of the appropriate person to write the plan and who can be called on to support a business process on short notice.

The Work Area Recovery Manager is also responsible for the ongoing maintenance of the office recovery site. This ensures that the space is not used as a dumping ground for excess furniture, obsolete computer servers, a parking lot for Christmas decorations, etc. The recovery site must be tested periodically to ensure that the network and telecom connections are functional and available when needed.

PANDEMIC EMERGENCY MANAGER Pandemics are a different type of emergency. They tend to be long lasting and cover a wide area. The Pandemic Emergency Manager must educate people on the potential for pandemic problems. They must also coordinate the authoring of plans that minimize contact between employees, vendors, and customers.

The Pandemic Manager applies medical expertise to guide the company through an extended medical emergency. Company policies must be adjusted and extensive sanitation measures applied across the enterprise.

Recovery Strategy

Insert the recovery strategy that was created in an earlier chapter. The recovery strategies are a high-level explanation of how the company will restore service within its recovery time objective. The different recovery strategies that are required are listed below.

IT RECOVERY STRATEGY Recovery solutions such as hot sites (a prepared data center filled with servers and disks waiting for someone to turn them on) are expensive. A popular solution is to establish a second company data center about one hour's drive from the main data center. This location should use a different power grid and telecommunications company link than the main facility. A one-hour drive enables workers to drive home at night. This is especially important for single parents.

To prepare the recovery site, move to the second data center all of the test servers for the critical IT systems. Also move servers for the noncritical systems. Include adequate disk and network support. To save time on recovery, mirror the critical data between the data center and the recovery site.

WORK AREA RECOVERY STRATEGY Like IT, the work area recovery plan must execute in a prepared site. It does not take that long to run electrical connections down the middle of a conference center, run some network wiring, and erect tables and chairs. The longest delay is the time required to add adequate bandwidth to the outside world (which includes the data center recovery site). Without this external connection of adequate size, the recovery is hobbled or delayed. If the disaster covers a wide area, it may be weeks before the telecom wiring is ready.

PANDEMIC STRATEGY The goal of the Pandemic emergency plan is for the company to continue operations at a level that permit it to remain in business. This will require that it take steps to prevent the spread of disease into and within the organization. Steps to minimize the spread of infection represent an additional cost for the company which must be borne until the danger passes. Pandemic emergency steps require different strategies for major stakeholders:

➤ Employees

◆ Those employees who can work from home should use a VPN connection to minimize the amount of time they spend in the office.

◆ The company sick day policy must be relaxed so that sick people are not forced to come into the workplace. Anyone who is sick should be encouraged to stay home. They should also stay home if they have a sick family member.

◆ Areas used by company workers must be cleaned thoroughly to address any infection brought in from the outside.

◆ Employees who travel into areas with a high rate of pandemic infection should work from home for the first week of their return.

➤ Customers

◆ Areas where customers enter the facility must be cleaned thoroughly to address any infection brought in from the outside.

◆ Provide complimentary hand sanitation at all store entrances.

◆ It may be necessary to bring in individual sanitation supplies for an extended period of time.

◆ All returned products should be sanitized before examination.

➤ Vendors

◆ Use video conferencing and other electronic tools to meet with vendors.

◆ Carefully select meeting places with a low incidence of pandemic.

Risk Assessment

A risk assessment is an analysis of the threats facing the organization. Controllable risks are mitigated to reduce their likelihood and impact. They may also be mitigated to increase the amount of warning prior to the incident occurring. For your administrative plan, use the same type of risk assessment discussed in Chapter 3.

Writing Recovery Plans

When an incident occurs, there a great need to take action. Recovery plans minimize the chaos by providing action guidelines and procedures to follow until adequate facts are available to select a course of action. For things to consider when writing your document, refer to the guidelines that you developed earlier, in Chapter 6.

It is impossible for the Business Continuity Manager to step into a department and write a viable business continuity plan. That person lacks the detailed knowledge of the process, including its variations and known quirks. Business continuity plans must be written by the people who work with a process on a regular basis. These plans are the responsibility of the department managers, not the Business Continuity Manager.

Three-Year Program Strategy

The three-year strategy explains how the BCP program will achieve its goals. It details how the program begins small in the first year and culminates in a full test by the third year. Many things must occur along the way and, once a plan is written, it becomes a maintenance burden on the team. As time goes on, there are more and more plans to maintain while others are still being written.

IT systems are a collection of interlocking technologies. They must individually be recovered and tested. Then, they need to be tested together with some of the interrelated systems. This type of test often reveals missed links and must be repeated, etc. The end is when all of the critical systems are tested together—a very expensive exercise. Without this progression of testing, it is unlikely a big test will ever be completed.

All IT systems begin and end with people. Business processes must likewise be tested. However, these plans are often tested informally due to day-to-day activity where one aspect or another fails.

"CRAWL"—THE FIRST YEAR This is the initial phase during which the foundation for the program is created. The company is examined using the Business Impact Analysis (BIA) and risk assessment to determine its recovery strategy. While the recovery site is selected and prepared, individual plans for business process recovery and IT system recovery can be written and individually tested.

During the first year, time must be set aside to train the various stakeholder groups so the entire company is following the same plan for business continuity recovery. If possible, begin on the work area recovery and pandemic emergency plans at the same time.

"WALK"—THE SECOND YEAR During the second year, continue writing the plan and raise testing to the next level. The recovery of entire IT systems (applications, databases, and network and operating support) are conducted. Business process plans are tested, and a work area recovery test is conducted for a limited number of people. A pandemic exercise can be tied into recent health threats or into a particular virulent flu strain. The point is to not focus exclusively on the IT recovery plans but to spread the exercises around to the work area recovery and pandemic emergency teams.

At this point, the program is matured enough that an outside organization can be hired to evaluate it and the testing procedures. This will inject some fresh ideas into the program and provide more assurance to the company executives that the plan is on the right track.

"RUN"—THE THIRD YEAR By the third year, the plan should be ready for a full system test. Shut down the office and IT and run the company from the recovery sites! (Such tests are rare.)

However, it may be possible to conduct a multisystem exercise that is coordinated with a test of a significant portion of the work area recovery plan. This should be timed to occur during the slow part of your business cycle. This also validates that the recovered offices can effectively communicate with the recovered data center. Some companies invite local news reporters to see the test to promote their public image.

Prepare a Document Repository

A business continuity program generates a lot of documents. Recovery plans, Business Impact Analyses, risk assessment, and results of testing are examples of the many things that must be kept handy. Further, many people contribute and maintain these documents. A central place is necessary to store everything, so that it can be found when needed. There are several popular options:

➤ Establish a file share with subdirectories to separate the technical plans from the public areas. This is inexpensive and access permissions are controlled by the Business Continuity Manager.

➤ Use a document management product, such as Microsoft's Sharepoint™. This also tracks who has which document checked out for updates.

➤ Another alternative is to purchase a purpose-built product such as Strohl's™ LDRPS (Living Disaster Recovery Planning System) which can be used to build an automated disaster recovery plan.

The challenge is to control access to plans so that the Business Continuity Manager ensures the quality and accuracy of anything accepted for storage. Some people will write little and call it enough. They will want to store it and declare the job complete. Other well meaning people may want to use their unique recovery plan format, which will also cause confusion. Whatever tool you use, set aside a submissions area to receive proposed plans for review.

To be useful in a crisis, the repository must be available at the recovery site. This may mean that it runs on a server at a third-party site or at the recovery site. This introduces other issues such as ensuring the network connection to the server is secured.

Training for a Consistent Product

Never assume that someone understands the basics of the business continuity program, what they should do, or how they should do it. Different people have different ideas about it based on their professional background and individual experience. Their intentions are good and their efforts sincere, but may be out of sync with the program.

Business continuity training provides many benefits, including:

➤ A consistent understanding of the essential business continuity issues.

➤ A common terminology for all team members.

➤ A framework so that plans follow a relatively consistent format.

Training is a never-ending challenge. It is a program's number one defense against poor quality. As soon as everyone has been trained on how to develop and maintain their business continuity plans, it is time to plan an annual refresher course. All training is based on:

➤ What must be learned and the best way to present it.

➤ How to prepare for it.

➤ How to present it.

➤ Handouts and visual aids.

➤ Practicing the presentation.

Well-prepared training focuses on its intended audience. It answers the basic questions of who must do what, when, and how. All of this is presented after explaining to the audience why the training is important and relevant to them. The instructor must answer the audience's question, "What's in it for me?"

Most BCP team members will perform to standard if they understand what the standard is and why it is important. Time spent training is time invested in an easier-to-manage program. It builds enthusiasm in the students, provides a sense of purpose in the team members, and ensures a consistent product.

Different groups of stakeholders need different types of training:

➤ **Company Executives.** Require an understanding of what a business continuity program requires.

◆ Goal: Explain what is required for a cost effective program.

◆ Method: Presentation and discussion.

◆ Frequency: Annually.

◆ Audience profile: Business focused.

◆ Main points

● Cost drivers.

● Value to the company and customers.

● Legal compliance.

● Strategic decisions.

● Regulatory requirements.

● What to expect.

➤ **Program Sponsor.**

◆ Goal: Gain support and make them a contributing member of the team.

- ◆ Method: Presentation and exercises.
- ◆ Frequency: Once.
- ◆ Audience profile: Result oriented.
- ◆ Main points
  - ● Three-year BCP strategy.
  - ● Conducting a risk assessment.
  - ● Conducting a BIA.
  - ● Oversight of the testing calendar.
  - ● Auditing plans.

➤ **Business Process Owners.**

- ◆ Goal: Keep business processes running even when things go wrong.
- ◆ Method: Presentation and plan development workshop.
- ◆ Frequency: Annually.
- ◆ Audience profile.
- ◆ Main points
  - ● Identifying vital business functions.
  - ● Process mapping to identify process chokepoints.
  - ● Writing a business process plan.
  - ● Testing a business process plan.

➤ **IT Technical Recovery Team.**

- ◆ Goal: Restart the data center in a new location.
- ◆ Method: Presentation and plan development workshop.
- ◆ Frequency: Annually.
- ◆ Audience profile.
- ◆ Main points
  - ● Documenting IT systems (there may be a company documentation standard in place).
  - ● Writing a technical recovery plan.
  - ● Testing technical recovery plans.

➤ **Executive Staff.**

- ◆ Goal: Demonstrate the executive's role in the early hours of an incident.
- ◆ Method: Small group presentation and discussion.
- ◆ Frequency: Semiannually.
- ◆ Audience profile.

◆ Main points

- Writing a corporate communications disaster plan.
- Writing a human resources disaster plan.
- Writing a payroll disaster plan.

Program Awareness

A successful business continuity program awareness effort can result in greater company-wide support for your program. It also reduces the reluctance of people to participate.

An awareness program is an ongoing process. It is best conducted a bit here and a bit there. Sometimes the message goes out one way and then another. Keeping the message fresh and relevant helps to maintain everyone's interest. The thing to avoid is an information void. People will fill an absence of information with their own fears. This will result in concern about the program rather than support for it. Ways to build awareness include:

➤ Success stories in company newsletters.

➤ Success videos on company TVs.

➤ Posters reminding key points.

➤ Discussions with departments.

➤ Dedicated quarterly newsletter with FAQ or Q&A.

➤ Company wiki or online forum.

Business continuity and disaster planning can generate a lot of employee interest. Harnessing this for the benefit of the program can provide some valuable support when fighting for priority support. The easiest way to encourage this positive energy is through a steady flow of program information.

BCP awareness can partner with other company functions to maintain a steady stream of information. A primary one is the information security team. Its members have the same challenge, which is to educate employees and demonstrate ongoing value to the company. A serious security breach disrupts company operations just like any other business disruption. Articles and presentations may be alternated or made at the same time.

The BCP awareness program is usually a never-ending series of small encounters rather than a single grand session. The BCP Manager must be the program's "evangelist," spreading the good word of the value and company benefits of the program to every employee encountered. This can be accomplished through a variety of channels.

COMPANY NEWSLETTERS Company newsletters work well because they have the potential to touch everyone at the same time with the same message. Most newsletters are starving for well-written stories relevant to the company's successes.

(This is not a place for editorializing or negative comments.) Newsletter stories can come from many sources:

➤ Profile a team member—everybody has some interesting facets.

➤ Talk about a specific aspect of the plan, such as the process of writing a recovery plan.

➤ Review the results of the latest plan test.

➤ Provide a year-end recap of program accomplishments.

➤ And a great one, after a major incident (such as a power outage, fire or other incident), describe how the event unfolded and its results.

➤ Remind everyone of their personal safety actions during an earthquake, fire, etc.

➤ Educate by detailing one subtopic in the recovery plan.

Newsletters have limited space. Keep the articles informative, upbeat, and tightly focused. This will keep readers looking forward to the next issue. Newsletters always present current events first and then fill the remaining space with non–time sensitive information.

Make up a stack of articles in advance. During a slow period, write up a half dozen or more and keep them in a folder. When time is tight, you can maintain a stream of copy to the newsletter staff.

PERSONALLY DELIVER THE MESSAGE There is no substitute for a face-to-face meeting. People are more convinced by a personal encounter, and it is an excellent way to obtain feedback on how the program is progressing.

Visit the various departments in the company and ask to speak to either the supervisor's staff meeting or an all-hands department meeting. A five-to-ten–minute recap of the program will be appreciated. This helps keep people focused on the program. Always leave time to answer questions. Feedback from the audience is valuable for gauging the clarity and usefulness of the message.

WHAT TO SAY Keep each article, poster, or presentation focused on a single issue. A single-page article is plenty. A five-minute presentation will be enough, particularly if the audience is not interested. Open an interested audience to questions after the brief presentation. The more that the message is tuned to the audience, the closer audience members will pay attention. Topics that involve their personal safety are of interest, as are topics dealing with the long-term health of the company.

Tie your BCP topics to current events. This could be a natural disaster of a type that could occur in your area, a significant fire at a company with a recognizable name or even an upcoming weather prediction. Each example makes the situation "more real" to your coworkers. The goal is not to scare anyone; it is just to gain a bit of their attention. In general, keep the message (or at least the closing lines) upbeat. Verify all of your facts to carefully protect your credibility.

Identify Critical IT Systems

In this section, insert your restoration priorities, based on the Business Impact Analysis. This consists of two lists. The first list is the business processes and their impact if unusable. The second list is the IT restoration priority list. This list begins with the infrastructure systems to be recovered and then progresses to the restoration sequence of the remaining vital IT systems. For example, a Windows domain controller must be restored before application software, etc.

Plan Distribution and Updating

Recovery plans have a balancing problem. On the one hand, they contain a significant amount of confidential information that can be used to harm the company. They must be kept locked tightly away. On the other hand, the plans must be readily accessible when needed or they are worthless. To address this, plans are broken into sections and distributed according to who will update or execute them. The primary sections are:

➤ **Administrative Plan.** Available to everyone. This describes the BCP program and contains many reference documents, such as contact information for service agreements.

➤ **Company Leadership Plan.** Describes the first few hours of the emergency.

➤ **Technical Recovery Plans.** Step-by-step instructions for recovering a business process or IT system.

➤ **Work Area Recovery Plans.** Recovering office worker spaces.

➤ **Pandemic Emergency Plan.** Actions during an extended health emergency.

It hurts the feelings of company executives to be denied access to something as important as a complete set of plans, but since it is doubtful that the CEO could personally understand or execute one of the technical recovery plans, possessing them provides little value.

Each company should determine the best mix of plan distribution. In general, those who execute a plan should have a copy at work and at home. Company executives should possess a copy of the company leadership plan, but not the technical plans, etc. Keep one complete set at the recovery site in a locked cabinet. The IT Director, Business Continuity Manager and the Business Continuity Manager's backup should each have a copy at work and at home.

A primary challenge with plan distribution is how to update the document. Updating binders can be troublesome. Often people will forget to insert the changes and remove the old pages. This results in inconsistent plans.

One solution is to always replace entire plan binders with updates. This is more expensive but ensures that plans are updated since the old binder must be submitted to receive the new one. Some companies provide the plans on memory sticks that the team members wear as necklaces or are attached to their car keys. The document on the memory stick must be encrypted.

Common mediums to use for distributing the plan:

➤ **Binders.** Easy to make up; physically available in a crisis. To update, must collect; don't tell anyone to insert pages because it won't happen. Best practice is to collect and exchange.

➤ **Memory Sticks.** Same or lower cost than binders. Must be encrypted. Can attach to key chains, etc. Requires a PC to read it.

➤ **Notebook PCs.** You have to hope employees take them home. They may be lost in an evacuation.

Assemble a Reference Section

The reference section of the plan contains information useful to managers in a disaster, as well as in day-to-day management. These documents speed problem resolution.

Out-of-date information provides a false sense of security. Be sure to update information quarterly. When the annual renewal comes around for a service contract, you can reflect on how often late time hours support was required so that hours for agreements can be lengthened or reduced. Typically a support contract for 24 hours, 7 days per week coverage costs twice as much as an 8:00 AM to 5:00 PM agreement.

Examples of items to include:

➤ **Vendor Contact List.** A listing of the vendors used by the company, including what they provide and how to contact them.

➤ **Service Agreement List.** A listing of all service contracts that support the company, along with the procedure for contacting someone about it. Be sure to include a 24-hour contact number even if support covers fewer hours.

➤ **Employee Skills Matrix.** This provides insight into who can be called on to help with a specific problem. This is essential when the regular support people are not available.

➤ **Organization Chart from the Top of the Company Down Three Levels.** This tool indicates who has what job assignment in each department. For example, if there is a problem with the system that receives incoming shipments of materials into the warehouse, the chart can provide names with telephone numbers and e-mail addresses.

➤ **Program Timelines.**

CONCLUSION

The administrative plan is the foundation for the business continuity program. It describes the framework for the overall program. It identifies tasks for the Business Continuity Manager to achieve, as well as describes ongoing program activities.

This document identifies the scope of the program. Knowing the limits of the plan helps to determine what areas are to be covered. The plan's scope is provided by the executive sponsor. This ensures the program covers all of the desired areas (lines of business, company sites, etc.). It also ensures that the program does not "wander off" into areas the company does not view as a priority.

Probably the best description of the administrative plan is that it holds material that is common to all programs. Its description of the program's fundamentals apply to each plan. The administrative plan provides reference materials required by all of the other recovery plans, such as employee recall telephone numbers, vendor contact lists, service contracts, etc.

Keeping everything in one place makes it easy for everyone to find. Since the plan does not include confidential information (like you will find in the IT recovery plan), it can be distributed to all team members.

CHAPTER 8

CRISIS MANAGEMENT PLAN
Minimizing the Damage

Lost time is never found again.
— Benjamin Franklin

INTRODUCTION

The first moments of an incident that disrupts the business are ones of executive anxiety. There is little reliable information and a great need to take immediate action. But what should be done? What is an overreaction, and what is too little too late? In an after-hours emergency, the first plan to execute is the Crisis Management Plan. It describes those first important steps to take until more specific information becomes available.

This plan describes the initial steps for dealing with an adverse situation. Guidelines are provided for initial notification and executive actions required during the incident as the functional experts begin the recovery processes. There is much to do in a short time! Customers must be reassured that their products will still be delivered on time—or assisted with finding alternate sources. Employees will want to know how they can help. The insurance adjuster may require that nothing moves until the company reviews the damage. The news media are arriving and deciding how they can tell your story for the greater entertainment of their audiences. The list of executive actions is long and the list contains little information about containing and remediating damage. That is left for other teams. The executive team must focus on external communications, overall coordination of the recovery, and taking care of the entire employee population.

The Problem

At the time of incident, minimal information is available. Is the damage big or small? Is it widespread or confined to one area? All of this is used to determine if "we can keep the doors open." Prompt action is required to quickly steer the company back to normality, but what to do? This plan begins at the point of incident and continues until either a disaster is declared or the situation is determined to be a local issue.

In a disaster, executives must continue their normal company responsibilities to communicate and control the situation. To do this, they need communication tools (telephone, e-mail, Web site, instant messaging, etc.) to pass on instructions or information bulletins. They must be aware of the response teams' progress without interfering with their work. Finally, they must provide the resources necessary to speed the recovery.

The Solution

A prompt response is the result of careful preparation. The first place to save time is in notifying the teams. Traditional call trees are unreliable and time consuming. Establish a contract with a company that provides an automated dialing system (autodialer). This service notifies many people at the same time.

Most problems are small. Rolling out the Crisis Management Team every time a squirrel chews through an electrical wire will soon diminish enthusiasm for incident response. A phased response requires one person to receive the call and to come in to investigate. Any additional support personnel can be contacted directly. However, if a major incident occurs, then the entire team should be activated.

Finally, the Crisis Management Team provides command and control during the damage containment and disaster recovery processes. The executive staff provides many important services to manage the public message, to address the needs of shareholders, and to satisfy the information needs of employees.

The phases in the executive recovery plan are:

➤ Receive notification and investigate its apparent seriousness.

➤ Alert the executive team and decide to work through the problem or declare a company "disaster."

➤ Activate the Command Center and summon the executive staff.

➤ Address external communications until the recovery teams restore minimal service.

➤ Continue supporting the recovery.

➤ Keep customers informed of their order status.

CRISIS MANAGEMENT PLAN ROLES AND RESPONSIBILITIES

There are several roles that must be fulfilled when the disaster first occurs to optimize the organization's response. These roles include:

➤ **First Point of Contact**. Usually the person who runs the facility's day-to-day maintenance. This person can look at a situation (like a gaping hole in the roof) and decide how to contain it (whom to call and what materials and tools to request, etc.) until it can be repaired.

➤ **Facility Manager.** Coordinates damage assessment, salvage, and restoration activities.

➤ **Executive Team.**

◆ **CEO.** Or, whoever makes the top business decisions.

◆ **CIO.** Makes the IT strategic decisions and advises top executives on the IT recovery progress.

◆ **Disaster Recovery Manager.** Advises executives on the disaster recovery plan execution and processes.

➤ **Executive Staff.**

◆ **Corporate Communications Manager.** Coordinates with the news media to ensure accurate reporting.

◆ **Human Resources Manager.** Coordinates communications and notification to all employees.

◆ **Legal Team.** Coordinates with the insurance company to meet assessment needs while speeding the company's recovery.

◆ **Purchasing Manager.** Quickly contacts suppliers and orders needed support.

◆ **Sales Manager.** Contacts customers to assure them of the timely delivery of their orders or to assist them in finding an alternative source of goods and services.

ESSENTIAL PLAN ELEMENTS

Every plan is unique to an organization and how it conducts its business. Privately held companies may see the owners onsite personally directing every action, while publicly traded organizations will need to keep their Board of Directors apprised of the situation.

Included on the CD included with this book is a sample Crisis Management Plan (Form 8-1). This sample plan is only a starting point. Customize it to meet your own company requirements. For instance, there are example risk assessments and restoration priority charts which you must replace with those based on your own information developed in other chapters.

Identify Assembly Points

To minimize confusion, ask everyone to automatically meet in a preselected place. Once notified of an incident, team members will not have to wait for further instructions; they will know where to go. The advantage of a prearranged rendezvous point is that no matter where someone is, in or out of the facility, he or she will know where to meet the rest of the team. The trick is that there are several situations to address:

➤ **During Working Hours**

◆ Isolated Incident. Assemble at some point in the facility that is prewired directly to external data and telephone service. It is usually a specific conference room. As the situation develops, this command center may move to a point closer to the recovery action.

◆ Building Evacuation. This is some point away from the building. For example, this might be in the southwest corner of the parking lot next to the light pole. The goal is to select a place that should not be blocked by emergency equipment in the event of a building fire.

➤ **After Working Hours**

◆ If the building is intact, then assemble at the same outside assembly point as if the building was evacuated. Only enter the building after it is structurally cleared.

◆ If the building is not available, due to a structural fire or other structural issue, select a nearby location (off of the company property) to assemble. For example, this might be a 24-hour grocery store. The location should be well lit at all hours, have a large parking lot so the team can assemble away from the front door, and be readily located by everyone.

As people arrive at the assembly point, begin organizing teams. The facilities team investigates the condition of the structure. The security team obtains clearance from the emergency services (fire, rescue, police) to enter the building to assess damage. The executive team may choose to relocate to a nearby hotel conference room to establish a temporary command center that is not affected by the weather. If the assembly point is then changed, issue another team announcement via the autodialer telling everyone where the new command center will be.

Assembly points should be identified for the general employees immediately involved in the recovery:

➤ **During Working Hours.** The assembly points should be identified in the company's building evacuation plan. (Predefined assembly points facilitate the determination of whether anyone remains in the building.)

➤ **After Working Hours.** Employees should be encouraged to stay home and near the telephone in case they are needed in the recovery. If they are already inbound, then identify a nearby property large enough to accommodate employee parking, which includes sanitation facilities and basic shelter from the weather.

Communications Plan

Communicating is the sharing of ideas, directions, and status information. Communications is the executive's way of moving people to action during an incident. It is essential for coordinating the efforts of many people in a short amount of time. To communicate with someone, you must have a communications medium and a message. What sounds so simple can become complex.

Communications planning is something that you can miss keenly when it is needed. Prior to an incident, determine who will be contacted in what situation. The most common method is by telephone. This means that an up-to-date telephone contact list must be created and maintained for use in emergencies.

The communications plan must consider the three phases of communication:

➤ **Initial Notification.** Using automatic notification.

➤ **During the Damage Assessment.** Using cellular telephones (in a wide-area disaster, the cellular system may be overwhelmed or damaged).

➤ **During the Recovery.** Person-to-person communications between the command center and the recovery site.

Maintaining a current telephone list is more difficult than it sounds. People come into and leave companies or departments all the time. They change residences and cellular telephone companies. (Although in most cases your telephone number can move with you, other circumstances may prevent it.) Employees may switch to an unlisted telephone number and, for personal reasons, never answer their personal phones directly. Every change means that an updated list must be distributed, and potentially requires a change to the autodialer database.

Some people are reluctant to provide their home telephone numbers for privacy reasons. Discontented employees and former employees may use it to harass company leaders. Others may use it to call during off hours to chat about minor business issues better left to working hours. Therefore, an emergency recall list is always considered company confidential information. Its distribution is limited to those people on the list.

Some companies maintain their telephone recall lists in their business continuity plan's administrative plan. This is because notification lists touch on all recovery plans.

Next is the choice of a tool to contact the recovery teams. It might be by telephone or face to face. In the early moments of an incident, face-to-face communication may be difficult, particularly if the team is scattered about the facility. After hours, this may be even more complex, as some people are at home, traveling, visiting someone else, or on vacation. Trying to phone each person is too time consuming. An essential tool is an automatic dialing system (also known as a robocaller or autodialer).

Automatic dialers save valuable time over "call trees." Traditionally, managers would call each individual on their list, dialing one person after another, trying each number on the list until that person was notified (and delaying notification of everyone else on the list). Each person would call four people, who would then call four others, and so on. This is less reliable than an autodialer because call tree participants may be difficult to contact or may neglect to call some of the people on the tree. They may not possess a current telephone list and lose time calling around to get the right number. When someone is contacted, a conversation may ensue about the problem, what to do, etc., which delays notification of others.

Time lost dialing staff members is time that could be used assisting with the recovery. With an autodialer, the manager calls one number and enters an access code. A message is recorded and instantly sent to everyone on that list.

One of the reasons to use an outside service for the autodialer service is accessibility. If the company's headquarters is up in flames or otherwise unusable, the autodialer would be out of commission if it was inside the building. Contracting for this service ensures that it is far away from the disaster site and unlikely to have been involved in it.

An autodialer provides the following essential services:

➤ One call notifies each person on the contact list simultaneously, eliminating delays.

➤ Enables the caller to record a message specific to the situation. This ensures that every recipient hears the same words the same way. When calling individuals manually, the message is sometimes altered in subtle or significant ways.

➤ Has a sequence of telephone numbers to call for each person (home, company cell number, personal cell number) until everyone is contacted.

➤ Will repeatedly try at a predetermined interval (such as once every two hours) for a set number of attempts.

➤ When a caller is reached, he or she presses the appropriate key on the phone to acknowledge message receipt.

➤ The autodialer can report who has not been reached. This alerts the team to notify that person's backup support.

Multiple Call Lists

Executive communications plans use multiple autodialer notification lists. These lists correspond to the various stages on the executive incident management plan:

➤ **Executives.** Used to notify senior executives, such as the CEO, the CIO, Controller, Data Operations Manager, etc.

➤ **Functional Staff.** Used to bring in the various department leaders, such as Facilities Management, Human Resources, Corporate Communications, etc.

➤ **Second and Third Line Managers and Supervisors.** Used to notify all company leaders of the situation and information to pass on to their employees.

➤ **All Call.** The general notification sent out to all team members.

Human Resources departments should periodically exercise the autodialer system for broadcasting information to employees. This validates the telephone numbers in the dialer and teaches the workers to wait for a message in a wide-area disaster. For example, in the event of a severe snow and ice storm, the company may cancel work and use the autodialer to notify everyone before they leave home, or even to state that the facility is still open.

In a disaster, the Human Resources Director can use this to ask that employees stay away from the work site until called back in. They may also use it to call everyone to a meeting to explain the situation and progress of the recovery.

Security

The company security team is the primary contact with local emergency services personnel. When police, fire, and emergency services personnel are on the scene in their official capacities, they have the authority to compel people to stay out of a building or area while they perform their duties. No employees may enter a structure until the police/fire release it. If it is a crime scene (such as an arson investigation), try to have as much of the facility released as practical.

During the course of emergency response, doors and gates may have been forced open. These entry points must be guarded until the company's security perimeter can be restored. If this requires more personnel than is available to the company, a private security company must be brought onsite. This security situation will be further aggravated if company property and papers have been scattered across adjacent properties by high winds or flood waters.

Since the outside security service cannot tell who should or should not be onsite, ask all employees to identify themselves with their company ID card. This will minimize the potential for looters to walk in amongst the chaos and steal company assets.

EXECUTIVE STAFF RESPONSIBILITIES

Executives all have the responsibility to respond once a disaster has occurred. Each has a role to play in responding to the disaster and making sure that the organization is functioning as soon as possible.

Facilities

The Facilities Director is the first person to inspect the structure, as that person has the most technical understanding of the structure (everything from where in the ceiling the network wire is routed to the point where the electricity enters the building to the location of buried utility connections). There is much to evaluate about a building before judging it fit to use, partially fit, or a danger to anyone who enters.

The initial facilities inspection begins by gathering opinions from the emergency services teams as to whether it is safe to enter the structure. Bulging walls and sagging roofs may not be easily seen in the dark, and an opinion might have to wait for daylight.

If the structure is usable, the next step is to verify that essential utility services are operational. The absence of one or more utility services can be mitigated and may not prohibit use of the building. Essential services include:

➤ Electrical

➤ Water

➤ Telephone

➤ Data

➤ Sewer

➤ Gas and other utilities

If the property is leased, then the landlord must document the plan to respond to an emergency within one hour. Know who in your company will be notified and at what point in the emergency. Be sure this plan is tested. Tenants must know the official assembly areas for a working hours and an after-hours emergency.

Once the structure can be entered, the first priority is to stop the spread of damage.

➤ Assess the situation.

➤ Plan the first recovery actions.

➤ Stop the spread of damage.

➤ Begin salvage.

  ◆ Indentify what is no longer usable.

  ◆ Remove salvageable assets.

Every utility service has a point in the building where it can be shut off. The trick is to know where it is. These places are usually locked. Obtain the keys from a custodian or Facilities Director or, if neither is available, use a bolt cutter. Knowing where the cutoffs are may minimize the spread of damage. For example, if a wall collapses in a storm and it severs a sprinkler pipe, then water will spew everywhere and soak down through all of the floors until the water is shut off to the sprinkler system or to the building.

Some of the tools you may find handy in a disaster include:

➤ Tarps to cover holes in roof and walls.

➤ Absorbent material to block water.

➤ List of equipment suppliers.

➤ Plenty of flashlights and batteries.

➤ A wet vacuum.

Executives

There is a fine line between "we can work around this during normal operations" and "we must pause company operations to work through this." Declaring a disaster means that the company is focusing most of its time, materials, and energy on recovering from a disaster. This is why only an executive can make this decision. Issuing this declaration to the recovery team means:

➤ Closing the business for a period of time to make the most of what is left.

➤ Moving some or all operations to recovery site(s).

➤ Initiating long-term recovery planning.

➤ Opening the Command Center.

Legal

We live in a lawsuit-happy society. The company's legal adviser must be alerted to any significant incident. There are many areas where a company may need to minimize its liability. Some companies contract to deliver goods or services on a schedule and now there may be a significant interruption. What is the legal impact? If someone is injured or killed during the incident, what legal issues must be carefully monitored? If there is a crime scene, could the company be liable in some manner?

Another area where the legal adviser is useful is during negotiations with the insurance company. Some insurance companies may want the incident site to be left untouched until it can be witnessed and assessed by its own adjuster. This will slow the use of undamaged machinery in the recovery. A delay by the insurance adjuster may be even greater in the event of a wide-area disaster.

Corporate Communications

Every company needs a designated spokesperson, who should establish a working relationship with the local news media well before any incident occurs. Small companies may hire a media relations service to provide the same support. The spokesperson is the company's "face to the world" and good relations before an incident will make the media more open to working with the company.

Always prepare basic announcements to be used on short notice. The news media have their own timelines to meet and will press for answers that the company may not be prepared to give. An example announcement might be, "Thank you for coming to this press briefing. I am the official spokesperson for my company. This morning, an alarm was monitored in the office area and the fire department was summoned. No company employees were in the building at the time. We have no further comment until the authorities complete their investigation."

The official company spokesperson must always be the only one to make official announcements. The news media should know the person. Otherwise, the company may lose control of its message as different executives "helpfully" provide their own opinions, not realizing that they may be interpreted as official announcements. A firm rule is that no one talks to the news media except the official spokesperson.

How seriously can things get out of hand? In January 2006, an explosion in a coal mine near Sago, West Virginia, trapped 13 miners. The news coverage was intense. After two days, rescuers reported to the Command Center that they had found the trapped miners. Someone in the Command Center interpreted this as meaning they were alive and passed an unauthorized message to the families. After several hours, it was confirmed that only one of the 13 miners survived. This unauthorized contact by someone in the Command Center made a very difficult situation much worse for the families (and the mine owners).

Inform the media when official announcements will be made. A reliable flow of status information reassures the public at a difficult time. Sometimes publishing a schedule for news updates is useful, so everyone can be ready at the same time to hear the same information. As a result, they may be less inclined to poke around.

During an incident, some of the news media may bypass the official communications channel and try to talk to company personnel working on the recovery. Every company has talkative employees, who readily express an opinion. If this cannot be stopped, at least make sure one of the company executives tags along to explain technical terms and to ensure that statements widely at variance with the official announcements are rebutted. No one wants an off-the-cuff remark repeated in a news report that might be presented later as a fact during a lawsuit.

Both Human Resources and Corporate Communications must have plans in place for how they will handle the injury or death of an employee on the job. This delicate situation must address how to notify the family prior to releasing names to the news media. It must also include ongoing family support after the notification.

HUMAN RESOURCES

Sometimes in the rush to recover a critical company function, we forget that a company is a collection of people. These people all have a stake in the company's survival (and their continuing paychecks). The Human Resources function addresses employee concerns during the crisis.

Dealing with Injuries or Fatalities

Once onsite, the Human Resources Director works with the Security Manager to determine if anyone (employee, rescue personnel, bypasser or criminal) was injured. If they have been, HR then must notify the company's legal adviser and promptly collect the following details:

➤ Type of event.

➤ Location of occurrence.

➤ Time of occurrence.

➤ Possible causes of the injury or death.

If there are injuries and/or fatalities the following details are required for the Legal department:

➤ How many persons were injured or killed.

➤ Names of all affected persons, if available.

➤ Disposition of persons seriously injured.

➤ Accounting for all staff who had been in the facility at the time of event occurrence.

Immediately contact the local authorities that may have jurisdiction over the incident and gather information about the incident and the injured. Find out where they were taken and if the families have been notified.

Using employment records and information provided by the worker's supervisor, reach out to assist the family and answer questions about company benefits. This will include medical or life insurance.

During this difficult time, families may ask many question about the incident, the people involved, etc. Working together with the company's legal advisers, craft answers to the sort of questions that may be asked before meeting with the family.

Reassigning Staff

In a disaster, many people are needed to help. However, most jobs require someone with a specific skill. In a wide-area disaster, some employees may be occupied with damages to their home or injuries to family members. These vital people will not be available when needed most. Therefore, the Human Resources department's Incident Response plan must include an analysis of employees with specific skills who can be called on in an emergency. Employees often move around in a company. For example, someone who spent five years in the payroll department may have spent the last year in sales. In an emergency, this person can bring his or her rusty payroll skills over to help where needed. This will only happen if Human Resources keeps track of individual skills.

The CD has three skills matrices (for IT personnel) that identify employee skills from different perspectives. Updating these matrices at least every quarter will provide valuable staffing information for assigning people during the recovery. These tables are also valuable during a minor crisis, when executives struggle to find "someone" to address an issue.

➤ **Form 8-2, Skill Matrix by Technical Skill.** Lists the programming languages and level of expertise.

➤ **Form 8-3, Skill Matrix by Job Process.** Lists business processes each person is skilled in using.

➤ **Form 8-4, Skill Matrix by Job Function.** Lists functional skills that may be useful in multiple processes.

Acquire Additional Personnel

During emergencies, various types of skilled labor must be found to begin work immediately. The best place to find skilled labor is other company sites. These personnel are already employees and no background check should be necessary. In some cases, they may be familiar with the areas in which you need help. As employees, they can be required to catch the next airplane. Otherwise, skilled help must be acquired from local contracting companies. However, bringing in a group of strangers who require training may take more time than would be saved.

Alternatively, employees could be reassigned to help with the recovery by doing jobs outside of their normal responsibilities. Most of a skilled worker's time is spent doing things that require much less expertise. Employees from other departments may therefore assist with these tasks.

Attendance in Difficult Times

During a crisis, payroll will be a primary employee concern. In the first few days after the incident, most companies will continue to pay employees until they determine how long they will be out of service. Good employees take a long time to find and train. If the company is no longer paying them, they will be forced to seek work elsewhere. Prior to an incident, establish a payroll policy to avoid worrying about this issue for the first few days. All supervisors will be permitted to recite the policy to their teams. For example:

➤ If employees are needed to assist with the recovery, they must come onsite and remain there for at least an 8-hour shift for each day requested by the company.

➤ If an employee refuses to attend or remain for the requested time, the company may end that person's employment.

➤ In the event that the employee's personal residence has been damaged or members of his or her immediate family have been seriously injured, then that employee will not be required to come to the recovery site.

Post-Traumatic Counseling

People deal with stress in their own ways. Employees may have witnessed a traumatic event or it may have impacted a dear friend. Just the potential of a job loss is stressful to most employees. This stress may result in lower productivity, attendance problems, and other difficulties.

To deal with this stress, engage a mental health counseling service well in advance. During normal operations, the same organization may also provide confidential employee counseling after hours for personal issues. Within 48 hours after an incident, the mental health counselor should meet with employees in small groups to discuss their concerns. The counselor should also return in approximately a month for a follow-up general counseling session. The need for additional sessions will depend on the nature of the incident and what was witnessed by the staff.

Contracting for mental health counseling in advance helps to ensure it will be available in a wide-area disaster, if needed. Trying to arrange for this service on the spur of the moment may provide uneven results.

SALES

The Sales department works endlessly to build up a set of loyal and profitable customers. It must work with these customers so that the company's disaster does not become the customer's disaster. To do this, the sales team notifies all critical customers of the situation and provides company approved updates as the recovery continues. If necessary, the sales team purchases products or services for the customer and sells them at the normal price. This will usually be at a loss but will keep the customer serviced until the recovery can be completed.

PURCHASING

The Purchasing function of the Accounting department must provide prompt issuance of purchase orders to keep the recovery moving forward. If the IT systems are inoperable, then the purchase orders must be cut manually. Purchasing may also be involved with bringing in contract workers, hiring additional security forces, etc.

SECTION I—NOTIFICATION AND INITIAL TRIAGE

When an incident occurs during normal working hours, the staff is already onsite and can skip ahead to Section II of the plan. However, problems arise in their own good time, so this plan begins in the dark of night in the middle of a holiday weekend when the company staff is away from the workplace.

It begins with notification that "something" has occurred. This might come from the night watchman or from an alarm service. The incident might be the ringing of a burglar or fire alarm, or almost anything else. At this point, the entire first response team can be rolled out (and be too tired to work the next day) or one person can drive in to see if the damage is widespread or contained to one small place.

If the incident appears to significantly impact the next day's operations, then the executive team must be notified. Record an incident status message on the autodialer system and summon the executive team. In some cases, this may be an alert that does not require immediate action, but they will know the problem must be addressed first thing in the morning.

After the incident and the initial notification, contain the damage so that it does not spread. Containment is normally done by the Facilities Director (which is why most companies use this person as their first responder). The Facilities Director will have a separate notification list on the autodialer.

Examples of containing the damage include:

➤ After a fire, installing a barrier to prevent water from spreading or to catch leaks if it seeps through the floor to offices below.

➤ Stretching tarps over holes in the roof created by high winds.

➤ Patching a hole in the perimeter fence if a car accident has punched through it.

➤ Securing a door forced open by a burglar.

If the damage is severe, it may require that the executive team come onsite. All jokes about lacking technical expertise aside, this group needs an early understanding of the situation. As previously described, they were notified via autodialer. Some of the reasons this team must come onsite include:

➤ There will be a significant interruption of some portion of the company operations. Arrangements must be made to continue the flow of goods and services to customers.

➤ The incident will require a prompt action to remedy, such as the loss of vital equipment, loss of the telephone switch, or relocation to the data center.

➤ Damage will halt most productive work for the next day so when the workers arrive, they must be told to go home or to the recovery site.

SECTION II—SUPPORTING THE RECOVERY TEAMS

When the executive team members arrive, they are briefed by the Facilities Director on the damage. Based on this discussion and their inspection of the situation, they decide to both patch things together and repair them the next day or to bring out the recovery teams. The key issue is the size of the operational impact (e.g., if damage is confined to one small work cell or encompasses an entire department).

If an incident requires immediate response, the first action is to open the Command Center. (If possible, use the onsite Command Center.) This is the "Go To" place for everyone involved in the recovery. Many people will want to help and their actions may undo or interfere with the careful work of others.

Next, use the autodialer system to call in the recovery teams. The recovery teams also include support staff to include:

➤ **Purchasing.** So emergency orders can be submitted for everything needed. (Be prepared to cut purchase orders manually!)

➤ **Corporate Communications.** It is better for a company to send out its own story and control the message than to let the local news channel inform your customers and suppliers of the incident. This message may be replayed later in a lawsuit, so the wording must be minimal and accurate.

➤ **Human Resources**. Handling the employees as they show up for work. Some will be needed for the recovery, and others must be sent home.

➤ **Payroll.** Payroll must know your policy. Do you pay the people sent home or is it a no-work day? In addition, if you only pay those onsite, how do you track who is here and for how long?

Disaster Declaration

Based on the situation, the Crisis Management Team decides to either work around the problem during normal operations or to declare a disaster. Declaring a partial or full disaster means that normal operations are halted. All attention is turned to restoring service at the recovery sites. Such a revenue ending decision may only be made at the highest levels.

The decision to declare a disaster is based on the length of time required to restore service. If it is longer than the company's published recovery time objective (RTO), then essential services can be restored quicker at the recovery site than the disaster site.

Supporting the Recovery

During the recovery, the Crisis Management Team and the company's executive staff continue to provide support services to the teams. It is important that communications are consistent and posted at published times. This reduces interruptions to the Command Center by ensuring that one person after another does not keep asking the same questions.

The tracking log ensures that Command Center personnel know who is onsite and where they are. If a family emergency arises (as might occur during a wide-area recovery), then that person can be quickly notified. Similarly, if someone is at the disaster site instead of the recovery site, then this updated document helps to locate them.

Another important service is to identify skills needed at a particular site and then calling this person to come in. This is most important for notifying the backup support person (or the closest that you can find one) to come in.

CONCLUSION

Disasters are a "come as you are" affair. Autodialers, assembly points, and policies must all be in place before they are needed. Executives have an important role to play in incident containment and recovery. A plan for company executives focuses their energies in areas where they excel and away from micromanaging the recovery teams.

The Crisis Management Plan develops the situation from the first notification through the disaster declaration. Time lost fumbling through the early hours might permit the spread of additional damage. Prompt action speeds a company to a quicker recovery. For example, if high winds blew the roof off, then a second storm an hour later poured a deluge onto the building. Losing the time in between compounds the problem.

Throughout the plan the emphasis is on communications. Executives do not turn their own screwdrivers. They coordinate the efforts of others to do so. In an emergency, coordinating the recovery teams is essential to avoid losing time. Every day the facility is inoperable is another day of all cost to the company without income.

The executive support team members, all of whom have vital functions to perform, must prepare in advance to provide on-demand services. Also, the IT systems may not be available so many processes may be manual or depend on files stored off-site.

During a disaster, much of the executives' efforts address external issues. Managing the news media, communicating with major customers and stakeholders, and addressing legal issues are vital parts of the long-term recovery. In the near term, the Security Team protects company assets while the Human Resources department protects the company's human capital.

CHAPTER 9

TECHNICAL RECOVERY PLAN
Putting Humpty Dumpty Back Together Again

Any sufficiently advanced technology is indistinguishable from magic.
— Arthur C. Clarke

INTRODUCTION

When people think about disaster recovery, they focus on technical recovery plans. Although these plans offer detailed instructions for how to re-create a technical function for a company, they are really more than instructions for rebuilding a computer server in IT. They can be for the recovery of anything vital to the business, including recovery of a single machine in the factory or an office process. Each company needs to determine which of its processes need a technical recovery plan.

This chapter addresses two types of technical recovery plans. The first explains how to recover something complex. In the examples used, it will be an IT system. The second describes the critical actions to be taken by the technical recovery team leader at the recovery site. For example, it details how to recall recovery media, what to expect from the delivery service, when it should appear, etc.

DETERMINING WHAT NEEDS A PLAN

In terms of the overall disaster recovery, only vital business functions are candidates for a technical recovery plan. This is because the creation and maintenance of these plans is time consuming and, therefore, expensive. However, department managers may find these plans useful for all of their primary business functions, even if the company does not consider all of them vital. The creation of recovery plans beyond the minimal helps to raise a company's business resilience from disaster recovery to business continuity planning.

Significant company disasters are rare. However, an isolated crisis, such as the failure of a company's e-mail server, can make a manager's life very stressful (assuming he or she is responsible for its care and feeding). In this situation, the company is still creating and delivering its products and services to customers, but without the assistance of this business function. A technical recovery plan provides a manager the tool to begin the recovery process while waiting for technical assistance to arrive. Some of the plans most companies require cover:

➤ All vital IT functions, as identified by the Business Impact Analysis.

➤ All vital business functions, as identified by the Business Impact Analysis.

➤ Telephone service, such as the main telephone switch, automatic voice mail routing, etc.

➤ Essential facilities services, such as water, electric, sanitary, etc.

➤ The office operations of vital business functions, such as how to recover a warehouse in another location during a disaster, how to maintain the customer service desk during a disaster, etc.

These plans cannot be written by anyone other than the person who supports them every day. Writing the plans takes time. Because few of these people have every written one, they will be reluctant to sign up for a task when they cannot gauge how long it will take.

The key to gaining their support is to make the process as easy as possible. Providing a recovery plan format and training them on how to use it relieves some of the anxiety. Beyond that, it is up to the company executives to free up the technician's time and to identify creating these plans as a priority.

Included on the CD attached to this book is a sample Technical Recovery Plan (Form 9-1). This sample plan is only a starting point. Customize it to meet your own company requirements. For instance, there are example risk assessments and restoration priority charts which you must replace with those based on your own information developed in other chapters.

CREATING RECOVERY PLANS

Many companies assign someone to run their business continuity program and then walk away thinking that the job is done. This person is expected to sit in a back room and create the company's response to a serious incident. For parts of the plan, this is true. This person can craft the administrative plan and even work through much of the Crisis Management Team's plan without significant input. However, the Business Continuity Manager cannot write the technical recovery plans. This must be done by the skilled technicians who support these systems. The problem is that these technicians are busy meeting other company priorities. Writing a plan for a disaster that may never happen is not high on their lists. Executive support is critical!

Overcome Objections

Asking technicians to write recovery plans is like asking small children to volunteer for a round of immunization shots. Few will step forward. That is why senior executive support is so important. However, in fairness, the technicians are also expressing their personal concerns, so the person coordinating the creation of these plans must address and eliminate as many of these objections as possible:

➤ "I can't write." Make plan writing easy through an approved "fill-in-the-blanks" plan template (see Form 9-1, Technical Recovery Plan, on the CD) and a brief class to show them what information goes into which space.

➤ "If I tell you, I lose my job security." You might explain that strong technical expertise is the best defense for job security. However, managers who permit workers to use this as an excuse are setting themselves up for blackmail at some future date (pay raise time, annual performance reviews, days off, etc.).

➤ "Someone will fool around with my systems." This can happen anyhow. Remind them that passwords typically protect systems, and they are not stored with the plans.

➤ "I know what to do and don't need a plan." The plan is a guideline for the technical backup person. Also, some software is so stable that it is rarely touched. This plan reminds the primary support person about its specific requirements for installation.

➤ "You never know what will happen so any written plan is useless." A technical recovery plan addresses the worst-case scenario by providing recovery instructions. No matter what the disaster, if the system needs to be rebuilt on different equipment, this plan will save the company a considerable amount of time and effort. If less than a full recovery is needed, then only part of the plan is used.

Passwords

IT systems are typically protected with passwords. In an emergency, the person recovering the IT system will need to know what the passwords are. However, writing down passwords to the company's most sensitive systems violates information security standards. Once written, they must be protected so that that are only available in a crisis.

Another problem is that passwords change. If your company is serious about its information security program, then all passwords expire at some point in time. With multiple servers, routers, and anything else protected by a password, this expiration date is variable. Passwords are also changed if the company's security is breached, if a key person leaves the company, etc.

There are as many different solutions to these problems as there are companies. Two of the most common solutions are:

➤ Keep the passwords in a locked container at the recovery site, and update its contents weekly.

➤ E-mail all changed passwords to the CIO's third party e-mail account (such as Yahoo or Hotmail).

Names or Position Titles

Some companies prefer not to include names within plans and instead refer to a system support chart. This makes maintaining the support chart simpler. Companies with lower employee turnover may prefer to have names in the plans, so leaders do not need to look up things in a chart that may be hard to find in a crisis. An example of a recall table is shown in Figure 9-1. This table is a simple way to collect and keep recovery recall information in one place.

PLAN FORMAT

Two important ways to encourage technician plan writing is to offer a plan template and a class explaining how to complete it. Some people find writing very

Title	Name	Company Cell	Home Phone
Primary Technical Support	Richard Reis	(614) 555-1212	(937) 123-4567
Secondary Technical Support	Whom Ami	(614) 555-1212	(937) 123-4567
Technical Support Manager	Greg Magee	(614) 555-1212	(937) 123-4567
Primary End User Support	Norm Fry	(614) 555-1212	(937) 123-4567
Primary End User Support	David McDermott	(614) 555-1212	(937) 123-4567
Primary End User Support	Mike Connelly	(614) 555-1212	(937) 123-4567

FIGURE 9-1: Example recall table from a technical recovery plan.

easy. Others stare blankly at an empty sheet of paper with no idea where to begin. Others fear that someone will criticize their writing and are afraid to write anything down. The Business Continuity Manager's approach to this is to be patient, firm, and helpful!

Plan Template

Use Form 9-1, Technical Recovery Plan, included on the CD. The plan template addresses the *who, what, where, when, why* and, most importantly, *how* to recover something. Although this template is organized for the recovery of an IT system, it could easily be reworked to recover a telephone switch, the company's data network, a special machine tool, or simply a process.

The front of the plan has a table of contents. No one reads these plans like a novel (front to back). Instead, they are often looking for something specific. The table of contents quickly points them to where they want to go.

The template steps through the various dimensions of what must be known or possessed to recover a particular IT system. The first part explains how the system supports the business. This is useful when making tradeoff decisions during a recovery. Farther down the list are technical requirements for a successful system recovery:

➤ **Purpose.** Set the context in which this system provides value. For example, the purpose of the materials management system is to control the quantity, location, and usage history of the company's manufacturing materials.

➤ **Scope.** What this system does and does not support. For example, this system supports the company headquarters, the Eldorado, Ohio factory, and the Abu Dhabi sales office.

➤ **Background.** Explain any business requirements that assist the reader in understanding why this server/application exists.

➤ **Assumptions.** A list of things that were assumed when this plan was written, such as, "The technical qualifications required for the person executing this plan," etc.

➤ **Dependencies**. Other servers must be in place, such as IBM's IIS server, a specific Oracle database server, etc. Essential IT servers, such as DHCP, Domain Controllers, etc., should be assumed as in place. Also skip the environmental concerns of air conditioning, filtered electrical power, etc.

➤ **Tech Support.** List the names and 24-hour contact numbers of the primary and secondary support persons for this system. Some companies refer to the employee recall list in the administrative plan for telephone numbers.

➤ **System Users.** List the primary end users for this system. These people will be called upon to verify that the system has been successfully recovered. They will more thoroughly exercise the system than will the IT technician.

"Systems Requirements" details specific technical requirements that must be in place before this IT system can achieve its minimal level of service. Since this is an IT example, a different set of criteria should be selected for recovering an office, a piece of machinery, etc.

➤ **Server Requirements** in terms of CPU, RAM, "C: drive" size and type, etc. Be clear about what is needed because these specifications may be used to order a replacement server that is the appropriate size.

➤ **Disk Space Requirements** lists the total disk storage required for local disks, SAN disks, etc. Any special configuration of these disks is also noted here.

➤ **Connectivity Requirements** describes the network configuration, such as VLANs, trusts, opened firewall ports, special firewall rules, etc.

➤ **Support Software** lists the many supporting utilities that may be needed.

➤ **Application Requirements** are listed in case a software application must be changed during recovery. The appropriate compiler version must be known to implement the repair.

➤ **Database Requirements** lists the type and version of the database program supporting this system. This will also include required permissions, databases, and table connections needed.

➤ **Special Input Data** beyond what is in the company's backup media, such as data stored in a different off-site location or an external data feed.

➤ **Licensing Requirements** may be relevant since in some cases, loading this system on new hardware may require a license change by the software manufacturer. For example, a license may be tied to a CPU serial number. If applicable, detail the instructions for obtaining it.

➤ **Special Printing Requirements** details instructions for setting up printed output for this application to include special forms.

➤ **Service Contracts** that support this system's components to include days and times of coverage, etc. Include the expiration date. Describe how to contact the vendor or whoever provides support. This information should be available through the command center and the administrative plan.

"Detailed Recovery" details the specific steps required to bring this system back up to a minimum level of service. This includes:

➤ Prerequisite Systems/Applications that are required prior to restoring this application.

➤ Successor Systems/Applications that are fed by this application.

➤ Application or Infrastructure Component License Requirements (necessary to accomplish the test).

➤ Architecture Diagram (insert a diagram that indicates where in storage the application is found, how to start it, how it relates to other systems and passes data between components).

Template Training

The people who know the most about your systems are often the busiest. Time spent writing your document is time not spent on actions the company judges to be productive. Therefore, only a few people at a time will be made available for writing plans. This is why template training is usually conducted in small groups. This allows for one-on-one questions to be quickly addressed. In larger groups, a few strong personalities may disrupt the meeting and many questions will go unanswered.

Walk the team through the template element by element. Ask for their ideas for improving it and seek to identify their challenges in filling it in. The most common problem is writing the step-by-step recovery. The easiest approach is to ask them to explain the recovery steps to you. Writing the steps is the same as speaking them to another person.

All plans are written for someone with at least a basic familiarity with that technology (UNIX, DB2, C++, etc.). To save on words, it is nice to include screen shots of what to enter where and software responses to look for. These screen prints should go into the recovery document. For example, instead of telling someone to look for the small button in the upper left corner and then describing the next field to enter, they can draw an arrow on the screen shot. This saves time to read and to execute it.

Screen shots can make the individual recovery plans rather large. However, a plan with clear illustrations speeds recovery.

Proofing with the Manager

Once the plan is drafted, it needs to be proofread by someone other than its author. This will help to correct grammatical errors and to identify logical gaps in the narrative. There are two logical candidates for this:

➤ **Author's Team Leader.** This is the person in the hot seat when it comes to ensuring that a workable plan is created. Proofreading the plan familiarizes the leader with the system in question and enables him or her to identify "best practices" that can be applied to other plans created by the team. The leader also has a "big picture" view of this system and adjacent software systems to point out connection points between them.

➤ **Backup Support Person.** This person may be the one called upon to execute the plan, so he or she has a personal stake in ensuring that it is understandable and complete.

Step-by-Step Specifics

How much detail is necessary? It is not practical to write a plan so detailed that any person walking by can execute it. That would take too long to execute and would be too unwieldy to keep current. Instead, write it at the level of someone familiar with the technology, but not necessarily with that IT system. This enables the use of other company employees or contractors to run with this plan in the event of a serious disaster.

When writing these plans, put yourself in the place of someone asked to recover this unfamiliar system. What would you want to know about? What aspect of the recovery would concern you the most? What is the logical way to sequence the recovery steps for a smooth recovery? How might the technician verify that required predecessors are in place before beginning?

RECOVERY PLAN FOR THE RECOVERY TEAM LEADER

A plan to manage the plans is important. During a disaster, the person leading the efforts at a recovery site will have his or her own specific recovery information steps and requirements. These should be included in a separate plan. In this case, use Form 9-2, IT Team Leader Recovery Plan, that is included on the CD. The purpose of this plan is to guide the technical recovery team leader on the actions required at the remote technical recovery site. This plan is intended to work together with the Command Center plan to ensure a smooth recovery.

Activity at the recovery site will be hectic with technicians coming and going—each with their own idea of what should be done next. The technical recovery team leader must focus this energy on the recovery effort at the time when it is needed.

Recovery Site Manager

The Recovery Site Manager is the CIO's representative at the recovery site. This person is charged with providing direction to all employees and contractors onsite. During a recovery, there is no time to argue over the boundaries of job responsibilities. The Recovery Site Manager has the authority to assign any employee or contractor onsite to any recovery task.

Organizing the local recovery efforts means wearing many hats. The Recovery Site Manager is both leading the recovery effort and activating a new company facility. This responsibility runs from reloading software to security to janitorial service and includes everything necessary to ensure a safe, sanitary, and operational facility. Most people assigned to this task have no problem with the technical side—it is the rest of the work that distracts them. If a facilities manager is onsite, that would be the logical person to address the facility issues.

To minimize distractions, the team must also be cared for. The recovery site should be located at least an hour away from the normal working site. This means that the surrounding countryside may not be familiar to team members. To keep the team focused on the recovery, food is usually purchased and brought in so no one needs go searching for it. Local hotel accommodations may also be needed. Specific responsibilities include:

➤ Appoint someone as the alternate site manager to answer questions in the Recovery Site Manager's absence.

➤ Ensure security of the site to safeguard company assets and data.

➤ Report progress once an hour to the company recovery Command Center on the IT systems recovery.

➤ Assign team members and contractors to whatever tasks need to be accomplished.

➤ Publish a rest plan to ensure the recovery can proceed around the clock.

➤ Ensure everything in the facility operates safely.

➤ Coordinate purchasing requirements through the Command Center. However, use the company credit card for small purchases such as food for the staff and miscellaneous supplies.

Several important tools will guide the Recovery Site Manager. These are typically found in the administrative plan as they are useful to more than one team.

Personnel Tracking

The Recovery Site Manager assigns workers to specific tasks as they arrive. Based on the situation, people may be assigned to areas other than their primary specialties. For example, once the networks are operational early in the recovery, the network technicians may be assigned to other duties.

Maintain a log of who arrived, and when. Know who is at the recovery site in case they are needed. When the crisis has passed, this can be used for a number of actions, such as "Thank You" notes, calculating labor used in the recovery toward the company's losses from the disaster, etc. This log enables:

➤ Tracking when people have been too long on the job and need to rest. Tired people make mistakes.

➤ Tracking who is in the disaster site to account for everyone. Know who went where and when so that someone can look for them if they are overdue.

Use Form 9-3, Technician Tracking Log, on the CD to track personnel. This sheet shows who arrived when. Late arrivals may explain some of the delays in starting specific recovery steps. It shows who is still onsite and can also be used to provide personnel status reports. The intention is to avoid time lost looking for someone. If they sign out then they are off-site and no further searching is required. It also serves as a record later for who was onsite, when, and for how long.

Recovery Activity Log

Use Form 9-4, Recovery Activity Log, on the CD to track recovery activities. It is used to record significant events occurring during the recovery. This document is valuable for later analysis so that recovery performance can be improved. Start this log as soon as the facility is open. Require all technicians to report when they begin their recovery work and when it is complete.

Examples of entries in the activity log are:

➤ Requests to Purchasing for additional supplies or services.

➤ Calls to external tech support.

➤ Status reports to the Command Center.

Recovery Gantt Chart

The Command Center's question is always, "When will it be ready?" The Recovery Gantt Chart will show where the recovery is in relation to its completion and provide some idea of when a specific application will be available for business use. There is a sequence to the logical recovery of IT systems. The network (internal and external) must be activated, then the supporting servers are restored (Domain Controller, DHCP, DNS, etc.), then the application and database servers are restored, and on and on. A tool to achieve this is a restoration priority list.

The Recovery Gantt Chart is created during plan testing. It is used to add up all of the estimated and actual plan test recovery times to see if the company can achieve its recovery time objective (RTO). The same document is an excellent tool for gauging progress. For example, if the CEO decides that he needs e-mail service restored as early as possible, then a review of the Gantt identifies those IT services that must restored before e-mail recovery can begin. As these services are restored, the remaining time for the rest of this recovery can be estimated.

The recovery timeline is a tool that enables the recovery team leader to monitor progress toward recovery completion and to estimate the remaining time required to complete the recovery. A copy of the timeline is maintained in the Command Center for the same purpose. The timeline helps the CIO project when specific IT functions should be available given recovery progress.

During the development of recovery plans, each author estimated the amount of time required to execute his or her plan. This information from all the plans was then added to the RTO Hour-by-Hour Recovery Plan. Each plan was placed in sequence according to its timing in the recovery. For example, the domain controller is recovered after the network is restored and before starting on application recovery. The sequence of restoration and the lengths of time required are formatted into a Gantt Chart using Microsoft Project.

Form 9-5, Hour-by-Hour Recovery Plan, is an example of a Gantt Chart that can be found on the CD. This is in Microsoft Project format.

To use the plan during recovery, follow the team's progress on the chart. If someone asked when a particular application will be ready, it can be traced back up the Gantt Chart to the point where the team is currently working. This backward check indicates the amount of additional time needed before that application can be used.

Another way this chart helps is if the recovery of one component is delayed. Looking ahead on the chart, this indicates the additional time required for subordinate recoveries. For example, if a domain controller was delayed by a half day, then all subsequent recoveries on the chart would be delayed by that much. The total of the delays is called the "accumulated delay."

Materials to Reference in the Administrative Plan

Keep a copy of the company's administrative plan in the recovery site. It contains much useful information for the Recovery Site Manager, such as:

➤ **Technical Support Chart.** A matrix indicating who is the primary and secondary support for every technology. This is used to determine whom to contact for recovering which system. If the primary support person is not present then the secondary person can be summoned.

➤ **Recall Roster.** A complete employee recall roster is located in the Command Center. If a particular person is needed, request him or her through the Command Center. The Human Resources representative in the Command Center also has a matrix of job skills. If the primary and secondary person are not available, then this chart can be used to identify someone else in the company who is familiar with the technology in question.

➤ **Vendor List.** 24-hour contact information for vendors. Although after-hours calls from a customer are severely discouraged, in a true emergency, a supplier looking to retain a valuable customer will step up and unlock business doors even in the middle of the night.

Emergency purchasing authority must be clearly described in the company's policies and Crisis Management Plan. No one wants to lose valuable recovery time waiting for a purchasing agent to appear.

Validating a Successful Recovery

When an application is restored, it is first tested by the technician who loaded it. Once the technician is satisfied that the application is ready, then the "power user" for that application should log in and exercise its many options. After that person is satisfied, the application is released for general use. This layering of testing catches errors and missing system interfaces before end users miss them. In addition, in a busy recovery, technicians are quickly assigned to recover other systems. There is little time to go back and troubleshoot a poorly restored software application.

Once a recovered application has passed all tests, inform the Recovery Site Manager. The result will be added to the Hour-by-Hour chart and reported back to the Command Center.

Security

Most recovery sites are not permanently staffed. When they are opened during a crisis, they need a team with the right mix of skills. The responsibility for ensuring this occurs usually falls to the recovery team leader onsite. This person must establish the basic support functions to make the site run smoothly.

The first person to arrive with a key establishes security for the front door. People will be going in and out for various reasons. Many of the team members will not have access via the electronic locks. Not everyone can be relied upon to verify the identity of someone before admitting them to the site. It is better to post one person at the door as a security check for movement in and out until a company security guard arrives. If the guard needs a break, they must call down to see if someone can watch the door for them.

Electronic locks make it easy to secure entrance to a few people during normal operation, and then enable many others to enter during an event. If possible, add the recovery team to the locks to minimize delays at the entrance.

Team Support

Identify in advance nearby hotels for rest and food so that team members are not missed while they wander around a strange neighborhood looking for an open restaurant. Find out who delivers to the recovery site. Through this all, an up-to-date telephone book or Internet access is essential.

The best time to set this up is during plan testing. When running a test, try out some of the local hotels and restaurants to see which provides the best service. Then when the crisis hits, the team will already know whom and where to call. The company may also keep the contact information for these sites close at hand and open purchase orders to cover requests.

Communications

As soon as the recovery site is opened for the technical team, the recovery team manager establishes communications with the primary Command Center. Report that the recovery has begun. Keep the line available so that the Command Center can call when needed. (IT recovery sites tend to be shielded and it may be difficult to gain cellular telephone reception.) Other important communications issues are listed below.

STATUS REPORTING It is important that the Command Center knows the current status of the recovery. As systems become available, users can be assigned to catch up on work to restore service to customers. Communications is a two-way street.

The primary Command Center will provide status of the disaster site's disaster containment and recovery.

Submit a status report to the Command Center on the hour containing some or all of the following:

➤ Progress in the restoration priority list and restoration timeline.

➤ Whether security has been implemented.

➤ Who is present at the recovery site.

➤ What resources are needed.

➤ What purchasing is needed.

The CIO in the Command Center reports to the Recovery Site Manager on:

➤ Progress in the disaster site assessment, as well as containment and salvage efforts.

➤ Status of resources at both sites.

➤ Status of purchasing requests from the recovery site.

COMMUNICATIONS TOOLS IN THE RECOVERY SITE The recovery site must be equipped with a range of communications devices. Given the short timeframe for a recovery, there is not time to work around a communications mismatch. Items needed include:

➤ Fax line for vendors requiring a faxed order with a signature.

➤ VPN line for contracted services to connect to the systems with minimal potential for interception.

➤ External network and modem connection. If the network connection is not normally live, the direct telephone line is, and external sources could dial in via modem.

Recovering Backup Media from Storage

The key to a prompt IT recovery is ready access to the most recent copy of the company's backup media. Every company has its own approach to storing this media. First, it must be stored off-site in a facility that has as rigorous security protection against theft and environmental controls in place as in the data center. Often this means that a secure courier is used to transport the media.

A part of this security is that only a few people can call out the media containers. Several of these people should be among the first dispatched to the recovery site. (Summoning several people is a good idea in case one or more cannot attend.) Ensure that team members know who is recognized by the off-site storage company as possessing the authority to recall the media.

In the plan, be sure to include:

➤ Media storage location.

➤ Who is authorized by the company to withdraw material. This person must be present at the recovery site to receive the material or the courier may not be permitted to leave it.

➤ Number to call to withdraw material.

➤ Pass codes to validate identity.

➤ A reminder to recall the latest weekly container and all daily containers since then.

Implement a Rest Plan

Recovering IT systems takes time. Tired people make more mistakes. So if the data center recovery will require more than one working day, the team leader must implement a rest plan for the group. This means that a portion of the techs will be in a quiet rest area (no loud music or anything to distract them). The remainder are working on assigned tasks. Although some people can sleep at anytime and anywhere, others will find it difficult to relax with so much excitement. Still, without a rest plan, everyone will run out of energy at about the same time and the recovery halts.

The rest plan is a published document that lists who is working what hours. Often this is determined by the sequence of events anyhow. The idea is if someone is not needed for a few hours, they should not get underfoot of the technicians working and should be in a separate area.

Janitorial Service

A facility that normally sits idle may not have a custodial staff. Someone is needed to clean the sanitary facilities, empty the trash, etc. Although this may not seem to be a priority for the team leader, think in terms of days. If the recovery is successful, then the recovery site will be the company's data center until service is restored at the primary site. To keep the recovery site safe and sanitary, a periodic cleaning is needed.

Plan Testing

The Business Continuity Manager must certify at least quarterly that the IT recovery site is capable of supporting this plan. For a recovery site to provide emergency recovery, it must have:

➤ Sufficient server capacity to load and run identified critical applications.

➤ The right type of back-end servers (Active Directory, Domain Controllers, Tape Management server, DNS, DHCP, firewalls, etc.) to support the recovered applications.

➤ Protected network connection to the Internet and Intranet.

CONCLUSION

Technical recovery plans are the heart of the recovery effort. They provide much of the "how" of the recovery. A plan must be written for every vital business function, not just for IT systems. There should be a plan for each business process in a work area recovery plan, telecommunications recovery, and every vital IT system. Companies aspiring to the level of business continuity planning should also provide plans for other important functions so they can be recovered from an incident more quickly.

Technical recovery plans must be tested regularly. Processes change over time and regular testing catches updates that have not made it to the plans. Exercising the plans is also the best way to train recovery team members. In a crisis, they will already be familiar with the content and recovery project workflow.

A separate plan is needed for the person managing the newly opened recovery site. Part of the plan is to open a miniature Command Center to control the site. Another part is to control the recovery team to ensure that the many personalities are working together instead of at cross-purposes. However, the primary purpose is to guide the sequence of recovery plan execution to speed the availability of these services to the company.

CHAPTER 10

WORK AREA RECOVERY PLAN
Getting the Office Up and Running

Ya gots to work with what you gots to work with.
— Stevie Wonder

INTRODUCTION

Work area recovery means preparing workspace in which to temporarily recover business operations. It usually involves offices, but it could easily encompass call centers, retail space, or factories. Whatever its function, a plan is needed to establish a place for people to work. Every day that your business is out of service is another day where:

➤ Your competitors' sales force is active while yours is idle.

➤ Bills are not sent to customers nor is there a place to receive funds.

➤ Bills are not paid and potentially become overdue.

➤ Customer orders are not received or processed, potentially leading to cancellation.

Some companies focus exclusively on recovering their IT operations and never think about applying the same effort to the people who are to use the IT services. Recovering one without the other will not restore service to your customers. Office space will not be recovered within the RTO without a tested plan.

This plan enables key personnel (such as the sales force and the tech support call center) to work during a disruptive event. Creating and testing this plan demonstrates corporate responsibility while simultaneously protecting your business reputation. A plan that promptly restores service minimizes the disruption of revenue and also protects customer relationships.

Work areas are more prone to disasters (small and large) than a data center. Rivers breach their banks, water pipes burst, small fires are turned into large water hazards by the fire department, and on and on. In a blizzard, the data center keeps chugging on, but the offices stop as employees are unable to come in to work. In a labor action, people cannot get in to the workplace, but the IT system runs on and on. So, planning for a loss of work areas is more practical and has a more likely payback than planning for an IT loss.

Customers are sensitive to supplier interruptions. Many long-term contracts require that the supplier demonstrate that a tested plan is in place. Everyone has at one time or another been disappointed by the failure of someone to deliver promised goods or services when ordered. For most companies, their office workers are their "face to the customer." When no one answers the phone during business hours, customers become very concerned about that company's reliability and look elsewhere for goods and services.

A challenge in working in recovered facilities is security of company information. Computers are always a target for anyone looking to make quick cash, but in a recovered site, confidential company documents must also be safeguarded. Many people may not be known to others, enabling curious strangers and criminally minded people to enter the facility and wander around.

The easiest team to recover is the executive staff. Some of them are already in the Command Center. The rest can work out of a hotel conference room from which they can use company cell phones for outbound calls. In many cases, their key customers already know their company cell phone number for inbound calls. Further, the hotel can provide an online connection.

Other departments, such as Customer Service, are heavily dependent on inbound telephone traffic. These groups must recover in a dedicated location so that the inbound telephone connections can be quickly changed. Like other transaction-based teams, the sales crew will require ready access to its data.

Included on the CD attached to this book is a sample Work Area Recovery Plan (Form 10-1). This sample plan is only a starting point. Customize it to meet your own company requirements. For instance, there are example risk assessments and restoration priority charts which you must replace with those based on your own information developed in other chapters.

WRITING A WORK AREA RECOVERY PLAN

The first question to answer is, why are you writing this plan? What problem are you solving? Is it to keep the Sales department always functioning? Is it a regulatory or contracted requirement? Whatever it is, write it down before starting your plan. This reason anchors the plan development and prevents it from drifting off target. It will vary from just someone to answer the phone to maintaining full customer service even during a disaster.

Based on this reason, select a strategy that describes the site where you will recover (in a company site, in a rented facility many miles away, or in local facilities acquired at the time they are needed). It details how many seats must be immediately available and, sometimes, how many more should be ready within an additional time period. Most importantly, it will identify the recovery time objective (RTO) for the facility to be ready.

The key elements to the plan are to select a recovery site, determine who should be there, equip the site, activate the site, and operate it during a company disaster. In a company-wide emergency, alternative work arrangements may be necessary, such as employees working from home or in scattered groups where facilities can be secured.

An important piece of the strategy is to enable employees to work from home. This requires advanced planning to provide them with Virtual Private Network (VPN) access. A VPN enables them to securely connect to the data center (or recovered data center) and continue their online work. To do this, companies must create a policy governing people working from home. Working from home should never involve company confidential material.

Recovered departments normally follow a hierarchy of importance. For example:

➤ Executive management, legal team, corporate communications, (core) Human Resources team—typically recovered near the Command Center and the disaster site.

➤ Human Resources (the remainder at the office recovery site).

➤ Customer contact team (Sales).

➤ Accounting (cash flow).

➤ Company operations.

Write a separate plan for each type of work area to be recovered, such as office, call center, warehouse, factory, retail, etc. Each will likely have its own recovery site and its unique requirements.

A Place to Work

Building the plan is a team effort. Include representatives from each of the critical departments during site selection and work area layout. If the departments don't like the layout, they won't use it. Their ideas and last-minute requirements are essential to make the site selection a success.

Review the vital business functions identified by the Business Impact Analysis with each department. Identify how many people need to be recovered from each team. Some will need to be recovered immediately, and some later. Be sure to include space for the supervisors and managers necessary for the team to function. Most recovery sites are wide open spaces, so carefully assign the few offices available. Executives will expect individual offices.

For each person, estimate 70 to 80 square feet of space. Multiply this times the number of people, and you will have the approximate minimum floor space requirements. This amount of space also accounts for hallways, conference rooms, reception, break room, and common areas. You can cram people into tighter space but productivity, already constrained by the basic work environment, will be further reduced at a time when more is needed. Sometimes the limiting factor is the local building and safety code for occupancy limits and mandatory ratio of sanitary facilities to personnel.

To stretch your limited assets, consider changing some departments to night hours. In this approach, customer-facing team members, such as customer service, technical support, or sales, are in the seats during daytime hours, while accounting, Human Resources, etc.—team members who are internally focused—work in the same spaces at night.

There are three kinds of "seats" that can be set up for recovery. "Hot seats" are fully equipped and ready to go. These are the most expensive to set up and maintain. "Warm seats" are missing some of the equipment, usually the personal computer and telephone. "Cold seats" are floor space and may or may not have a table and chair. This space may be set aside for team members who can wait several days before recovering.

In general, a work surface should be 36 inches wide and 24 inches deep. This provides sufficient depth for the PC and keyboard and some space to the side for shuffling papers and writing. Of course, a comfortable chair to accompany the worktable is important. Adequate lighting either from desk lamps or overhead light (preferred) is essential. Take care that data, telephone and power cords are carefully routed to avoid tripping anyone.

To allocate scarce resources in a chaotic time, establish a restoration priority for your recovery site. A restoration priority ensures that the recovery team is always focused on the highest value actions for that moment. This is as simple as a sequence of what to do next. Be sure this priority list is well communicated to the teams.

One author developed a plan to recover a technical support center that required each technician to use two dial-out telephone lines for modems to connect to customer PCs. This requirement was uncovered by inspecting a "typical" workstation and was not provided by local management.

Make sure to carefully consider the environmental control needs for people and technical equipment. The facility must be able to hold the temperature and humidity within an acceptable range. This avoids problems with equipment and with people becoming ill in the midst of a company disaster. How important can this be? Imagine someone trying to recover offices in an empty warehouse in the middle of winter. Everything else can be there except the ability to hold heat within the work area.

Other aspects to consider in selecting a recovery site include:

➤ Easy access to airports, major highways, or public transportation.

➤ Adequate parking.

➤ Loading dock for deliveries.

➤ Nearby lodging and food establishments.

➤ Storage space for preprinted forms and reference materials onsite for ready use.

The key to the success of the facility selection is the careful management of end-user expectations. Emphasize that it provides a basic work area with limited service. As the plan is tested, each department will better understand the situation and become your champion to finance facility improvements. The size, location, and desk setup will all drive the solution's cost. The executive approval process often cuts back on user requests.

Recovery Options

The criteria used for selecting a site for recovering your workers is similar to that of selecting an IT recovery site. It should be far enough away to avoid damage from the same incident. Beyond that, it can be quite close or two states away. If the recovery will be in a commercial site, then it may be several states or more away. Commercial recovery sites are sprinkled around the country, and the nearest available site may be across the country. The first company to declare a disaster has its pick of sites. In a wide-area disaster, the nearest available site may be far away. For this reason, when a hurricane strikes, some companies declare a disaster immediately. Figure 10-1 lists the issues you need to consider when evaluating recovery options.

DIFFERENT COMPANY SITE Using a different company site is a simple way to go. This site should be close enough for people to drive to it. If it is also used for IT training classes, then it can be quickly converted to a recovery site by canceling the classes and reimaging the computers. Using a company site means you know it has an active network and telephone connections, the security is already in place, and you can pre-position materials for emergency use. For the desktop PCs, you might use the last generation of units that you were going to scrap.

Using a company site brings the risk that some executive will try to use it for an operational activity. When a disaster strikes, it will be difficult to kick them out. Therefore, closely guard the facility's uses. Do not dress it up so much that it is too attractive to someone. Its layout should be dictated by how it will be used and is not designed for aesthetics.

CONTRACTED HOT SITE A contracted hot site is the "least-grief" approach because you pay someone to take on all the maintenance. The terms of the agreement depend on the vendor and the level of service you hire, but it typically includes test time and a set number of seats in a recovery. Any variation from the standard desktop and single line telephone must be coordinated with the vendor. These sites are close to public transportation and already have arrangements for local lodging and food.

	Security	Inbound telecom	Data bandwidth	Time to activate	Potential problems	Relative cost
Different company site	Total control	Control over capacity	Known	Minimal, a few hours if properly equipped	Clearing out whoever is using the equipment	Expensive, unless the facility is used for low value uses
Contracted hot site	High	Available capacity	Available capacity	24 hours	Nearest available site may be far away	High
Mobile recovery equipment	Your responsibility; total control but perimeter is open	Limited to equipment capability	Limited to equipment capability	24 hours	If the company site is unavailable, must find another quickly	High
Scramble at the time of incident	Multiple sites mean minimal control	Too dispersed to easily swing the inbound calls to a site	Dispersal should provide adequate bandwidth to each site	Long; this is an untested plan	Recovery delayed while locating a site, which may require preparation	Zero until it is needed and then high

FIGURE 10-1: Recovery options.

Contracted hot sites can be expensive. Testing time must be reserved far in advance and may be preempted if another customer declares a disaster and occupies the space. Testing time may also require an additional fee. Finally, in a disaster, the closest recovery facility may be occupied and the nearest available seats several states away.

MOBILE RECOVERY EQUIPMENT Mobile recovery equipment comes to the disaster site. These are expandable trailers that contain almost everything needed in a disaster site. Each trailer includes its own generator, telephone switch, and a satellite uplink for communications. When a disaster is declared, the trailers are pulled to the customer site and activated. If local electricity and data communication connections are available, then so much the better.

An immediate advantage to this approach is that all employees sleep at home. This enables a high level of employee participation (depending on the type of disaster). In an incident such as a structural fire, using trailers provides an onsite presence that may be comforting to customers.

A trailer's usefulness may be limited in a wide-area disaster like a flood. If the company's building is inundated with flood water, so is the parking lot, so the trailers must be parked somewhere else. If the company lacks distant property, then a site must be rented. Still, employees can likely drive to the trailers and back home at night.

SCRAMBLE RIGHT AFTER THE INCIDENT Some companies feel that the local real estate situation is such that buildings with adequate space and facilities can be found on short notice. Then, the workplace is set up with a damn-the-cost speed. Overall, the company then saves the annual expense of subscribing to recovery trailers or to a hot site.

The first problem with this approach is that it leaves all planning to the point of incident, when there is so much to do. Without a test site, the plan cannot be validated or the team members adequately trained. Second, it ignores that more is needed than four walls and a roof. External data and telephone connections are required, as well as properly configured desktop equipment. Finally, it underestimates the time required to settle the real estate details even if everyone is pressing for an immediate resolution.

Pre-position special forms and reference material needed by the work groups during their time at the recovery site.

Employee Notification

Immediately after a disaster is declared (an incident that activates this plan), the facility preparation crew is notified. In most cases, this is the team leader for each recovery team. This crew opens the facility and prepares it for the recovery teams. If the recovery is in a commercial site, some of this may be done by the service provider, based on terms of the service agreement.

The crew is notified by the company's automated notification "telephone blast" system, which sends a notification to every person on a particular list. (Alternatively, the slower and less reliable telephone call tree may be used.) This crew includes team leaders for:

➤ Security.

➤ Facilities.

➤ Each supported department.

➤ Onsite IT support.

➤ Onsite telecommunications and network support.

If there was an IT disaster as well, then there will be a time delay before the IT systems are usable and can be used. If so, the main crew for the recovery site should be alerted through the automatic notification system (or other process) to arrive about 24 hours before all systems are scheduled to be recovered. This minimizes idle time at the site waiting for IT application availability.

Tools to Work With

A personal computer with a network connection and a telephone are the primary tools provided to an office worker. The first challenge is to provide the equipment. Keep spare units onsite ready to exchange in case of a failure. In a chaotic recovery, there is no time to wait for a repairperson.

Work together with each recovery team to develop a "standard" workstation layout. This will ease unit setup and IT support. A standard unit will also make it easy to move equipment between the teams as the recovery team makeup shifts.

Each department must create checklists for activation of their teams. These lists will ensure that the required materials are stored in the facility for ready use. They will also provide a list of items to monitor for updates, such as procedure manuals, quality checklists, routing forms, etc.

DESKTOP PCS With an unlimited budget, a quick trip around town can collect enough PCs to support all of your recovery sites. The challenge is to load the company's desktop PC software image onto those devices. This can require an hour per unit (assuming that a copy of the image was maintained at the recovery site). If there are hundreds of units to load, the process can be quite tedious. The software image contains the operating system and its configuration settings, specific device drives for the onboard components, information security settings, copies of all standard software, etc.

If the PCs being used are not the exact same model as the company standard, then a software image must be created for each model (or variation on a model) potentially requiring several hours. A new image is required to ensure that all of the necessary hardware drivers are installed and configured as well as all security settings installed. If the emergency purchasing process brought in many different models, then the problem grows.

Some companies bypass the PC imaging issue by using a virtual environment for their desktops. Virtual environments can run on any typical PC and configuration. Using this technology, the PC's "desktop" is a session inside of a computer room server. Once that server is recovered (and the user's data is restored), the employee will see his or her electronic desktop as before. In essence, the PC runs a browser into the server, so little local configuration is required.

As an interim to the data center recovery, many companies establish a file server at the recovery site. This unit provides a local "public disk" for file sharing and local reference information. It can also be used to hold the latest software "image" and any other files that would be locally useful in a recovery. A maintenance item is to keep the information on this device current.

If office workers back up their PCs to the data center regularly, then their data will be available to recover.

TELEPHONES Few office workers can complete their daily tasks without ready access to a telephone, with its quick access to coworkers, customers, suppliers, etc. Given the close working quarters in the recovery site, speaker phones are impractical. Therefore, each desk should have a hands-free headset.

Some workers, such as those in Customer Service, depend heavily on inbound telephone traffic. They will require an Automated Call Director (ACD) device to route incoming calls to the proper place. (This is another reason for not allowing people to sit anywhere they wish.) Outbound callers can supplement the recovery center's phones with company cell phones. This will also free the facility's telephone trunks for inbound calls.

Because everyone working in the facility is new to the building, provide a preprinted telephone directory to each seat (but do not print it until the center is activated). This will be based on previous seating assignments and not on who actually appears.

PRINTERS There are times when a printed document or label is essential. Each department must identify its printing requirements in terms of types of printers, volume (so adequate printer materials and paper stock can be stored in the center), workstations each must connect to, etc. This may lead to requirements for special printers, which then leads to the requirement to store printing supplies (toner, ink cartridges and ribbons) onsite.

The other half of printing is the material to print on. This could be special sizes or colors of paper, multiple part forms, stickers, etc. An alternative to preprinted forms is a template on which the employee enters the information. A laser printer then prints the completed form. This avoids the need to stockpile expensive preprinted documents that eventually become obsolete and must be refreshed. Printing supplies should be adequate for as long as it takes to order a resupply plus at least one day. These supplies will age and must be rotated back for use in the primary facility over time. The more specialized these materials are, the longer that it may take to obtain them.

Some offices use many printed reports. The ideal solution is to convert these documents to online viewing and only print the small portions that must be on paper. If that is not practical, then high-speed printing may be required at the recovery site. This may require a large impact or laser printer, raising the competency level required for onsite IT support.

A corporate companion to a printer is a shredder. This tool reduces the chance that confidential printed company information can be retrieved from the trash. The shredder location should be marked on the floor plans and placed somewhere to minimize its contribution to the noise level.

REFERENCE MATERIALS Many office workers use reference materials in their work. This includes physical documents, as well as electronically stored data runs from sales tax tables to a catalog of industrial suppliers to telephone numbers for local trucking companies. Each department should include on its activation checklists the reference materials necessary to function. There may be an opportunity to consolidate some of these documents for fewer copies. The reference materials held in the recovery facility should be provided and maintained by each department.

Some of the company's reference materials may be confidential "vital records." These may include financial information, customer data, or even the health records of employees. In each case, the vital records must be protected from internal compromise just as they would be in the normal company offices. This may require locked doors or locked cabinets in the work areas. Where possible, obtain or convert reference documents to CDs or obtain them via the Internet. This is another point in favor of an onsite recovery facility file sharing server.

Provide reference material detailing the recovery facility which:

➤ Explains the layout of the facility.

➤ Shows the arrangement of departments in the facility seating.

➤ Includes a telephone number chart for the recovery area (especially valuable if each of the seats is designated for a specific person).

Collocate Interactive Teams

Selecting who sits where can be emotional for some people. Some wish to sit by windows, others away from the door, etc. Bring in representatives from each department that will work in the recovery center. Some groups naturally work close together. They pass physical documents or exchange information on a routine basis. These teams should be located adjacent to each other. Other teams, such as the company legal department, require privacy and value isolation. When laying out your recovery area, keep in mind the specific needs of each team. A carefully designed and executive-approved floor plan can minimize arguments and political posturing.

It may seem easier to locate different teams in different recovery sites. However, this compounds the security issue, as someone must protect the materials and documents at each site around the clock.

Once the seating is settled, create signs for each of the work areas. When the recovery team begins arriving at the facility, its members will need to know where to work. If this information is hard to find, then people will start sitting wherever it strikes their fancy, disrupting all of the careful planning. To reduce this confusion, install lots of signs. You should:

➤ Label every door in the building.

➤ Label every cabinet as to its contents.

➤ Label every desk in the recovery center as to the department using it and those dedicated desks that no one else should use.

➤ Suspend signs from the ceiling to indicate the location of each department.

Telecommunications and Data Systems

A recovered work area site must have a data connection to the recovered IT site. The bandwidth must be adequate to support the number of workstations at the site. In addition, telephone service must be provided to the desktop. Adequate inbound service can be an issue. Inbound telephone lines must be rerouted to the recovery site for the duration of its use. Outbound traffic is less of an issue as cell phones can be used.

The difficult parts of the plan to execute are moving the inbound call lines from the damaged work site to the recovery location. This includes fax machines, inbound local telephone lines, and inbound toll-free numbers.

The telecommunications support team must work with the telecom provider in advance to understand the steps to do this. As always, the question is how long will this take and will it still meet your RTO? Specific information may be required, such as the phone numbers involved, the service provider's contract number, and whom to call to request this immediate service.

Several important telephone features to include are conferencing and voice mail. These functions are common in offices, and their absence will be an employee productivity concern.

The recovery site activation team sets up signage so everyone knows where to go, where to sit, and where to secure supplies. They verify that each workstation, telephone, printer, fax, copier, shredder, etc. is ready to go. They pull from storage any reference materials, special forms, etc. so that each desk is ready to begin when the recovery team arrives.

In a crisis, think imaginatively. Office workers can use their personal cell phones for outbound calls. The company can reimburse them for by-the-minute plan or provide a flat reimbursement such as an average month's usage.

Security

Activating a recovery facility transforms it from an empty or lightly occupied building into a hub of activity. It will attract a lot of attention. Few people in the company can recognize every employee. There will be many strange faces in the crowd. This is an opportunity for a stranger to walk in and leave with company property under his or her arm. The recovery site requires both physical security to protect assets and information security to protect its data.

An easy way to control access is to use the same key card access as used in the primary facility. This will require adding employees to the local security server. If you keep a backup copy of the primary facility's key card access list, it can be added locally along with the security zones into which they are welcome. Otherwise, post a security guard at the employee entrance. No one enters the building without a card key, a company ID card, or without being escorted by a company employee.

In addition to security for the building, there is also security for company documents created during the recovery. This might be anything pertaining to legal compliance, call logs, customer information, etc. Ensure there is adequate shredder support onsite in sound-deadening rooms.

Another issue is that the workstations are close together. While in the primary facility there may be sound deadening walls and cubicle barriers, everything is now wide open. Ask everyone to speak quietly since others may be on the telephone nearby. For security, be careful about what is spoken out in the open.

If you are using a commercial hot site, security to the facility will be provided for you, as will the external data and telephone connections.

TESTING

Before a plan can be declared as operational, it must be tested. This trains the participants, as well as demonstrates that the plan can meet the RTO. Over time, be sure that each department has a team participating and observing the tests. This familiarizes them with the recovery site, the area around it, recovery processes, tradeoffs, limitations at the site, etc.

Recovery site testing is often conducted in small groups. It is very difficult to swing inbound lines into the center, but teams who primarily use outbound lines can test the plan by working onsite for several days. This also works well for internally focused (noncustomer facing) teams.

MAINTAINING THE RECOVERY SITE

If your company is providing its own recovery site, it will require regular maintenance. The revision level of the recovery site must match that of the site it is supporting. As the organization changes or as the emphasis of the business evolves, so must the recovery facility. This eliminates one more distraction when recovering the facility in this site. Maintenance should be performed at the following intervals:

Annually

➤ Executives must determine if the Business Impact Analysis has materially changed from the previous year.

➤ IT validates that the desktop computer hardware is adequate and still meets corporate standards.

➤ Telecom support team reevaluates if the telecom arrangements need to be changed.

Quarterly

➤ Each department reviews its desktop requirements with the IT team, which ensures that the desktop computers in the recovery facility still meet everyone's needs.

➤ The IT team verifies that the software in the recovery units is adequately patched with bug fixes and security patches.

Periodically conduct tours of the facility. This will acquaint employees with where they may work in an emergency and familiarize them with the facility's layout. This is an opportunity to remind everyone that this facility's value is to always be ready in an emergency and that it is not available for use as a "production" facility.

One idea is to "brand" the facility to help place its recovery function in people's minds. For example, "People and Infrastructure Recovery Facility (PIRF)" or "The ORB (Office Recovery Building)." Another idea is to create an employee information brochure that describes the facility's capabilities. The brochure includes a map and driving directions to the recovery site.

CONCLUSION

Every company depends heavily on its IT department. Its prompt recovery is critical to the company's continued viability. However, some companies overlook the fact that recovered computer databases are of little value if no one is available to use them. A work area recovery plan is an essential complement to any IT recovery plan.

Recovering a workplace is not trivial. People need an adequate place to do their jobs, with a minimum of environmental distractions. Adequate data lines must be installed in advance, as they cannot be prepared on short notice. Similarly, telephone service must be in place so that when the incident occurs, the inbound lines can be quickly redirected from the damaged facility to the recovery site.

Selecting a recovery strategy will likely follow the same strategy as the IT recovery plan. It may be another company site, a third-party facility, or bringing fully equipped trailers to the disaster site. Each approach has its advantages and disadvantages in terms of convenience, cost, and capabilities.

Recovery sites are busy places. It should be very easy to find your way through the recovery site. Signs should be everywhere informing recovery team members where to go, where to find things, and where not to go.

Be sure to test everything at the recovery site as soon as you arrive. The RTO is measured from the time of the incident, not from when you were alerted. Early detection of problems enhances the chances of a timely recovery.

Finally, if you have designated a company site for recovery, never let your defenses down for a moment. Name it something that positions it in people's minds as providing value as the recovery site. Never let it be used for even a small production function. Regularly scheduled testing helps to keep it active enough (and annoying enough) that production functions look elsewhere for a quieter setting.

CHAPTER 11

PANDEMIC PLAN

Epidemics have often been more influential than statesmen and soldiers in shaping the course of political history, and diseases may also color the moods of civilizations.
—Anonymous

INTRODUCTION

Up to this point, every plan has been based on an incident that adversely affected the operation of a company process—or even the company itself. These events triggered activation of the incident response plan. With work and a bit of luck, the incident's impact was quickly minimized and the company moved on.

A pandemic requires a very different type of plan. It fits under business continuity planning as a disruption of the flow of business. Unlike the sharp suddenness of a disaster, a pandemic may appear gradually and then run for several months or even years. The disease follows its favorite season around the globe and ends up again on your doorstep—often more virulent than before.

A pandemic refers to an infectious disease that is spread by contact with people. Therefore, minimizing contact with people is essential. This might be between employees, as well as between employees and customers. For some businesses, this is not a problem. For others that depend on face-to-face customer contact, it requires a well-considered plan to minimize contact and to sanitize areas.

A pandemic affects more than people. It can change the demand for the goods and services offered by your company. If your services are offered person to person, it might reduce demand, as people seek to minimize personal contact. Are your products something that are used as people interact? Are they something used at home where people may shelter their families from others? Do your products provide something to ease the pandemic such as improved personal sanitation or face masks?

Disease has always been part of human history. Pandemics of differing severities occur several times each century. A seasonal flu outbreak is not a pandemic, even if widespread. Each pandemic is unique.

WHAT IS A PANDEMIC?

A pandemic is an infectious disease that strikes a significant portion of a population over a wide area, often over continents. The disease must be infectious (you catch it from other people). It must be widespread and not a local outbreak. This is different from an epidemic, in which there are significantly more cases of a particular disease among a specific group of people over a period of time. Figure 11-1 lists the differences between a normal seasonal flu and a flu pandemic.

At any given time, a number of pandemics for various diseases are declared. For example, HIV/AIDS is an infectious disease that spreads from person-to-person contact and reaches across continents. However, avoiding risky behaviors makes this less of a business concern. Many of the current pandemics are limited to a particular climate zone, such as the tropics.

Some health issues are not infectious, even though they can disrupt your business. For example, Legionnaire's Disease (caused by the legionella bacterium) is not passed person to person, but can disrupt business and dampen travel to an area.

Pandemics strain the local healthcare system. Hospitals, clinics, and other healthcare organizations are not staffed for peak demand. We take for granted their availability in case we need them. However, a large number of cases pouring into them in a short time may mean that treatment for ill employees is only provided to the most serious cases.

The Spanish Influenza pandemic in the early twentieth century is the catastrophe against which all modern pandemics are measured. It is estimated that approximately 20 to 40 percent of the worldwide population became ill and that more than 20 million people died. Between September 1918 and April 1919, approximately 500,000 deaths from the flu occurred in the United States alone. Many people died very quickly. Some people who felt well in the morning became sick by noon, and were dead by nightfall. Those who did not succumb to the disease within the first few days often died of complications from the flu (such as pneumonia) caused by bacteria.

One of the most unusual aspects of the Spanish flu was its ability to kill young adults. The reasons for this remain uncertain. With the Spanish flu, mortality rates were high among healthy adults as well as the usual high-risk groups. The attack rate and mortality was highest among adults 20 to 50 years old. The severity of that virus has not been seen again.

http://www.hhs.gov/nvpo/pandemics/flu3.htm#9

Seasonal Flu	Pandemic Flu
Outbreaks follow predictable seasonal patterns; occurs annually, usually in winter	Occurs rarely (three times in 20th century—last in 1968)
People may have some immunity because of previous exposure	No previous exposure; little or no preexisting immunity
Healthy adults usually not at risk for serious complications; the very young, the elderly, and those with certain underlying health conditions are at increased risk for serious complications	Healthy people may be at increased risk for serious complications
Health system doctors and hospitals can usually meet public and patient needs	Health system likely will be overwhelmed
Vaccine developed based on known flu virus strains and available for annual flu season	Vaccine probably would not be available in the early stages of a pandemic
Adequate supplies of antiviral medications are usually available	Effective antiviral medications may be in limited supply
Average U.S. deaths about 36,000 annually	Number of deaths could be quite high (e.g., U.S. 1918 death toll was approximately 500,000)
Symptoms: fever, cough, runny nose, muscle pain; deaths often caused by complications, such as pneumonia	Symptoms may be more severe and complications more frequent
Generally causes modest impact on society (e.g., some school closing, encouragement of people who are sick to stay home)	May cause major impact on society (e.g., widespread restrictions on travel, closings of schools and businesses, cancellation of large public gatherings)
Manageable impact on domestic and world economy	Potential for severe impact on domestic and world economy

FIGURE 11-1: Seasonal flu vs. pandemic flu.

Source: http://www.odh.ohio.gov/ASSETS/652D0F0FDDF64B40BE6834674214C25F/
SeasonalVSPandemic.pdf

WRITING A PLAN

The first step is to appoint a Pandemic Plan Administrator. Because this is primarily a health issue, the Pandemic Plan Administrator is usually a staff member with a medical background. If the company lacks someone with these qualifications, then appoint a business leader. Pandemic issues involve Human Resources and Facilities management so either might be suitable.

Define the roles and responsibilities of the Pandemic Administrator in a job description. This includes details concerning planning, testing, and preparing for a rapid response to a pandemic.

Included on the CD attached to this book is a sample Pandemic Management Plan (Form 11-1). This sample plan is only a starting point. Customize it to meet your own company requirements. For instance, there are example risk assessments and restoration priority charts which you must replace with your own information developed in other chapters.

Round Up a Team

Writing a plan is a team effort. Anyone who is expected to execute the plan should be involved in its creation. The Pandemic Administrator will require close assistance from the company's Human Resource Manager, IT Manager, and Facilities Manager. If your company has multiple sites that are far apart, you may want a different team for each location. Dispersed sites provide the potential that some locations may only be lightly affected. Your company may also consider hiring a local healthcare adviser to assist the planning team.

In addition, consider including:

➤ Business managers responsible for areas containing vital business functions.

➤ Union officials, if the company uses represented labor.

➤ Critical suppliers and long-term contracted labor.

➤ Logistics providers.

Tie the Plan to the BIA

As always, anchor your plan on supporting the company's vital business functions identified in the BIA. A primary business complication of a pandemic is extensive employee absence. If workforce attendance is low, you may need to choose between which functions will be done and which must wait. Prioritize company activities based on the highest value BIA processes. At the height of an influenza pandemic, employee absenteeism (for all reasons) may reach as high as 40%.

Unlike the sharp and comparative short-term impact of a disaster, a pandemic may last 18 months or more. Sometimes an employee is ill; sometimes it is an employee's family member. Also, the priority list of vital business functions may shift as one function is fully staffed and one with less urgency suddenly acquires urgency. For example, shifting staff to assemble goods in a factory may be a first priority, but then you need to shift the team to the shipping department to move the goods out the door.

Review Contractual Obligations

Make a list of each contractual obligation. Add them to your risk assessment. Some contracts contain penalty clauses if promised products are not delivered. Preparing for a pandemic and taking steps to minimize its impact must be completed before claiming that the failure to fulfill a delivery is beyond your control.

PANDEMIC RISK ASSESSMENT

Based on your BIA, evaluate the challenges specific to your company from a pandemic. One concern is extended absences of workforce or key personnel. However, are your revenues dependent on people-to-people contact? (Who knows what germs are on the credit card handed over by a customer?) Determine the impact of a pandemic on different product lines and/or production sites. Do your company's products or services depend on crowds? For example, consider a hotel adjacent to a convention center. If people avoid crowds, then convention attendance will be low and food service demand will be diminished. Contrast this to a factory with little direct customer contact.

Risk management identifies the potential interruption to continued performance of essential functions, the degree of its impact, and strategies to mitigate those risks. Gather the pandemic planning team and perform a risk analysis on how a pandemic might impact your business operations. Refer to Figure 11-2 and the list below for an example of a pandemic risk assessment.

➤ **Employee-to-employee contact.** How close to one another do company employees work? If it is elbow to elbow or face to face, then the risk of infection is high. If they sit in isolated cubicles all day long, then their contact with others is much less.

➤ **Employee-to-customer contact.** Salespeople deal directly with their customers. Close contact is essential. Basic courtesies and business rituals, such as shaking hands, may put the sales team at risk. Other examples of risky professions are security guards, cashiers, and taxi drivers.

➤ **Contact with infected items.** Do customers use your product and then return it? Do you work in a hotel where items that have been in contact with people are collected? Are you an airline baggage handler or even an accounts receivable clerk handling checks?

➤ **Contact from travel.** Airplanes are stuffed with coughing strangers and the swirl of germs in the cabin is enough to make anyone sick.

	Product	Process	Likelihood	Impact	Mitigation
Employee-to-employee contact		X	4	4	Increased sanitation, generous sick leave, work from home
Employee-to-customer contact		X	7	8	Increased sanitation
Contact with infected items	X		4	5	Increased sanitation on items returned or handled by a customer
Contact from travel		X	8	7	Stay home and use teleconferencing
Impact on raw materials		X	2	8	Monitor key supplier Web sites, monitor outbreak areas
Impact on customer demand		X	2	2	Minimal impact

FIGURE 11-2: Pandemic risk assessment.

> **Impact on raw materials.** You may be fine, but what if the population around a key supplier is hard hit?

> **Impact on customer demand.** What if your product depends on crowds—the very thing that people are avoiding?

Companies are typically in multiple lines of business. Each must be evaluated for the impact of a pandemic (reduced employee attendance, potential supplier disruption, etc.). A good example is a contract to deliver materials to a customer as a just-in-time company. In this situation, a failure to deliver the agreed materials at the agreed time may trigger financial penalties.

Suppliers may also be an issue. Most products are assembled from many components. If any one of these is missing, then a larger product may not be assembled. We live in a global economy and materials may come from a foreign source. If that area of the globe is particularly hard hit, the local companies may not be able to provide the necessary materials. The borders may also be temporarily closed to slow the spread of infection.

Understand the Threat

Consider the various scenarios that may occur. A severe outbreak may occur in your area, in your target market area, or in a key supplier area. Could a government-ordered quarantine on the movement of people or large assemblies impact your business? Will any situation you can foresee change the demand for your product—or will the pandemic become a business opportunity?

During the height of the annual influenza season, schools will sometimes close for several days. This breaks the infection cycle. With a two-day incubation, people can now be treated so that they do not infect others. This also gives schools time to sanitize all common surfaces. However, some of your employees will stay home to watch their children until the schools reopen.

Pandemic Techniques

There are four actions that your pandemic plan must include. Each action will have its own section in your plan.

➤ **Social Distancing.** Infectious disease is spread by person-to-person contact. The farther apart people are, the less likely it is that they can pass germs to others.

➤ **Sanitation.** People touch many things, such as banisters, doorknobs, vending machine buttons, etc. These must be properly cleaned at least daily to reduce the passing of germs through touch.

➤ **Communications.** Keep your workforce and the public informed about the pandemic, explaining what each individual should do and what the company is doing about it.

➤ **Timing.** Know when to activate your pandemic plan and when to close it down.

The Politics of Pandemics

Governments are caught in a bind. If they do nothing and disease rages out of control, then they are "idle." If they vigorously attack the problem, they are "alarmist." Further complicating this are politicians who seek to create a crisis so they can be seen as "solving" it.

Another aspect is money. In a "crisis," money flows into public health organizations, but a pandemic really opens the flow of money. Over the coming years, expect to hear the term "pandemic" more and more often. The World Health Organization's designation of a disease as "pandemic" focuses on its global nature rather than on its severity. The H1N1 (swine flu) pandemic was declared when the disease spread from North America to Australia.

THE PLAN

At some point, it is time to put pen to paper. With the team well in hand, create a written plan for your company to execute when a pandemic is declared. As the plan develops, try minitests to validate each component and identify additional planning requirements.

Although a pandemic plan is different from other incident management plans, it should still follow the same format. State the problem (which you can refer to for events not covered by the plan), state actions to take (just guidance because each situation is unique), and assign tasks to different functional areas or team members.

Triggering the Plan

Pandemics have a beginning and an end. Identify the action that will trigger your plan. This usually depends on how dispersed your company sites are. For example, a nationwide retail chain of stores, warehouses, and regional offices might trigger its plan based on a declaration of a pandemic by the U.S. Centers for Disease Control and Prevention (www.cdc.gov). Companies whose operations, suppliers, and customers are located within a single geographic region (such as a restaurant chain) might trigger their plans based on their state's department of health's determination.

Large companies generally follow the six phases of a pandemic as published by the World Health Organization (www.who.int). This is because their operations are dispersed, they participate in international markets, and employees often travel internationally. The six phases of an influenza pandemic as described by WHO are:

➤ **Phase I.** Influenza circulates among animals, with no human infections.

➤ **Phase II.** Animal influenza infects humans.

➤ **Phase III.** Limited human-to-human transmission.

➤ **Phase IV.** Community-level outbreaks indicating a significant increase in the risk of a pandemic.

➤ **Phase V.** Human-to-human spread between two countries in the same region—a pandemic is imminent.

➤ **Phase VI.** Community-level outbreak in a different region—a global pandemic is under way.

As the number of cases decreases, the time will come to deactivate your pandemic plan. Monitor the same service that you used to start your pandemic plan for a sign that it can be ended. If you have widely dispersed sites, then each area will end its pandemic emergency based on the local situation.

Find the Latest Information

Identify local sources of information on infections in your area. This might be the state or county department of health. Document these sources so their location is well known to the team. Check with these sources frequently to see how the pandemic threat is emerging in your operating areas.

Local sources will also provide information about the availability of immunizations. Pass this on to employees and encourage them to immunize themselves and their families. Some examples of resources include:

➤ U.S. Centers for Disease Control and Prevention - www.cdc.gov

➤ WHO - www.who.int/en/

➤ U.S. Department of Health and Human Services - www.HHS.gov

➤ State sites, such as Ohio's at www.odh.ohio.gov/

An example of local information can be found on this Franklin County, Ohio, Web site: http://www.columbuspandemicflu.org/.

THE PANDEMIC BUSINESS CLIMATE

Will a pandemic be an opportunity for your business? For example, demand may increase if you make hand sanitizer or sell entertainment products used at home (since people may avoid crowds). Other examples might be videoconferencing companies or telephone companies that rent telephone conference numbers (as people seek to avoid crowded transportation).

The opposite of this would be if the pandemic damaged your business. To avoid crowds, people may avoid concerts, the beach, restaurants, malls, schools, casinos, movie theaters, or other entertainment venues. In extreme local pandemics, such public venues and assemblies may be banned by the government.

You might change the way that you conduct normal business. For example, at a college graduation, instead of shaking hands with each student, you might smile and give a "thumbs up" or other positive gesture. Retailers may be sensitive to handling credit cards or money from someone who looks ill.

Some companies might disperse employee seating to reduce the amount of direct contact between workers or erect sneeze shields between close-set workstations. Frequent fliers might prefer to use teleconferencing. Shared workstations and cash registers should be minimized and equipped with hand sanitation.

COMMUNICATIONS

The company's Pandemic Administrator will possess more relevant information about the situation than the workforce. For this information to benefit the company, it must be shared. How this information is communicated differs according to the type of workers receiving it. In the end, the greatest coverage results from the use of multiple communication methods. For example, office workers sitting in front of computers all day long have constant access to e-mail. Factory workers or people who move a lot during their work might be easier to reach through posters and individual copies of information handed to them.

It is important to also communicate with the families of employees. An illness in their household can spread to the workplace through the worker. Also, employees may lose work time tending to sick relatives. Therefore anything to help keep the worker's family healthy (including inoculations) will pay off in reduced absence.

COMMUNICATIONS PLAN

Develop a communications plan to ensure that the right information is provided to the right audience in a format most likely to reach them. Overlapping delivery approaches is a good practice as when dealing with wide audiences, each individual has their own way of absorbing information. See Figure 11-3 as an example.

Before It Strikes

The purpose of communicating before the pandemic strikes is to prepare employees for the coming disruptions. Opening this communication channel early acquaints everyone with a source of factual information that will be available for them to check (such as a Web site). Establishing this communication link may reduce employee fear and anxiety by providing information and explaining defensive measures that they and their families can take. In the absence of information from an authoritative source, people's darkest fears will take control.

As a disease approaches a pandemic state, warnings are posted on the public health Web sites. Pandemics start in one place and then spread. When a pandemic is close to being declared, begin an information program for executives and for the workforce. Company executives will want to know the severity of the pandemic and how it will impact company operations. As the pandemic progresses, update this estimate at least monthly. Employees will want specific information on what the disease is, symptoms to watch for, and preventative steps they should take. They will also be interested in actions their families should take to minimize the likelihood or impact of an infection.

Depending on how your company is organized (geographic dispersion, size of individual sites, degree of person-to-person contact required), you may choose to use any one of a variety of media. Each has its own advantages:

Stakeholder Communications Plan

Stakeholder	Reports	Content	Best Format	Frequency	Delivery
Executive	Weekly status	Attendance, updated risk analysis, government projections	Brief executive staff meeting	Weekly	e-mail
Pandemic team members	Weekly status	Status on key communications points	Bullet points	Weekly	e-mail
Employees	Weekly update	Impact on company, steps to take at work and at home	Company newsletter, bulletin board postings, team meetings	Weekly	Web site posting and team meetings
Customers	Semimonthly	Steps taken by company	Single page recap of actions taken	Monthly	e-mail and Web site posting
Suppliers	Semimonthly	Company status and requirement forecast	Single page recap of actions taken	Monthly	e-mail and Web site posting
Company Sanitation Team	Weekly	Focus areas for regular cleaning	Team meeting to announce status and hear about obstacles	Weekly	Team meetings
Employee families	Weekly	Steps to take at home to reduce the chance of infection	Narrative and "success" stories	Biweekly	e-mail

FIGURE 11-3: Communications plan.

➤ **Team Meetings.** Provide the latest information and are an opportunity to hear questions and concerns from target audiences.

➤ **E-mail Updates.** Sometimes are ignored by busy people but provide the same information to everyone at the same time.

➤ **Web sites.** Enable people to access as they wish, but they are passive ways to communicate and are only useful if someone reaches out to it.

➤ **Status Reports.** Time consuming to prepare and should be targeted narrowly (e.g., factory floor, factory office, factory supervision would all need succinct information relevant to them).

➤ **Videotaped Reports.** Provide visual impact but are not suitable for any fast-breaking information.

➤ **Instructional Videos.** Can be used to address proper sanitation during the pandemic.

➤ **Hotlines.** Used to answer questions from employees and their families.

Begin monitoring various government Web sites closely. Determine which ones provide various points of view with minimum redundancy. Some sites will repeat what is posted on the primary national and international sites. This will help to narrow the list of sites to monitor.

Do not wait until the pandemic is at its height to purchase materials such as extra tissues and hand sanitizer. They may be in short supply and the price may be significantly higher during the threat of a pandemic.

Take advantage of available sources of information. Your health insurance provider may provide ongoing pandemic mitigation techniques. Arrange for a local medical consultation to supplement your pandemic plan.

Use your communications to form a partnership with employees for their better well-being. Begin by explaining the actions being taken by the company, such as social distancing, additional sanitation, etc. Provide information that employees can pass on to family members about the pandemic and home treatment of symptoms.

During the Pandemic

When the pandemic sweeps through a company location, it is time to kick communications into high gear. People who ignored the earlier information are suddenly interested in detailed information. It is not unusual to repeat the same information in different formats.

Encourage healthy habits among employees through posters and e-mails. These topics may include the most effective way to wash hands, how to cover a cough, and how to identify flu symptoms. Encourage use of large and airy rooms instead of small "huddle" rooms for meetings. Installs signs in restrooms showing the proper way to wash hands.

During the pandemic, the information to publish includes:

➤ What is the disease, and what symptoms should you look for?

➤ An explanation of the different ways infectious diseases spread.

➤ Ideas for minimizing the spread of disease specific to your workplace, such as how to sanitize your work area, dealing with customer contacts, sharing objects, etc.

➤ Where to go for inoculations (or provide company-sponsored inoculation clinics).

➤ Simple actions to minimize contacts that might spread the disease, such as appropriate hand hygiene, coughing/sneezing etiquette, contingency plans.

➤ Relaxed attendance policies if you feel ill or a family member is ill.

Local Sites to Obtain Immunizations

People have their own opinions about inoculations. Some fear the sting of the needle. Others object to injecting something into their body whose long-term effect is unknown. Whatever your opinion, to minimize the potential of significant absence and the absence of key personnel, promote voluntary inoculation.

Creating vaccines requires time. As a new strain of virus appears, there is a delay of four months or longer to produce the first doses that may prevent it. In the beginning, immunizations will be in short supply and restricted to high-risk groups. Over time, they will become generally available. The Pandemic Administrator can monitor the situation to be ready to arrange employee immunizations when the supply allows it.

Prepare employees for the time when inoculations will be generally available. Promote the value of these immunizations through your company communications. To minimize liability, coordinate with a nearby healthcare provider to provide the inoculations. People like free things, and they appreciate free things that are convenient. Arranging for a nearby facility to provide the shots makes it easy for the company to cover the expense.

After the Pandemic

As the pandemic diminishes, remind everyone that it is still not completely gone. Keep your guard up as the number of reported cases winds down. Do not slack on communicating the status until the pandemic is officially declared ended.

Pull all of the team members together for a pandemic plan performance assessment and critique. Recap the plan and how well it worked. Compare company performance to that of similar companies nearby. This could be a list of the actions taken, such as a company-sponsored immunization day, the family information helpline, or total number of sick days taken compared to previous (nonpandemic) years.

Collect teams' ideas and publish them in a report to management. The various team members will have much to say about their individual efforts. Include details of what worked well and what must be changed. Pandemics do not come along every year. After the conclusion of a pandemic emergency, gathering this information is essential. It may be years before such an emergency arises again. This report should be the first document reviewed in the next emergency.

Report items might include:

➤ An official announcement that the pandemic emergency plan was closed.

➤ Thanks to the many different people involved.

➤ A review of the effectiveness of the pandemic actions taken (social distancing, sanitation, communications).

➤ Impact on employees and their families.

➤ Impact on sales of products and service.

➤ Impact on production.

➤ Impact on suppliers.

Another postpandemic activity is to examine how well the relaxed attendance and the work from home policies worked. Employees will have become accustomed to the new rules. Before rescinding them, determine the impact on company operations and morale.

THE ROLE OF THE HUMAN RESOURCES MANAGER

A common factor in infectious diseases is that they are spread through people-to-people contact. The Human Resources Manager must identify which company policies impact its pandemic plan. This involves social distancing by enabling people to work from home and a relaxation of the company's sick leave program.

Review Policies Concerning Virtual Workers

Working from home is not new. In recent years, it has become more practical through the widespread availability of high-speed Internet connections. If a worker is concerned about commuting on public transportation and demands to work from home, should that request be honored?

Under what circumstances should someone be permitted to work from home? Should it be based on the type of work they do or specific company positions? Should the option be open to all office workers (except those in production, as hands must reach the materials!)?

Attendance Policy

Minimize employee-to-employee contact. If someone is ill, the company must require that person to go home until the illness passes. An obstacle to this is limited sick leave time. If an employee does not have available sick leave time, they may come in while ill and spread the disease around the department (similar to one person with a cold infecting everyone around them).

A similar requirement is someone with a sick family member. That person could easily bring the infection into the workplace if company leave (paid or unpaid) was not available. Spell out when the company feels that an ill person is recovered enough to return to the workplace.

In severe situations, the government may step in and close parts of public institutions. This might be public assemblies, such as celebrations or sporting events. They might close public transportation, schools, or even government offices. Employees unable to travel to work must not be penalized.

During a pandemic emergency, the local government may call for everyone to minimize their movement, sort of like a "snow day." Decide how the company will address paying employees for any government-imposed "stay home" days.

Trained Substitutes

Identify key personnel who can keep the company going. Each of them must have a trained backup. This provides ongoing service during vacations, illnesses, and other absences. (Some may become nervous that the company intends to replace them.) In a pandemic, the trained substitute means you are more likely to have someone onsite to maintain a vital business function. When selecting backup personnel, consider your many company locations or regular business travel destinations.

Company Travel

The immediate area around your offices may experience little of the pandemic. However, most companies have employees who regularly visit distant or international locations. Travel often includes sitting in a crowded airplane in tiny seats, standing close to others in lines, and eating in cramped restaurants. This exposes the traveler to a greater potential of catching a disease.

To minimize the chance that a traveler is bringing back pandemic germs, set a company policy that anyone returning from a trip will work from home for four days before coming into the office. The idea is to give the disease (if present) some time to make itself known.

On occasion, distant sites will be particularly hard hit by the pandemic. Avoid travel to these locations, as the traveler may arrive there only to be placed in an extended quarantine as local officials struggle to contain the outbreak. Check the local news at the intended destination or Web sites such as the World Health Organization (www.who.int).

Consider Working Alternate Shifts

Separate employees by having them work different shifts. Not all work must be completed during the traditional 9 to 5 timeframe. If a person in a particular position primarily works alone, then the work can be completed on an alternate work shift and then passed on to the next person. This might be a valuable tool if the local schools close, allowing spouses to share childcare responsibilities without affecting your production.

TECHNOLOGY CAN HELP

The IT department is responsible for pandemic planning prior to an outbreak. Technology can be used to reduce face-to-face contact with coworkers, suppliers, and customers. A computer network does not care if you are sitting in an office, your home, or the next continent. In any case, your workstation connects to the network, and then to the appropriate IT services. It is important to install this technology before the onset of a pandemic. Then everyone will be familiar with the technology and ready to use it as needed.

As an added bonus, these IT actions will reduce the amount of pollutants generated through normal business practices. In some cases, they will directly save the company money.

Virtual Private Networks (VPNs)

Employees with high-speed Internet access in their homes can work from there. To maintain the privacy of company data, the communications from the employee's home to the company data center is encrypted, thereby making the network "private." This is similar to a secure session in which you enter credit card information into a vendor's site, except that the encryption starts when the employee logs on.

Even when a pandemic is not looming on the horizon, a VPN can enable employees to work from home when caring for a sick family member or when they are too sick to come in to the office but well enough to work with a computer. Some employers readily accept this, while others feel that sitting at home offers too many distractions that will result in less than a full day's work. Still, people who spend their days working with computers and passing work objects electronically are suitable for this option if the individual has a high-speed data line at home. Positions that require exchanging work objects (such as documents) with other people do not always fit this model.

Working at home does present some pitfalls. Primarily they deal with the security of company information. Data can still be printed locally or downloaded to local PC storage. Employees should be instructed that this insecure environment should never be used for critical company data or customer data of any type.

How many people will require VPN support in your pandemic plan? VPN systems have technical limits to the number of users they can support. Even if a company has an existing VPN capability, the next step is to ensure that it is adequate for the number of simultaneous users required in your pandemic plan. In addition, most use a physical "authentication token" to identify a person. An adequate supply of these must be available when needed. Many companies provide these all of the time as this service also supports other business continuity plans.

VPNs also add to a company's "green" credentials since fewer people are commuting to work. For details on the use of VPN and its green impact, read our book *Green Tech* (AMACOM, 2009).

Virtual Meetings

Teleconferencing is another social distancing technology tool. Instead of crowding into a tightly packed aircraft full of coughing and sniffling people, use teleconferencing to conduct meetings with distant workgroups. Online products, such as Microsoft's NetMeeting™, can show the same presentation slides as if you were standing there, while you provide the audio narrative over a phone line.

Teleconferencing lacks the face-to-face communications and, admittedly, it denies participants the ability to interpret body language, which is an important part of a discussion. However, an online meeting saves the time lost to travel, the expense of travel, and all of the potential infectious contacts with fellow travelers or business partners. It also adds to a company's green credentials through reduced employee commuting.

SANITIZE COMMON AREAS AND OBJECTS

Often, employees or customers are infected before they know it. Their constant contacts with various fixtures around the facility are potential places for passing infections on to others. The company's Facilities department must step up its level of sanitation efforts during a pandemic to reduce the spread of germs through contact with contaminated items.

Some of the areas that must be sanitized daily include:

➤ Door knobs and push plates.

➤ Banister rails.

➤ Light switches.

➤ Lunchrooms.

➤ Vending machines.

➤ Shared workstations and tools, for example, the electronic card catalog in a library.

Provide employees with hand sanitizer, tissues, and even face masks. Place the hand sanitizer in prominent locations for use by employees and guests. This increases their confidence in the company management and reduces the spread of germs. There is expense for providing these items, but it is offset by even a slight reduction in the number of employee sick days.

BUSINESS DEPARTMENTS

Each business department must focus on continuing the flow of products and services to the customer in the face of significant absenteeism. As always, prioritize team members to work on the vital business functions and not spend time on noncritical actions.

One aspect of this is if a geographic area is particularly hard hit by absences. Many companies specialize functions among their many sites. In this case, the headquarters building may be relatively disease-free but the distant accounts receivables office could be in the middle of a pandemic emergency.

Assemble each business team and explain the relaxed attendance policies. Educate everyone on proper individual sanitation steps. These meetings are an opportunity for the company's management team to demonstrate its commitment to the steps necessary to minimize infection. It also allows time to answer employees' questions and pass their concerns on to the pandemic planning team.

If a department's work involves a lot of face-to-face contact with customers, then appropriate sanitation must be readily available. Greeting a customer while wearing a face mask and surgical gloves is no way to close a sale. Provide hand sanitizer for all encounters (for the customer, as well as the employee). Most customers will appreciate your concern for their well-being as well as that of your own staff.

If there is a concern that the local pandemic outbreak will be severe, for the sake of business continuity, consider evacuating key personnel to other cities. Pandemics can sometimes hit one city much harder than another.

A College Adjusts Its Graduation Ceremony

At the height of the H1N1 pandemic, a university was faced with a dilemma. Graduation is an important milestone for students. Yet shaking hands as the diplomas were handed out could potentially spread infection from a student to the dean and then to subsequent graduating students (a typical social distancing problem). Rather than risk the health of the faculty and students, the school personnel handed over the diplomas and gave every student "a knuckle bump" as he or she crossed the stage.

TESTING YOUR PANDEMIC PLAN

Pandemic plans are normally tested using a tabletop exercise, They do not require reassembling office or data centers. They are focused on people and avoiding the passing of infection.

Implement an exercise/drill to test your plan, and revise periodically. Testing a plan is the best way to train plan participants on their roles during an emergency. It also exposes gaps in planning and demonstrates if the plan is keeping current with changes in the company's organization, mission, and direction. Test the company's pandemic plan at least annually. Otherwise, it will become a shelf ornament. Without regular exercising and updates, it will become worthless when needed.

From time to time public organizations conduct tests of their pandemic plans. They like the chance to integrate a company's reactions into the overall game plan to add twists to the exercise that they had not foreseen. Working a pandemic plan with other groups is a great way to add some realism to your company's test and to bring fresh ideas into your pandemic action plan.

CONCLUSION

Pandemic planning is a subset of business continuity planning. Unlike the sharp point in time during which a disaster occurs, a pandemic is like an ocean wave. It slowly appears, overwhelms the population, and then gradually recedes. A typical pandemic will run for about a year and a half and strike in two waves, where a typical disaster is over in a few weeks.

Social distancing is an important mitigation step. Pandemics require loosening the company's absence policy to ensure that sick people stay home. Time must also be allowed for tending to family members as employees may carry the infection from the family member to the workplace.

Use technology to enable people to work from home and stay separated from potential infection. This will also enable someone providing home care for a sick relative to still provide essential services. As a side note, this will also improve a company's green credentials.

Establish a communications plan for passing information to employees, pandemic staff members, customers, and suppliers. Explain the steps you are taking and individual actions everyone should perform. Also provide information about detecting the symptoms and how to treat them at home. Communication plans must be in place before they are needed so that everyone knows where to look for what they need.

Finally, arrange for the immunization of employees and their families. This might be coordinated through local clinics and your health insurance provider. This will reduce the likelihood of an employee infection, and therefore reduced sick time absences. Some companies pay for the immunization to increase employee participation.

CHAPTER 12

EMERGENCY OPERATIONS CENTER
Take Control of the Situation

Congress can make a general,
but it takes a radio operator to
make him a commanding general.
— USMC Radio Operator School slogan

INTRODUCTION

After you have developed your disaster recovery plan the final step is the creation of your Emergency Operations Center. The terms *Emergency Operations Center, war room,* and *Command Center* all invoke images of serious-faced people feverishly scurrying around trying to address one major problem or another. These terms imply action and direction of resources toward a goal. For the Emergency Operations Center, the goal is the return to service from a business emergency. In this sense, an Emergency Operations Center is a temporary tool to coordinate your containment and recovery efforts.

The radio school quote at the top of this page, trite as it is, provides a great deal of insight into a serious problem. Unless leaders can communicate with their workers, they are unable to lead. Imagine a horde of well-meaning technical people (and a few who amuse themselves with mischief) all scurrying around trying to fix a problem regardless of what the person on their left or right is doing. Some people would be wiring equipment up, only to have someone come in behind them and disconnect everything. No coordinated action, no focused activity, just confusion. Of course, you would have no clue as to the progress being made while your boss demands an accurate update every hour. Not a pretty sight.

Now consider the alternative. A disaster occurs, and everyone knows where to report. Someone at the recovery site is documenting who is available and assigning them to teams based on the problem and each individual's expertise. As a team is created, they are dispatched under the direction of a single person. As the teams leave, their locations and composition are noted on a status board. Relief teams are sent out so the teams assigned earlier can be rested. The status board and the disaster coordinator are up to date to answer executive questions about the recovery. Sound like a control freak's dream? No, it is just a focused effort.

A disaster recovery Emergency Operations Center is essential when addressing serious or wide-scale disasters. An Emergency Operations Center allows a company's management to reestablish organizational leadership, allocate resources, and focus on emergency containment and recovery. This Command Center minimizes the disruption of management and leadership caused by the chaos of the emergency. From a business perspective, it is a command and control center that is essentially a temporary project office to manage the special project of addressing the emergency. An Emergency Operations Center must be preestablished and presupplied, with its location well known to everyone before it is needed.

An Emergency Operations Center takes time and effort to start up and close down. Before a disaster strikes, you should have three Emergency Operations Centers identified. The first is the obvious place to which people go in a limited emergency. For short-term, contained disasters, you probably already have a place where "everybody knows and everybody goes." This could be the security office with its radio network or the data processing help desk with its data network monitoring capability. Wherever your choice, it should have a telephone number that people would think to call during an emergency. Even smaller disasters have their own natural Emergency Operations Center of sorts. If your company lost its data network, then the Network Manager's office is turned into the hub of activity as a small team works to restore service. This works because the response team is a small group and the Network Manager's office is a natural place for them to work.

The second Emergency Operations Center addresses big problems and is the primary subject of this chapter. Imagine a winter storm that collapses the warehouse roof. Resolving this problem requires many people with a wide range of skills. Because the roof collapse was unforeseen, a plan to limit the damage and begin repairs would be created quickly and modified as the recovery progressed. This type of Emergency Operations Center will be in use for many days and is therefore worth the effort to set up. The size and composition of the Emergency Operations Center team depends on how widespread the damage was and how many people are needed to address it.

The third type of Emergency Operations Center is a backup facility for the primary Emergency Operations Center. This facility would only be used if the primary Emergency Operations Center was unusable; for example, if a fire burned that part of the building and the rest of the building was in danger of collapse. You need a place to contact customers, suppliers, employees, etc., to keep them aware of the recovery progress.

A further variation on the Command Center is a mobile Command Center that uses a camping trailer or self-propelled recreation vehicle to bring the solution to the problem. This is a good solution for a large company with many sites, such as a large chain of department stores.

WHAT IS A DISASTER RECOVERY EMERGENCY OPERATIONS CENTER?

A disaster recovery Emergency Operations Center is a physical place where all the communications of the recovery effort are focused. Sometimes called a "war room" to dramatize its importance, it provides a known place where all interested parties can report on the status of the recovery effort. The Emergency Operations Center also provides communications to all stakeholders external to the recovery process, such as company executives, the general public, suppliers, and customers. Another key function is to provide administrative support to the recovery effort, such as purchasing, public relations, safety, and site security.

The phrase "a known place" is important. When disaster strikes, there is no time to announce to everyone where the Emergency Operations Center will be. It is too late then. In your company, the Emergency Operations Center should be some logical place where people would turn for information or assistance. Two logical places are the facility's security office and the data center's help desk.

An Emergency Operations Center has three essential functions:

1. **Command and Control.** This is where you will find the person in charge of the containment and recovery efforts. This person will set objectives and priorities and has overall responsibility at the incident or event.

2. **Operational Control.** Hour-by-hour control is exercised from here by the various functional areas, such as security, human resources, purchasing, communications, logistics coordination, etc.

3. **Recovery Planning** (which is separate from emergency containment) will begin here but quickly transfer to its own office.

If you would like to see what an Emergency Operations Center might look like, contact your local Federal Emergency Management Agency (FEMA) office. See how their model office is set up to get some ideas for your own. Find out where in your state the next Emergency Operations Center exercise will be held and ask if you could observe the exercise. You may also receive some advice on the resources an Emergency Operations Center in your geographic area might require. If possible, ask for help in selecting a site for the Emergency Operations Center within your facility. Your local FEMA office will be a wealth of knowledge as you work on your disaster plan, and it is a good idea to build a working relationship with its personnel before disaster strikes your facility.

A Personal Experience

Imagine for a moment you are in a very large automotive factory with thousands of workers and lots of heavy machinery—a very busy place. Everyone is focused on keeping the production line moving, focused on doing their job right the first time. It's a weekday afternoon about 1:45 and—you lose electrical power. The assembly line stops, the overhead lights blink off, a roar of surprise arises from the assembly line workers, and then silence falls because all the noisy machinery has also stopped.

For the data center, the excitement has just begun. Computer programmers, whose workstations are now dead, begin walking up offering to help. Some of the battery-operated emergency lights failed to come on. All the internal data processing offices were plunged into blackness only faintly lit by a small amount of light through the glass in the office door, which everyone migrated toward. The emergency lights had failed. Total chaos!

Meanwhile, in the main computer room, people are milling about wondering aloud how long the Uninterruptible Power Supply (UPS) battery backup units would hold and should they begin turning off servers and minicomputers. More volunteers came flooding in, all with their own advice, some forcefully offered.

The Data Processing Manager personally went to the UPS units to try and determine how their displays worked in an effort to learn if they could estimate how long they would last. Still more volunteers were coming in, and others were leaving, loudly telling everyone that a bunch of idiots were in there since they did not act immediately on their advice.

Eventually everyone calmed down and began switching off noncritical system monitors used primarily to observe processes. All printers, test servers, and servers to systems that could be restarted quickly were shut down. Without air conditioning, the equipment was beginning to heat the dimly lit (from emergency lights) computer room.

Eventually others joined the Data Processing Manager to help figure out how much power was left. A few more flashlights appeared. Finally, building services called to say that the cause of the problem was discovered and everyone should be back online within an hour. An estimate, not a promise!

Outside the computer room, people were beginning to grab their coats and head outside into the daylight, loudly contemplating going home since there wouldn't be much of a workday left if the power came on in an hour. More confusion as people are reminded of their working hours—electricity or not. The group supervisors were unsure what to do and could not offer any other advice to their people but to wait and see how long it would take.

Finally, the various system administrators were rounded up from the crowds and reminded of how ugly these systems become if the UPS runs out of power before the servers are shut down gracefully (they kept hoping the power would reappear momentarily). You begin shutting down servers according to how long it would take to restart them. Your goals were to reduce the drain on the UPS batteries and extend the UPS battery support for the most critical equipment.

In the end, you worked through the issues and learned a few lessons that are included in Chapter 14, on electrical service. The points relevant to this chapter are that:

➤ You did not have a predesignated Emergency Operations Center for a problem like this, so key people did not know where to report. In the end, the help desk proved to be the perfect place because it had plenty of telephone lines and everyone knew the number.

➤ The prime decision maker (the Data Processing Manager) was absent from the Emergency Operations Center, trying to learn about the UPS system because no one knew the details about it. This left decision making in limbo and fueled chaos. Managers need to focus on making decisions, setting priorities, and allocating resources. A technician should have been assigned to investigate the UPS units.

➤ Guesses were made about which systems to shut down instead of following a predetermined plan. Also, as some system passwords were not available, those machines, even if noncritical, were left drawing critical power from the UPS.

➤ Emergency lights failed because no one bothered to check them on a regular basis.

➤ The only people with flashlights were the ones who went through a similar facility blackout 5 years before. Basic tools were lacking when they were needed most.

➤ Many well-intentioned and skilled people were ready and interested in helping in any way possible, but when they saw the chaos around the manager, they left in disgust.

➤ Because the data processing people were focused on the computer room, we forgot that the telephone system was also on a UPS system but the telephone manager handled the problem on her own initiative. We just were not feeding repair progress information in that direction.

Where to Locate Your Emergency Operations Center

An Emergency Operations Center should be located as close to the problem site as is safe. This is rarely practical. If you knew for sure where a disaster would take place and what it would involve, you would take steps to prevent it. So unless you are the cause of the problem, you don't know where it will be. Therefore, when establishing an Emergency Operations Center, evaluate the possible sites based on a few criteria, although the actual site is usually based on what is available.

Few companies can afford to leave a fully equipped room sitting idle just in case it is needed. What most companies do is convert an existing facility to an Emergency Operations Center as needed. For example, a personal computer training room is already wired for data and equipped with computers. If extra telephone lines were run to this room in advance, then with some rearranging of tables and plugging in of telephones, it can quickly be converted to an Emergency Operations Center. If a training room is not available, perhaps a large conference room was wired long ago to support a company activity. Ask your building services manager for some suggestions.

When picking a site, consider how close it is to a building exit and how likely it is to be flooded. A typical center is between 500 and 2000 square feet. It should have a large closet (with a strong door lock) to hold supplies for setting up your

Emergency Operations Center. It must be easily accessible by road, have convenient materials loading and unloading available, and have ready access to delivery services, food service, and hotels.

Now you also need to set up a backup Emergency Operations Center. The backup center should be on a different power company electrical grid and be serviced by a different telephone central office. If you have another facility across town or in a nearby city, this makes a perfect choice. In this case, your primary Emergency Operations Center becomes their backup Emergency Operations Center, and their primary Emergency Operations Center backs up your operation. This saves money for the company and keeps your company's recovery actions "in house" rather than in the public eye. Another advantage is that your backup site is already connected into your company's wide-area telephone and data communications network, allowing for faster Emergency Operations Center activation.

If this is not possible, consider partnering with another company for a backup facility. A close supplier or customer makes a good choice. Be sure to work through how telephone service can be rerouted to this location and complete a clear legal agreement about company confidential information. Another alternative is a hotel that is wired for PC training and has sufficient outbound telecommunications capacity to support your telephone and data traffic. However, a backup Emergency Operations Center in a hotel might be in use by someone else in a wide-area emergency, so use this plan as a last resort.

A note on using a backup Emergency Operations Center to control your recovery operations: expect to relocate it closer to the disaster site within 48 hours, as it will quickly become unwieldy to control operations from a distance. However, for the first few hours, even a remote facility will be of immense value.

On the morning of September 11, 2001, the City of New York's Emergency Operations Center was preparing to execute a biohazard incident exercise. After the first aircraft struck one of the World Trade Center towers, the Emergency Operations Center sprang into action. Many key personnel were already onsite for the exercise. When disaster struck, additional teams were called in, and they began to coordinate containment and recovery actions. When the twin towers collapsed, the city lost its emergency "nerve center." Backup centers were quickly established, but rescuers struggled to make up for the equipment and trained staff tragically lost in the wreckage.

Mobile Emergency Operations Center for Large or Dispersed Companies

Depending on the number of sites you are supporting, you might consider a mobile Emergency Operations Center. Such a tool is normally a large "camping" trailer or self-propelled recreation vehicle. This vehicle is preloaded with everything necessary to establish a Command Center, including a generator and tent for expanding the work area outside of the vehicle. This reduces the number of Emergency Operations Centers required for dispersed companies. For example, if your company owned freight delivery hubs in major cities and one had a major fire, then you would immediately activate the mobile center and send it to the disaster site. The emergency staff could fly in or drive themselves over.

The mobile Command Center (lacking an immediate local telephone capability) will require multiple cellular phones for voice and data access. As you do not know in advance where you will be going, it should also include digitized floor plans and wiring drawings for every building, along with door keys to access critical places or clear instructions on how to gain access. It should also include temporary security passes for the entire staff. To save space in the mobile unit, include electronic telephone books for all areas serviced to speed the location of local support services.

EMERGENCY OPERATIONS CENTER PRIMARY FUNCTIONS

When an Emergency Operations Center is activated, there are two parallel teams working at the same time. The containment team works to stop the spread of damage. The recovery team works to restore a basic level of business service. One team has all the resources initially, while the other may start with a single person. As the disaster progresses, the personnel gradually shift to the other team.

Containment Team

A containment team is formed as soon as the disaster is called. The members begin work immediately to minimize damage from the disaster. This might involve draping large tarps over holes in the walls to keep the rain out; it might involve pumping water out of the building or even salvaging soggy equipment from a computer room fire. The containment team quickly establishes a security cordon around the site and forms the initial damage assessments.

In the beginning, the containment team is the "main effort," as the early hours are occupied with minimizing the damage caused by the emergency. This will consume all your labor resources as you struggle to stop the damage from spreading. The Emergency Operations Center described in this chapter is primarily for damage containment.

As the spread of damage is stopped, the containment team will also take steps to safeguard assets (you don't need anyone taking any valuables home as "souvenirs of the great fire"). Sometimes helpful employees might sincerely try to safeguard their computers by taking them home so as to ensure the data on their hard drives do not get lost. Whatever their reasoning, nothing can be removed from the site until cleared by law enforcement authorities, your insurance adjuster, and then by your security force.

Even though the spread of damage has stopped, there is still much work to do. There are equipment and materials to sift through to determine what is salvageable. There may be artificial walls to erect (usually canvas or something to protect the contents), there are rooms to inventory, etc.

Recovery Team

The leader of the recovery team may begin work even while the damage is still spreading. This team is charged with restoring the facility to a minimal level of service as quickly as possible. Usually, this begins as a team of one and gradually gains labor resources as the events come under control.

The recovery team leader contacts the insurance company immediately and is their primary point of contact. Even as containment activities continue, this person is scurrying around taking pictures and documenting damage to aid in the damage assessment and the insurance claims. This person works closely with the insurance agent to ensure they gather the critical information for filing their claim. You will need the insurance money to rebuild and need it fast!

The recovery team begins to fill out as soon as the initial damage assessments are ready. Starting with a small group, they begin the planning of how to return the damaged area to full service. This might involve shifting the operation to another location or bringing in replacements for a few pieces of damaged equipment. As the containment effort winds down, executive management will shift their attention to the recovery effort and may replace the recovery manager with a more senior executive. This is normal to monitor the large flow of cash required to restore a severely damaged facility to service.

Emergency Operations Center Specific Functions

The Emergency Operations Center performs three essential functions. They are to command, to control, and to communicate. Keep these basics in mind as you tailor a plan to support your facility. Some functions are listed here for you to think about, but what you actually need depends upon your own situation. The best way to find out what your Command Center requires is to run several exercises based on different types of disasters.

COMMAND A disaster, like any traumatic surprise, is full of chaos. A lot of chaos! The person in charge of the Emergency Operations Center must make decisions about containment activities based on very limited amounts of information. Indecisive people should never be placed in this position. If your Command Center does not pull all important decision making into it, then you will have small pockets of people making potentially hazardous and expensive decisions for you. There will be no vacuum of command, just whether the company's representative exercises it or decisions are made by individual employees. This person will set objectives and priorities and has overall responsibility at the incident or event.

Disasters never seem to happen the way they are planned for, and this person must adapt plans as events unfold. When the problem occurs, the first action is to open the disaster recovery plan to see if that situation is specifically covered. If it is, then adapt the plan to the situation. If it is not, then develop a short-term reaction plan based on anything else in the plan that may be close to it. Emergencies vary according to their circumstances, priorities, and needs. Disasters are never as clear cut as the recovery plans seem to make them. As the problem unfolds, decisions must be made that may be different from the approved recovery plan. Keep in mind the plan is only a guideline and was never intended to be followed mindlessly.

Command activities include:

➤ Gathering damage assessments.

➤ Developing action plans based on current information.

➤ Assigning scarce resources where they will do the most good at that point in time.

CONTROL Control involves obtaining and dispatching resources based on the direction of the Emergency Operations Center manager. Control handles all the administrative duties that are the tools for implementing the directions of the manager.

Control activities include a wide range of support activities:

➤ Ordering materials from food for the crews to pumps for pumping out flood water to tarps for covering equipment.

➤ Tracking the recovery effort to ensure all personnel are accounted for at all times.

➤ Implementing the allocation and reallocation of resources as circumstances require.

➤ Gathering raw information and summarizing it for the manager's ongoing damage assessment.

➤ Controlling information about the facility to ensure it is available for all to use and not letting it be borrowed and lost.

COMMUNICATIONS Communications is the primary tool for the commander to control resources. Beyond this, the Command Center will also communicate with the news media, with vendors, with customers, with the community, and with a wide range of very interested stakeholders. Communications becomes the primary tool of the leader to mobilize teams toward a specific action. As was noted at the beginning of this chapter, it takes a radio operator (a communications medium) to make someone a *commanding* general.

ADMINISTRATIVE FUNCTIONS A primary Emergency Operations Center function is to receive information about the status of the problem. The first action is to identify the problem. We'll use the electrical outage example to illustrate our points. The first information you need to know is what the problem is. The problem is not that the lights went out. That is a symptom. The problem was a loss of electrical power. Proper identification of the problem allows you to focus on solving the problem rather than treating the symptoms.

Here is a list of some of the things that might be needed based on the type and severity of the problem. A key consideration of the administrative function is to ensure that records are maintained on what was done, when it was done, and how money was spent. Otherwise, at a later date, the "armchair quarterbacks," in their comfortable, no-pressure surroundings, will begin criticizing your actions. Administrative records also allow the company to later acknowledge their gratitude to those who did so much for them during the disaster.

➤ Keep a log of the steps taken toward problem resolution so you can later conduct an after action: lessons learned.

➤ Keep a list of who was working on the problem and when. A thank-you is in order later.

➤ Keep track of who is in each repair team and where they are. Use this to ensure teams are rotated and rested. Tired people make mistakes.

➤ Track expenses: Sometimes we cannot wait for purchasing to issue POs. In the heat of the moment, money may flow for supplies, but all of that will be forgotten next month when the bills become due. Keep track of all expenses!

➤ Maintain communications logs for telephone traffic, radio traffic, electronic mail, and faxes; any message traffic into or out of the Emergency Operations Center. This enables you to later refer back to who said what, and when.

➤ Ensure the essential human functions of food, water, and rest are addressed. Cater in food, order plenty of bottled water, and make arrangements with nearby hotels for the crews to rest. In the cases of being "locked in" your facility by flood, hurricane, blizzard, etc., this support must be provided from in-house services.

➤ Carefully track the location of the company's vital records that are governed by legal or regulatory agencies. If they must be relocated away from their usual storage area, a guard may be required.

➤ Maintain a list of injuries and any follow-up actions taken.

➤ Assist in documenting the damage for the insurance adjusters.

➤ Provide material safety data sheets to damage control teams and emergency service providers.

PREPARING AN EMERGENCY OPERATIONS CENTER

A disaster is not the time to figure out what you need in your Emergency Operations Center. Careful planning before a disaster will help ensure you have what you need to get the business back up and running.

Basic Emergency Operations Center Materials

There are many things that will be required to operate your Emergency Operations Center facility. Here are some items to consider. The more time and resources you have, the more you can improve on this basic list.

➤ **Electricity.** The Emergency Operations Center will need a steady, reliable supply of electricity. This may mean a portable generator and a UPS battery system. The size of these units is based on the amount of electricity they will be called on to provide. Be sure to consult closely with your equipment suppliers about this.

   Before you can size your electrical support units, you must know what they will need to support in the Emergency Operations Center. Hopefully you won't need them, but be prepared for the worst. If in doubt, go for larger units. Once you start adding copiers, personal computers, cellular telephone chargers, etc., to the load, you will appreciate the extra capacity.

   If you are located in an area that is prone to wide-area disasters, such as flooding, hurricanes, or earthquakes, then your own emergency power generation capability is essential and might be required to run for up to a week.

➤ **Emergency Lighting.** You will need to provide emergency lighting for the Emergency Operations Center in the event that power is lost and the generator is not ready yet. Emergency lights are battery operated and come on automatically when normal lighting is lost. These lights must be installed well in advance and checked regularly to ensure they will be ready when you need them.

   Other forms of emergency lighting are flashlights (keep plenty of batteries on hand) and light sticks. Both batteries and light sticks lose their potency over time, and your emergency stock must be replaced at least every other year. Pack plenty of these away in your Emergency Operations Center supplies storage closet. Remember that recovery efforts are an "all-out" affair and will consume supplies around the clock. In a wide-area disaster, it may be some time before you can obtain additional supplies such as flashlight batteries.

➤ **Readily Available Sanitary Facilities.** If your Emergency Operations Center is open for any length of time, then sanitary facilities are essential. If water pressure is lost, then some sort of external facility must be obtained for the duration of the emergency.

➤ **Medical Kits.** It is always useful to keep several medical kits on hand for medical issues. These kits should be used by trained personnel to apply first aid until proper medical help arrives. Include blankets to keep patients warm. In addition to the kits, encourage employee first aid training and make a list of any trained Emergency Medical Technicians (EMTs) on your payroll. Many rural communities make extensive use of volunteer emergency services, and you should know if any of these trained people are on your staff.

➤ **Office Supplies.** Every office lives on a steady diet of paperwork and a disaster is no exception. Ensure there are sufficient materials packaged and stored in your materials closet so you don't lose time chasing them down in a crisis. As you detail what you might need to recover and who might need to help, it becomes obvious what sort of supplies might be needed. Some common materials required include:

◆ PC workstations and printers, connected to a data network. If necessary, connect via cellular modems. Notebook PCs make it easy to take the PC to the work site. Be sure all PCs are preloaded with your standard software. If your key disaster recovery staff members are issued notebook PCs for use in their normal work assignment instead of desktop PCs, they can bring them to the Emergency Operations Center.

◆ Chairs, tables, secure filing cabinets, folding tables, bookcases, and wastebaskets.

◆ Portable radios and battery chargers.

◆ Telephones, telephone books, fax machines, copiers, paper shredder.

◆ Video cameras and still cameras.

◆ Copies of the business continuity plan.

◆ Local maps, building floor plans.

◆ Basic office supplies, such as pens, paper, staplers, paper clips, tape, notebooks, and special company forms, checks, postage, etc.

Communications

Communications are critical to focus the maximum effort where it is needed. In an Emergency Operations Center, this will consume most of your effort. Ideally, your communications network will allow for rapid discussions with all members on your team. Emergency Operations Center communications also include company executives, news services, the public, suppliers, customers, and other groups.

When reporting the recovery project's status, be sure that your information is correct and complete. Make a note documenting who is reporting each information element that flows into your official management updates. If you pass on someone else's bad information, then the integrity of the entire containment and recovery project will be questioned.

Basic infrastructure needs include:

➤ **Telephone.** There must be multiple telephone lines into the Emergency Operations Center. At a minimum, you need one line for incoming calls, one for outgoing calls, and one for the disaster containment manager. The more telephone lines in service beyond this minimum, the better the information will flow. In case the loss of telephone service is the problem, make a list of who on your staff carries a cellular telephone so the traditional telephone equipment can be bypassed. If necessary, add external cellular antennas to the roof of the building to ensure a clear signal. Note that in a wide-area disaster, the cellular telephone network may quickly become overloaded.

➤ **Radio Communications.** It is essential to maintain contact with work crews in the field. If the problem is with a data hub in a closet on the 22nd floor, there is probably not a telephone connected in the closet. However, if the repair technicians carry a radio, then this problem is solved. Your security force normally already has a radio network in place for communications within the facility. If your location is remote and prone to wide-area disasters, such as flooding, you might also want a shortwave radio to maintain contact with emergency services in your area. Be aware that radio communications can be intercepted and interrupted by third parties. As such, it is not a good medium for passing sensitive information.

➤ **Data Communications.** Data communications are essential for communicating with other sites and systems. In addition, it provides an e-mail pipeline for publishing press releases on recovery progress.

➤ **Web Site.** A Web site can be a valuable tool to communicate with employees and the public. Be sure to use lightweight pages that are quick to load and easy to update. Keep the information current and the tone compassionate.

➤ **Messengers.** Messengers are sometimes a vital communications link when the amount of information is large and it is already written down. It is also a more private way to communicate information that should not be sent over the public radio waves.

➤ **Television and AM/FM Radios.** It sometimes helps to hear what the rest of the world is hearing about your problem. In addition, if this is a wide-area disaster, such as a blizzard or hurricane, then there may be important public announcements broadcast over the television and radio.

Information flow is critical every step of the way. Ensure you are using the appropriate communication channel when communicating with stakeholders.

➤ To contact management and request people, equipment, tools, material and money, use regular voice communications such as direct or conference telephone calls. To provide management updates, use periodic updates via e-mail or voice mail box. This should be a different voice mail box than the one for all employees.

➤ To employees not present at the recovery site and their families, use a voice mail box or Web site with regularly updated announcements. Be sure the telephone number or Web site address is widely published before an emergency occurs.

➤ To apprise customers of the status of their orders, try to call each one individually to assure them about the shipment or to advise them of the estimated delay. If there isn't sufficient time or telephone lines available to call them individually, consider a "fax or e-mail blast" to broadcast the same message to everyone.

➤ To let the public and news media know what is happening with the recovery effort, get your message out via e-mail, fax, and onsite interviews. If things are going well, this is a chance to showcase the management expertise of your company. Public messaging Web sites such as Twitter can also be useful for getting basic status information out to a large number of people efficiently.

➤ To the people working on the recovery, use a large whiteboard with the status of the various efforts. Choose your words carefully.

➤ To notify suppliers, materials managers must have telephone access. Let suppliers know to hold shipments if appropriate or to assure other suppliers that you still need their goods on time.

➤ To insurance companies, use telephones. They will want to know immediately of disasters, as they may want to send in their own damage assessors before any cleanup effort begins.

Ignorance flourishes in the absence of truth. Time must be spent ensuring that factual information concerning the scope of any disaster is properly communicated. Your corporate communications staff must handle all communications external to the facility (especially to public news services). An ambiguously worded announcement can do more damage than no news at all.

To maintain a flow of information to employees who are not on the site, establish a password-protected Web site and post updates on the progress of the recovery. It should include information on the type of emergency, locations, time of occurrence, injuries, extent of damage, possible cause, and what action is being taken. These people are worried about their coworkers and their ongoing employment. Keep them on your side by updating this message often. The best way to make this work is to use this Web site for routine company announcements on a regular basis. Then when a disaster strikes, everyone knows where to turn for information.

If you set the standard of publishing regular updates, then the calls from executives will be fewer. If you force management to call for updates, then the staff will waste a lot of time responding to the same questions repeatedly. Try to stick to a containment and recovery progress announcement schedule even if there is nothing new to report.

An Emergency Operations Center needs a few basic items to efficiently channel information in and out. Things to think about include:

➤ **Status Board.** Rather than field many of the same questions repeatedly, set up at least one large marker board. Marker boards make great temporary posters for sharing information of interest with a wide range of people. A marker board reduces calls to people doing the work asking, "Are we there yet?" If your small children have ever repeatedly nagged you during a car trip with "Are we there yet?" then you can imagine what it is like for workers laboring through a problem to be interrupted and inundated with progress report requests from a wide range of people. Post the progress on this board and refer all inquires to it.

A status board is invaluable for seeing the "big picture" of what is happening and how the recovery is unfolding. Some of the things you may want to post on your recovery progress board are:

◆ An updated status of the recovery.

◆ The name of the current recovery manager on watch.

◆ Any important upcoming activities.

◆ Key telephone numbers.

Decisions are made and actions are taken based on information provided by everyone on the recovery team. It is important that this information be complete and accurate. When using a status board, only the clerk assigned to update the board should write on it. Inaccurate information may lead to major delays or costly mistakes. The clerk controlling the status board should log the origin of every piece of information used to update the board.

If practical, use two status boards. The one in the Emergency Operations Center is for keeping track of fast-moving details. The one posted outside of the Emergency Operations Center is to inform whoever walks up of the progress of the recovery effort and is a tool to reduce casual demands for information.

➤ **Inbound Communications.** The purpose of the Emergency Operations Center is to command, and the key to commanding is communications. Using telephones, radios, e-mail, fax machines, and any other communication tools at hand, information will pour into the center. It is important that every inbound communication be logged and identified with a number (usually based on a date/time stamp). This will make it easier to later track back to see who said what, and when.

Inbound communications might include such things as:

◆ Work crews reporting the status of their recovery efforts.

◆ Requests for tools, specific people, or skills from work crews.

◆ Current locations of crews.

◆ Status of inbound materials to aid in the recovery.

◆ Inquiries from the local news services.

◆ Offers of help.

◆ Questions by the police and fire department.

◆ Injury reports.

➤ **Outbound Communications.** A large recovery effort will generate a steady stream of outbound messages to a wide range of stakeholders:

◆ Status updates to executives. Keep them informed or they will show up asking questions.

◆ Public Relations spokespersons. They need the facts in case the disaster is considered a public event.

◆ Suppliers. They need to know if they should hold shipments, or even turn around loads on the road.

◆ Customers. They need to know if their goods will still arrive on time, especially if this facility provides just-in-time service to another company. If you are a just-in-time supplier, then it is crucial that you must maintain a steady flow of recovery progress reports to your customers.

Emergency Operations Center Security

It is nice to have a lot of help, but too many curious people will just get in the way. If someone is not assigned to the Emergency Operations Center staff, they should not be there except by invitation. This isn't intended to cover up anything or to keep the truth from anyone. It will cut down on the casual questions and well-intended actions that interfere with work.

Assign someone to oversee (and keep under control) visitors to your site. Visitors should have a comfortable place nearby to congregate and to be briefed on progress. These people might be a valuable labor resource to draw from as the recovery progresses. As employees show up to volunteer their services, log them in and note their departments and the areas in which they normally work.

The primary source of identification during a disaster is your company ID card. If possible, hand the responsibility for the Emergency Operations Center and recovery work site security over to your facility security force. If you do not already have a company security force, then you should arrange an on-call support agreement with a local firm. With a standing agreement, this reduces their response time to your site and frees your staff to concentrate on the recovery.

Beware of people walking through your area looking for some loot to take home. It is prudent to limit the number of access points at a recovery site. Nothing should leave without a materials pass. Remember that a flash drive or CD full of customer information is easily picked up and fits neatly in a thief's pocket.

EMERGENCY OPERATIONS CENTER STAFFING

It is important to identify the Emergency Operations Center staff well in advance of a disaster. They need to know to automatically head for the Emergency Operations Center when a disaster occurs. There is no time to go looking for them. To facilitate this process, periodic recovery Emergency Operations Center staff exercises should be held. If you practice it, you'll better understand what to do at a time when your thoughts are distracted by the emergency and concern for others.

Who should be in the Emergency Operations Center? The number one person is the Disaster Containment Manager. This person is like an orchestra conductor who keeps everyone focused on the task at hand. There can only be one boss, and that boss should have a direct communications pipeline to the top executives. If some well-meaning vice president comes onsite, he or she deserves a briefing on containment and recovery efforts but should not be allowed to begin issuing orders. The caveat to this is if they are advising on their own area of responsibility; then, their advice is valuable and should be seriously considered.

The company must decide in advance who the Disaster Containment Manager will be and what authority that manager will have. Because a disaster can happen to any part of the business, this should be a senior executive who has broad experience in the company. In a crisis, it must be someone who can be spared from his or her regular job for up to several weeks to focus exclusively on disaster containment and recovery. This person must be authorized to spend money on the spur of the moment to bring in emergency assistance and materials without lengthy consultations with top management. Given this description, a company is wise to identify this person in advance and ensure the person is intimately involved with the facility's disaster recovery and mitigation planning. The greater this manager's prestige in the company, the greater the support will be for your mitigation, training, and testing programs.

Declaring a disaster invokes a prewritten directive identifying the Disaster Containment Manager and placing the manager under the direct control of the top company executive until relieved. Such a directive must be prepared in advance and distributed to all company officers. It is issued by the Disaster Containment Manager when activating the Emergency Operations Center. This action eliminates confusion among the employees. Typically, this prewritten declaration is intended to authorize prompt action for the first 24 hours or until the top executive decides to appoint someone else or to reaffirm it as ongoing through the recovery period.

An important staffing consideration is for every person to have a predesignated and trained backup. Every effort must be made to cross-train the staff on the other functions of the recovery effort. Remember that your Emergency Operations Center will quite likely be tasked to run around the clock to speed the recovery. If you are only "one deep" in job skills, that person will quickly burn out. Everyone in the Emergency Operations Center must be prepared to wear several hats at once.

A recovery staff "rest plan" should be in effect for around-the-clock efforts. A rest plan ensures that recovery teams are rotated regularly to allow for rest. Team members on their rest break should sleep or otherwise rest their minds and bodies. They should not assist in other recovery activity. Tired people make mistakes and get hurt.

Disaster Containment Manager Responsibilities

The Disaster Containment Manager is responsible for protecting and preserving the company's assets and resources. The manager has the dual role to ensure the impact of a disaster is minimized and to begin recovery operations. This position is most crucial during the first few hours of the recovery. As the containment phase passes into a recovery phase, this person may be replaced by one of the company executives to oversee rebuilding the damage areas.

The Disaster Containment Manager makes the tough decisions, sets the recovery effort objectives, directs staff toward priorities, and keeps the recovery team focused. The manager is also your primary contact with public emergency services on the disaster site. These organizations (fire, police, and government agencies) are legally mandated to control the site, safeguard lives, contain the incident, and preserve any criminal evidence. By working closely with these organizations, the manager can determine which parts of the site can be entered and addressed at that point in time. They can also pull together a damage assessment and begin recovery planning.

Disaster Containment Manager responsibilities include:

➤ Declaring that a disaster exists and identifying which outside assistance is required. This includes the need to activate an off-site data center. Note that this declaration to an off-site data center service provider incurs a major cost as soon as this call is made.

➤ Coordinating with any emergency services onsite to gain access to the site as soon as possible.

➤ Making an initial damage assessment and beginning planning for emergency containment. As the event unfolds, the manager updates the damage assessment and uses that as the basis for all future recovery actions.

➤ Selecting a site for the Emergency Operations Center by determining if the primary site is suitable, if the backup site must be activated, or if there is an opportunity to set up an Operations Center very close to the disaster.

➤ Activating the disaster recovery teams, assigning people to either business continuity or business recovery efforts.

➤ Personally ensuring that adequate personnel safeguards are in place.

➤ Assigning staff to maintain a 24-hour schedule for containment and recovery. Drafting and enforcing a rest plan.

➤ Maintaining the official status of the recovery for executive management.

➤ Coordinating incoming material with the materials receiving staff.

➤ Coordinating use of skilled trades with the facility engineering management such as for contract labor, electricians, welders, and millwrights.

➤ Assessing personnel strengths and weaknesses in terms of knowledge, skill, and performance to balance labor expertise and staffing.

➤ Watching for signs of excessive stress and fatigue. Even exceptionally good performers grow tired and reach a point where they no longer can think clearly and are prone to serious error.

➤ Identifying "at-risk" employees, that is, those deeply affected by traumatic stress. Moving them to a safe environment under the care of counselors or friends, and assessing the need for professional intervention.

➤ Designating a backup person to assume the Disaster Containment Manager's role while they are resting or not on the disaster site.

Facility Engineering Manager Responsibilities

The Facility Engineering Manager's responsibilities include:

➤ Ensuring floor plans are current as to electrical, data network, fire, and environmental considerations, and that copies are maintained both in the Emergency Operations Center and in the off-site vital records storage facility.

➤ Prearranging for on-call contract skilled labor to supplement the facilities repair staff and to fill in any gaps in expertise.

➤ Ensuring the facility's safety alarms and emergency lights are in good working order through periodic testing.

➤ Restoring utilities—electrical, water, sewage, telecommunications, and HVAC—as soon as possible.

Other Essential Emergency Operations Center Staff Members

Everyone in the company can play an important role in helping the firm recover from a disaster. This includes:

➤ **Purchasing Agent.** The purchasing agent must have the authority to spend whatever funds are necessary to assist in the immediate containment and recovery effort. The purchasing buyer will need a checkbook for situations where a purchase order is not appropriate. Some companies also use a company credit card for this function. The purchasing agent is responsible for tracking the expenses incurred during the containment and recovery.

➤ **Public Relations Coordinator.** This person controls all official announcements concerning the disaster. This person is critical if injuries have been suffered by anyone during the disaster. Accidents can also occur during recovery, so this person must be fully aware of what is happening so that a minimal but truthful statement can be issued to the press.

➤ **Human Resources Manager.** This manager makes the decisions on personnel issues that are consistent with company policy. This person will probably be the one who calls in emergency staff from home and deals with employees who refuse to assist in the after-hours recovery. The Human Resources Manager is also the one who can send people home (with or without pay according to your company's disaster guidelines). They ensure that employee engineering and skilled trades skill assessments are up to date.

➤ **Security Manager.** This person will be fully occupied securing the disaster site to prevent material from being stolen. If you do not have one, then appoint someone to this important post and hire a security service to safeguard your equipment.

➤ **Safety Person.** This person is very concerned that anyone entering or exiting the damaged area is accounted for on the status board and provided with the proper safety devices. The safety person briefs the teams on safety issues before they enter the disaster area and debriefs them after they come out (to learn if there are any new hazards).

➤ **Materials Manager.** You will need someone to contact all inbound materials shipments and have them held at the terminal or redirected to a warehouse for temporary storage. Shipments that have not left the suppliers' dock may be canceled. This person should be skilled at traffic management for expediting shipments of emergency supplies.

➤ **Sales Manager.** This manager needs to get on the telephone to critical customers and keep them apprised as to the viability of their orders. Customers may see a splashy news report that sounds like your facility has been flattened when in reality all you lost were a few offices. Timely calls will prevent nervous people from canceling orders at a point when a continuous flow of business is very important.

➤ **Facilities Engineer.** If there was any structural damage, no one should enter the building without engineering approval. If heavy equipment is needed to move debris, this person will be very busy directing that operation.

➤ **Data Processing Support Manager.** Needed for the operations center and the recovery effort.

➤ **Medical Director.** Needed if you have an in-house medical staff.

➤ **Vital Records Manager.** This person provides advice for recovering vital records or safeguarding undamaged records.

As time moves on, don't forget to reach out and request help from your vendors. Just as you will "go the extra mile" for your customers, so will they for your future business. As you make emergency material orders, bring their sales representatives onsite for advice. They may even send over technical experts to help you recover. After all, if you don't recover well, then you won't be a very good customer in the future. However, your vendors will not know you are having a problem *unless you tell them!*

EMERGENCY OPERATIONS CENTER: WHEN A DISASTER STRIKES

Now that your Emergency Operations Center plan is ready, what do you do when an emergency strikes? It takes time to bring together the proper people to begin addressing the problem. This time gap between when the disaster strikes and when the disaster recovery team is assembled is a critical time during which events must not be allowed to take their own course. When a disaster strikes, the Disaster Recovery Manager must take immediate and decisive steps to protect people and property. This prompt action buys time to organize a proper reaction. Drilling the Disaster Recovery Manager and his team during disaster plan testing will make this an automatic process.

When the problem strikes, you have three major actions to accomplish at the same time. These may occur in rapid succession and overlap. In an emergency there will be massive chaos, so be prepared! Your three initial actions are to protect human life, to contain the damage, and to communicate with management and fellow employees.

Protect Life

Your first action is to provide for the safety of all employees, visitors, and bystanders—everyone! Work in the area of the disaster stops, and people are evacuated while an assessment is made. This can be expensive but is a very wise precaution. If, for example, this is a 10-story building and there is a fire on the second floor, everyone on the floors above needs to get out in case the fire climbs higher and to avoid smoke inhalation. Everyone on the floors below must leave due to water damage (from the fire hoses) and to avoid the potential of a building collapse (full or partial). By evacuating everyone, you can account for who is missing and may need to be rescued inside. You can also identify which managers and supervisors are onsite and ask them to keep their staffs together. You may need their help in the immediate recovery efforts.

Predesignate rendezvous areas by department. Someone (or several people) should be assigned as assembly area leaders whose job it is to account for everyone. They will need a roster of all active employees to check off names. Many companies identify the rendezvous points by attaching signs on the parking lot light posts. People need to know where to go!

To signal an evacuation, use an in-building page to alert everyone. In a noisy factory, you may need to set off the fire alarm—even if the problem is not a fire— just to get their attention. The important thing is to get everyone out safely with a minimum of panic. It is better to use a prearranged signal but in an emergency you must use whatever is at hand.

Besides a fire, you might need to evacuate due to a toxic material leak, a sudden structural problem, or even someone waving a gun around in an office. There are many reasons why this might be necessary. Everyone must know what an evacuation alarm sounds like and what to do when it goes off.

Contain the Damage

Once everyone is out, a quick assessment can be made to determine the extent of the damage. How this assessment is done depends on the nature of the problem. The first action is to call for help. If there is a fire, call for the fire department. If it is a toxic leak, activate your environmental hazard containment team (you should have one if you keep toxic material onsite). The on-scene manager must be sure the call gets through and must not delegate this important task without following up.

Next, notify top management of the situation. If this is a weekday, executives may already be there. However, if this is a Saturday night and you just evacuated the building, then they need to be tracked down and told. This is not a time to be a go-it-alone hero. You need their support for the immediate recovery steps.

Determine if there is anything you can safely do to contain the damage. This is a judgment call. If everyone is out of the building and accounted for, then you might want to await emergency support. If anyone is missing, try to determine where they may have been in the building so this information can be passed on to the rescue crews. They have the equipment to go in there and you do not. If the building has structural damage, do not reenter it without the clearance of a structural engineer.

As you work to contain the damage, you need to establish security around the building. Chaos is a momentary opportunity for a thief to snatch and run, so try to identify anything leaving the building and who has it. Use your idle employees to assist your security team. Ask for volunteers. Make a list of who is helping with this before they move out.

Communicate

For the first few moments, people will tend to follow whoever seems to be in charge and knows what to do. In times of crises, leaders tend to emerge. Unfortunately, some of these will be misguided and could tend to pull people in the wrong direction. So after the previously mentioned actions are taken, get an announcement to every assembly point that:

➤ Briefly describes the problem. Don't speculate. If you don't know, say so.

➤ Tells them what actions you need from them. If the problem appears severe and it is close to quitting time, ask the assembly point leaders to account for everyone. If you know whom you need to stay and help or if you want to ask for volunteers, do so now. Send the rest of the people home. Keep all the department managers onsite so they can better understand if they should call their people to cancel work for the next day.

Keep the executives informed with hourly status reports. The hourly status report should include:

1. Assessment of the extent of the damage.

2. List of what is needed to recover the site in people, data, hardware, and software.

3. The decision to recover onsite or at the alternate site.

4. Keeping everyone informed of the situation. Use the Public Relations department as a spokesperson for all external contacts.

5. Activating the Emergency Operations Center and assembling the recovery team.

6. Requesting priority on purchasing support from the facility's accounting manager.

CONCLUSION

The goal of the Emergency Operations Center is to help return the business to normal as quickly as possible. While you can't eliminate the damage to your business from a disaster, a well-designed plan for managing the recovery will dramatically reduce your recovery time and speed the return to business as usual. As with most management functions, communications is the key to the commander controlling the situation and leading the recovery to a successful conclusion.

CHAPTER 13

TESTING YOUR PLANS
Test, Test, Test

Action is the foundational key to all success.
— Pablo Picasso

INTRODUCTION

Writing a recovery plan is only half of the challenge. The second half, the real challenge, is to periodically test it. Everyone can relate to writing a recovery plan. "Testing" a plan sounds like you do not trust it. Testing requires expensive technician time, the equipment and facility resources to conduct a test, and the expertise to plan the exercise. Gathering all of this into one place can be difficult.

Arranging for expensive technician time was tough enough to secure for writing the plans. The most knowledgeable people are usually the busiest. Getting them to give the time to sit down long enough to test a plan is difficult—yet essential. Testing validates that a recovery plan will work. A plan that is tested has a much higher possibility of succeeding over a plan that has never been proven. The many benefits to testing include:

➤ Demonstrating that a plan works.

➤ Validating plan assumptions.

➤ Identifying unknown contingencies.

➤ Verifying resource availability.

➤ Training team members for their recovery roles.

➤ Determining the true length of recovery time, and ultimately the ability to achieve the desired company RTO.

The Many Benefits of Plan Testing

Recovery plans are tested for many business reasons. An untested plan is merely process documentation. Testing a plan ensures that the document provides the desired results. The benefits of testing include the following.

TESTING REVEALS MISSING STEPS When people write a plan, they think about a process or IT system, and then write the plan so that they will understand what is explained and the steps to take. In this sense, the plan is a reflection of their experience. However, in a crisis, they may not be the person who will execute the recovery. Further, some people cannot break down a process to include each of its individual steps. In action, they will pick up on visual cues to take a specific action to fill a gap.

Therefore, the first purpose of a recovery plan test is to ensure that it includes all of the necessary steps to achieve recovery. Missing steps are not unusual in the first draft of a recovery plan. Other missing information may be IT security codes, the location of physical keys for certain offices or work areas, or the location of vendor contact information.

TESTING REVEALS PLAN ERRORS Writing a plan sometimes introduces misleading, incorrect, or unnecessary steps. Testing the plan will uncover all of these.

TESTING UNCOVERS CHANGES TO THE PROCESS SINCE THE RECOVERY PLAN WAS WRITTEN A plan may have been sitting on the shelf for a period of time without review. Over time, IT systems change server sizes, add disk storage, or are upgraded to new software versions. Business processes move machinery and change the sequence of steps, and key support people leave the company.

TESTING A PLAN TRAINS THE TEAM After a plan has been debugged, exercising it teaches each recovery participant his or her role during the emergency. It is one thing to read the words on a page and another to actually carry out the steps.

Types of Recovery Plan Tests

Exercises can consist of talking through recovery actions or physically recovering something. Discussion-based tests exercise teamwork in decision making, analysis, communication, and collaboration. Operations-based tests involve physically recovering something, such as a data center, telephone system, office or manufacturing cell. This type of test uses expensive resources and is more complex to conduct.

Everyone has their own name for the various types of testing. Tests are categorized by their complexity in setting them up and in the number of participants involved. These tests are listed here in a progression from least complex to most difficult to run:

➤ **Standalone Testing** is where the person who authored the plan reviews it with someone else with a similar technical background. This may be the manager or the backup support person. This type of testing is useful for catching omissions, such as skipping a process step. It also provides some insight into the process for the backup support person.

➤ **Walk-Through Testing** involves everyone mentioned in the plan and is conducted around a conference room table. Everyone strictly follows what is in the plan as they talk through what they are doing. This also identifies plan omissions, as there are now many perspectives examining the same document.

➤ **Integrated System Testing** occurs when all of the components of an IT system (database, middleware, applications, operating systems, network connections, etc.) are recovered from scratch. This type of test reveals many of the interfaces between IT systems required to recover a specific IT function. For example, this would be to test the recovery of the Accounting department's critical IT system, Human Resources IT system, the telephone system, e-mail, etc.

➤ **Table-Top Exercises** simulate a disaster but the response to it is conducted in a conference room. A disaster scenario is provided and participants work through the problem. This is similar to Walk-Through Testing, except that the team responds to an incident scenario. As the exercise progresses, the Exercise Coordinator injects additional problems into the situation.

➤ **Simulation Exercises** take a Table-Top exercise one step further by including the actual recovery site and equipment. A simulation is the closest that a company can come to experiencing (and learning from) a real disaster. Simulations provide many dimensions that most recovery plan tests never explore. However, they are complex to plan and expensive to conduct.

Validating the Recovery Time Objective

Testing recovery plans ensure that it can achieve the required recovery time objective. Since plans are tested in small groups, the actual RTO is determined by tracking the amount of time required to recover each IT system and business process. These plans fit into an overall recovery sequence (developed by the Business Continuity Manager). Once in this framework, the time required to complete each plan is added up (many plans execute in parallel) to determine if the RTO can be achieved.

Is it a "test" or an "exercise"? A "test" implies a pass or fail result. An "exercise" implies using something and is less threatening to participants.

WRITING A TESTING STRATEGY

Testing distracts an organization from its mission of returning a profit to shareholders. Everyone is busy meeting his or her own company objectives. Somehow, time must be found within each department's busy schedule to test its recovery plans. To maximize the benefit to the company while minimizing cost, develop a testing strategy for your company. This strategy describes the type and frequency of test for recovery plans. An executive-approved testing strategy provides the top-level incentive for management compliance. The testing strategy is inserted into the administrative plan.

The testing calendar should reach out over several years. Keep in mind that different departments have their own "busy season" and trying to test at that time will be difficult. For example, the Accounting department will be occupied before and after the end of the company's fiscal year. Payroll needs to submit tax forms at the end of the calendar year, etc. By using an annual testing calendar, it is easier to gain commitment from the various departments to look ahead and commit to tests on specific days.

Testing follows a logical progression. It begins with the individual plan. The next level is a grouping of recovery plans to test together. This is followed by a simulation of some sort. Executives become frustrated by the length of time required to properly test all of the plans in this sequence, but they are more disturbed by the cost to test them faster.

Begin by Stating Your Goals

As with all things in the business continuity program, begin writing the testing strategy by referring back to the Business Impact Analysis. If the recovery time objective is brief (measured in minutes or hours), then the testing must be frequent and comprehensive. The longer the recovery time objective, the less frequent and comprehensive the testing may be. Considered from a different angle, the less familiar that the current recovery team is with a plan, the longer it will take them to complete it.

Another issue is the severity of an incident. While the overall plan may tolerate a long recovery time, there may be specific processes whose availability is important to the company. This might be the Order Entry IT system or a critical machine tool. Consider testing those few highly critical processes more frequently than the overall plan.

The testing goal may be stated as, "Recovery plans are tested to demonstrate that the company's approved recovery time objective of (your RTO here) can be achieved" and that all participants understand their roles in achieving a prompt recovery.

Progressive Testing

Testing follows a progression from simple to complex. Once a plan is written, it begins at the Standalone Test level and progresses from there. Any process or IT system that is significantly changed must be retested beginning at the Standalone level. The progression of testing is as follows:

➤ **Standalone Testing** is the first action after a plan is written. It reveals the obvious problems.

➤ **Walk-Through Testing** exercises a group of related plans at the same time, conducted as a group discussion.

➤ **Integrated System Testing** tests a group of related plans at the same time by actually recovering them on spare equipment.

➤ **Table-Top Exercises** test a group of related plans at the same time, based on an incident scenario.

➤ **Simulation Exercises** combine many groups for an actual recovery in the recovery sites, based on an incident scenario.

Creating a Three-Year Testing Roadmap

Some tests only involve two people, while others can include most of the IT department. All tests require preparation time. This is necessary to coordinate schedules for people, exercise control rooms, and equipment. Copies of plans must be printed and distributed and exercise scenarios created. At a minimum, every plan should be tested annually. This can be accomplished by the manager and the process owner performing a Standalone Test to see if anything significant has changed in the process.

Few companies halt operations for several days to conduct a complete disaster simulation. Instead, they test "slices" of the recovery program. For example, the test might focus on a recovery of the Operations department or Shipping department. On the IT side, this would be a group of related systems that regularly exchange information, such as order entry, materials management, and billing.

Too much testing can reduce interest in the program. Practically speaking, testing is a preventative measure (all cost and no immediate payback) and does not increase a company's revenue. Depending on the industry, testing may never progress beyond the table-top exercise stage. The Business Continuity Manager works with the program sponsor to identify the adequate level of testing for the organization and then spreads it throughout the year.

When developing a testing calendar, executives will vent their frustration. They will want something that is written, tested, and then set aside as completed. They do not like to consider that completed plans must continue to be exercised regularly. There are many plans and combinations of plans to test: business processes, IT systems, work area recovery, pandemic, etc. A typical testing schedule includes:

➤ Quarterly

   ◆ Inspect Command Center sites for availability and to ensure their network and telecommunication connections are live.

   ◆ Data Backups

      ● Verify that data backups (on each media type) are readable.

      ● Ensure that every disk in the data center and key personal computers are included in the backups.

      ● Inspect safe and secure transportation of media to off-site storage.

      ● Inspect how the off-site storage facility handles and secures the media.

   ◆ All business process owners verify that their employee recall lists are current.

   ◆ Issue updated versions of plans.

➤ Annually (spread throughout the year)

   ◆ Conduct an IT simulation at the recovery site.

   ◆ Conduct a work area recovery simulation at the recovery site.

   ◆ Conduct a pandemic table-top exercise.

   ◆ Conduct an executive recovery plan exercise with all simulations.

   ◆ Review business continuity plans of key vendors.

   ◆ All managers submit a signed report that their recovery plans are up to date.

   ◆ Practice a data backup recall from the secured storage area to the hot site.

A partial plan exercise calendar might look like Figure 13-1.

TESTING TEAM

Testing a recovery plan is a team effort. The best results come from a clear explanation of the responsibilities of team members and some training to show them what to do. This enables each person to contribute expertise to the exercise while learning by doing. Training for individual team members is the responsibility of the Business Continuity Manager.

The duties for each of the testing team members will vary according to the type of test, with a full disaster simulation requiring the most time from everyone. Possible team duties include:

➤ Business Continuity Manager

   ◆ Develops a long-term testing calendar, updated annually.

   ◆ Develops or updates a testing strategy.

Business Continuity Testing Calendar

	2010				2011				2012			
	Q1	Q2	Q3	Q4	Q1	Q2	Q3	Q4	Q1	Q2	Q3	Q4
Materials Management												
Shipping	S		I	I	T				SIM			S
Receiving	S		I	I	T				SIM			S
Picking		S	I	I	T				SIM			S
Put Away			S, I	I	T				SIM			S
Order Processing												
Order Receipts	S			I		T		O		SIM		S
Order Exceptions		S		I		T		O		SIM		S
Backorders			S	I		T		O		SIM		S
Accounting												
Accounts Receivable	S		T		I		O			SIM		S
Account Payable	S		T		I		O			SIM		S
Billing	S		T		I		O			SIM		S
Customer Service	S		T		I		O			SIM		S
Pandemic												
Accounting				T							T	
Sales				T							T	
Manufacturing				T							T	

Chart Legend
S = Standalone
T = Table-Top
I = IT Integrated
SIM = Simulation
O = Office Recovery

FIGURE 13-1: Example of a three-year testing calendar.

- ◆ Schedules tests.
- ◆ Prepares test areas and participant materials.
- ◆ Explains testing process to team prior to start of exercise.
- ◆ Presents scenario.
- ◆ Logs events during the exercise.
- ◆ Keeps exercise focused for prompt completion.
- ◆ Injects variations to scenarios during simulation testing.
- ◆ Conducts after-action critiques of recovery plan and a separate discussion of the test process.
- ◆ Provides a written test report to the program sponsor.

➤ Sponsor
  - ◆ Reviews and approves recovery plan test calendar and testing strategy.
  - ◆ Approves initiation of all tests.
  - ◆ Provides financial support for tests.
  - ◆ Ensures internal support of test program.
  - ◆ Observes tests in progress.
  - ◆ Reviews written report of test results and team critique.

➤ Exercise Recorder
  - ◆ Records actions and decisions.
  - ◆ Records all assumptions made during the test.
  - ◆ Drafts narrative of what happened during the test for the after-action review.

➤ Exercise Participants
  - ◆ Prepare for the test by reviewing the recovery plans.
  - ◆ Participate in test by following the plans.
  - ◆ Offer ways to improve the recovery plans during the test.
  - ◆ Participate in the after-action critique of the recovery plans and the testing process.

➤ Nonemployee Participants
  - ◆ Where practical include people from other organizations who have a stake in your plans, such as the fire and police departments, power company.
  - ◆ News reporters to report on the exercise and to participate by exercising your corporate communications plan.
  - ◆ Visitors, such as customer or supplier representatives.

EXERCISE SCENARIOS

A disaster scenario is a hypothetical incident that gives participants a problem to work through. The scenario may describe any disruption to the normal flow of a business process. The scenario should be focused on the type of problem that a particular group of people may face. For example, the problem and its mid-execution "injection of events" should encompass all participants.

Every simulation starts with a scenario, a hypothetical situation for the participants to work through. Scenarios that reflect potential threats also add an air of reality to the exercise. A good place to look for topics is in the plan's risk analysis section or program assumptions. Another place to look is in the recent national or local news.

For example, who has never experienced a power outage or a loss of data connectivity? How about severe weather like a hurricane or a blizzard? Or consider tornados and earthquakes. Human-created situations, such as fire, loss of water pressure, or a person with a weapon in the building, are also potential scenarios.

The planning expertise of the test coordinator is crucial. The coordinator must devise an exercise schedule to include a detailed timeline of events, coordinate and place the resources involved (people, equipment, facilities, supplies, and information), establish in everyone's minds their role, and identify interdependencies between individuals and groups.

In theory, a business faces a wide range of threats from people, nature, infrastructure, etc. In reality, few of these will occur. Some are dependent on the season and changes in the political environment. Whatever the crisis, the recovery steps for many threats are the same. A data center lost to a fire is the same as a data center lost (or made unusable) because of a collapsed roof, a flood, etc. In each of these cases, there will be many steps unique to that event. However, the initial actions in each case will be the same. It is this similarity that enables disaster recovery planning. A disaster plan is most useful in the first few hours when there is limited information, but the greatest benefit from containing the damage and restoring minimal service to the company.

Include in the scenario the incident's day of week and time of day. The weekend response will differ from the work-time response. Consider declaring the scenario to include the company's worst time of the year (such as the day before Christmas for a retailer). Also, the severity of the damage can at first appear to be small and then grow through "injects" provided by the exercise controller. Consider the example of a small fire. When a large amount of water was sprayed on the fire, it ran down the floor and saturated the carpet in the nearby retail show room. It also leaked through the floor into the data center below, soaking the equipment.

Ask the program sponsor to approve the scenario used in an exercise. This will minimize participant discussion during its presentation. It will also help to avoid scenarios that executives feel are too sensitive.

Some potential testing scenarios might be:

➤ Natural Disasters

◆ Hurricane or heavy downpour of rain

◆ Tornado or high winds

◆ Earthquake

◆ Flood

◆ Pandemic

◆ Fire

◆ Severe snow or ice

➤ Civil Crises

◆ Labor strike (in company or secondary picketing)

◆ Workplace violence

◆ Serious supplier disruption

◆ Terrorist target neighbor (judiciary, military, federal, or diplomatic buildings)

◆ Sabotage/theft/arson

◆ Limited or no property access

➤ Location Threats

◆ Nearby major highway, railway, or pipeline

◆ Hazardous neighbor (stores or uses combustibles, chemicals, or explosives)

◆ Offices above 12th floor (limit of fire ladders)

◆ Major political event that may lead to civil unrest

➤ Network/Information Security Issues

◆ Computer virus

◆ Hackers stealing data

◆ Data communication failure

➤ Data Operations Threats

◆ Roof collapse (full or partial)

◆ Broken water pipe in room above data center

◆ Fire in data center

◆ Critical IT equipment failure

◆ Environmental support equipment failure

◆ Telecommunications failure

◆ Power failure

◆ Service provider failure

◆ Loss of water pressure which shuts down chilled water coolers

Select scenarios so that the problem exercises multiple plans. Choosing the right scenario can engage the participant's curiosity and imagination. It converts a dull exercise into a memorable and valuable experience for its participants. A good scenario should:

➤ Be realistic—no meteors crashing through the ceiling.

➤ Be broad enough to encompass several teams to test their intergroup communications.

➤ Have an achievable final solution.

➤ Include time increments, such as every 10 minutes equals one hour, etc.

Prior to the exercise, draft the scenario as a story. It begins with an initial call from the alarm monitoring service with vague information—just like a real incident. To add to the realism, some people will use a bit of photo editing to illustrate the scene. Imposing flames over the top of a picture of your facility may wake some people up!

As the exercise continues, the Exercise Coordinator provides additional information known as "injects." This predefined information clarifies (or confirms) previous information and also raises other issues incidental to the problem. For example, if there was a fire in the warehouse, an inject later in the exercise may say that the warehouse roof has collapsed injuring several employees or that the fire marshal has declared the warehouse to be a crime scene and the data center is unreachable until the investigation is completed in two days.

Injects, like the scenario, must make sense in the given situation and may also include good news, such as workers missing from the warehouse fire are safe and have been found nearby. Unplanned injects may be made during the exercise if a team is stumped. Rather than end their portion of the test, state an assumption as fact. For example, the Exercise Coordinator could state that, "The data center fire was concentrated in the print room and no servers were damaged."

Try to insert some humor into a tragic situation. For example, state that a fire started by a lightning strike in the boss's office or the Board of Health condemned the food vending machines or no one can enter the building.

TYPES OF EXERCISES

There are various types of recovery plan tests. They range from easy to set up and quick to complete to full simulation requiring months of planning. Each plan starts with Standalone Testing. Unfortunately, many companies never test their plans in a full simulation.

Standalone Testing

Standalone Testing is the first level of testing for all recovery plans. It is also required when a significant change has been made to the IT system of a business process.

Standalone Testing exercises individual IT components or business processes to estimate the time required for recovery. It provides the first level of plan error checking. The scenario of a Standalone Test is to recover an individual IT component or business process from nothing. (It assumes the process or IT system has been destroyed or rendered totally unusable.) A recovery plan is written so that someone other than the primary support person can understand and follow it. It also familiarizes at least one other person with the plan's contents.

Recovering business processes often requires that many plans work together. Standalone Testing examines the individual building blocks of the overall effort. Later tests examine the interactions and interfaces among the individual plans.

The result of a Standalone Test should be a recovery plan that is in the company standard format. This ensures that anyone unfamiliar with this process can find the same type of information in the same place. The plan should be approved as complete and accurate by the plan's author and plan reviewer. The plan's author also provides a time estimate as to how long the recovery plan should take to complete.

PREPARATION Schedule a conference room away from an office's distractions. If the document is large, break it into one-hour meetings to keep everyone fresh.

MATERIALS TO PROVIDE A copy of the standard plan format and copies of the plan for each participant.

TESTING TEAM Consists of the document author and a reviewer (may be the backup support person or the process's owner).

THE MEETING AGENDA The meeting agenda should be as follows:
- ➤ Review ground rules.
  - ◆ This is a draft document and anyone can suggest changes.
  - ◆ Suggesting a change is not a personal attack.
  - ◆ All comments are focused on the document and not on the author.
- ➤ Review document for:
  - ◆ Proper format.
  - ◆ Content.
  - ◆ Clarity.
- ➤ Estimate time required to execute each step in this plan and the plan overall.
- ➤ Set time for review of changes suggested by this test.

FOLLOW UP Continue Standalone plan reviews until the document conforms to the company standard format and the participants believe that the document reflects the proper recovery process.

Integration Testing

Integration testing (or Integrated System Testing) exercises multiple plans in a logical group. This might be an IT system with its interdependent components (a database server, an application, special network connections, unique data collection devices, etc.).

The purpose of an Integration Test is to ensure that the data exchanges and communication requirements among individual components have been addressed. These interdependent components require each other to provide the desired business function. This type of test is normally used by IT systems. For example, the Order Entry system may require access to multiple databases, files, and applications. To test the recovery of the Order Entry system, all of the three other components must be recovered first.

The ideal place to execute this plan is at the IT recovery hot site that the company will use in a crisis. If that is not available, then use equipment that is as close in performance and configuration to the hot site as practical. This will help to identify differences between the hot site and the required data center configuration.

Another advantage to using the hot site is to provide an actual recovery time for validating the recovery time objective (RTO). This result is added to other test results to see what the company can realistically expect for a recovery time, given the current technology.

Integration testing is usually conducted by the backup support person(s) for each recovery plan. The Business Continuity Manager observes the test and records the actual time required to recover the IT system or business process.

In most IT recoveries, the server administrator builds the basic infrastructure and then provides it to the recovery team. For example, an operating system is loaded onto "blank" servers and then turned over to the recovery team. The time to prepare these devices is part of the RTO calculation.

PREPARATION Schedule time at the hot site or the use of equipment in the data center.

TESTING TEAM The testing team should consist of the following people:

➤ Backup support person(s) for each device to be recovered.

➤ Network support technician to isolate the test network from production and to load the DNS server.

➤ System administrator to load the operating systems and establish the domain controller.

➤ Applications support team to load and test their systems.

➤ Optionally, a database administrator.

➤ Reviewer (IT Manager or Business Continuity Manager).

➤ Business process owner to validate a good recovery.

➤ Business continuity program sponsor.

MATERIALS TO PROVIDE These include the following:

➤ The business continuity program sponsor approves timing of test and required funding.

➤ Nonproduction (spare) IT equipment, based on the list of required equipment as detailed in the recovery plans.

➤ Copies of the recovery plans to be tested.

THE TEST PROGRAM The program should include the following:

➤ Review ground rules.

◆ Write down all corrections as they are encountered.

◆ Record the amount of time required to complete each step in the plan and the total in the plan. This may isolate steps that take a long time as targets for improving the speed of the recovery.

◆ Given the amount of time required to set up an Integration Test, if time permits, rerun it after the plans have been corrected.

◆ The support team (network, database, systems administrators) remains close at hand to address problems after the applications recovery begins.

➤ Prepare for the test.

◆ Set up a network that is isolated from the world since some applications may have embedded IP addressing.

➤ Conduct the test.

◆ Set up the infrastructure.

● Set up required infrastructure, such as DNS and domain controllers.

● Load a basic operating system on the recovered servers.

● Provide adequate servers and disk storage space.

◆ Using the recovery plans, follow each step.

◆ Note all corrections.

◆ Using these corrections, restart the test from the beginning.

◆ Once the system is ready:

  ● Applications support runs test scripts to ensure the system has been properly recovered.

  ● A business process owner validates that it appears to function correctly.

➤ Review the results.

  ◆ Update any plans as required.

  ◆ Determine a realistic recovery time for this process.

➤ Conduct the after-action review.

  ◆ Identify plan improvement needs.

  ◆ Identify areas to research to reduce the recovery time.

  ◆ Identify improvements in the testing process.

➤ Business Continuity Manager writes a report of test results to the program sponsor.

➤ Set time for review of changes.

FOLLOW UP Collect all plan corrections and reissue updated documents. If a plan required significant changes, then it should be reviewed in a Standalone Test before using it in another Integration test.

Just as recovery plans are exercised, so is your ability to plan and conduct a test. After the plans are updated, ask the participants to review the planning and testing processes for ways to improve them.

Walk-Through Testing

The purpose of a Walk-Through Test is to test a logical grouping of recovery plans at one time. It is similar to an Integration test except that no equipment is involved and the recovery is theoretical. A Walk-Through recovery plan exercise familiarizes recovery team members with their roles. It is useful for rehearsing for an Integration test, for testing when an Integration test is not practical, and for reviewing business process recovery plans.

Integration testing is valuable since it involves an actual recovery. A Walk-Through also provides many benefits, but without the expense of actually using equipment.

Walk-Through recovery plan testing is conducted in a conference room. Participants explain their actions as they read through the recovery plan. The goals are to improve plan clarity, to identify gaps in the plans, and to ensure that all interfaces among individual plans are addressed. These interfaces may be the passing of data from one IT component to another or the passing of a document between workers.

A Walk-Through Test does not provide a real RTO for the collective plans. However, estimates may be provided by the recovery team members.

PREPARATION Schedule time in a conference room.

TESTING TEAM The testing team should consist of the following people:
➤ Backup support person(s) for each plan to be recovered.
➤ Exercise Coordinator (IT Manager or Business Continuity Manager).
➤ Business process owner.
➤ Exercise recorder to capture action, decisions, and assumptions as they occur.

MATERIALS TO PROVIDE Include copies of the recovery plans to be tested.

THE TEST PROGRAM The program should include the following:
➤ Conduct the test, following the recovery plans.
  ◆ Set up the infrastructure.
    ● Set up required infrastructure, such as DNS and domain controllers.
    ● Load a basic operating system on the recovered servers.
    ● Provide adequate servers and disk storage space.
  ◆ Note all corrections.
➤ Review the results.
  ◆ Update plans as required.
  ◆ Team members are now more familiar with their recovery roles.
➤ Conduct the after-action review.
  ◆ Identify plan improvement.
  ◆ Identify areas to research to reduce the recovery time.
  ◆ Identify improvements in the testing process.
➤ Business Continuity Manager writes report of test result to program sponsor.
➤ Set time for review of changes.

FOLLOW UP Collect all plan corrections and reissue updated documents. If a plan requires significant changes, then it should be reviewed in a Standalone Test before using it in another Walk-Through exercise.

Simulations

Up to this point, all tests have been based on recovering a business process or IT system from scratch. The reasoning is that if the plan has adequate information to recover from nothing, then it will have the information necessary to recover from a partial failure. However, it is this partial failure that is more common.

A simulation test brings all of the plans together. In a real crisis, rarely is the recovery isolated to a single plan. IT systems recover the data center, work area recovery plans recover office processes, and the supporting plans for Human Resources, Corporate Communications, Facilities, Security, and a range of other departments are all in play. A simulation not only invokes these many plans but forces them to work together toward the common goal.

A simulation test begins with a scenario (such as a partial roof collapse from a severe storm or a person entering the building with a gun). In both of these examples, most of the facility is intact yet may be temporarily disabled.

Simulation adds to plan exercises the elements of uncertainty, time pressure, and chaos. No situation comes with complete and verified information, yet managers must react correctly to minimize damage to the company. Chaos comes from inaccurate and incomplete information yet decisions must be made. Unlike the smooth pace of a Walk-Through Test, simulations add to the element of chaos in which events surge forward whether someone is ready for it or not.

Simulation tests can be simplistic, such as Table-Top exercises. They can also be complex (and expensive), such as relocating the entire data center or work area to the recovery site and running the business from there. Most simulations only address a portion of the company, usually a group of related business processes. This keeps the recovery team to a manageable size and the recovery exercise focused on a set of plans.

Make it fun! Send out pre-exercise announcements as if they were news elements related to the scenario (clearly marked as exercise notices for training only). At the beginning of the exercise, state the goals to instill a sense of purpose in the group. At the end of the exercise, restate the goals and ask the group how well it measured up. After all, these people gave up some hours of their lives, so show them how important it was to the company!

Simulations can also add the dimension of external agencies to the recovery. Firefighters, reporters, police officers, and other emergency groups can be invited to keep the chaos lively while educating participants of each agency's role in a crisis. The Exercise Coordinator may also include employees at other company sites via conference call.

The purpose of the exercise is to validate that the plans are workable and flexible enough to meet any challenge. Participants will depend on the plan to identify actions to take during an incident. (However, just as in a real crisis, they are free to deviate from them.) Notes will be collected, and the plan will be updated as a result of the exercise. Participants will note areas for improvement such as corrections, clarity, content, and additional information.

There is no "right" answer to these exercises. The goal is to debug the plans and seek ways to make them more efficient without losing their flexibility (since we never know what sorts of things will arise). "Rigging the test" to ensure success should not be done. Conducting the exercise at the recovery site will minimize distractions from electronic interruptions.

About one week before the exercise, verify that participants or their alternates are available. This is also a good time to rehearse the exercise with the testing team and to handle minor administrative tasks such as making copies of plan and tent cards identifying participants and their roles.

People will react in different ways. If someone on the team will be declared injured or killed during the exercise, ensure that they agree to this prior to the start of the exercise.

Table-Top Testing

A Table-Top Test is a simulated emergency without the equipment. It exercises decision making: analysis, communication, and collaboration are all part of the plan. Table-Top exercises test an incident management plan using a minimum of resources. The size of the incident is not important. It is the fog within which early decisions must be made until the situation becomes clearer.

A Table-Top exercise tests a logical grouping of recovery plans with a realistic disaster scenario. One or more conference rooms are used to control the recovery. The primary difference between a Walk-Through Test and a Table-Top Test is that a Table-Top Test uses a scenario, midexercise problem injections, and, often, external resources.

A Table-Top exercise is much less disruptive to a business than a full simulation. A Table-Top exercise typically runs for a half day, where a full simulation can run for several days.

The goals are to train the team members, identify omissions in the plans, and raise awareness of the many dimensions of recovery planning. Each participant uses the recovery plan for guidance but is free to choose alternative actions to restore service promptly. The goals are to improve plan clarity, to identify gaps in the plans, and to ensure that all interfaces between individual plans are addressed. These interfaces may be the passing of data from IT component to another or the passing of a document between workers.

A Table-Top Test does not provide a real RTO for the collective plans. However, estimates may be provided by the recovery team members.

The exercise coordinator keeps the group focused on the test. It works best if someone else is designated as the exercise recorder. The recorder writes down the events, decisions, and reactions during the exercise, freeing the exercise coordinator to work with the team. These notes are valuable later when considering ways to improve the recovery plans and the Table-Top exercise process.

PREPARATION Schedule a conference room.

TESTING TEAM The testing team should consist of the following people:
➤ Backup support person(s) for each plan to be recovered.
➤ Exercise Coordinator (IT Manager or Business Continuity Manager).
➤ Exercise recorder.
➤ Business process owners.
➤ External resources, such as news reporters, firefighters or police officers.

MATERIALS TO PROVIDE Materials to provide include:
➤ Copies of the recovery plans to be tested.
➤ Scenario and incident "injects."
➤ A clock projected by a PC onto a whiteboard.

THE TEST PROGRAM The program should include the following:
➤ Explain to participants the rules for the exercise:
◆ Time is essential; decisions must be made with incomplete information.
◆ Everyone must help someone if asked.
◆ Everyone takes notes for the after-action critique.
◆ No outside interruptions are permitted—cell phones off.
◆ If an issue is bogging down the exercise, the Exercise Coordinator can announce a decision for the issue or set it aside for future discussion.
➤ Introduce each of the team members and explain their role in the recovery.
➤ State the exercise goals (familiarize the team with the plan, gather RTO data, improve the plans, etc.).
➤ Introduce the scenario to the team.
◆ Clarify group questions about the situation.
◆ Ensure everyone has a copies of the appropriate plans.

➤ Conduct the exercise.

   ◆ Select several of the primary recovery team members to step out of the exercise; their backup person must continue the recovery.

   ◆ Inject additional information and complexity into the exercise every 10 minutes.

   ◆ End the exercise at a predetermined time, or when the company is restored to full service.

➤ Conduct the after-action review.

   ◆ Identify plan improvements.

   ◆ Identify areas to research to reduce the recovery time.

   ◆ Identify improvements in the testing process.

➤ Business Continuity Manager submits a written report of the test result to the program sponsor.

FOLLOW UP Collect all plan corrections and reissue updated documents.

Two types of plans are best tested as Table-Top exercises. A crisis management plan is easily tested in a conference room. The types of actions required can be discussed rather than acted out. A pandemic can range over 18 months, so a full simulation is not practical. Both can be conducted in the Command Center for additional realism.

Disaster Simulation

The purpose of a Disaster Simulation is to test a logical grouping of recovery plans with a realistic scenario. Essentially, a Disaster Simulation is a simulated emergency that includes the people and equipment necessary to recover IT equipment or a wide range of business processes. Running a simulation is expensive in time and equipment, so it should be approved far in advance. A simulation may be disruptive to a company's normal business and should be planned for the company's slow time of the year. It may run for several days.

The goals are to train the team members, identify omissions in the plans, and to raise awareness of the many dimensions of recovery planning. A key advantage of a simulation is that it provides the actual time required to recover a process. It also adds in the pressure of chaos to the recovery.

The Exercise Coordinator keeps the group focused on the test. Appoint an exercise recorder for each recovery team. That person writes down the events, decisions, and reactions during the exercise. These notes are valuable later when considering ways to improve the recovery plans and the exercise process.

Always preannounce a simulation; there should be no surprise alerts. Before engaging outside participants, the DR core team should perform the simulation exercise, as a dress rehearsal to "polish" the sequence of events.

Real tests provide the most realistic results. Avoid the temptation of the IT team to make a "special" set of backup media just for the test. The true recovery time comes from sifting through the many backup tapes to find the files that you need.

A simulation begins with the initial incident alert by the night watchman or by an alarm that automatically alerts a manager. Full-scale testing involves pulling the plug on some part of the operation and letting the disaster recovery plan kick in. For obvious reasons, this is rarely done.

Simulation tests should be conducted at the recovery site at least once per year. Recovery plans are used as guidelines, but participants are free to deviate from them. The goals are to improve plan clarity, to identify gaps in the plans, and to ensure that all interfaces between individual plans are addressed. These interfaces may be the passing of data from one IT component to another or the passing of a document between workers.

PREPARATION Schedule a conference room. Ensure the participants understand the exercise is a rehearsal and not a test. A rehearsal allows people to play out their actions; a test implies pass or fail. For each recovery team:

➤ Create a log sheet to document the communication among recovery teams (see Form 13-1 on the CD).

➤ Create an observation log (see Form 13-2 on the CD).

TESTING TEAM The testing team should consist of the following people:

➤ Backup support person(s) for each plan to be recovered.

➤ Exercise Coordinator (IT Manager or Business Continuity Manager).

➤ Business process owners.

➤ Exercise recorder.

➤ External resources, such as news reporters, firefighters or police officers.

MATERIALS TO PROVIDE Materials to provide include:

➤ Copies of the recovery plans to be tested.

➤ Scenario and incident "injects."

➤ A clock projected by a PC onto a whiteboard.

Task Name	Duration	Start	Finish	Processors	Resource Names
Hour-by-Hour Recovery Schedule	0 hrs	8:00	8:00		
Arrive at hot site facility	0.13 days	8:00	9:00		
Arrive at hot site	0 hrs	8:00	8:00		Recovery Team
Meet with site management	1 hr	8:00	9:00		Recovery Team
Organize materials	1 hr	8:00	9:00		Recovery Team
Server hardware review	0.13 days	9:00	10:00		
Review Unix servers	1 hr	9:00	10:00	4,5	UNIX Admin A
Review Windows servers	1 hr	9:00	10:00	4,5	Windows Admin A
Review network equipment	1 hr	9:00	10:00	4,5	Networking Tech A
Network configuration	1 day	8:00	17:00		
LAN recovery	1 day	8:00	17:00		Networking Tech A
Partial LAN recovery (within hot site)	2 hrs	8:00	10:00		
Complete LAN recovery (hot site and work area site)	6 hrs	10:00	17:00	12	
Configure Internet and create public DMZ	12 hrs	8:00	12:00	11	Networking Tech A
VPN remote access restore	0.38 days	8:00	11:00	10	
Restore VPN concentrator	0.38 days	8:00	11:00		Networking Tech B
Restore radius services	1 hr	8:00	9:00		Networking Tech B
VPN remote access restore complete	0 hrs	11:00	11:00	15	Networking Tech B
WAN (hot site to work area) restore	8 hrs	8:00	17:00		Networking Tech B
Domain controller/active directory replication	0.56 days	10:00	15:30		
Install OS	2 hrs	10:00	12:00	8	Windows Admin A
Replicate active directory with alternate facility	1 hr	13:00	14:00	12,21,33	Windows Admin A
Seize FISMO roles	1 hr	14:00	15:00	22	Windows Admin A
Test connectivity	0.5 hrs	15:00	15:30	23	Windows Admin A

FIGURE 13-2: RTO Hour-by-Hour Recovery Plan for a Data Center.

THE TEST PROGRAM The program should include the following:

➤ Explain to participants the rules for the exercise:

  ◆ Time is essential; decisions must be made with incomplete information.

  ◆ Everyone must help someone if asked.

  ◆ Everyone should take notes for the after-action critique.

  ◆ No outside interruptions are permitted—cell phones off.

  ◆ If an issue is bogging down the exercise, the exercise coordinator can announce a decision for the issue or can set it aside for future discussion.

➤ Introduce each of the team members and explain their role in the recovery.

➤ Introduce the scenario to the team.

  ◆ Clarify group questions about the situation.

➤ Conduct the exercise.

  ◆ Select several of the primary recovery team members to step out; their backup person must continue the recovery.

  ◆ Inject additional information and complexity into the exercise every 10 minutes.

  ◆ End the exercise at a predetermined time, or when the company is restored to full service.

➤ Conduct the after-action review.

  ◆ Identify plan improvements.

  ◆ Identify areas to research to reduce the recovery time.

  ◆ Identify improvements in the testing process.

  ◆ Collect RTO metrics.

➤ The Business Continuity Manager gives a report of the test result to program sponsor.

➤ Set time for review of changes.

FOLLOW UP Collect all plan corrections and reissue updated documents. If a plan required significant changes, then it should be reviewed in a Standalone Test before using it in another Integration test. In addition, update the RTO Hour-by-Hour Recovery Plan.

SOMETIMES NATURE TESTS THE PLANS FOR YOU

There are numerous incidents that pop up from time to time that are not significant emergencies but that provide an opportunity to test parts of a plan. For example, if there is a power outage at work, use the plans to minimize the disruption. Do the same for a loss of data communications, a tornado warning, or a snow storm emergency. Relocating a business process or significant portion of the data center is similar to a disaster.

Another opportunity that can trigger a test plan is facility construction. An example of this is if the electricity to a building must be turned off for work on the power main. Use the recovery plans to locate and turn off all of the equipment, noting anything found that was not in the plan. When the work is over, use the plans to turn back on all of the equipment. Then test each critical system to ensure it is operational. Following the plans for restarting equipment may uncover equipment tucked away in offices or closets that are not in the plan.

Relocation to a new facility is a great opportunity to completely test your disaster recovery plan. Many of the activities necessary during relocation are the same as those required in a disaster: new machines may need to be purchased, servers are down for some period of time, new communications infrastructure needs to be built, data need to be restored, etc. In fact, if a relocation project is not done properly, it may turn into a real disaster!

Whenever such a problem occurs:

➤ Focus people on referring to their recovery plans. The value of a plan is to reduce chaos at the beginning of a crisis. Plans are no good if no one uses them.

➤ Begin recording what has occurred and people's reaction to it. These notes are used to improve our plans (and never to criticize anyone).

➤ Conduct an after-action review the next day to gather everyone's perspective.

➤ A plan that is used for a real event has been tested just as surely as a scheduled exercise. Mark that plan as tested for the quarter!

Whenever a significantly disruptive incident occurs, such as a power outage, loss of external network, or a computer virus outbreak, begin taking notes during the event. These notes should be a narrative of times and actions taken—who did what, when, and the result. See if anyone thought to break out the appropriate recovery plans and follow them.

Within two working days after the incident, convene a group to conduct an after-action review. This review is intended to capture everyone's perspective of the incident to improve plans for future use.

Debriefing Participants Using an After-Action Review

Whenever an incident occurs (such as a power outage, fire in the computer room, etc.) that is covered by a recovery plan (or should have been covered by a plan), conduct an after-action review on the next work day after the recovery. This is an open discussion of the event and how to improve future reaction.

Someone is appointed as the review coordinator (usually the Business Continuity Manager). It is helpful if someone else records the discussions, so that the review coordinator is free to focus on the discussion.

What happened – it is important to gain agreement on what occurred, as further discussion is based on this. Each person will define the problem from his or her own perspective. Sometimes agreement on a point takes a lot of discussion.

What should have happened – this is where positive things are listed, such as the recovery plan was easy to find, etc.

What went well – not all is doom and gloom. Now that the crisis has ended, take credit for the things that went well. Acknowledge those people who contributed to the recovery.

What did not go well – this is the substance of the review. Once you list what did not work out, you can move to the last step. Take care never to personalize the discussions. Focus on the action and not on a person. Otherwise, people become defensive and no one will participate in the discussion.

What will be done differently in the future – list the solution to each item identified in the previous step. Assign action items to specific people each with a due date.

An example after-action report for a power outage:

What happened – The power for the building went out and everyone stopped working. The office people flooded out to the factory because there was light there through the windows. People milled around outside of the data center to see if they could help. The emergency lights failed in most of the offices and everyone was in the dark.

What should have happened – The emergency lights should have worked. Everyone should have known where to meet for further instructions.

What went well – Nobody panicked. The UPS system kept the data center running until power was restored.

What did not go well – No one knew what to do. Different people were shouting out different directions, trying to help but really confusing everyone. We could not find the system administrators in case the servers needed to be turned off.

What will be done differently in the future – We will identify assembly areas for everyone. Supervisors will be responsible for finding out what has occurred and passing it on to their people. The emergency lights will be checked monthly.

DEMONSTRATING RTO CAPABILITY

During the Business Impact Analysis, an RTO was established by the company. It was selected based on the impact to the company, not on what the company was capable of doing. Testing recovery plans and recording the time is the place where the company proves it can meet the RTO. If not, something must change to meet it.

Some RTOs are obvious. A company that expects to recover from tape backup requires days. If the organization requires recovery in a few hours, then stop the testing and rework the data storage strategy. However, if a company has a reasonable strategy based on its RTO, then only testing can prove if this is achievable or not.

Figure 13-2 shows the first page of a possible RTO Hour-by-Hour Recovery Plan for a data center. (A similar chart should be built for work area recovery.) This chart collects the recovery times from plan exercises. In the IT world, most recoveries must wait until the basic infrastructure is in place (network, firewalls, DNS, domain controllers, etc.). The plan for recovering each infrastructure component is placed in sequence at the top of the chart. Below that are the applications, databases, etc., that must be recovered in the appropriate sequence. For example, a LAN recovery must be in place before the domain controller can be recovered.

Use this basic plan as an outline for building your own recovery timeline. As you enter the times from actual system recoveries, you can prove or disprove the company's ability to meet its desired RTO. Actual recovery times are always preferred to estimated values.

If the RTO is not achievable or if you wish to shorten it, use this plan to identify places to make changes. Look for tasks that could run in parallel instead of sequentially. Look for the ones that take a long time and seek ways to shorten them (use faster technology or redesign the process). Of course, the best way to reduce the time required is to eliminate noncritical steps.

During a recovery, company executives can use the RTO Hour-by-Hour Recovery Plan to follow along with the recovery's progress. Based on where the team is in the recovery, they can look at the times and see how much longer before (for example) the e-mail system should be available, or that the billing system should be operational.

CONCLUSION

No plan can be called complete until it has been tested. Beyond the initial testing, ongoing testing is critical to ensure that the plan is kept up to date. As the organization grows and evolves, the plan must be updated to incorporate the necessary changes. Periodic testing validates these changes and keeps everyone aware of their responsibilities when a disaster strikes.

There are different types of tests from simple one-on-one Standalone Tests to full simulated disasters. Tests should follow a progression from simple tests to complex. Trying to jump too quickly into simulations will result in people sitting around while muddled plans are worked through. Participants will conclude that the tests themselves are the disaster.

The people participating in the tests are a valuable source of information. After each exercise, promptly gather their ideas in an after-action meeting. They should advise the Exercise Coordinator of ways to improve the plans, communications among the testing teams, and everything that can speed a recovery. In a separate meeting, ask them to critique the testing process. This will improve their participation and cooperation in the future, as well as make your tests run smoother.

There are times when company activities or Mother Nature tests your plans for you. Immediately focus everyone on using their plans. After the event has passed, pull everyone together for an after-action meeting to collect their ideas. (This is also a great time to slip in a plug for the value of plans when disaster strikes.)

The outcome of each test should be used to update an RTO Hour-by-Hour Recovery Plan. It is one thing for a company to declare an RTO but that chart illustrates whether it is likely or not.

CHAPTER 14

ELECTRICAL SERVICE
Keeping the Juice Flowing

Nothing shocks me. I'm a scientist.
—Harrison Ford, as Indiana Jones

INTRODUCTION

This chapter is provided so you will have a basic understanding of electrical power support for your critical equipment. Use the information as a background when talking to your facility electrical engineer and your UPS supplier. While you'll not want to work on high-voltage circuits or equipment yourself (leave that to trained professionals), an overall knowledge of how your electrical systems work will help you to write a better plan.

ELECTRICAL SERVICE

Imagine a business in which if you create too much product it is immediately lost forever. A business where people only pay for what they use, but demand that all they want be instantly available at any time. A product they use in varying amounts throughout the day. A product that requires an immense capital investment but is sold in pennies per unit. Welcome to the world of electricity. Electrical service is so reliable, so common, that people take it for granted that it will always be there whenever they want it. Electricity is an essential part of our everyday existence. Few businesses could run for a single minute without it.

Side-stepping the issue of the huge effort of the electric company to ensure uninterrupted service, let's consider the impact of electricity on our business. Without a reliable, clean source of electric power, all business stops. We have all experienced an electrical blackout at some point. When we add together how important electricity is and that we believe a blackout is likely to occur again, we meet all the criteria for requiring a disaster recovery plan. Because we cannot do without it and there are economically feasible disaster containment steps we can take, a mitigation plan must also be drafted.

In addition to recovering from an outage, our mitigation plan will reduce the likelihood of losing power to critical machinery. There are many other problems with electrical power beyond whether we have it or not. Therefore our mitigation plan must address ensuring a clean as well as a reliable electrical supply.

In the case of electricity, we need a process that:

➤ Monitors the line and filters out spikes.

➤ Provides additional power in case of a brownout or partial outage.

➤ Provides sufficient temporary power in case of a total outage.

➤ Makes the transition from normal power supply to emergency power supply without loss of service to critical devices.

Whatever power support plan you select, keep in mind that it must be tested periodically. With luck, you will be able to schedule the tests so that a power failure will have minimal impact. With a touch of bad luck, nature will schedule the power outages for you and, again, at that time you will know how well your power support plan works.

RISK ASSESSMENT

What sorts of problems are we protecting against? In an ideal situation, North American electricity is provided at 120 volts, 60 cycles per second, alternating current. If we viewed this on an oscilloscope, the 60 cycles would display a sine wave. There are many variations from "normal" that will play havoc with your reliable power connection.

The most common electrical power problem is *voltage sag,* or what is more commonly known as a "brownout." Generally speaking, this is a reduced voltage on the power line; you can see a brownout when the room lights dim. They can cause some computer systems to fail and occasional hardware damage by forcing equipment power supplies to work harder just to function.

Sags can be caused by turning on power-hungry equipment. As they begin operation, these power hogs draw the amount of electricity they need to run from the power grid. This sudden electrical load causes a momentary dip in the line voltage until the electric company compensates for it. These power drains might be anything from heavy machinery to the heater under the desk next door. Most sags are of short duration.

Brownouts can also be caused by utility companies switching between power sources and, in some situations, it can be an intentional voltage drop by the electrical company to cope with peak load conditions. An example is the summer of 2001 power crisis in California with its rolling brownouts when the electrical utility company could not meet peak demand. The demand for electrical power is growing, but the supply of electricity is not.

Once a voltage sag ends, there is typically a corresponding "spike" of "overvoltage" that can further damage equipment. Sharp or extended overvoltages can severely damage your electronic systems, which are not designed to receive and handle large voltage variations.

Another common electrical power problem is a *voltage surge,* which is a short-term substantial increase in voltage caused by a rapid drop in power requirements. A typical surge lasts for 3 nanoseconds or more (anything less is known as a spike). Surges are caused by major power users being switched off. For that brief moment, the power available for that item is still being supplied but is no longer needed and must be absorbed by other devices on that line. Examples of large users that may be switched off are factory equipment, air conditioners, and laser printers.

Surges frequently occur and usually go unnoticed. Some can be handled by the equipment's power supply, some must be absorbed by a surge protector, and the rare major surge will wipe out anything in its path. A common example of a major power surge is a lightning strike that surges down power and telephone lines into nearby equipment.

Noise is seen as jitters riding along on the 60-cycle sine wave. It is electrical impulses carried along with the standard current. Noise is created by turning on electrical devices, such as a laser printer, an electrical appliance in your home, or even fluorescent lights. Did you ever see "snow" on your television screen when using an electrical appliance? That is an example of line noise sent back into your electrical system. What you see on the screen is electrical noise riding on your local wiring that is too powerful for your television to filter out.

Noise is one source of irritating PC problems, such as keyboard lockups, program freezes, data corruption, and data transfer errors. It can damage your hard drives and increase audio distortion levels. The worse part of the problem is that in many cases you aren't even aware of what is happening when it occurs.

Voltage spikes are an instantaneous increase in line voltage that is also known as a "transient." A spike may be caused by a direct lightning strike or from the return of power after a blackout. Think of a spike as a short-duration surge that lasts for 2 nanoseconds or less. Spikes can be very destructive by corrupting data and locking up computer systems. If the spike hitting the device is intense, there can be significant hardware damage.

An *electrical blackout* is a total failure of electrical power. It is any voltage drop to below 80 volts since, at that point, most electrical devices cease to function. Blackouts have a wide range of causes from severe weather to auto accidents to electrical service equipment failures.

A blackout immediately shuts down your equipment, and it is time consuming to restart most machinery from a "hard stop." Even though most blackouts are of a very short duration, from a business perspective a momentary blackout can be just as serious as a 2-hour outage. In addition, some equipment may not have been turned off for years—and for good reason. There may be some doubt as to whether it will even start again!

Blackouts are very damaging to computer systems. Anything residing in memory, whether it is a spreadsheet or a server's cache, is immediately lost. Multiply this across the number of people working in a single building, and you can see the lost time just for one occurrence. Compounding the data loss is the damage and weakening of your equipment. A further issue is that, from a recovery perspective, there may be network devices working out of sight in a closet deep within the building. If you don't know these exist or where to find them, just the process of restarting equipment can be very troublesome.

When recovering from blackouts, beware of the corresponding power surge that accompanies the restoration of system power. So when a blackout strikes, turn off your equipment and do not restart it until a few minutes after power is stabilized.

YOUR BUILDING'S POWER SYSTEM

Many years ago, your company's delicate data processing equipment was concentrated in the facility's data processing center. Often one whole wall was made of glass so everyone could see this technical marvel in action (hence the term "glass house" for computer rooms). This concentration allowed the equipment to be supported by a few Uninterruptible Power Supply (UPS) units and power line conditioning devices.

Now, the primary computing muscle for most companies is spread all over the facility in the form of PCs and departmental servers. Instead of a carefully conditioned and electrically isolated power feed, your equipment shares the same power circuits as soda pop machines, copiers, and factory machinery—all of which add noise and surges to the power line. None of this is good for your computer systems and network devices!

This variety of computing power creates a need to monitor electrical service to ensure maximum network and computer capabilities. The emphasis is on network because while personal computers are located comfortably on office desktops, network hubs, routers, and bridges can be found stuffed in any closet, rafter, or crawl space, or under a raised floor. This makes the automatic monitoring of electrical service across your facility an important network management function.

Filtering the electricity as it enters your building is a good practice to minimize external influences. Sometimes, however, the problems are caused by equipment inside your building; this might be arc welders, heavy machinery, etc.

BUILDING A POWER PROTECTION STRATEGY

Power protection for business continuity is a five-step process.

1. The first step is to isolate all your electronic equipment from power surges by use of small surge protectors. Power surges sometimes occur internal to your building. Surge strips are inexpensive and simple to install.

2. The next layer is line conditioning. A line conditioner smoothes out voltage variation by blocking high voltages and boosting the line voltage during brownouts. This filtering should always be applied to the power line before electricity is passed to your UPS.

3. An Uninterruptible Power Supply provides electrical power for a limited time during the event of a power outage. The UPS battery system can also help to protect against brownouts by boosting low voltages. A UPS is a critical device for ensuring that key components do not suddenly lose electrical power.

4. One of the best solutions for companies that cannot tolerate even small power outages is an onsite electric generator. These backup units instantly start and begin generating electricity to support your facility. Imagine a hospital's liability if all their life support equipment suddenly stopped from a lack of power. This added security is not cheap to install or maintain. Keep in mind that electrical generators of this sort are internal combustion engines and must conform to local air pollution and building regulations.

5. The last step, not directly related to electricity, is the physical security of the electrical support equipment. Few people require access to this equipment, and it must be safeguarded against sabotage. This equipment is unique in that if someone disabled it, the entire facility could stop with lost production quickly running into the thousands of dollars per minute. Additionally, the "hard stop" on machinery and computer servers will result in lost or corrupt data files.

However you secure this equipment, keep in mind the cooling and service clearance requirements for the UPS system. The UPS control panel must also be available to the disaster containment team in a crisis.

Surge Protection

One of the most common electrical protection devices is a surge protector power strip. Computer stores sell these by the bushel. For your dispersed equipment, a surge protector can provide some measure of inexpensive protection. A typical surge protector contains circuitry that suppresses electrical surges and spikes. All electronic devices should be attached to electrical power through a surge strip to include all your PCs, network equipment, printers, and even the television used for demonstrations in the conference room. Even if your facility's power is filtered as it enters the building, a direct lightning strike can ride the wires inside the building and still fry your equipment.

There are many brands of surge suppressors on the market. There are places to save money and places to lose money. The old saying goes "for want of a nail, the battle was lost." When protecting your equipment from power problems, you may not want to skimp too much. Here are some things to look for when buying a surge strip:

➤ **Joule Ratings.** A joule rating is a measure of a surge protector's ability to absorb power surges. A joule is a unit of energy equal to the work done by a force of 1 Newton through a distance of 1 meter. Generally, the higher the rating the better. A good surge suppressor will absorb between 200 and 400 joules. If greater protection is needed, look for a surge suppressor rated at least 600 joules.

➤ **Surge Amp Ratings.** The amount of above-normal amps the surge protector can absorb. As with joules, the higher the better.

➤ **UL 1449 Voltage Let-Through Ratings.** Underwriters Laboratories™ tests to determine how much of a surge is passed by the surge protector on to the equipment it is protecting. The best rating is 330 volts. Any voltage rating less than 330 adds no real benefit. Other ratings of lesser protection are 400 and 500. Be aware that UL 1449 safety testing does not test for endurance.

➤ **Response Time.** The response time of the surge protector is important. If it blocks high voltages but is slow to react, then it is of marginal usefulness. Adequate response time is 10 nanoseconds or less. The lower the number, the better.

➤ **All-Wire Protection.** A high-quality surge protector guards against surges on the ground wire, as well as the current-carrying wires.

➤ **Telephone Line Support.** To protect your modem from power surges riding on the telephone wire.

➤ **Clamping Voltage.** The voltage at which the surge suppressor begins to work. The lower the rating, the better. Look for a rating of 400 volts or less.

Some surge protectors provide basic line conditioning against noise on the line. This circuitry can smooth out minor noise from the lines.

An interesting thing about the ubiquitous surge protector strips is that in addition to protecting equipment, they make handy extension cords. Over time, these surge strips may silently have absorbed any number of electrical "attacks" that have eroded or destroyed their ability to protect your equipment. Most people cannot see this because they still function quite nicely as extension cords.

Surge protectors often have lights to tell you when they are energized or not. High-quality surge protectors will have an additional light to let you know if their surge-fighting days are over. This light may say something like "protected," "surge protection present," etc. If your surge protector has such a light and it is no longer lit when running, then you may have a false sense of security that it is functioning as something other than an extension cord, because that is all it now is!

People traveling around the country using a notebook computer would be well advised to carry and use high-quality surge protectors when plugging their equipment into the local power grid. When you consider how big a typical surge suppressor is and how tiny notebook PCs have become, you can guess at how little room there is for surge suppression circuits in the notebook PC chassis. This is especially important for international travelers, as the power in some countries is a bit rougher than it is in the United States.

A few more things to consider when using surge protectors. As great a tool as they are, they cannot stop a nearby lightning strike from damaging your equipment. When a lightning storm approaches, unplug both the power strip and your network cable from the wall. (This is good advice for any sensitive electronic equipment that depends solely on a surge protector to defend against lightning.)

Also, never use a ground eliminator with a surge strip (a ground eliminator converts a three-prong plug into a two-prong plug for use in an older building). Doing so will make it difficult if not impossible for your surge protector to resist a major line surge.

Line Conditioning

Line conditioning ensures that your equipment always receives the same steady voltage. It also screens out noise on the power waveform. Line conditioning involves passing your normal electrical service through filtering circuitry before it is used. Many people don't realize that the "old reliable" electricity that magically comes out of the walls is susceptible to a wide range of influences. These influences take the "pure" 60-cycle alternating current and introduces fluctuations in the voltage or current as it passes down the line.

These fluctuations can have many sources but one that we especially want to avoid is lightning. Lightning can cause a localized one-shot power surge to roar down the electrical line into your equipment. When this happens, equipment power supplies and integrated circuits can quickly melt.

Line conditioning is also advised for analog telephone lines connected to PC modems. The same lightning strike that induces an electrical charge in your electrical power lines can throw a jolt down your telephone line. Unfortunately, PC modems have little protection against a power surge, and they are very easily destroyed. Many surge suppressors now include a telephone line surge suppression jack to filter these problems out.

A line conditioner should always be installed between a UPS and the electrical power source to reduce the load on the UPS batteries. Some UPS units include a line filtering capability. Check your model to see what it is capable of doing. A line conditioner reduces the number of times that the UPS jumps on and off of battery power (which shortens the life of your batteries).

A line conditioner is an essential component when generating your own emergency power. Use it to filter the electricity provided by the generator before it is passed on to delicate computer hardware. The power delivered by a generator is not as clean as that normally delivered by the power company.

Uninterruptible Power Supplies

An Uninterruptible Power Supply provides several essential services and is best used in conjunction with surge protection and line conditioning equipment. A UPS can help to smooth out noisy power sources and provide continuous power during electrical sags. Its primary benefit is to provide temporary electrical power during a blackout. Depending on the model, it may also provide some measure of line conditioning protection.

Uninterruptible Power Supplies come in three basic types, based on their features.

1. The basic UPS is a "standby" UPS. A standby UPS provides battery backup against power outages (blackouts and brownouts) and a modest amount of battery-powered voltage correction.

2. The "line interactive" UPS is a step above the basic unit. It provides voltage regulation as well as battery backup by switching to battery power when line voltages move beyond preset limits. This type of UPS converts a small trickle of electricity to charge its batteries at all times. When power fails, the line interactive UPS detects the power loss and switches itself on. A line interactive UPS has a subsecond switching time from line power to battery power.

3. The third type of UPS is an "online" UPS that sits directly between line power and your equipment. The online UPS is always providing power to your electric circuits and has a zero transfer time between the loss of line power and the start of battery power.

UPS BATTERIES UPS systems provide power during a blackout by drawing on their battery electrical supply system. Most of these batteries are sealed lead acid batteries. Unlike the batteries found in many notebook PCs, these batteries do not have a "memory" and should be completely drained as few times as possible. Depending on how often your UPS draws on its batteries, they should last up to 5 years. Remember that brownouts and short-duration blackouts all wear on the batteries, so if your local power fluctuates very much, the life of your batteries will be reduced. The speed at which your UPS batteries age is also determined by their environment. Extreme heat or cold are not good for your batteries. Refer to your manufacturer's guide for the recommended operating temperature range.

As batteries age, their power-generating capability will decrease. Therefore, regular preventative maintenance is important. Preventative maintenance should include changing the air filters to help keep the UPS unit cool. At that time, all the batteries should be checked for damage, leaks, or weak cells. You should also consider a service agreement that includes the replacement of damaged batteries.

UPS systems use "inverters" to convert the DC battery power to AC power. An inverter is electrical circuitry to change the direct current to alternating current. High-quality UPS systems use a dual inverter system for smoother power conversion.

UPS "SIZE" The first question people ask about UPS units is, "How big does it need to be?" This all depends on several things:

➤ What must be supported? This translates directly into how much electricity must be supplied at a given point in time.

➤ How many minutes must the battery pack provide this level of support?

➤ Is your area prone to power problems?

➤ Will this UPS be managed remotely through manufacturer-provided software?

UPS units are rated according to the number of volt-amps they can deliver. Volt-amps are different from watts and you cannot equate the volt-amps provided by a UPS with the watts used by an electronic device. Typical power factors (which is watts per volt-amp) for a workstation is 0.6 or 0.7. So if your PC records a drain of 250 watts, you need a UPS with a 417 volt-amp rating (for a 0.6 power factor). Always be careful to never overload a UPS beyond its rated capacity. Doing so will severely damage it.

Most UPS manufacturers have a software tool for estimating UPS sizes. Where possible, use their programs to size your UPS. In the absence of that tool:

1. Begin with a list of all equipment for which you will need to provide electricity. This may include personal computers, monitors, servers, critical printers, network hubs, and telecommunications equipment—whatever will be supported by the UPS.

2. Determine the wattage ratings on all these devices by checking their nameplates. The numbers may be expressed as watts. We need the numbers in volt-amps (VA) since that is a more accurate number for UPS sizing. Multiply the watts by 1.4 to get the volt-amps load.

3. If the power usage is provided in amps, then multiply that number by the line voltage (120 volts in North America and 230 volts for Europe) to get a volt-amp rating.

4. Total the volt-amp requirements for all the supported equipment.

This is the amount of load you need to support. From here you check with the manufacturer for the size of unit to support this load for the amount of time you select.

SWITCHING TO BATTERIES A UPS uses power line filters to address minor power disturbances, but its main weapon against a power loss or severe brownout is a near-instantaneous switch to battery power. This is good for keeping your systems alive but hard on the batteries. If your UPS must often switch to batteries because of poor power regulation in your area, then your battery life will suffer significantly. As the batteries rapidly age in this environment, they would not provide protection for the length of time you may be counting on from your UPS.

Recharging the batteries is another issue. Some UPS systems allow you to choose between a fast recharge or a slow recharge. The frequency and duration of outages in your area should determine if you must recharge your batteries as fast as possible or use a more gentle slow recharge process. Fast recharging puts a large drain on your restored power supply.

If you switch to generator power, you do not want the batteries to recharge from the generator as it might take away too much of the power needed elsewhere. If you plan to recharge the batteries from the generator, be sure that is included in the power load plan when sizing the generator, and that the batteries are on a slow recharge cycle.

UPS LOCATIONS If you have concentrated your data processing main computers and servers into one room, then selecting a location for your UPS will be easy. Electricians will run a separate electrical circuit from the UPS to the equipment to be protected. Electrical codes require these outlets to be a different color so you will know which circuit you are plugging into.

Some critical machinery and computers will be located away from the central computer room. For these devices, consider smaller UPS units located adjacent to the equipment. These units will not have a long battery life and will be used to keep the machine operational long enough to shut it down gracefully. Be sure not to lose sight of these satellite units as they will need to be tested and their batteries maintained over time. Remote monitoring software is ideal for this situation.

ADVANCED UPS FEATURES Modern UPS units offer much more than battery backup. They possess microprocessor logic to support a wide range of services. They can provide alarms of error conditions both on the unit and through your data network. This is a very useful feature since they are often stuck in some dark back room where an audible alarm only serves to annoy the mice.

The network signaling of power conditions is a very useful feature. Depending on the capabilities of your UPS and data systems, a UPS can start the orderly shutdown of equipment to protect it before the UPS batteries are exhausted. This feature is very useful over weekends and holidays when no one is around. In some cases, it can order a restart when power is restored. A more sophisticated UPS system stores a log of the power supply status for later analysis. Do you know how noisy your power lines are? Do you know the frequency and magnitude of sags and spikes that occur on your electrical power lines?

A UPS is a critical component of a data network. Remote monitoring software allows a network control analyst to monitor the status of each remote UPS and display the current line voltage and the voltage/current draw on the equipment. This helps to track which lines seem to have the most variation and potentially drive it back to a root cause in your facility. If some electrically driven machine in your facility is causing problems in your internal power grid, it needs to be identified and provided with better electrical isolation.

UPS TESTING It is great to have a UPS system set up and running, but it needs to be tested if there is to be a credible plan. So on a weekend in your slow time of the business cycle, you should plan for a UPS load test. This will demonstrate your power support system capabilities before a blackout strikes.

To set up the test, shut down the programs on all your computers but leave the computer running. The idea is to not lose any data but to still pull each system's normal electrical load. Bring in your UPS service technician to address issues during and after the test. Warn management you are going to do this. When all is in place, have an electrician cut the power to the UPS in that part of your facility and see what happens.

This test has several goals:

1. The first is to see what is not on the UPS that should be. Once the power is cut and the batteries are humming, you will see which server, computer, network device, etc., has been overlooked. Now look to see which low-value items are connected and wasting valuable emergency power.

2. Second, you need to know how well your UPS will support the load you have attached to it. If it is overloaded, you must plug some equipment into other power sources or get a bigger UPS unit.

3. When you shut down the servers' operating system, bring along a stopwatch and write down how long it takes. This will tell you the minimum amount of time the UPS must hold for you to perform orderly system shutdowns. If your servers are far apart in different rooms and the same person is expected to shut them all down, that may add travel time to the time you must allow on the UPS. Plan your time for the worst case.

4. Observe exactly what information the UPS displays about the remaining minutes of power given the current consumption rate. Compare this to the operator instructions you have provided to the after-hours support team. Be sure to also train the facility electricians on how to read the UPS display panel.

5. Exercise your power shedding plan while someone observes the impact on the UPS. How much additional time do you get for each level shut off?

POWER GENERATORS

If your facility absolutely must maintain its power supply in the face of any sort of electrical problem, then you will need your own electrical generation system. This is a large leap in complexity above UPS systems and takes extensive planning. There are some industries that quickly come to mind as requiring this level of support. Hospitals need it to support electronic medical equipment, food storage sites need it to prevent spoilage, and even Internet hosting providers need it to ensure maximum application availability to their customers.

On the other hand, it is kind of nice to switch from having a problem to being in control of it. A properly sized and installed electrical generation system can return some benefits in the form of keeping your company running while other companies cope with a rolling blackout, by the potential of selling electrical power back to the utility company, and by running your generator during peak electrical usage times thereby avoiding the highest cost electrical power.

Sizing Your Generator

Once you decide the need for maximum power availability, you begin with determining what it is you need to support. If it is everything within a building or an isolated part of a building, you could contract for an electrician to monitor the amount of electricity used in that building or part of the building and use that as a starting point for sizing your equipment. If the generator is only supporting one portion of the facility, you must have a way to isolate it from the rest of the structure.

Next, you need to know how long your generators must provide electricity. If you live in an area that experiences widespread natural disasters, such as floods, hurricanes, earthquakes, or blizzards, then you might want to allow for running this system for several days at a time. A good place to start here is to use your personal experience for the frequency and length of outages in your area to plan on system size. This will help to determine the size of your fuel storage system for running the generator.

Switching Time

Some industries, like hospitals, have a standard amount of time they can be without electrical service. Their generator must switch on automatically. However, mechanical engines take some time to start and run up to operating speed (ever start your car on a cold day?). Some of the fastest generators can automatically sense the loss of electrical power and start providing stand-by power in less than 10 seconds.

The question here is how long of a gap your company can tolerate. During this brief outage, UPS systems can maintain power to critical devices. Some equipment, like refrigerators, can tolerate a brief gap since they are already chilled down. Some equipment, like lights, can ever so briefly be out if supported by a backup emergency lighting system. So when deciding how long your company can function without electrical power, be very specific of what is needed and why.

The alternative is to always run generators together with pulling power from the power grid. As you can quickly discern, this is yet another step in complexity that distracts you from your core business. Rather than take this step, most companies settle for quick-switching generators supplemented with UPS support at critical points.

Generator Testing

More than any other power support system, the engines on your generators will take regular care. Begin by running them monthly to ensure they function on demand. Next, they need to be tested under load. This can be arranged for a weekend where everything they are to support is turned on and the electricity disconnected for a few hours from the power grid. Periodic testing under load is a critical component of your power backup system credibility.

During your testing, monitor the actual fuel consumption to generate a given unit of power. Fuel consumption is also a matter of air temperature (height of summer or the depths of winter). Aside from the manufacturer's claim, use this to determine how long your onsite fuel supply will last for delivering electricity.

Testing also exercises the people supporting your generators. By drilling them on their duties, they will be able to respond more quickly in a crisis. Be sure to rotate personnel to provide sufficient trained backup staff.

Working with Your Public Utility

Unlike a UPS or line conditioner, a generator has the potential to help pay for itself. During peak electrical usage periods, such as the depths of winter or the oppressive heat of summer, running your generators will reduce your draw on the community's power grid. Some utilities base their year-long electrical rates on the peak usage at any point over the year. By using your generators on these days, you contribute to the overall containment of electrical rates. And even then the units don't need to run all day, just during the peak usage hours of the day. If your generation capability is sufficient to run your entire company site, then the utility may call you and ask that you run your generators at those times to reduce peak usage.

Another aspect of running your own generators is the selling of power back to the power utility. This must be investigated with your local board of public utilities as to how much you would be paid and what conditions must be met. But if you are in an area of unreliable power, you might be able to address your own problems and cover some of your costs at the same time.

Environmental and Regulatory Issues

Like all good things, there are some downsides. Running an internal combustion engine to make electricity puts pollution into the air. Some jurisdictions limit the number of hours per month that a generator can be run (except in a crisis). Before purchasing your generator, check for any requisite permits for such things as fuel storage, air pollution, taxes, etc.

ACTION STEPS FOR YOUR PLAN

If you have a UPS, be sure that it is properly maintained. Most UPSs require regular preventative maintenance, such as changing the air filters and checking the condition of the batteries. If you skip this step, then you are destined to discover how important it is the next time your UPS is needed.

Most large UPS units come with a small display panel that indicates the condition of the UPS's ability to supply power. Master this panel and all controls before an emergency arises. Never open the front of the UPS as the unit is an electrical shock hazard. The unit should only be opened by trained electricians.

In the event of a power outage, the front panel display can tell you how long the UPS batteries will be able to supply power to all the devices attached. This is a very important piece of information. Most computer servers take a long time to recover if they suddenly lose power. They require time to shut down "gracefully." You need to know the typical amount of time required to shut down each critical server.

Most UPS units include an audible alarm for when they are on battery power. It is important to know what these alarms are and what to do when you hear them. If the UPS units are in a place where a security guard can hear them after hours, be sure the guard knows what to do.

EMERGENCY LIGHTING

In a large building, it can get very dark very quickly in a blackout. Even if flashlights are readily available, you need to be able to find them. Also, a sudden blackout can be very disorienting to some people. This only adds an element of panic to the moment. To address this, most legal jurisdictions require the installation of emergency lights that come on whenever power to the building is lost. This provides some light for the safe evacuation of offices and workplaces.

These lights depend on a battery to power the lights in a blackout. To be sure that the lights and the battery are ready when they are needed, they must be checked monthly according to the manufacturer's testing steps.

SOMETHING FOR YOUR SUPPORT PLAN

Following are three notices for you to consider as additions to your power support plan.

The first is an insert for your immediate steps contingency plan to be kept at the help desk and posted on the computer room walls. When power drops, employees should execute the steps on this notice to contain the problem while the technical staff is called in.

The second is a wall notice on priorities—which equipment to turn off in what order so that your UPS and generator system can be freed to support the most critical systems.

The third is a set of instructions for making up the power shedding tags described on the Power Shedding Priorities page.

Power Outage Action Plan

1. Immediate Action.

  a. Notify your facility's Maintenance supervisor immediately.

  b. Notify your Supervisor.

               Primary: **(name and number here)**

               Alternate: **(name and number here)**

  c. Determine the scope of the problem.

  ➤ Look outside the office. Is there power everywhere else in the building?

  ➤ Send someone outside to see if the electricity is on outside of the building. (Do not go yourself. You must sit by the phone to coordinate action until your supervisor arrives.) Are there lights on in any other buildings? Are traffic signals working? Are street lights on?

  d. Notify the facility's Disaster Recovery Manager.

  e. Begin a log sheet of all events to include when the lights went out, who was notified and when, any communications with the power company, etc.

2. Physical Layout.

  a. UPS Room

  ➤ Send someone to look at the UPS. Note how long the display indicates the batteries are projected to last.

  ➤ Execute the power shedding plan.

  ➤ Keep monitoring the UPS and continue shedding power using devices. When the UPS time falls below 20 minutes, begin shutting down all the servers.

  ➤ Call all system administrators and the network manager.

Power Shedding Priorities

When electrical power fails or when the power company notifies you that a failure is imminent, the drain on the UPS batteries is minimized by turning off equipment according to its power shedding priority. After reliable power is restored, turn equipment back on according to its priority. Start the most critical systems first.

When a power outage occurs or is anticipated, notify the Help Desk, Facility Security, your supervisor, and the Data Processing Manager. Monitor the UPS systems to see how much time is remaining on the batteries (instructions are posted on the UPS devices).

This approach uses Power Shedding Priorities A through D, with A being least critical and D being most critical equipment to keep running. Priority is set according to:

➤ Which systems directly support facility production.

➤ Which systems will cause widespread problems if they stop working.

➤ Which systems are difficult to restart if they stop suddenly.

1. As soon as you lose electrical power, shut off nonessential systems and equipment identified with a green "A" power shedding label, such as CRTs, terminals, printers, card processing equipment.

   ➤ Notify other company sites on your network.

   ➤ Update the Help Desk, Security, and the Data Processing Manager.

2. When the UPS units show 15 minutes of power remaining, shut off low-priority CPUs and devices identified with a Yellow "B" power shedding label. When you progress to this step, notify:

   ➤ The Help Desk and the Data Processing Manager.

3. When the UPS units show 5 minutes of power remaining, shut off all remaining equipment and servers identified with a red "C" power shedding label. When you progress to this step, notify:

   ➤ The Help Desk and the Data Processing Manager.

4. Let equipment identified with a tan "D" power shedding label "die" on their own as power drops off. This is equipment that can tolerate a sudden power drop.

Communication is important!

Ensure that management and the appropriate support people know when you start the next step of shutting down or restarting systems. Data Processing Management will call in the required system support people for a proper restart.

Power Shedding Tag Instructions

Labeling your equipment: Make up labels on colored paper and then laminate them.

A = Green   B = Yellow   C = Red   D = Tan

Power Shedding Priority A	**Power Shedding Priority B**	**Power Shedding Priority C**	**Power Shedding Priority D**

Resources:

Liebert	www.liebert.com
American Power Conversion	www.apc.com
Tripplite	www.tripplite.com
Underwriters Laboratories	www.ul.com

CONCLUSION

Electricity is a powerful resource necessary to operate the modern business. As with any resource, you need to be familiar with its role in your operation and how its absence will affect your company. In the absence of clean power from the electric utility, the main sources of electrical power are a battery-operated UPS and a generator. A thorough understanding of the electrical requirements of your organization will help you to design the most cost-effective plan to protect against its absence.

CHAPTER 15

TELECOMMUNICATIONS AND NETWORKING
Your Connection to the World

Everything is connected . . . no one thing can change by itself.
— Paul Hawken

INTRODUCTION

All of us are becoming more interconnected, as people and companies make increasing use of telecommunications networks to connect to suppliers, customers, business associates, and friends. Telecommunications has enabled our businesses and personal lives to be "just-in-time" no matter where we might be in the world. We use telecommunications networks to talk, share data, run applications, download files, organize schedules, exchange e-mail, and access the Internet. We use these networks to connect us with our coworkers and to collaborate with customers in doing the business of the firm. This chapter reviews the dangers that threaten our telecommunications networks and the attributes unique to these networks that require special processes to restore them after a disaster.

Most organizations have two distinct telecommunications networks: one for voice communication that uses the standard telephone system (also known as the public switched telephone network, or PSTN) and another for all electronic communication that uses one or more computer networks that are typically connected to the Internet. While the need for two distinct networks is slowly changing with the increasing use of VoIP (Voice-over-Internet Protocol) for sending voice communications over the Internet, many organizations will have to maintain both for the foreseeable future. Fortunately for our planning purposes, both types of networks have very similar issues that affect disaster recovery.

PUBLIC SWITCHED TELEPHONE NETWORK

How important can a telephone line be? What's the cost of a telephone call? What is the value of a missed call? How much would you pay for 100 percent telecommunications reliability? Is such a thing even possible?

Consider this scenario. You are the Plant Materials Manager sitting at home in your living room. As you watch the evening news, you see a video of flames rising out of the roof of a key supplier's main factory. You don't need trouble like this. What should you do? You try calling your salesperson and the company offices but no one answers. First thing in the morning and all the next morning you try calling them. The company is more than an hour drive away, you can't get away from the office for that long, and your calls still go unanswered.

Looking through your contact list, you select another supplier and place an order for a 2-month supply of goods to replace the supplier that had the fire. The set-up costs are a killer but it is worth the money if you can keep your factory running. At least this problem is contained. Trouble is, the fire you saw on TV was isolated to the front offices and the factory is fine. The warehouse is bulging. At a time like this, the supplier needs the cash, but employees can't call out until the telephone switching room is replaced! The company took care of the fire but forgot all about its customers.

All companies strike a fine balance between the cost of reliable telephone service and the cost of downtime. In a time of tight budgets (which is always), you balance the cost of premium services against the potential loss of telephone service. The more reliable that you want your telephone network to be, the more you must spend. Telephone service is central to the conduct of business in most companies. A failure isolates customers and suppliers from your company—and that can quickly become a very lonely feeling.

Some companies are even more dependent on telephone service than others are. If you work at a factory, you use the telephone to conduct business, but your main concern is moving products down the line. The loss of telephone service does not slow down the assembly line one bit. However, if your facility is a call center for sales or service, then 100 percent reliable telephone service is crucial to your ongoing business. In the factory example, if the conveyor on the main assembly line breaks, the workers have nothing to do. In the call center, if the telephone service is interrupted, then they are likewise idled. How your facility utilizes its telephone service has a great deal to do with how crucial it is for your operations.

The North American telephone network is designed to carry traffic from about 10 percent of all telephones in a given area. This approximates its load at its busiest times. In a wide-area disaster, this capacity is quickly swamped, as people everywhere call to check on their loved ones. The cellular network doesn't fare any better because portions of it also use landlines and it has its own capacity limits. In today's fast-paced business environment, how long can your business afford to be without telephone service?

The disasters that can befall your delicate communication lines are legion. Anywhere along its path the wire can be broken, switching equipment can lose power, or problems can even occur within your building. The high level of telephone communications reliability of our modern telecommunications networks is the envy of the world. You must ensure that your company has reviewed the risks to its telecommunications pipeline and has taken steps to reduce the likelihood of failure. Our job here is to identify those risks and build a wish list of mitigation actions to make your company's telephone communications even more rock solid than ever before.

The next few sections of this chapter review the basics of how your telephone system works. If you are already a telephone system expert, you can skip these sections. If you are charged with writing a plan in an area in which you are not a full-fledged expert, then you should read on. A basic understanding of the main components will make it easier for you to develop an appropriate plan.

PSTN Basics

The world of telephonic communications all begins with the telephone instrument on your desk. This modern marvel connects you to the world at large. The telephone is connected by wire to the wall jack, which in turn is connected to a wiring closet. A wiring closet may be one of those locked doors on your office building floor that you never get to look into. The same function can be served by running wires to a specific place on the wall of a factory (which is generally a wide-open space). In either place, you would see brightly colored wires running in spaghetti-like fashion to a telephone wire "punch-down block" or punch block.

If you look at a punch block, it seems to be a "rat's nest" of colored wire routed in an orderly fashion, yet going in all directions. Each office telephone has at least one pair of wires running from its wall jack all the way back to the wiring punch block. The punch block also has wires running to the telephone switch for your building. This is where the two are connected to each other. If an office no longer needs a telephone line, the punch block is the place where it can be disconnected.

Private Branch Exchange

From the wiring closet, large bundles of wires run to the company's telephone switching equipment. In a larger company this would be a Private Branch Exchange (PBX). A PBX replaces the long-gone company telephone operator who would connect internal calls with a plug patch panel. The patch panel physically connected the wires from one telephone instrument into the wires of another. This is really a basic operation, but until electronics matured, it was the only way to do it. This is now all done electronically. In today's offices, a PBX takes these incoming wires and, using the signal on them, provides electronic switching of calls within the building. A simple way to think about a PBX is to consider it a special-purpose computer with all the support needs of a minicomputer.

The PBX determines which calls are intended for external telephone numbers and connects to the local telephone company central office using "trunk" lines. Trunk lines are used for inbound or outbound calls. The number of trunk lines the PBX has connected to the central office determines the maximum number of external (inbound or outbound) calls you are capable of supporting at a given moment. Modern PBX systems offer a wide range of additional services such as:

➤ Voice mail.

➤ Telephone conferencing.

➤ Call transferring.

➤ Music on hold.

Based on this, from a business continuity perspective, you have a large single point of failure device. You must plan to recover from a catastrophic failure of the PBX (e.g., burned to a cinder in a fire). A close examination of the PBX room and its ancillary equipment will show that it is essentially a computer room, requiring the same electrical and climate stabilization actions as any computer room. Backup copies of the configuration data must be made for each device and handled with the same care as the backup data from your computer system. These data should be securely stored off-site and available when needed. Up-to-date backed-up data are the key to a prompt recovery.

Internal to a company, the telephone signals can be analog or digital. Digital PBX systems provide a wide range of services beyond simply routing calls. Most PBX systems use digital signals to communicate with the telephones. This allows for additional services, such as one-touch dialing, preprogrammed telephone numbers, voice mail, etc. This is significant in the case where you want to use a modem to dial out of the office. A fax machine or a direct modem connection requires an analog line. If you have a digital PBX, then you will need separate analog lines.

Rather than run a multitude of analog telephone lines, most companies access the Internet via their external data network. This works fine for most office dwellers. However, some devices still need these analog lines and you should keep track of where they are. Examples of analog dial-out lines might be for an alarm service, which dials out to notify the repair service of an out-of-tolerance condition, or for validating a credit card in stores at the point of purchase.

OTHER VITAL EQUIPMENT LOCATED IN THE PBX ROOM Other important equipment is typically located in the same room as your PBX. After the critical devices are identified, make sure they are protected and draft a plan to fully recover them. These devices may include:

➤ **Interactive Voice Response (IVR).** Gives callers information based on what the caller enters using the telephone keypad. You have heard the messages— please select 1 to talk to sales, select 2 to talk to . . . These audio tracks should be backed up and the queuing logic documented.

➤ **Automatic Number Identification.** This is the business version of what is sold to consumers as "caller ID."

➤ **Intelligent Port Selector.** Connects the incoming call to the first available line. This is used when you have multiple people answering inbound calls, as in a hotel chain's reservation center.

➤ **Call Management System.** Used to monitor the volume of telephone calls during peak periods, to identify the number of telephone operators needed, and to track operator efficiency.

➤ **Call Accounting.** Tracks calls made and assigns them to a billing account. This is also known as a "Station Message Detail Recording" (SMDR). This is used in various ways. Lawyers might use it to bill their time to a specific client. Some companies use this to track employees' long distance usage, etc.

➤ **Call Monitoring.** Tracks the level of call activity by showing the status of the trunk lines, the number of calls in progress, the number of calls waiting in queues, the wait time, the number of abandoned calls, and the status of the operators.

The Telephone Company's Central Office

Soon after telephone service was first created, it became obvious that every person could not be wired to every other person they might possibly want to call. This would result in an impossible maze of wires. To call someone new, you would first need to run a wire from your telephone to their telephone. Imagine the problems in asking a girl for her telephone number in those days!

To simplify this problem, all the telephone lines were run into a centralized building and then the switchboard operators would physically patch your telephone line into the switchboard, making the connection. These buildings would be located at various places around the city and were the central place where connections were made. Eventually, automated switching made it easier, but buildings were still needed to switch the calls. In more recent years with the advent of solid-state circuits, the floor space required for these buildings has shrunk dramatically. You still see them around: small buildings without any windows, usually neatly trimmed grass, and a small telephone company sign by the front door.

The central office provides a service similar to your PBX by switching your call to another local telephone, to a different central office far away, or to a long-distance carrier's point of presence (POP). The long-distance company then routes the call through its switching center and back to a distant central office and down to the far-away telephone.

Interexchange Carrier Point of Presence

With the breakup of the AT&T long-distance monopoly in 1982 came the creation of independent long-distance telecommunications providers. These non-AT&T

long-distance providers are known as Interexchange Carriers (IXCs). Along with this choice came the opportunity to split your long-distance service across different carriers in hopes that all of them would not be knocked out in a disaster and therefore your communications traffic could flow out on the alternative pipeline. For that to be true, a lot of careful planning is necessary.

First, you must ensure cable separation so that you have a different wire path from your facility to the IXC's point of presence. Most companies are a mix of owning the network in high-traffic areas and renting from another carrier in a low-traffic area. This means your traffic separation may only be on paper. If you are in a high-traffic area, the carrier may run a separate cable to your facility. If you are not, then you will probably connect to the IXC in the nearest central office. Do not take for granted that because you use two companies you are on two different wires. Ask them if they share lines and ask to see the route of the cable.

Some telecommunications experts believe that route separation is much more important than using multiple telecommunications companies. They feel it is easier to manage one supplier so long as the cable issue is addressed.

When evaluating networks, the first thing to consider is whether they rent their network or own it. Most are a mixture. The more of the network equipment that they own, the more control they can exercise over it. When choosing an IXC, things to consider include:

➤ What is their system availability time, and what they will guarantee?

➤ What are the consequences to the IXC of downtime? You can ill afford it. A few extra free minutes of service every month is poor recompense for missed customer calls.

➤ What is the restoration priority for the sections of the network that you will be using?

➤ What are their alternate routes for the places you normally communicate with? Don't automatically assume a new carrier will be a better alternative to your existing carrier. Is your service route a spur (single-threaded) service? Is it a ring architecture, which at least gives you two paths in case one has a problem?

➤ How often does the carrier practice its disaster recovery procedures?

➤ How easily can the IXC shift your inbound calls to another site?

OK, well, this all sounds pretty straightforward. After all, telephone service has been around for well over 100 years and its technology is pretty well known. *What could possibly go wrong?*

COMPUTER NETWORKS

All but the smallest firms today have one or more networks within their organization. A network consists of one or more servers that are connected to one or more workstations and allows users to share information and resources. This connection can be by copper wire, by fiber-optic cable, or even by radio frequency (RF, or wireless). Rarely are workstations connected directly into a server. Typically they plug into the wall jack, which is connected to a wiring closet. In the closet will be one or more "hubs" that will connect the local devices to a hub in the computer room. This room is often the same closet as contains the telephone wiring.

In the computer room (either a central location or possibly sprinkled about the facility) sit the servers. A server is a computer that runs software to provide access to resources attached to the network, such as printers, disk storage, and network applications. A server can be any type of computer that supports the sharing of resources: it may be a standard desktop PC, or a dedicated device containing large amounts of memory and multiple storage devices that can support hundreds of PCs at the same time.

The next section reviews the basics of how your computer network works. If you are already a network expert, you can skip this section. If you are charged with writing a plan in an area in which you are not a full-fledged expert, then you should read on. A basic understanding of the main components will make it easier for you to develop an appropriate plan.

Computer Network Basics

The term local area network (LAN) is typically used to describe workstations and servers that are all physically in the same location. A LAN can be implemented using two main architectures:

➤ **Peer-to-Peer.** Each computer on the network communicates directly with every other computer. Each computer is treated equally on the network. Communication between computers is coordinated using a network hub.

➤ **Client/Server.** Each end-user PC is connected to a central server, which coordinates communication and supplies resources to the end users. Typically the server contains file storage, printer, backup, and other resources that are shared by the end-user client computers.

Figure 15-1 shows a typical client/server LAN, with five PCs connected to a server. The server has attached a network printer and a backup tape drive that can be accessed from any end-user client computer on the network.

A wide-area network (WAN) is a data communications network that consists of two or more local area networks connected to allow communication between geographically dispersed locations. Most companies have some sort of WAN connection, either connecting to other locations within the organization or to the public Internet. There are several different types of WAN communication links available. The most common ones are:

➤ **Dialup.** This is the most basic type of connection, using a modem and a PSTN line. This is also the slowest and most unreliable type of connection available, supporting up to 56 kilobits per second (kbps).

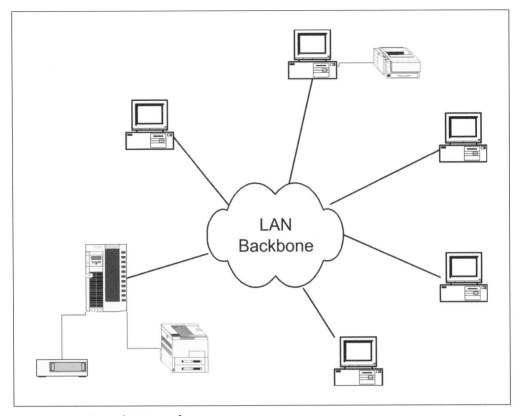

FIGURE 15-1: Typical LAN configuration.

➤ **ISDN.** An ISDN (integrated services digital network) connection uses a PSTN line using an enhanced communication standard to speed up the connection to 64 or 128 kbps.

➤ **T-1.** A dedicated connection that supports data rates up to 1.5 megabits per second (mbps). A T-1 line consists of 24 individual channels, each supporting 64 kbps of data.

➤ **T-3.** A dedicated connection that supports data rates up to 43 mbps. A T-3 line consists of 672 individual channels, each supporting 64 kbps of data.

➤ **Frame Relay.** This is a packet switched protocol for connecting devices on the WAN. It supports data transfer rates up to T-3 speed.

➤ **Cable Modem.** Using the same digital or fiber-optic network as cable TV, cable modem Internet is capable of speeds up to 60 mbps.

➤ **ATM.** ATM (Asynchronous Transfer Mode) is a means of digital communications that is capable of very high speeds; suitable for transmission of images or voice or video as well as data.

➤ **Wireless.** A wireless LAN bridge can connect multiple LANs for distances up to 30 miles with a direct line of sight.

➤ **VPN.** A VPN (Virtual Private Network) uses encryption in the lower protocol layers to provide a secure connection through the public Internet.

Figure 15-2 shows a corporate wide area network, with two remote locations linked to the headquarters, which is in turn connected to the public Internet. Just as your phone system has a room for patching users into the telephone network, your computer network also has a central location where individual pieces of equipment are connected into one or more servers. This might be the same room as your telephone patch panel, or it could be part of a separate dedicated computer room.

It starts with each piece of equipment on the network being connected by wire to the wall jack, which is in turn connected to a wiring closet. A wiring closet for your computer network is typically located in or next to the computer room where your servers are located. The wiring closet consists of many different cables running in spaghetti-like fashion to a network cable "punch-down block" or punch block.

The network cable punch block is similar to the telephone wiring punch block discussed earlier. It has network cables routed in an orderly fashion, yet going in all directions. Each piece of equipment on the network has at least one cable

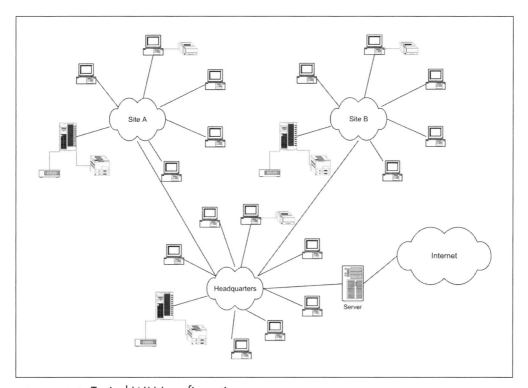

FIGURE 15-2: Typical WAN configuration.

running from its wall jack all the way back to the cable punch block. The punch block also has wires running to the computer servers. This is where the two are connected to each other. If a piece of equipment needs to be removed from the network, the punch block is the place where it can be disconnected.

Internet Service Providers

Internet Service Providers (ISPs) connect your organization to the Internet. You are connected to your ISP via one of the network connection options listed in the previous section. Most organizations will have only one physical connection between its network and the ISP for Internet access. If Internet access is critical to the operation of your business, you should consider a connection to a second ISP to give you a second pathway to the Internet. There are, however, several things to evaluate and plan for when considering a redundant ISP. (This is similar to considering multiple telecommunications companies.)

First, you must ensure cable separation so that you have a different wire path from your facility to the ISP's point of presence. Most ISPs are a mix of owning the network in high-traffic areas and renting from another ISP in a low-traffic area. This means your traffic separation may only be on paper. If you are in a high-traffic area, the ISP may run a separate cable to your facility. If you are not, then you will probably connect to the ISP's nearest point of presence. Do not take for granted that because you use two ISPs you are on two different wires. Ask them if they share lines and ask to see the route of the cable.

Some telecommunications experts believe that route separation is much more important than using multiple ISPs. They feel it is easier to manage one ISP so long as the cable issue is addressed. When choosing an ISP, things to consider include:

> ➤ What is their system availability time, and what they will guarantee?

> ➤ What are the consequences to the ISP of downtime? You can ill afford it. A few extra free minutes of service every month is poor recompense for missed sales due to the Internet being unavailable.

> ➤ What is the restoration priority for the sections of the network that you will be using?

> ➤ What are ISP's alternate routes for the places you normally communicate with?

> ➤ How often does the ISP practice its disaster recovery procedures?

RISK ASSESSMENT

When developing your disaster recovery plan for your telecommunication services, look for single points of failure that will adversely impact your critical business processes. These critical processes should have been identified in the Business Impact Analysis. External threats to telecommunications include cables being cut, interference from electromagnetic sources, attacks by hackers and other intruders, and damage from natural hazards, such as fire or water. Internal threats include many of these same dangers; cables can be cut by remodelers and leaky water pipes can damage cables and equipment. In an ideal world, you would have duplicate service running to each telephone or desktop. Externally, an issue with multiple Internet connections is that there are now two points of potential entry for hackers; be sure to work closely with your security team to adequately protect your WAN. Internally, it is usually not cost-effective to run duplicate cables; an alternative is to install an extra jack every few cable drops. If a problem occurs in an end-user's cable, the extra jack would be available as a backup until the problem cable is repaired.

It is also important to review your vulnerability to problems with the devices that connect your telecommunications network together, such as routers, switches, and hubs. Your Business Impact Analysis should determine the level of threat that these devices pose if they fail. Look at having redundant devices installed that can take over if the primary device fails.

Wireless telecommunication connections can provide an effective backup strategy if the wired network fails. Wireless networks have no wires to fail and can be quickly installed if needed after a failure in the wired system. The major drawback to using a wireless network is that the transmissions can be intercepted; make sure encryption and other security measures are implemented to avoid others intercepting your network traffic.

You should also consider using network monitoring software that can detect problems on the network. Network monitoring software can alert you immediately if a node on the network is having problems or has failed, which will allow you to restore service more quickly and help prevent problems from cascading. Most network monitoring software can be configured to look for system parameters that fall out of the desired range and then generate a message to a support person to take action.

Natural Hazards

Now that you know the basics of how your telecommunications systems work, what are the risks to these systems? Chapter 3 discussed natural hazards in detail, so this section only addresses those natural hazards that have a major impact on your telecommunications systems.

- ➤ **Ice Storms and Blizzards.** Ice can coat cables strung from telephone poles and, if the weight is great enough, potentially bring them down.

- ➤ **Thunderstorms and Lightning.** Severe rain can weaken the ground around a pole and cause it to sag when there are high winds at the same time pushing against it. Lightning can strike telephone poles and send a major charge flying down the line, burning up wire and equipment along the way.

- ➤ **Tornadoes.** A powerful destructive force that can snap lines and rip up telephone poles. High-risk areas are prime candidates for buried lines.

➤ **Hurricanes and Floods.** Can cover a wide swath of land and not only bring down a telecommunications network but also prevent crews from promptly addressing the problems.

Human-Created Hazards

People are just as big a danger to your telecommunications systems as nature can be. Human-created dangers include:

➤ **Breaks in Buried Lines.** Sometimes emergency excavation is necessary (such as repairing a broken gas main). Sometimes the local government is cleaning trash out of the ditches alongside the road. Sometimes a well-meaning person just digs without asking (including on your own property). In any of these cases, there is the chance that your tiny little cable will be dug up and severed.

➤ **Accidents.** Sometimes people miss the tight turn and break off a telephone pole. If this is your only line to the central office or your ISP, your service is gone until the pole is replaced.

➤ **Central Office or ISP Failure.** A problem in a central office or with your ISP can quickly shut down your telecommunications unless you are wired to a second provider.

➤ **Denial of Service Attacks.** Hackers can use various techniques to render your Internet service unusable. A Distributed Denial of Service (DDoS) attack uses the computing power of thousands of vulnerable, infected machines to overwhelm a target or a victim.

Telecommunications Equipment Room

The room that houses your telecommunications equipment may not be as safe as you think it is. Dangers to your telecommunications room include:

➤ **Temperatures** that are too hot, too cold and that swing widely are all hard on your telephone switching equipment. Extreme temperatures stress the printed circuits. Large swings in temperature (hot to cold) cause expansion and shrinkage of circuit cards and again can weaken components over time.

➤ **Humidity** has an effect on temperature and the growth of mold on your equipment.

➤ **Loss of electrical power** will definitely stop a PBX, routers, switches, and other telecommunications equipment. Pay phones and direct lines out should still be operational since the telephone circuits supply their own power.

➤ **Water pipes overhead** in your telecommunications room could release water onto your equipment. The same goes for your cable panels. Overhead pipes along external walls could potentially freeze and leak when thawing. Leaks from rooftop air conditioning compressors are also a problem.

➤ **Security may be a factor.** This room is not set up to accommodate tourists and they should not be allowed in. Keep the door locked at all times.

➤ **Fire is a possible danger.** This equipment generates heat and is in danger from fire or the sprinklers used to extinguish a fire. Typically this room is unattended and a slow-starting fire may go undetected. Gas fire suppression is expensive but may save your equipment.

Cabling

The discussions earlier about wiring closets had a purpose. Imagine the mess if an isolated fire in the wiring closet melted all these wires. In terms of structural damage, you got off pretty easy. But in terms of damage to the telecommunications system, that entire area of the facility will be without service for some time. New cable would have to be run from the PBX or Internet server to the closet and from the wall to the closet. The alternative is to splice an extension onto each cable and run it into a punch block. Either way is time consuming and expensive. So you can see how the wiring closet can be a single point of failure for your telecommunications systems. This makes it a good idea to keep everyone out of it and to not store anything in the closet that might cause a problem.

INTERNAL CABLING For disaster avoidance, concerns begin with the wiring closet and patch panels. Take a walk with your telecommunications specialist and identify the location of all telecommunication patch panels in your facility. Things you are looking for:

1. In a closet

➤ The door and any windows are kept locked.

➤ There is fire suppression equipment (usually fused link sprinklers).

➤ There is nothing else in the closet except telecommunication and/or data communications equipment. Combustible materials stored in the closet threaten your equipment. This is not the place to store holiday decorations, old files, office supplies, janitor supplies, etc.

➤ Very few people have keys—telecommunication support staff, security, and no one else.

➤ There should be sufficient light to work in the closet.

➤ There will often be data network wiring and telephone switching equipment together in these closets. They are a natural fit here. The issue is that where the patch panel is simply a physical connection for wires, the network equipment is energized electronics, which will generate heat and introduce a potential fire source.

2. Outside a closet

➤ Be sure it is covered and the cover is locked. Same rules for the keys as for the wiring closets. Enough keys for the right people and none for anyone else.

➤ All cables and wires leading into the external panel are encased in heavy conduit to inhibit tampering.

➤ If this is located in a warehouse or factory, be sure it is strongly protected from environmental influences (leaky ceilings, etc.) and from being crushed by a forklift or toppling stacked material.

EXTERNAL CABLING The first rule of outside cabling is "cabling and backhoes don't mix!" A chain is only as strong as its weakest link. Your servers and PBX are snugly locked up in their room, and the ISP's office and the telephone company's central office are also secure. But the wire in between is exposed to the ravages of weather, people, and machines.

Experienced telecommunication professionals have their own name for backhoes—cable locators!

External cabling, which is the cable that runs from your wiring closet to the telecommunication provider's office, is your biggest concern. The wire runs from your building to an access point along the road, usually on a pole. Then the wire runs through the countryside (usually along a road or railroad) to a point of presence or central office. In the city, it might run through underground pipes to the point of presence or central office. You have no control over where the wire is run and no capability to protect it! In some areas, you will even have separate cable runs to be concerned about—one for the local telephone company, one for the Interexchange Carrier (long-distance service), and yet another for your Internet service.

A common term used when describing part of a telecommunications network is "the last mile." The last mile describes the wire from the telephone company's central office or the ISP's point of presence to your structure (and is usually more than a mile). This is also known as the "local access" or the "local loop." This part of the network is the most vulnerable. It is often carried on telephone poles (susceptible to ice storms and errant vehicles) or underground (susceptible to damage from digging).

ROUTE SEPARATION The best path to telecommunications reliability is redundancy. This can include redundant equipment, redundant technicians, and redundant cabling. The more alternate paths that a signal can be routed, the more likely it is to get through. The principle of cable route separation should be an integral part of your telecommunications network design. Essentially this means that you have more than one cable between your building and your telecommunications providers. This prevents a total communications outage from a single cable cut.

Few companies can afford to take this to the extreme, but you can look into some steps. Begin by asking the telecommunications provider to show you the route that your cable takes from the wall of your building to their office. This will also show you how exposed the cable is to auto accidents (are the poles close to the road), to backhoes (is the cable buried along the road in some places), or any other number of threats.

With this experience in mind, negotiate with the telecommunications provider a fresh cable run from your building (exit from the opposite end from the other cable) to a different central office or point of presence. This will keep you operational in case your usual point of presence is damaged or experiences an equipment failure, or if the cable to the point of presence was broken. How likely is that to happen?

In May 1988, there was a fire in the Illinois Bell central office located in Hinsdale, IL. The two-story building was completely gutted. This building was an important hub for Illinois Bell, as well as for major long-distance carriers, such as MCI and Sprint. In addition to cellular service and data networks, approximately 40,000 subscriber lines and 6 fiber-optic lines lost service.

To reduce the chance of a total system failure similar to the Hinsdale disaster, the telephone companies have gradually migrated their central office structure from a spoke-and-hub approach (with its obvious single point of failure) to a ring or mesh approach, in which multiple central offices are connected to each other. In this scenario, calls are routed around the damaged central office in a manner that is transparent to the caller. This is an ongoing process and may not yet have been completed in rural areas or small towns. If possible, you want routing separation with the wire running from your facility running to two different central offices on separate routes.

Route separation is more important than having multiple vendors. Most cable routes follow railroad rights of way and the major carriers' lines commonly converge at bridges. Imagine the number of places there are to cross a major river, highway, etc. There aren't many to choose from. The lines from various companies often come together here and cross under the same portion of the bridge. What could go wrong? Vehicles crossing bridges might catch on fire, river barges can break free and strike bridge pilings, and major bridges are tempting terrorist targets.

Many telecommunication providers define cable separation as a distance of 25 feet or more between cables. Others ensure cables are at least 100 feet apart and have at least a 2-foot separation at cable crossovers. Ask your Internet, local, and long-distance telephone carriers how they define cable route separation and how faithful they are to that standard. When using multiple vendors, even if their cables are separated, they share a common weakness if they join at the same point of presence or cross a river under the same bridge. Upon close investigation, you may even see that where you are using two companies, one is leasing part of the same wire from your other provider!

What to do? Find out how many access points there are for your telecommunication service. Does it enter the building at more than one place (again, trying to separate the cables)? Ask the telecommunication provider to identify the route that the cable takes from their office to your facility. Drive along this route and look for potential problems.

In terms of your long-distance provider, where is their point of presence located? Where is the point of presence of their competitors? You can consider running a separate connection to a second point of presence to provide for multiple circuits. Depending on the distance, this separate line may be quite expensive to run and maintain.

MAP IT OUT Now that you know the cable route to the telecommunication provider, map it out—from where it enters your wall to the provider's point of presence. You might think, "Isn't that the telecommunication provider's responsibility?" The answers is yes, but type up that excuse and paste it to your wall in case the line is cut. Try it on your boss! If you drive to work using the same route as your cable, you might see construction crews digging near where the cable is to repair a water main, snapped poles, or sagging wire due to accidents or severe weather—any number of threats too close to the wire for comfort.

So draw out a map of where your wire runs from the telephone pole outside to the telecommunication provider's office. Then make a detailed map of the run from the pole to the wall and on to the wiring closet room. Indicate which lines terminate in equipment provided by the telecommunication provider and which lines provide essential services.

DEVELOPING A PLAN

This sections describe issues to consider as your develop a disaster recovery plan for your telecommunication assets.

What Are We Protecting?

As you know, the first step in building a plan is to make an inventory of your telecommunications assets. You will assemble at least three lists. The first lists every major item and who to call if it breaks. The second shows where the main cable runs are located in the building. The third includes all the telephone numbers used by the facility. In a crisis, you may need to reroute some of these to another location.

1. Begin with a list of all major devices in your telephone switching room and network room, such as the PBX, IVR, Internet server, etc. Include on this list:

   ➤ A description of each device.

   ➤ The serial numbers of the main equipment and any major components.

   ➤ The name, 24-hour telephone number, contract number, and contract restrictions for whomever you have arranged to service that item.

   ➤ The location of every item, including a simple floor map of all telecommunication rooms.

   ➤ Be sure to back up your entire configuration data, either on magnetic media or, if the file is small, print it off and store it safely away.

2. Now make a wiring inventory of all the cable runs within your facility. You do not need to show individual runs to the offices. In a crisis, you can always shift someone to another office. This is best accomplished with computer-aided drafting software on a digitized version of the floor plan.

   ➤ Indicate the runs on maps of each building or floor of a multistory building. Knowing the location of these cable runs is important to quickly assess damage.

   ➤ Indicate where the telecommunication service enters the building and its route to the telephone exchange and network rooms. Note any hazards along the cable path.

   ➤ If you have pay phones, indicate them on the map.

   ➤ If you have any independent direct lines that bypass your telephone switch, mark them on the map.

3. Make up a telephone number inventory with all the telephone numbers assigned to your building/facility.

   ➤ DID (Direct Inward Dialing) lines.

   ➤ Dedicated telephone lines that bypass your PBX, such as fax machines.

   ➤ Pay telephones.

   ➤ Foreign exchange lines.

Identify Critical Telephone Circuits

Telephones are used to communicate, and every part of the company uses them differently. In an emergency, salespeople will need to contact customers, the warehouse will need to call suppliers, and the people at the disaster site will want to call home. In a disaster, you won't be able to please everyone right away, so you need a restoration priority guideline to know which circuits to recover (or protect) and in what order.

Start this analysis by reviewing the critical functions identified by your executives at the beginning of the business continuity planning project. Next, meet with representatives from each department and ask them to identify their critical telecommunications needs and at what point in the disaster containment/recovery they would be needed. For example, early in the emergency, the Human Resources team might need to notify employees to not report to work or to come in at certain times, etc. Each department must prioritize its communications needs.

With your critical communications functions identified, you can determine which circuits support these key functions. If you trace out the top three or four circuits, you may see some of the same hardware, some of the same cables, and circuit paths common to them all. Working down your list, you can see which of your hardware devices (or cable bundles) has the greatest benefit to being restored first.

You must also include in your plan how you will relocate operations to another site. This is a twofold issue. In the first case, if a department must be moved off-site due to damage to its offices, you need to be able to shift its inbound calls to the new location quickly. In the second case, if your telephone equipment room is destroyed, you must quickly restore a minimal level of service. Some people might plan to build a new telephone room onsite. Others will contract with a service company that will bring a telephone equipment room to your site already set up in a large trailer. The company needs to plug into your wiring (no trivial task). This could buy you time until your equipment room is rebuilt. If you elect to bring in the configured trailer, this agreement must be made in advance, and be aware that these might not be available in a wide-area disaster.

Review Network Security

Your network has some unique security issues to consider. The first is physical security. No one but the network support staff should be allowed in the network closets. The network administrator must work with the facility's security manager to ensure that these doors are always locked. Depending on the airflow in the closet, some vents may be added to the doors. These rooms are not for storing holiday decorations, old documents, unwanted furniture, etc.

Sometimes network equipment is in freestanding cabinets instead of closets. These cabinets must be locked just like the closets and the keys held by only a few people. In a large facility, this can add up to a lot of keys. Your goal is to minimize the number of keys by using a submaster key for all closets and, if possible, a submaster key to all cabinets. These keys must be tracked and, if lost, a determination made whether to rekey the locks.

The next area to consider is logical security. The network software on the servers and in the network devices will be, in some cases, password protected. These passwords should be protected like any other and known only to the key network support staff. However, they should also be written down and locked in the data processing manager's office in case the network staff is unavailable. (In a wide-area emergency, the network manager or key staff members may not be available or able to come in.)

Another issue to consider is having a policy that no one is permitted to plug anything into the network. That is the exclusive job of the network support team. This is to stop people from plugging in their home notebook PCs and bringing down your network. In addition, contract employees should never be permitted to connect into your network. The same policy should cover your wireless nodes.

Because servers can support a large number of users and are used to host critical applications, loss of a server can have a severe impact on the business. Some processes to ease the restoration of servers include:

➤ **Store Backup Tapes and Software Off-site.** Follow the procedures discussed in Chapter 17 for handling and storing backups. Backups of data and application installation media should be stored off-site in a secure, environmentally controlled facility.

➤ **Standardize Hardware, Software, and Peripherals.** Standard configurations of these items will make restoration much easier. The standard configurations for hardware, software, and peripherals should be documented in your plan.

➤ **Document the Network.** The physical and logical network diagram must be kept up to date. The physical documentation should include a diagram of the physical facility, where the primary cables are routed. The logical diagram shows the network nodes and how they interconnect. Both diagrams are critical in restoring the network after a disaster.

➤ **Document Vendor Information.** Maintaining up-to-date information on the vendors you use for hardware, software, and peripherals will make it easier to restore your operations.

➤ **Work with Your Security Team.** The more secure your systems are, the less likely you are to have a data loss due to a security breach. You'll also want to be sure you can restore the latest level of security if you must configure new servers after an emergency.

Telecommunications Mitigation Plan

With these risks in mind, along with due consideration of the identified priority circuits and equipment, you can assemble a mitigation plan to reduce the likelihood of a threat or its impact if it occurs. The key to telecommunications mitigation is redundancy. Redundancy in equipment in case one machine must be repaired. Redundancy in communications routes in case a cable is severed or interrupted. Redundancy in communication methods, such as radios, cellular telephones, or satellite communications, will provide at least basic communications support.

CABLE MITIGATION PLAN Your cable mitigation plan should consider the following.

➤ Multiple paths for the "last mile." Investigate the path from your telecommunications equipment room all the way to the central office or point of presence. Ask the telecommunications provider to make another connection from your PBX or Internet server out through the wall of your building at a point distant from the other exit point and on a different route to a different point of presence. Be sure that your in-house wiring staff understands what you are asking for before they start.

➤ Multiple paths for Interexchange Carriers. Investigate the path from your telephone equipment room to your service provider's point of presence. Avoid the same route as used for your local telephone service.

➤ From the pole to your wall, if the cable is underground, ensure it is clearly marked with "do not dig" indicators or other obstacles to keep digging equipment away (or at least delay them until the cable can be marked).

TELECOMMUNICATIONS EQUIPMENT ROOM MITIGATION PLAN Think of your telecommunications room like a computer room. Their environmental and security needs are almost identical.

➤ **Uninterruptible Power Supply (UPS).** When you lose electrical power, this is what will keep your PBX or Internet server active until external power is restored or until your facility's electrical generators kick in. Conduct a power loss test to see which equipment is not connected to the UPS. If the device isn't essential or time consuming to restart, take it off the UPS. The fewer machines on the UPS, the better. When conducting the power test, see how long the batteries can support the load. Be sure the UPS is properly maintained by your service company.

When Hurricane Hugo struck the southeast United States in 1989, it surged hundreds of miles inland with huge amounts of rain and wind. The storm downed so many trees that it was days before electrical power was restored to some areas. Even the emergency batteries at the central offices were eventually drained. So, do not depend solely on your UPS for emergency power. Consider other power sources as well.

➤ **Fire.** This room requires the same fire protection as a computer room. An early-warning fire alarm system and gas fire suppression system are highly recommended.

➤ **Security Access.** This room is normally unattended. It should be locked as no one has any business strolling around in this room. The telecommunications system administrator can normally perform his or her administration duties via terminal over the network.

➤ **Structural Investigation.** Although you can rarely select the room, a close inspection can identify problems. Water pipes running along the walls or along the ceiling are a potential source of problems. They may freeze or leak. They should be watched carefully. Consider installing a plastic shield attached to a drain placed under them to catch condensation or leaks. A roof-mounted air conditioner may cause a roof leak. External walls may stress the air-handling equipment as outside temperatures heat or cool the walls.

➤ **Temperature Variability.** Your equipment must be in area that maintains a specific operating temperature and humidity range for maximum life. This is also essential to maintaining your service agreement coverage. Proper air conditioning, heating, and humidity control equipment must be in service and well cared for.

➤ **Alarms Such as Humidity, Temperature, Fire, and Electric.** A bank of alarms will help you monitor the condition of the room. These alarms must sound within the room, as well as at the security guard station as the room is normally unattended. Early detection will reduce the likelihood of significant damage. Include automatic paging equipment for notifying the after-hours support team of problems. Consider installing automatic shutdown software for your equipment. This signals your hardware to shut itself down gracefully in the event of a problem.

➤ **Data Backups.** Like a computer, your switch and configurable devices need to back up their configuration data whenever these change. Store copies of these files in a secure off-site location.

➤ **Housekeeping.** Keeping the door locked will help to prevent others from using the switch room as a storage facility. Nothing should be stored in this room that does not pertain to the equipment. This will reduce the amount of combustibles available to a fire. Do not let this room become another storage or janitor's closet.

ALTERNATE COMMUNICATIONS METHODS You must have written procedures for quickly routing Interexchange Carrier traffic to the local telephone service in the event that your IXCs have major problems. How hard is this to do, and then to switch it back again? Is it easier (or cheaper) to do this by splitting the load across two carriers and then shifting the entire load to the functional carrier? Other items to consider include:

➤ Do you have company-owned cell phones and cellular modems for communicating when the telephone system is inoperable?

➤ Develop written procedures for how to work with the telephone company to shift specific telephone numbers or all incoming calls to a different company site.

➤ Do you have any employees who are ham radio operators? It is nice to have alternative channels when the primary ones are not available. In a wide-area emergency, radio communications will also get congested. Radio conversations are not secure and anyone with the proper equipment can listen to them. Radio communication is also slow and not suitable for large data volumes.

➤ Other communications alternatives include satellite and microwave, both susceptible to problems if the antenna has been shifted by a storm or earthquake.

ACTION STEPS FOR YOUR PLAN

Most companies contract emergency recovery of their telecommunications equipment through the same company that services their equipment. A problem arises if there is more than one service company involved. An alternative is to arrange with a company to come onsite if your telecommunications equipment room is destroyed and to set up a trailer adjacent to your building with a ready-to-go telephone switch and Internet connection. To support this, companies often run cables to the front of the building for a quick connection.

Another consideration is that pay phones do not route through your PBX. They are direct lines to the outside service. So, if your PBX is inoperative, use pay phones. Keep a list of where they are and their telephone numbers.

Cell phones are also common. Cellular traffic can be somewhat limited in a wide-area emergency as the local cell towers become saturated with calls. Use this as an alternative communications channel, not as the primary backup.

A branch office is an ideal place to shift operations to until the disaster-struck site is recovered. The key is how far away the backup facility is located from the affected site. It should be far enough away to be unaffected by the same disaster. There is no set mileage distance but it should at least be on a different power grid and telephone central office. If it is too far, then you must also provide lodging for the relocated people.

One problem is how to relocate to these sites in a crisis. If this is during an area-wide disaster, mass transit such as air travel may be disrupted and driving there yourself may be difficult. One side aspect of the attack on the World Trade Center in September 2001 was that it shut down all air travel. Companies scrambling to activate their out-of-state recovery sites had a difficult time shifting key personnel and material to the site. No one had planned for a complete shutdown of the air transportation system.

Things to consider after a disaster:

➤ Do not make any unnecessary calls—only for emergencies.

➤ When calling, you may need to wait several minutes to get a dial tone. Do not hit the switch hook, because every time you do, you are placed at the end of the line for the next available dial tone.

➤ When you receive a dial tone, quickly dial your number. In a time of low telephone service availability, the dial tone is offered for a much shorter time.

TESTING

Plans are written by people with the best of intentions but, unless they are tested, you will never know what you don't know. Testing a plan exposes gaps and omissions in the process steps. It points out incorrect emergency telephone numbers and emergency equipment that no longer exists.

Test exercises are a great way to train the people on what to do. The more that they practice their emergency steps, the faster they will be able to perform them as they become familiar actions instead of something new. Where possible, include your emergency service providers. They will be a great source of recovery information.

When testing your plan, include some of your contract service providers. They may be able to point out some gaps in your planning or things that can be done in advance to make their assistance to you flow much easier.

Also, over time, your communications flows will shift. As this occurs, update your testing accordingly.

CONCLUSION

The modern business relies on telecommunications to perform its role in the marketplace. Like any resource, we need to be familiar with its role within our operation and how its absence will affect us. Redundancy is your best defense against a disaster removing your ability to communicate with customers and suppliers. A thorough understanding of the telecommunication requirements of your organization will help you to design the most cost-effective plan to protect against its absence.

CHAPTER 16

VITAL RECORDS RECOVERY
Covering Your Assets

Every vital organization owes its birth and life
to an exciting and daring idea.
—James B. Conant

INTRODUCTION

What are your personal vital records? Are they your car title, your home's deed, a marriage license, or even a divorce decree? Whatever they are, you spend a lot of time and effort to be sure they are safe because you know they may be difficult and time consuming to re-create later. The same holds true for your company's business records. They need a well-thought-out emergency management program if they are to be there when you need them.

Throughout this chapter, the references to documents and records apply to information stored on any media, including paper, magnetic, optic, or microfilm. There may be a bit of difference in how they are stored, but the issues for their handling and management are essentially the same.

This chapter focuses more on mitigating actions than on recovery, as that will address most of the emergency situations that you will encounter. Also included are recovery actions for small, contained records damage. There is always a chance that an emergency will overpower the best defenses and a recovery action will be needed. Few facilities are staffed or equipped for a large-scale recovery. Your best plan is to prearrange for a professional recovery service to come onsite to assist. Such a service is also a resource for designing your records mitigation processes. Remember that in a wide-area disaster, an outside service may already be engaged, so be prepared to take the initial preservation actions on your own.

A professional storage facility can be a safe and secure place for storage of documents not needed to run the business day-to-day and can also be a good source of information. Companies that provide this service include:

Fireproof Records Center—www.fireproof.com
Iron Mountain—www.ironmountain.com
Archive America—www.archiveamerica.com

The whole point of storing your vital records is that they will be available when you need them. If they are not accessible, then why are you spending all this time and money to store them? Every company has a set of records that it must safeguard for future reference. These records might be contracts, customer lists, or personnel files. Vital records can encompass just about anything.

But typically, vital records refer to documents that your company must retain to comply with legal requirements. This could be accounting records to support tax reporting, hazardous waste disposal forms, or even quality verification records to defend against future product liability lawsuits. Other types of vital records might be engineering plans and drawings, product specifications, trade secrets, and computer database backup tapes.

Vital records can be stored on many different forms of media. They can be on paper, microfiche, CDs, data backup tapes, or removable disks. On which media are your company's vital information stored? The answer is probably all of these. Where are they stored? All over your facility! They are squirreled away in closets, under desks, on CDs, and sometimes at employees' homes. Even the vital records that are properly situated in routine storage—how well are they climate controlled for preservation? If they are stored off-site, who ensures they are well cared for? Will they be accessible and readable when you need them?

Whatever the media your vital records are stored on and wherever they are stored, you must have a plan for safeguarding them and recovering them in the event of a disaster. Each type of media requires its own recovery strategy. Each type of document has its own level of recovery urgency.

Our goal is to safeguard these documents, whatever media they are stored on. In an emergency, your best plan is to call in a records recovery company that you previously contracted with on an as-needed basis. In an emergency, you will not have the leisure time to shop around for the best service and the best price. Every hour counts.

Our plan reviews the different types of primary vital records storage media, action steps you can take to safeguard them, and steps you can take to recover them yourself. Even if you have a company lined up for an emergency, they may be busy with another customer when you call if this is a wide-area emergency (such as a flood or earthquake).

A company's records retention plan should address destroying out-of-date documents, explain how to store records, and detail how to identify each container. If we uncover out-of-date or unmarked documents, we can use the records retention plan as authority to get the records custodians to clean up the storage areas. It is also a chance to educate people about the records retention and storage standards. This information will be very valuable as you work to build your plan.

If your company does not have a written records management and retention program, you may need to write one. It will make your recovery planning a bit easier.

VITAL RECORDS INVENTORY

By now you know that the first step is to make an assessment of what you are going to protect. This will tell you how big the issue is. In the case of vital records, you need to know at a minimum four essential things. Refer to Form 16-1 on the CD-ROM. The inventory, also known as a shelf list, can be combined with the risk assessment spreadsheets. Other information elements may also be useful, such as the document's expiration date, but you want to keep this plan basic:

➤ **Records.** What are these documents about? Are they customer records with credit card numbers, personnel files with legally protected information, or legal documents referring to lawsuits and court actions? The information content of a record will help determine its recovery priority.

➤ **Media.** Is this information stored on paper, magnetic tape, CD, microfilm? This will tell you what its storage conditions should be to protect its readability.

➤ **Originating Department.** This helps you track down someone who may know something about this document to properly prioritize it in the event of a recovery.

➤ **Location.** Vital records turn up in the strangest places, so you need to know where they are all stored. Otherwise, you may lose those vital first few hours after an emergency and the records will be damaged or unrecoverable.

Locate Your Records

The location for storing your records is extremely important. If most of your vital records are stored far away at some distant corporate headquarters, then that saves us from a lot of mitigation and recovery actions. Mitigation and recovery will be the responsibility of people at headquarters. You can then focus your efforts on ensuring a safe delivery to them for storage.

The best place to begin your vital records inventory is with your company's records retention plan. This will detail what types of records you are expected to keep and how long each type of record must be maintained. If you are lucky, then most of these records are stored in the same place, or in only a few places. The key thing is that you know where they are. Ask your records custodian for a copy of the records inventory or a listing of what types of documents are stored at which locations. Your next step is to visit these file rooms and see how much volume is involved. Vital records tend to be bulky collections, so expect to see a lot of boxes.

Companies that keep records in top shape should be admired. Most companies probably have outdated records lingering everywhere. The concern here is not housekeeping, but rather that excess records distract you from dealing with the truly vital records. Once the records custodian sees that you are looking at the records, he or she should wake up and purge the storage areas of outdated documents. Just like cleaning out the garage or seeing the dentist, some people won't do what they should until they must.

It is time well spent to speak to the originators of these records. They can explain to you what is vital and why. Add to your documents inventory the retention period for each document type. Try to uncover any other vital records storage sites not listed, such as interim storage sites, various offices where vital records are stored for office use, and any other records storage. Most departments keep their own cache of records regardless of the need to safeguard or environmentally protect them. Now is not the time to fight that battle. Some of these are in boxes under a desk. Some are in the bottom of coat closets. Some are even stored in people's homes, as if that would be any safer. As you work with each department, find where these records are stored and add them to your records inventory.

Make a list of the locations and the types of media stored in each. Knowing which type of media is stored there helps you to quickly form a containment and recovery plan based on whether the room suffered water damage, smoke damage from a fire in an adjacent room, deep-freezing due to loss of power in the winter, etc. Each type of media has its own preferred storage conditions to protect readability. Paper can tolerate freezing so long as it is not wet. Airborne particles and pollution can damage microfiche. Extreme heat or cold can damage magnetic media such as tapes, diskettes, and fixed disk cartridges.

So now with the records inventory list in hand of the types of media you need to protect, the quantities of material and the locations, we can begin to figure out how to protect these records in an emergency.

Prioritize Your Records

The biggest time saver you can do for your vital records disaster recovery plan is to classify your records according to how valuable they are to your business. This single action will help everyone involved to know which records are to be kept safest or to be recovered first. Skip this step, and valuable time may be wasted on low-value records.

Record priority can be determined by legal requirements. It may be based on the cost to reproduce the same information from other sources. It can be determined by who the originating department is. Select a system that suits your business. Be sure you understand the legal retention period for all document types. If in doubt, consult a lawyer. Do not guess!

Once priority has been established, tag every record or record container. Priority tags should follow a simple color code to speed the containment effort. Consider using 1-inch-square stickers with different colors to indicate priority, such as red for top priority, black for do-not-recover records that have copies at a backup site, etc. Post the color code explanation on the walls and be sure it is documented in your plan. Color coding is especially helpful when there is a fire and someone other than the company employees (fire/police) is performing the salvage operation.

Next, ensure that all your top-priority records are stored in the safest locations. This might be in a fireproof cabinet or in special moisture-proof containers. Typically, the safest place for your documents is on the middle shelf—midway between the floor (moisture, vermin, etc.) and the ceiling (sprinkler heads).

With all the records marked with their recovery priority, make up a floor plan for each storage site indicating the location of your top-priority records. Keep this plan posted in all copies of your recovery plan books. The facility security office should have this also for immediate action during a late-night disaster.

Another classification is by originating department. A visual identification tag is needed so you know which records belong to Human Resources, Finance, Legal, etc. Refer to your company's records retention plan for your standard marking information block. As these documents are recovered, be sure the originating departments are involved in the effort. They may be reluctant to have others perusing their stored documents for reasons of legal or privacy issues.

You might mark or stamp the originating department's name in the recovery priority colored tab.

RECORDS TRANSPORTATION

Just as important as your storage process is how your records are handled during transportation. Do you have an off-site storage facility? Most companies have off-site storage for backup computer media. Imagine how valuable this information would be to an outsider. They can't hack through your network defenses but could they easily snatch your tapes while en route to or from the storage room?

Just because records are traveling to somewhere, don't let your guard down about their security or environmental controls. Once outside the cozy confines of your storage room, they are susceptible to the ravages of all sorts of environmental dangers. Their security must be safeguarded just as well as when they are locked in your storage room. Their environmental "comfort" must also be protected. Improper handling can negate all the careful handling we have used so far. Prudent actions when shipping these records will ensure that they return to you as fresh as they were when they were sent out.

Security

Security during transit is not a lot different from security in your storage room. Keep the curious and the criminal away from your documents. Safeguard the documents from environmental threats so they will be readable upon arrival. Limit access to your records by starting with locked shipping containers. If the records are of very high value, employ a courier to personally carry these records to their destination.

Shipping of vital records should be by an overnight express delivery. This minimizes the amount of time the records are exposed to security and environmental threats. Shipments should be adequately insured to cover the expense of re-creating the material and should be in as inconspicuous a container as possible. Always require a signature from the receiving party. The shipper should provide a tracking number so the progress of the shipment can be monitored. This provides valuable clues when looking for materials missing in transit.

Magnetic Recordings

If a magnetic recording is being sent to someone to review, make a copy of it and send them the copy. Never ship the original. Other things to consider when shipping magnetic media include:

➤ Open-reel magnetic tape should be wrapped in bubble wrap or shock-absorbing material and packed snugly into containers. This will reduce their movement within the container and reduce the likelihood of damage during transit. It also acts as an insulator against temperature swings.

➤ Cassettes with a locking hub should have their hubs locked and be placed in a rigid container for shipping.

➤ Temperatures in transit should not exceed 110 degrees Fahrenheit. The best time of the year to ship these materials is the spring and the fall.

➤ Tapes and cassettes should be shipped in the same way that they are stored, on their edge. The weight of the media should be supported by the hub.

RECORDS RETENTION

Every company has its own records retention requirements. If your company does not have any, then either you are accumulating massive amounts of paper (creating a fire hazard, housekeeping issues, and storage charges), or you are throwing out documents that you should be retaining to meet legal requirements. Either situation is a problem.

The details of the many things that go into a records retention plan are beyond the scope of this book. An important issue is the elimination of obsolete documents. This means we will have fewer documents to protect and to recover. Some organizations like historical societies try to keep everything. That is the nature of the service they provide. But a business cannot afford to hang on to stored documents that have no value. It takes floor space to store them. It takes energy to maintain them within an acceptable environment. It takes people to move them around. Check with your lawyers, check with your accountants, and properly dispose of the excess. Some laws and regulations may require that the original documents be retained even if they are also recorded on other media.

As you implement your plan, work to identify those critical records that must be restored after a disaster. This is a very time-consuming and expensive process. But it begins with being able to quickly find these critical documents. The less clutter there is to wade through, the easier the plan will be to exercise.

The records retention plan will detail a standard way to identify documents. Know what each of the markings mean and where they are supposed to be placed. Be sure that all the high-priority records encountered are properly marked according to this standard.

When documents reach the end of their useful life, they are destroyed. When this happens, a record is made of the event so we know what happened to that document. A portion of a records retention plan will deal with how your company will record document destruction. In an emergency, documents not at the end of their useful life may be destroyed. A part of your recovery effort will be to make a list of what was destroyed. Be sure that your emergency procedure for reporting accidentally destroyed records agrees with your overall records destruction documentation policy.

MEDIA STORAGE

Most business records have a fixed useful life, usually less than 10 years. If your records collection includes documents of historical or artistic value that you must retain indefinitely, then the storage and recovery of those types of documents are beyond the scope of this book. Always consult a restoration professional for questions about storing or recovering these types of artifacts.

In general, your vital records can be reasonably stored at room temperature. This is true for records whose useful life is 10 years or less. The ideal situation is for your records storage facility to be a separate room or set of rooms, with its own air filtration, heating, air conditioning, and humidity controls. The storage environment of your records will be the major determinant of their useful life. The more controlled the environment, the longer they will be readable.

In general, your storage room should be between 62 and 68 degrees Fahrenheit with a relative humidity of 30 to 40 percent all year long. Temperature and humidity should not vary more than 10 percent from your established settings. If your room is cooler than this, allow magnetic media time to slowly warm to room temperature before use. Temperature and humidity will vary in different parts of the storage room so keep the air circulating with a strong air-handling unit.

As the seasons change, so will the weather outside. Be sure your environmental control equipment can compensate for the temperature and humidity variations of the change of seasons and those that occur between day and night.

To monitor the climate in your storage area, install a thermograph and hygrometer. They will chart the conditions inside of the room over time. Pay particular attention to how well the humidity and temperatures stay within tolerance between daylight and nighttime hours—and between winter and summer. If something occurs when no one is around, these charts will indicate when the problem began. You might discover someone is turning off the heat to your storage room over the holidays and weekends, not realizing the impact on stored magnetic media.

Many smaller companies will assign a trusted employee to take the backup tapes home as a remote storage solution. This is not a good idea, as there are security and accessibility issues and risks involved. While you would like to trust all your employees, corporate espionage and damage caused by disgruntled employees are not unheard of. You wouldn't want to be in a position where you have to deal with performance issues with the employee who is storing your corporate data at his or her home. A private home is also not going to be as secure as a professionally managed storage facility. Accessibility could be a problem if a disaster occurs and the employee is not at home due to vacation or other reasons. Listed below are some of the different media types you may have in storage and their particular requirements:

➤ **Paper Document Storage.** Paper is sensitive to humidity and to temperature. It slowly deteriorates. Rapid swings in either or both accelerate this process. If the documents are exposed to low humidity and high temperatures, they gradually dry out and become crumbly. If they are exposed to high humidity and warm temperatures, they become susceptible to mold.

To protect your most important records, store them on the middle to lower-middle shelves. This keeps them well off the floor in case of a flood or pipe leak and away from the sprinkler in case of a fire. It also keeps the records in the middle of the room's temperature range (cooler near the floor, warmer near the ceiling).

➤ **Microfilm Storage.** The first key to safeguarding your microfilm is to store it in an airtight container. This will protect it from dust, humidity, and impurities in the air. The container should be made from a noncorroding material, such as anodized aluminum or stainless steel. If your microfilm is on a roll, the reel should be made of the same material as the container. Always use lint-free gloves when touching the film.

Store your microfilm on shelving and storage racks made from noncorroding material. Special cabinets designed for protecting microfilm can be obtained from industrial equipment suppliers. If possible, do not store your microfilm in rooms containing pressboard or particleboard as these may give off fumes that will damage the film.

The storage room should have its own temperature and humidity controls. Humidity should be between 30 and 40 percent, and it should never change more than 5 percent within a given day. Large swings in temperature and humidity are damaging to microfilm. The temperature should stay around 65 degrees Fahrenheit and vary no more than 5 percent in a given day.

Fire is always a threat to a storage facility. If possible, install a gas fire suppression system. Water from sprinklers is very damaging to microfilm. If you choose to use fireproof cabinets, be sure they are rated for microfilm storage. A cabinet designed to keep paper from burning will not be able to keep damaging heat away from your microfilm. The cabinet must be able to hold the internal temperature below 150 degrees Fahrenheit.

➤ **Magnetic Media Storage.** Magnetic storage media requires every bit as much care as printed documents. The useful life of a tape can be sharply reduced by improper storage or handling. Unlike paper, you cannot readily look at a tape and determine if it is still readable or not. Improper handling can result in a tape becoming unreadable.

Steps must be taken to ensure that no contaminant of any kind comes into contact with the recording media. You should never touch the magnetic surface at any time. Therefore, magnetic media, such as reel tapes, cassettes, floppy disks, etc., should only be stored and used in a very clean environment. In these rooms, smoking, eating, and drinking must be prohibited. Ideally, an air filtration system will be employed to screen out airborne contaminants.

Magnetic media are susceptible to variations in temperature and humidity. If storage and operating temperatures vary more than 15 degrees Fahrenheit, you must allow time for the media to adjust to the different conditions. Allow 4 hours for every 15 degrees Fahrenheit of temperature difference. Strong sunlight will also damage magnetic tape.

The components that make up magnetic tape will react with moisture and slowly begin a process of breaking down the chemical bonds. Carefully avoid water and moisture when tapes are exposed.

Before using a tape, inspect it for surface damage. Look for any debris on the tape (but never touch the media itself without lint-free gloves). If in doubt, clean the tape surface before use. Always return tapes promptly to their protective containers. Minimize how much tapes are handled. Ensure that any tapes being returned to service are first thoroughly bulk erased.

Magnetic tapes should never be dropped or treated roughly. When in storage, they should always be stored on end and never stored "flat" (with the reels parallel to the table). Magnetic tapes are susceptible to damage from magnetic fields. Never store tapes on or near machinery, on windowsills, or on top of electronic devices.

Magnetic media is worthless without the proper equipment required to read the media. As your storage media ages, periodically check to make sure you still have the proper equipment for reading the media. Work with your data processing hardware support team to make sure you are involved when new backup hardware is being considered. Software can also be an issue, as formats may change slightly as backup software and operating systems are upgraded. You may need to copy the old media to a new format as the technology changes.

RISK ASSESSMENT

This is a good place to conduct a risk assessment of the threats facing your vital records. Refer again to Form 16-1 (on the enclosed CD). Use the inventory list of documents to fill in the left side. Once all the documents are listed, identify the storage risks faced by these documents, based on the type of media and where they are stored.

If life were fair, you would be able to select your own storage facility. It would be a secure place without water pipes in the ceiling, with a reliable, steady environmental control system, and no external walls. The facility would be located in a place not susceptible to natural disasters, with a separate clean room for magnetic media storage. Unfortunately, vital records storage is usually on the low end of the floor space priorities, and you must compete for adequate floor space with everyone else. Vital records storage is an overhead cost and does not bring in any revenue. Therefore, it is treated like the coat closet, important to have but must fit in wherever it can.

A key part of the risk assessment is to identify the types of documents to retain and their priorities for restoration. With computers, many of these records can be duplicated from stored media—unless it was in the midst of the fire zone.

Storage risks include:

➤ **Water.** This could be caused by a leaking roof, a burst water pipe, a sheared-off sprinkler head, a water leak on the floor above—any number of things. If this storage area is below ground, is it susceptible to flooding? Are the temperature and humidity automatically controlled? Never establish a records storage area in a room under a rooftop air conditioner, as they tend to collect water. Also, keep away from rooms with overhead water pipes, steam pipes, and exterior walls. Spot coolers used in storage rooms collect water and are a haven for mold and bacteria. Subfloor cooling in computer rooms also collects water.

➤ **Smoke.** If there is a fire in this room, what is the potential for smoke particles to penetrate the packing crates?

➤ **Structural Problems.** Does the roof leak? Is it strong enough to withstand a very heavy snowfall or an unusual downpour? Look at the ceiling. Is it discolored at any place as if moisture was collecting there or had previously leaked?

➤ **Fire.** Is there adequate fire suppression? Does this include fire-suppressing gas or are you relying solely on sprinklers? Is the room clear of clutter? Is anything stored against an electrical appliance or receptacle? Are extension cords in constant use? Are the walls fireproof? Is a fire hazard on the other side of any of the walls?

➤ **Humidity.** How much humidity is floating about in this room? Does it vary appreciably during the year? Is a functioning humidifier/dehumidifier in operation?

➤ **High Heat and Deep Cold.** Excess heat or cold can be very damaging to stored documents—especially for magnetic media and microfiche. Is this room well insulated and climate controlled?

➤ **Wide Temperature Swings.** Wide temperature swings can age your material and cause humidity variations. The best long-term storage environment for your materials is a stable one that varies in temperature no more than 5 degrees Fahrenheit.

➤ **Theft.** If there is something of value in these documents, you must take steps to reduce the likelihood of theft. This can be personnel information, credit card numbers in your customer files, or any number of things. Securing the room with a lock and key is a good start.

➤ **Sabotage.** Similar to theft, except in this case, they just want to destroy what you are safeguarding. Like theft, sabotage may be difficult to detect.

➤ **Insects and Rodents.** No food or drinks should ever be allowed in the storage area. Look around for signs of animal or insect infestation.

➤ **Magnetic Fields.** If you are storing magnetic tape or diskettes, your materials may be susceptible to damage from magnetic fields. Be sure there are none present in your storage areas and also be aware of what is going on in adjacent rooms. Over-the-weekend construction work may not be reported to you yet could damage your media. This hazard includes small magnets and magnetized tools in the storage room.

MITIGATION

Now you need to identify the mitigation actions to be taken to minimize the identified threats. Risks to your records depend on the types of media that they are stored on, how carefully they are stored, and how accessible they need to be.

Use the table in Form 16-1 (on the enclosed CD), where you have previously identified the threat to each document. Now identify the mitigation actions you will use to reduce the impact or likelihood of that threat.

Fire Control System

➤ **Smoke Alarms and Fire Detection System.** Early warning is your best deterrent against losing records to a fire—and most likely is mandated by the local fire code. These alarms must not only alert anyone in the storage area of the danger, but also your facility's security team so that the local fire department is dispatched immediately. These alarms are often used to trigger the gas fire suppression system. Special fire alarms are available that detect fires in their earliest stages. This permits quick intervention with a fire extinguisher before the sprinklers can kick in.

➤ **Sprinklers.** These are necessary to contain fires and save the building. They also provide valuable time for people to escape an inferno. Most of the material stored in the records room will readily burn, so sprinklers are essential. A problem is that the tool you are using to save the room is damaging to what is stored there. Sprinklers are an inexpensive fire suppression tool and regulated by local fire code. Do not defeat the sprinklers' action by lining your shelves with plastic. It will only allow the fire to grow larger before the plastic melts (and is likely a violation of local fire codes).

➤ **Gas Fire Suppression.** Gas fire suppression is the best first line of defense against a fire. It can snuff out a fire before the sprinklers' fusible link melts. Although the gas discharge may spew some particles in the air, the damage is far less than from sprinklers. A gas fire suppression system is expensive and requires a sealed room for best effect, so be sure the doors close automatically and snugly.

➤ **Fire Extinguishers.** These come in several types based on the type of fire. In general, they should be of the "A" type, which is for combustible materials. Fire extinguishers must be inspected monthly. Employees should know where they are and how to use them.

➤ **Fireproof Containers.** Use these for cash, checks, and vital records that cannot be replaced. After a fire, never open these containers until they are completely cooled, inside and out. If the inside is still hot, sudden exposure to fresh air may cause a flash fire. Documents protected from a fire by a fireproof container may be charred but readable.

➤ **Fire Drills.** Drills should be conducted at least every 3 months, or more often if required by your local fire code.

➤ **Good Housekeeping.** This minimizes the amount of rubbish in your storage areas. Rubbish accumulation is nothing more than fuel for a fire or food for vermin. Be sure it is removed daily. If possible, do not allow trash cans in the storage areas at all.

➤ **Electrical Equipment.** Minimize electrical equipment in the storage areas. This is a potential source of fire and magnetic pollution.

◆ Move all possible electrical equipment out of and away from your storage area. This reduces the possibility of a fire starting in this equipment. Also, some equipment, such as copiers, stir up paper dust.

◆ Electrical outlets should not be overloaded as this could start a fire. Always use equipment with properly grounded plugs.

◆ Extension cords are another potential fire source. Be sure to only use heavily insulated extension cords and never on a permanent basis.

Environmental Issues

➤ **Moisture Sensors and Alarms.** These alarms alert you to the presence of moisture in your storage room. These are very useful if you have a raised floor or an area that is difficult to see such as a drain in the room. These alarms may alert you to water buildup or excess moisture due to temperature changes.

➤ **Humidifier/Dehumidifier.** This device will help to keep your records storage area within the proper humidity range.

➤ **Temperature Control.** Some records may be stored on media that is susceptible to temperature damage. Actually, all media are susceptible, but some, like magnetic media, have little tolerance for high or freezing temperatures. These extremes even work to degrade your paper records but not as severely. Steady temperatures will reduce the load on your humidifier/dehumidifier.

➤ **Magnetic Check.** Wherever magnetic media is stored, be sure to run a periodic check of magnetic influences on the storage area. Magnetic influences are difficult to see but will degrade or damage the data stored on magnetic tapes, diskettes, cartridges, etc.

Other Issues

➤ **Secured Access.** Eliminate the people problem by limiting who has access to the storage areas.

➤ **Off-Site Duplication of Key Records.** If you have very critical records, one of your best solutions is to store copies of these records off-site. Then, if a crisis occurs, you will not need to labor through an expensive records recovery process. This would require, however, that you maintain the off-site storage facility to the same high standards as used in your primary records storage facility.

➤ **Pest Extermination.** These creatures are not welcome in your storage area. Insects, rodents, and anything else that might want to dine on your documents must be vigorously kept away from your records.

➤ **Proper Storage**

◆ Identification tags must be attached to every container. In a crisis, these tags will be used to prioritize the records to be recovered. Records recovery is an expensive and time-consuming process. Proper identification allows everyone to focus on the most critical records first.

◆ Any documents containing water-soluble ink should be stored on microfilm. If these documents get wet, they will probably not be recoverable.

◆ Store your most critical records on the middle shelf. This keeps them off the floor in case of a water problem, and the records above will slow down the flow of water from a sprinkler or broken water pipe.

◆ Store all vital records at least 4 inches above the floor. If shelving is not available, use clean pallets.

◆ Do not store anything within 6 inches of the ceiling or lights.

◆ Do not store anything within 18 inches of a sprinkler head. That would interfere with the sprinkler's ability to put out a fire.

◆ Do not store anything in contact with an electrical device or obstructing any of the air-handling ducts.

A quick note on alarms. We talked about moisture sensor alarms, excess temperature alarms, and fire alarms. Alarms are useless unless people know what they mean and what to do when they hear one. During your training exercises, let your staff hear each kind of alarm and explain what to do when it sounds. Repeat this step with every exercise! Ensure that alarms in the closed storage room can be detected and acted on during the weekends and evenings.

Security Mitigation Actions

Unfettered access can lead to theft problems, increased insect issues (people bringing in food), potential for sabotage, and, in some cases, just nosy people rifling through documents. Always secure your vital records storage areas. If they are climate controlled, then the less often the door is opened, the better.

Begin with controlled access to your vital records. This may be as simple as locking the door to the storage closet. Controlling access is important to prevent someone from these actions:

➤ **Reading Your Records.** If these are trade secrets, such as customer lists, you may not want anyone to casually peruse them. Someone reading your records and copying the information can be difficult to detect. If documents are worth keeping, they are worth keeping in secured storage.

➤ **Stealing Records Is a Form of Employee Sabotage.** If these records are required for regulatory compliance, a disgruntled employee could attempt to damage a company's reputation or an executive's job performance by removing records. This can go undetected for a long time. Sometimes companies victimized in this way find out as the documents are published online. An angry employee could also steal the records in an effort to damage your ability to prove company compliance with legal requirements or even to hide their own crimes.

➤ **Damaging Your Records Is a Variation of Employee Sabotage.** Similar to stealing, someone trying to hide their own actions or trying to damage a company's reputation could damage records. Often this is done on a wide scale rather than stealing a few select documents; the miscreant may opt for damage through arson or heavy water damage.

Rodents and Insects Mitigation

Your vital records may be very appetizing to insects and rodents. Basic housekeeping steps can minimize your exposure to these pests. Clutter, dirt, and dust should never be allowed to accumulate. Eating and drinking should never be allowed in your records storage area. Break rooms and cafeterias should be as far from the storage room as possible to reduce exposure to these pests.

These pests also like to be comfortable. They prefer high temperatures and high humidity. Keep your storage room at the optimal temperatures for storing your media; this provides a built-in defense against pests. Ensure that there are no "dead spots" in your air circulation that might create a safe haven for these creatures.

A key way to prevent these creatures from setting up housekeeping is to not invite them into the room in the first place. Doors, windows, and vents should be opened as little as possible. Seal cracks in the walls and ceiling promptly. Inspect incoming materials for signs of insects before admitting them to your storeroom. Remove packing material before entering the storeroom as that is a conduit for the spread of insects.

If an infestation is discovered, the quickest method is to bring in a professional exterminator. Rodents are easier to treat as they can be trapped. Poisons should be avoided as a contaminant to the room's atmosphere.

Insect eradication is a tougher job. If possible, take an example to the exterminator so they can apply the proper solution. Isolate all documents around the infestation. The best solution is to carefully freeze infested paper documents and all the containers around them to kill the insects.

ACTION STEPS FOR YOUR PLAN

In an emergency, you will have an immediate need for damage containment supplies. These supplies should be purchased in advance and stored in a locked room far across the facility from the records storage area. The goal is that an emergency in the storage room will not also destroy your containment supplies. If possible, store the emergency materials on a cart for rapid deployment.

A list of the recommended supplies is found in Form 16-2 (on the enclosed CD). What you need for your site depends on your risk assessment (things likely to go wrong) and your inventory (what types of media you are protecting).

The materials needed for an emergency fall into several general categories:

➤ General items are basic items needed to clean up a mess. Some of these materials age over time (such as flashlight batteries) and should be rotated at least annually (out of the closet and into general use, fresh batteries into the closet). Some of these items may be in regular use in departments across the facility from the storage area and a separate storage stockpile may not be necessary. Not listed here but useful will be a wide range of hand tools.

➤ Portable equipment is the heavy tools you may need to address more severe problems. Smaller items, such as water vacuums and portable dehumidifiers, may be kept in your storage closet. Larger items, such as water pumps, may need to be obtained from the facility's maintenance department. In addition, you must list the telephone numbers of ALL local companies that will rent trucks with freezer compartments in case you must freeze and/or ship documents for off-site recovery.

➤ Individual equipment is the safety equipment for the recovery team. Be sure to inspect this annually and rotate out the older materials to the facility's cleaning staff.

➤ Drying and cleaning materials will be quickly consumed in a large emergency, so be sure you know who the local suppliers are.

➤ Containment material: if the flood waters are rising, if the roof or wall is missing, if the fire is now out, these materials can slow the spread of damage or prevent additional damage from occurring.

Maintenance Activities

Now that you have your storage facility safeguards in place, ensure that you don't let your guard down. Plan to make these activities a part of your normal routine:

DAILY ACTIONS

➤ Trash emptied.

➤ During off hours and weekends, ask your security guard to step into the room and see if it feels too hot or humid.

➤ Check locks on windows and doors.

➤ Look for ceiling leaks, especially after a major storm.

EVERY WEEK

➤ Housekeeping inspection: ensure all trash is promptly removed.

➤ Change the paper on the hygrothermograph's plotter.

➤ Check the corners of the room for warm, moist air circulation "dead spots."

QUARTERLY ACTIONS

➤ Pest control. Check sticky traps, doors, foundations, walls.

➤ Test fire and humidity alarms.

➤ Test water detection sensors.

➤ Fire extinguishers inspection.

➤ Magnetic check; also do this whenever neighboring rooms change, including the floor above and below.

➤ Meet with local emergency officials.

➤ Rotate supplies out of your emergency stock. Be sure that emergency recovery supplies are stored away from the vital records storage so they aren't lost at the same time.

➤ Be sure air filters on all equipment (such as air conditioning) are changed.

You may also want to consider hiring a records storage professional to perform an audit on your off-site storage location, the security procedures in place, and the retrieval process. Whether you perform the work yourself or use a dedicated storage company, this can help you to identify gaps in the company's storage and retrieval process.

IMMEDIATE ACTIONS IN AN EMERGENCY

In an emergency, the first concern is the safety of your people. You must wait until the vital records areas are structurally safe to enter. Buildings are substantially weakened by fire, flood, and any major shock to their structure. In the event of a fire, you must check with the on-scene fire marshal in case the site needs to be sealed for a criminal investigation. This is where your predisaster liaison with local emergency services will pay off. An investigation may not start for days. Work with local officials to gain access to remove your undamaged records—but only do so with the permission of the proper authorities. Before entering, put on the hard hats stored with your emergency supplies. Ceilings are easily weakened in a structural emergency.

In the meantime, scramble around to line up emergency supplies to be ready to act once the go-ahead to enter is given. Contact your company security team and inform them where your records recovery operation will take place so they can assign a detail to keep the curious away from your documents. Immediately call sister companies requesting help from their records custodians. Begin setting up your damage mitigation area so recovery operations can begin as soon as the teams are ready.

When entering a damaged area begin your initial damage assessment. This is a quick walk-through to see which records are obviously damaged. Determine which vital records are damaged. Use the color coding on your containers to see the recovery priority of all damaged containers and their type of damage (heat, water, exposed to air, etc.).

Before opening any file cabinets, use your hand to feel their outside temperature. If they are still hot, allow them to cool thoroughly before opening.

A fireproof cabinet prevents a fire by sealing the contents from an oxygen supply. If the contents are sufficiently hot, and you open the cabinet too soon, you will see your documents turn into a flash fire and quite possibly injure someone.

Based on your initial damage assessment, divide your helpers into teams. There is no set size on a team since each emergency is unique:

➤ **Damage Containment Team.** These people focus on containing the damage. If there are now holes in the walls or ceiling, they should hang heavy-ply plastic to keep out further weather damage. If documents are strewn about on the floor that are too numerous or for whatever reason cannot be picked up, the damage containment team will locate and lay plywood to protect the documents from foot traffic.

➤ **Assessment Team.** These folks will identify the records to be retrieved from the storage area based on their preestablished priority color code. They should take many photographs during all phases of the operations. Assessment pictures can be reviewed for understanding the amount of damage and may be useful to the insurance company. Pictures taken during the recovery can be used as source material for the after-action report.

➤ **Shuttle Team.** These are the people who are carrying documents from the storage room to the recovery area or for transportation to the off-site storage location.

➤ **Triage Team.** This team will log all documents as they are received from the damaged store room to begin tracking them through the recovery process. They will examine incoming documents and assign them to three categories: not damaged, damaged, or beyond recovery. Damaged documents will be categorized by the recovery technique to be used. They also ensure that the priority documents are addressed first. The triage team will monitor the flow of documents to the recovery team and may identify documents to send on for immediate freezing and later recovery.

The triage team will also identify those documents that are unlikely to be salvageable. They may be charred beyond recovery, or deteriorated due to water or physical damage. Note these on your recovery log, tag them and, if made of paper, freeze them for later evaluation.

Some teams may use a color code for documents to indicate their disposition. Take care not to confuse these with the color codes assigned to the documents in normal storage. Use whatever color system suits your situation, but a suggested one is this:

➤ Green for undamaged documents: send these on to storage.

➤ Red for priority documents: to be recovered first.

➤ Yellow for lower-priority documents: to be frozen and reviewed for potential recovery later.

➤ Black for documents beyond hope of recovery.

What If the Emergency Missed Me?

In many instances, your building may be damaged but your records are intact. In those cases, you must decide if they are safe where they are or if they must be evacuated to a safer place. Safety involves both physical security and environmental security. If the air conditioning system still works, plan to stay where you are. Work to return the storage area to its proper environment to inhibit the growth of mold.

Before the emergency, you had a secure building. There were secure walls, locks on the doors, guards at the front door, and other security measures. Once a major structural emergency is contained, there may be holes in the roof or walls, strangers wandering about, and less than adequate physical security for your records. In addition, power may not be functioning in the building until major repairs are completed. You must decide to stay or go.

If you stay, and if your temperature and humidity control equipment are not working, then it is just a matter of time until problems begin. Insects may begin to creep in, mold begins to grow, and your records begin to deteriorate. Still, it is a major effort to pack everything up and move out. Packing, transportation, reestablishing a controlled atmosphere at the new site, and then moving everything back later is a frighteningly difficult challenge. What to do?

The key to this question is how soon electrical service, air conditioning, heating, and humidity control can be restored to your storage areas. If your rooms are unharmed, turn off the air circulation immediately until the air has settled. This should prevent circulating smoke fumes throughout your storage areas. After the emergency has been contained, try to maintain the flow of clean, filtered air at the proper temperature and humidity levels to avoid a forced move of your records.

If you stay, ensure there are adequate air filtration, ventilation, and climate controls in your storage room. This may require the use of a large portable electrical generator and portable air-handling units. With wire runs all the way from the generator in the parking lot up to your storage area, and then with the expense and effort involved with portable air-handling units, you can quickly see what a major job this will be.

If service restoration is likely to be soon, then seal the storage area as tightly as possible and press for prompt temporary repairs to the storage area.

What If the Emergency Hit Me?

There are detailed recovery steps later in this chapter, but the issue here is that if your storage facility is unusable, you must relocate it to an off-site facility. This off-site facility must have security for your documents. It should have as much of the climate control capabilities as your old site as possible. On short notice this could be a problem, so if possible, contract with a storage company to be used on an as-needed basis. If practical, ship the documents to another company site. This will greatly simplify the security arrangements.

Once the disaster has passed and the document recovery process is underway, the new records storage room must be carefully prepared. Be sure that it is completely dry. All the old carpeting, shelving, furniture, and anything else that may harbor mold or fungus must be replaced. Walls, floors, and ceiling must be treated for mold and fungus before returning documents to this room. Be on the lookout for hidden water under tile or raised floors.

Allow fresh paint to dry for at least 2 weeks. This allows the solvents to dissipate and the airborne paint particles to settle.

When all the excitement is passed, sit down and write an after-action assessment. This is where you can recognize the people who helped through the crisis and critique how realistic your plan was. Include the photographs taken during the emergency. You should also review actual expenses incurred for future budgeting.

RECOVERY TECHNIQUES

There are many recovery processes that can be used. Most companies turn this over to a professional recovery service as they lack the expertise and equipment to do this in the face of a major emergency. Document recovery is a very delicate business that, if not properly done, will complete the destruction of your vital records. If you expect to recover your own documents, here are some of the steps to take. You should also study the finer details of document recovery from books dedicated solely to that subject. Time spent practicing before an emergency is an excellent idea.

Water Damage to Paper Records

Water is a threat to all your vital records. Just about any paper documents can be recovered from water damage (except those containing water-soluble ink, which should be microfilmed before storage) if promptly treated. Paper records begin deteriorating in as little as 3 hours. Within the first day, mold, fungus, and bacteria begin growing on paper. Recovery is basically to remove the documents from the water, and then remove the water from the documents. If the document is not to be immediately recovered, then it should be quick-frozen until it can be processed. Freezing can protect a paper document for up to 5 years.

Begin your paper recovery process by stabilizing the atmosphere in the work area to between 50 and 60 degrees Fahrenheit, with a humidity level between 25 and 35 percent. Temperatures and humidity in a room tend to vary based on how close you are to the heater or dehumidifier, so use fans to circulate the air and equalize the conditions. Remove from the room any wet things that are not the documents being treated, such as wet clothes, unneeded packing material, etc.

Review paper documents for damage. Water-soluble inks will not likely survive a good soaking. The wettest records are usually the ones that were on the lower shelves or directly under the fire sprinkler (so be sure not to store your most valuable records in either location!). Among your priority records, process the wettest ones first.

Remove all metal fasteners from the documents. This will prevent rust from forming on the fastener and then spilling over onto the document. Use plastic milk crates or similar containers to transport documents because they allow for some of the water to drain off. Never pack them more than three quarters full as the weight of the wet papers will further damage your documents. For the same reason, you should not stack books atop each other in these crates.

Wrap the documents in freezer paper before placing them in the crate, about 200 sheets at a time. Wrap books and set them in the crate with their spine toward the bottom. Always make a list of any documents you have found, their condition, and where you sent them. Mark the identity of the documents on the outside of the freezer paper.

AIR-DRYING PAPER RECORDS Air-drying is the easiest but most labor-intensive process for recovering paper documents. It is most suitable for small amounts of documents or lightly damp books. Drying documents in the open air requires a lot of space and time. After drying, the documents will never look the same and may be permanently stained by soot and water. Note these considerations:

➤ Wet paper is easily torn. Handle every document very carefully.

➤ Individual sheets of coated paper are very difficult to air-dry. Send them to a freeze-dry facility. If they are to be air-dried, carefully separate them immediately. Books printed on coated paper should never be air-dried. They should be frozen immediately and sent for professional recovery.

➤ Books suffer the most from air-drying. Most will be distorted from the moisture and will require rebinding. Very wet books should always be freeze-dried. If you decide to air-dry books, interleave absorbent paper every few pages. Do not stress the spine. Place absorbent paper inside the front and back covers. Change the absorbent paper every several hours. Dampness will persist in the spine and the covers for quite some time, so you must check often for mold. Never return books to shelves until fully dry to reduce introduction of mold into your facility.

➤ Air-dried documents, especially books, are susceptible to mold.

➤ Mud can be brushed from dry documents. Trying to remove mud while the paper is still wet simply pushes the mud into the document fibers.

As you begin your recovery efforts, use the nylon fishing wire in your emergency supplies to string some drying lines. Take care where you place the wire as it is hard to see, especially in low light, because people may run into it. Separate the sheets of paper and hang them on this drying line.

In your drying room, keep temperatures lower than 70 degrees Fahrenheit and humidity below 50 percent to inhibit the growth of mold. Use fans to circulate the air to the dehumidifiers to accelerate drying. If your drying efforts are conducted outside, keep in mind that prolonged exposure to sunlight will accelerate the aging of paper.

An alternative to a drying line is to spread the documents out on tables covered with absorbent paper. Interleave sheets of paper with absorbent paper if they are very wet or in a book. Change this paper as needed, depending on how wet the documents are. Use your fans to keep the air circulating around the room to the dehumidifier.

Other recovery methods include photocopying damaged documents and discarding the original. This solution may depend on any legal requirements for maintaining the original document. Another is to use a low-heat clothing iron to gently heat the moisture from the paper.

Dried records always require more storage space when finished. Photocopy water-damaged documents if possible and keep the copy (assuming there is not a legal requirement to keep the original).

FREEZE-DRYING PAPER RECORDS Freezing is a way to stop the progress of damage to your damp paper-based documents. Those documents that cannot be recovered quickly or those which will be transported off-site for recovery should be frozen. If the quantity of documents is small, use dry ice to freeze them during transport. If the quantity is large, call in freezer trucks. Freeze documents to between 20 and −40 degrees Fahrenheit. Freeze as quickly as possible to prevent damage from the formation of ice crystals.

If a commercial recovery service is used, they will freeze your documents and possibly vacuum dry (freeze-dry) them. This process reduces stains and odors caused by smoke and also eliminates mold. Freeze-drying is a passive process and may take several weeks or more to complete. Freeze-drying is the best solution for recovering wet books. In the case of slightly damp books, this will kill any mold. In the case of very wet books, this will reduce the damage to the book in addition to killing any mold.

Wrap bundles of documents in freezer paper and place in interlocking milk cartons. Document bundles should be about 2 inches thick. The milk cartons allow for air circulation and moisture drainage. Be sure to label the bundles so you know what they are without unwrapping them. Books should be wrapped separately. Never fill the cartons more than three quarters full, as damp paper is weak and easily damaged.

When preparing books for shipment to a freeze-drying facility, support the bindings to reduce the likelihood of swelling. This will reduce the amount of rebinding required for your recovered material.

Even though your records are in a recovery facility, you must still ensure their security. Depending on the sensitivity of your data, you might want a security guard present in the drying room at all times. Now is not the time to drop your guard.

UNRECOVERABLE DOCUMENTS The destruction of any document must be carefully recorded. Be sure to clearly identify what the document was, any identifying titles or routing codes, and why (or how) it was destroyed.

Fire Damage of Paper Records

Fire damage to your records can be just as severe as water damage. Fire will char documents, cover them with soot, and make them more brittle. They may also be wet and smell of smoke. Even portions that are not burned may be darkened by heat and smoke. If you can do without the original document, make a photocopy and discard the original. Handle these documents as little as possible as they may be quite brittle and crumble in your hands.

Place every fire-damaged document on paper towels or absorbent paper. Move these documents by picking up the absorbent paper, not by touching the document itself. The absorbent paper will also pull some of the moisture out of the document.

Microfilm

Wet microfilm must be delivered to a film duplicator as soon as possible. Line containers with clean trash bags and fill them with clean cool water. Submerge the film in the water and deliver them to a professional recovery service within 48 hours. The recovery service will professionally wash the media and dry it.

Optical and Magnetic Media

Wet magnetic media should be placed in bags of cold water for transportation. The media should never be frozen. Use distilled water when rinsing magnetic materials. Tap water may contain chemicals or other materials that would dry on the media. Air-dry the magnetic media in a clean room within 48 hours. Conduct a quick check of the recovery area and ensure no magnetic sources are present, including magnetized tools.

Once magnetic storage media is dry, promptly copy it onto fresh media. Clean the read heads frequently.

➤ **Tapes.** Immediately rinse dirty water and mud off magnetic tapes. Be sure to never touch the magnetic media with your bare hands. When touching the media, use lint-free gloves and handle as little as possible. Whenever possible, handle the tapes by the hubs or the reel. Air-dry in a clean room to prevent the settlement of dust and other particles on the media.

➤ **Compact Disks.** Handle the CD carefully to avoid scratching. Air-dry to remove moisture.

➤ **Floppy Disks.** Pack wet disks vertically in bags of cold water. Rinse thoroughly before air-drying.

CONCLUSION

Vital records protection is not difficult, but requires some thought and action before a disaster strikes to keep the damage to a minimum. The key is a good records retention policy, so that you are storing as little as possible and destroying records you no longer need.

CHAPTER 17

DATA
Your Most Irreplaceable Asset

640K ought to be enough for anybody.
— Bill Gates, cofounder of the Microsoft Corporation, 1981

INTRODUCTION

Most of what you lose in a disaster is relatively easy to replace. Buildings can be rebuilt or new offices leased, furniture is easily replaced, and even new computers can be purchased at the click of a button. What is not easy to replace is your competitive advantage, which is stored in the files and databases within your computer systems. This critical information is in accounting files, customer lists, part lists, manufacturing drawings, etc. This information is unique to your company; it is what makes your company special to your vendors and customers. It is the very essence of your company. Unlike physical assets, this information is difficult, if not impossible, to re-create once it is gone.

There are two types of risks to the infrastructure that supports your data assets: (1) physical loss due to a device failure or a disaster at your location and (2) logical loss caused by an application or user error. Physical loss is the less likely of the two, but it is potentially the most damaging. It includes incidents such as a hard disk failure, server failure, or an environmental disaster, such as a fire or flood. It can affect just a single device or your entire location. Physical loss accounts for approximately 20 percent of all incidents affecting information technology resources. In contrast, logical loss includes incidents such as application errors, user errors, or a security breach. Logical failures account for approximately 80 percent of all incidents. A logical failure can be easier to repair, but it may also not be noticed for some time.

COMPONENTS OF AN INFORMATION TECHNOLOGY INFRASTRUCTURE

A modern corporate computing environment consists of components that build on each other to support the functions of the business. You must understand each of these components and how they relate to your business process to create an effective recovery strategy. At the foundation of this infrastructure are data. Figure 17-1 shows the typical components of an information technology (IT) infrastructure.

Each layer builds on the layer below, building up to the application that the user sees. The applications interact in varying degrees depending upon the requirements of the organization. But no matter what the specific architecture, the foundation is the data that are stored on various media somewhere within the organization.

RISK ASSESSMENT

Your data are susceptible to loss or damage or both from several sources. Some key causes of data loss include:

➤ **Viruses.** These malicious programs can get into your system at any time and strike when you least expect it. Once you're infected, the virus can spread from system to system, destroying data along the way.

➤ **Natural Disasters.** Fire, flood, and high winds can all cause physical damage to systems and make your data unavailable or unreadable.

➤ **Human-Created Outages.** Systems can be damaged by a sudden loss of power, or worse yet, a small part of a data stream can be lost, causing damage that may not be readily apparent.

➤ **Hard Drive Crash.** It's not *if* a hard drive will fail, but *when*. A hard drive is most likely to fail within 90 days of being placed in service and after about three years of average use (see Figure 17-2).

➤ **Laptop or Smartphone Loss or Theft.** The value of the data stored on a laptop or other portable device usually far exceeds the cost of replacing the hardware.

Market research firm IDC estimates that approximately 60% of all corporate data reside on laptop and desktop PCs.

➤ **Software Failures.** Operating systems and storage area network software can fail, corrupting existing data.

➤ **Application Failures.** Applications are not guaranteed to be bug free; a bug in an application can cause incomplete or incorrectly formatted or calculated data to be written into your files.

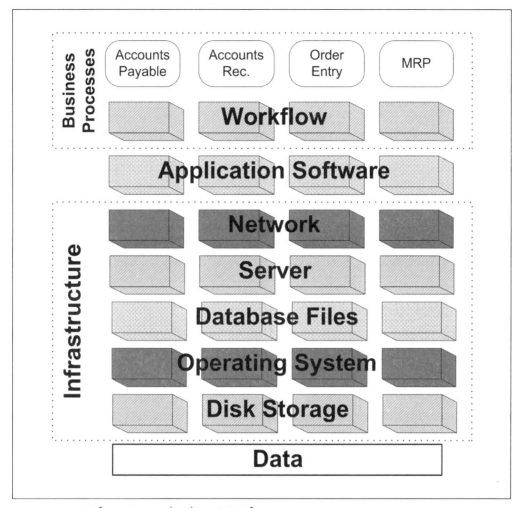

FIGURE 17-1: Information technology (IT) infrastructure.

➤ **Vendor Failure.** If you are hosting e-commerce or other applications with an SaaS (Software as a Service) vendor, your data could be at risk if the vendor suddenly goes out of business.

Approximately 20% of application downtime is attributed to a "disaster."

    40% is caused by application code failures.

    40% is caused by operator error.

    20% is caused by system/environmental failure or other disasters.

Source: Legato Systems

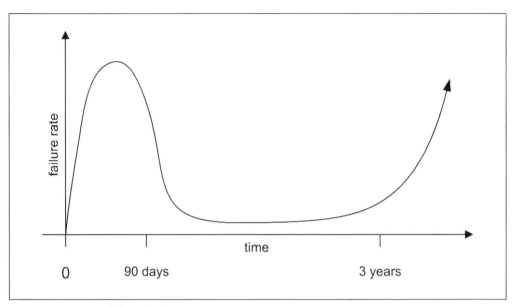

FIGURE 17-2: Hard drive failure rates

There are both tactical and strategic issues surrounding the loss of critical corporate information. Tactical issues include:

➤ **Compromised Information.** Your valuable information could fall into the hands of competitors if stolen by hackers or by losing a portable device. Your competitors having this information could be more damaging than if it were simply destroyed.

➤ **Lost Productivity.** Re-creating lost data can be very expensive, especially if it must be re-created from paper records.

➤ **Employee Downtime.** Employees need their information to do their jobs; this includes people in the sales, customer service, and accounting departments.

➤ **Loss of Customer Information.** Loss of important customer records can seriously hinder your ability to serve your customers.

➤ **Increased Help Desk Support Required.** Not only might your help desk people be needed to help restore your data, but they will be bombarded by users requesting assistance and information.

In 2007, TJX, the parent company of TJ Maxx and Marshalls, reported that hackers had gained access to approximately 45.7 million unencrypted credit and debit card numbers. Estimates of the cost of the breach range from $250 million to as much as $1 billion.

Strategic issues surrounding data loss are those that have an impact on some critical operation within your business processes. This might include:

➤ **Loss of Opportunity.** Without up-to-date and accurate information about your customers and your company, data loss can result in lost sales. If you don't have accurate inventory information, customers may order from someone else who can guarantee delivery from stock. Follow-up calls to customers might be missed if your CRM data are lost; this may also resulting in lost sales. Future sales could also be in jeopardy.

➤ **Decreased Operational Efficiency.** The lack of access to data will result in a greater reliance on manual processes, which will drastically decrease your operation efficiency.

➤ **Inability to Support Customers.** Without access to customer data, you will have a difficult time supporting your customers or will incur unnecessary costs providing support to which they are not entitled.

➤ **Increased Systems Costs.** Your total cost of ownership (TCO) will increase, making it more difficult to make money if margins are thin.

➤ **Noncompliance Issues.** Without accurate data, you might not be able to prove compliance with government mandates, resulting in fines and legal fees.

Other costs you may incur from a serious data loss incident include:

➤ **Customer Notification.** Many states now require that companies notify all customers potentially affected by a data breach.

➤ **Litigation Expenses.** Lawsuits resulting from a data loss incident can be very expensive.

➤ **Internal Investigations.** Time and resources will be required to clean up after a data breach.

➤ **Forensic Experts.** You may need to hire outside forensic experts to help identify any existing security weaknesses.

➤ **Software Updates.** In many cases numerous software updates may be required to patch security holes.

➤ **Subpoenas by Government Authorities.** You may be required to respond to subpoenas from state Attorneys General or by the Federal Trade Commission.

➤ **Stock Price.** If you are a public company, your stock price may go down after a data breach becomes news.

➤ **Reputation.** Data breaches affecting credit card information can be especially damaging to a company's reputation with its customers.

CREATING YOUR DATA RECOVERY PLAN

Just like any other project, there are several distinct steps required to develop your plan to successfully recover your data after a disaster. The recommended steps, as shown in Figure 17-3, are:

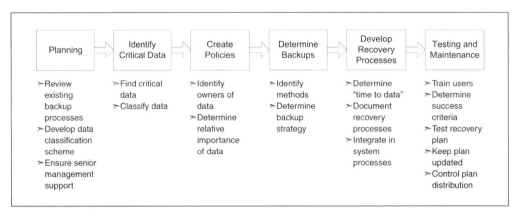

FIGURE 17-3: Data recovery steps.

1. Planning.

2. Identify critical data.

3. Create appropriate policies and procedures.

4. Determine type of backups.

5. Develop recovery processes.

6. Plan testing and maintenance.

PLANNING

As with any project, a successful data recovery plan begins with proper planning. Your first step should be to review data recovery expectations with key stakeholders. Find out what their business needs are, and if there are regulatory requirements about which they are concerned. Few organizations have not done any data recovery planning, so your next step should be to review the existing backup and restoration strategies. Find out what is currently being backed up and how often. Are there procedures in place to periodically test the backups? How are the backups transported and stored? What new systems have come online since the backup documentation was last updated? Are old files being backed up that could be archived and removed from the live systems?

Begin researching the most efficient and effective ways to store your backed-up data. Do you have multiple facilities that can store each other's data? Make sure that the data being stored cannot be destroyed in the same disaster; they should be at least 20 miles apart.

You must also plan for an analysis and classification of data. What is the importance to the firm of each file being backed up? The cost of protecting the data should be proportional to the value of the data. You don't want to spend a lot of time and resources protecting data that are easily restored by other means.

There are numerous strategies for backing up and restoring of data. They include traditional offline storage methods, such as hardcopy printouts, magnetic tape, CD-ROM, portable hard drives, and microfiche. However, online methods, which include disk mirroring, storage area networks and Internet backups, allow for faster restoration of your data. The evaluation and selection of the appropriate strategies are critical to the success of your recovery plan. Other things to consider are whether your backup hardware and software tools are the latest versions from the manufacturer. Many firms have had a disaster only to discover that the software needed to read their backup media was outdated and difficult and expensive to obtain, or simply no longer available.

Where your data will be stored is also an important consideration. It's most convenient if your firm has multiple locations that can store each other's data. You might also have a reciprocal agreement with another noncompeting firm to store data for each other. Of course, you need to be reasonably sure that both locations won't be affected by the same disaster. You'll also need to make sure that both locations can handle the extra workload if one site is down. This option is difficult to manage and does not always work well in practice.

Another option is to use a commercial storage company that will have an environmentally controlled facility to protect the integrity of your media. It will also have tested procedures for storing and retrieving data in an emergency and can offer advice on your disaster recovery plans.

If you lose not only the data but the hardware on which it is stored, you will also need a place to set up replacement hardware. One option is to have a contract with a vendor to have an off-site facility ready if your location experiences an incident. There are several basic types of remote sites:

➤ **Cold Site.** A cold site is simply a place to store your data. It should have adequate space and infrastructure (power, communications, and environmental controls) to support your systems. This is the least expensive option, but it requires the most time to get up and running in the event of a disaster.

➤ **Warm Site.** A warm site has systems and communications ready to go, but it requires that data to be restored on to them before they are ready to use.

➤ **Hot Site.** A hot site is an active duplicate of your live systems, with both systems and data ready to go at a moment's notice. Hot sites are usually staffed 24 hours a day, 7 days a week, and are prepared for immediate action if an incident occurs.

➤ **Mobile Site.** A mobile site is a self-contained transportable office custom fitted with IT and communications equipment. It is usually transported by truck and can be set up at the desired location. The mobile site needs to be configured before it is needed for it to be a viable recovery solution. If using an outside vendor, a service-level agreement is necessary to make sure the vendor is committed to meeting your needs in an emergency.

➤ **Mirrored Site.** A mirrored site is an exact duplicate of your production site, with data stored there in real time. This is the quickest way to get your business back up and running, but it is also the most expensive.

The different recovery site options offer different cost and recovery time tradeoffs. Your organization's restore time requirements and the results of your Business Impact Analysis will determine which option you choose. Figure 17-4 compares the resource requirements for the different recovery site options.

Restoring data in the fastest time possible will minimize the revenue loss caused by damaged or lost data. "Time to data" is a critical metric to evaluate when creating your recovery plan, and is defined as how much time it takes for your users to have access to their data after a disaster occurs.

Rapid "time to data" is fundamental in achieving reduced downtime and maximizing productivity and system I/O rates.

Source: Strategic Research Corporation

Asset management is an important key to recovering your systems. You'll need an accurate and complete hardware and software inventory list. You'll need to know when and where it was purchased, as well as the warranty status. You'll need to know where the hardware was located and how it was configured. Your original software licenses will be necessary to facilitate getting new media from your software vendors. You'll also want to research what the vendor's policy is in a disaster situation. You'll want to know what to do if you need to quickly obtain replacement software.

IDENTIFY CRITICAL DATA

The first problem you'll face in creating your data recovery plan is *finding* the data. The amount of data being produced by business today is growing rapidly. These are not just data stored in traditional databases, but also include graphics, word processing files, spreadsheets, sound clips, and other enhanced forms of data. In many organizations, terabyte (approximately 1 trillion bytes) databases are becoming common; petabyte (1,024 terabytes) size databases are right around

Type of Site	Cost	Equipment	Communications	Setup Time	Location
Cold	Low	None	None	Long	Fixed
Warm	Medium	Partial	Partial – Full	Medium	Fixed
Hot	Medium-High	Complete	Full	Short	Fixed
Mobile	Medium-High	Servers only	Varies	Varies	Mobile
Mirrored	High	Complete	Complete	None	Fixed

FIGURE 17-4: Recovery site selection criteria.

the corner. And, of course, paper is still an important repository of data; these paper files are stored in file cabinets, desk drawers, etc. Microfilm and microfiche are also still used in many organizations. For data that are stored electronically, there are products available for automatically discovering files and databases throughout your network.

The next issue after you have found the data is *categorizing* the data. Like paper files, much of the electronic data that are created are never referenced again. You'll need to identify the critical data required to restore critical business operations. Don't forget to review ancillary data and documentation and data that must be preserved due to legal requirements.

Nonessential Data

Much of what is stored on your file servers by users is data that are not essential to the operation of the business. This includes space-wasting data such as e-mail attachments, Internet cache files, and personal files such as digital pictures. This nonessential data can add to the cost of backup and recovery in many ways. If you have a hot-site facility, it will require more disk storage space. If you are performing backups using tapes or CDs, additional media will be required for backups. If you are using replication to a remote location, additional bandwidth may be required to support the transfer of all these files.

A place to start in reducing the volume of unneeded files is to have policies in place that prohibit the storage of personal files on company servers. Strict enforcement of these policies can dramatically reduce the amount of data that are backed up. You should also consider limiting the amount of storage place available to each user, which will force them to consider carefully what to store in their personal folders.

CREATE APPROPRIATE POLICIES AND PROCEDURES

Most companies do not have policies and procedures for storing and classifying data. And many that do have policies do a poor job of enforcement. Having policies that aren't enforced can create a false sense of security, which can be worse than having no policies at all.

The first step in creating policies for storing and classifying data is to identify the owners of information. All data in the company should have an identified owner who is responsible for understanding the importance and use of the data.

Once the owners of the data have been identified, develop a policy for determining the relative importance of data. You can then develop an information classification scheme. Some categories you might use include business critical, sensitive, legally required, and noncritical.

➤ **Business Critical.** These are data that you must have to run your business. This can include customer lists, production drawings, accounting files, etc.

➤ **Sensitive.** These are data that you would not want your competitors to see. This might include customer lists, employee lists, production process documentation, etc.

➤ **Legally Required.** This is information that you need for compliance with government regulations, such as Occupational Safety and Health Administration (OSHA) compliance data, Environmental Protection Agency (EPA) information, hiring data, etc.

➤ **Noncritical.** This is information that you can live without. Up to 90 percent of all information stored in file cabinets and databases is never retrieved, so this category can include a lot of data.

DETERMINE TYPE (OR TYPES) OF BACKUPS

Different types of data and different time to data requirements will require different backup processes and media. Types of backups include:

➤ Regular backup to tape or other removable media.

➤ Remote mirroring.

➤ "Electronic vault" storage via a wide area network or the Internet.

You will probably use a combination of techniques, balancing time to data versus cost tradeoffs. Traditional tape backups are still widely used and can be effective, but they can create transportation issues, storage issues, and restoration issues. If not handled and stored properly, tapes can fail without warning. They require that the application also be reloaded, and software to read the tapes must be available. Electronic vault storage allows you to save your data over a wide area network, such as the Internet, and can be easier to restore than tape. Remote mirroring ensures that there is little or no data loss, but it is the most expensive option.

DEVELOP RECOVERY PROCESSES

The last step is to develop and document the process for both backup and recovery of data. It does no good to have a plan in your head or one that sits on the shelf. Schedules will need to be developed to ensure that backups are made in a timely fashion. Some criteria to be considered when evaluating which recovery techniques to use include:

➤ **RTO (Recovery Time Objective).** How quickly must the data be restored before business is adversely affected?

➤ **RPO (Recovery Point Objective).** How much data can you afford to lose before the business is adversely affected?

➤ **Availability.** Can the system be down while you create the backups?

➤ **Restoration.** How sure do you have to be that you can restore the data?

➤ **Value.** How much is it worth to protect the data?

➤ **Performance.** What are the performance requirements of the application?

You must also consider how effective each recovery technique is in protecting from the different types of loss. Each business process may have a different recovery process.

DATA STORAGE OPTIONS

There are numerous options for data storage, each with its own advantages and disadvantages.

Tape Backup

Tape backup is almost as old as computing itself. Tape has a low cost per gigabyte, and it is relatively easy to transport and store. Tape has been a reliable workhorse for the storage and archiving of important data, but it is not foolproof. Tapes can fail, so it is critical that backup tapes are periodically audited. The audit should be done by randomly selecting a tape and verifying that it can be read and restored using different equipment than that used to create it. An emergency is not a good time to discover that the tapes are unreadable or can only be read by the equipment used to create the backup.

If the data are important enough to back up, then they are important enough for you to implement the appropriate levels of physical and logical security. Ensure that the tapes are stored in a climate-controlled location free of dust and other sources of contamination. You should also make multiple copies of the tapes that can be stored in different locations to increase the chances of the data surviving a disaster.

Almost as important as how and where the tapes are stored is creating a tape rotation schedule. It is impractical in all but the smallest organizations to back up everything each time a backup is performed, so the normal practice is to perform a full backup periodically (e.g., weekly) followed by regular backups of any changes that have occurred since the full backup. The most common tape rotation strategy is called the Grandfather-Father-Son (GFS) backup scheme. It offers the following benefits:

➤ A minimum number of tapes is required to keep all the system's data backed up.

➤ It is easy to understand and perform, making it more likely to be followed.

➤ It is relatively easy to restore lost data from backups using this process.

➤ It minimizes the wear and tear on both the tapes and the equipment.

The most common GFS backup process is to use a seven-day schedule where a full backup is created once a week (usually over the weekend). Incremental backups are then made each of the other days. Tapes can be rotated and reused at specified intervals, depending upon how many copies you wish to store. An example GFS backup strategy is:

1. Create an initial complete backup. Label this tape "Month 1" and store off-site. This is the first "Grandfather" tape.

2. Create a full backup at the beginning of the week. Label this tape 'Week 1" and store off-site. This is a "Father" tape.

3. On each of the other days, perform an incremental backup using a different tape for each day. Label each tape with the appropriate day of the week. These are the "Son" tapes.

4. On the same day of the week that you did the first full backup, perform another full backup and label the tape "Week 2."

5. Repeat for each week of the month, reusing the incremental backup tapes each week.

6. After 4 weeks, make a full backup and store this tape off-site. This becomes the second "Grandfather" tape. The first "Grandfather" tape can now be reused.

7. Repeat the weekly process, reusing the "Father" tapes from the previous month.

Disk Mirroring

With disk mirroring, data are written to two different disks to create two identical copies to increase the odds that at least one copy of the data is available at all times. The main disk used to store the data is called the protected disk, and the disk to which the data are replicated is called the backup disk. The two disks can be in the same location or in different locations. A WAN is used if the backup disk is at a different location from the protected disk. Installing the backup at a different location provides protection against a disaster that occurs at the location of the protected disk. While this is an effective approach, beware of its impact on your network traffic load.

Two different types of disk mirroring are available, synchronous and asynchronous. Each provides a different time-to-data recovery, and each has different performance considerations.

Synchronous mirroring works by writing to the backup disk first, then writing to the protected disk once it has been confirmed that the write to the backup disk was successful (see Figure 17-5). This type of mirroring ensures that the backup data are always up to date, but it is slower and more expensive than asynchronous mirroring. Special disk controllers are required to enable the two-way communication between the disks, and there is inherent latency between the writing of the data to the backup disk and waiting for the confirmation.

Asynchronous mirroring (or shadowing) works by sending the data to both the protected and backup disks at the same time (see Figure 17-6). It is cheaper than synchronous backup, and more than one system can write to the backup

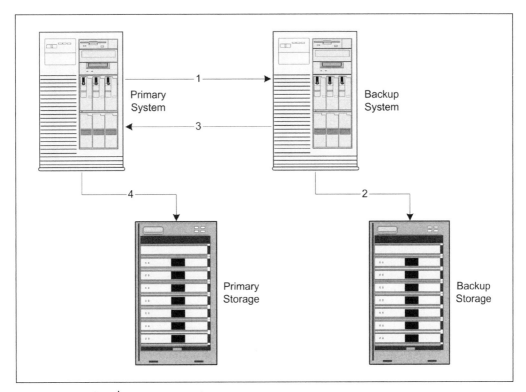

FIGURE 17-5: Synchronous mirroring.

disk. It is also quicker, since the application does not have to wait for a confirmation on the write to the backup disk. The downside to asynchronous mirroring is that you cannot be guaranteed that the last transaction before a disaster was successfully written to the backup machine.

RAID

RAID is an acronym for redundant array of inexpensive (or independent) disks and is used to provide fault tolerance to disk storage systems. RAID works by combining a collection of disks into a logical array of disks using a special disk controller that does not require all disks to be functioning to maintain data integrity. It can be implemented using either hardware or software. The RAID drives are seen as a single device by the operating system. RAID also increases disk performance and reliability by spreading the data storage across multiple drives, rather than a single disk. The terms used when describing a RAID implementation are defined below:

➤ **Duplexing.** Disk duplexing involves the use of two RAID controllers writing the same data to two separate disks simultaneously. A system using duplexing can survive the failure of either a disk controller or a hard disk.

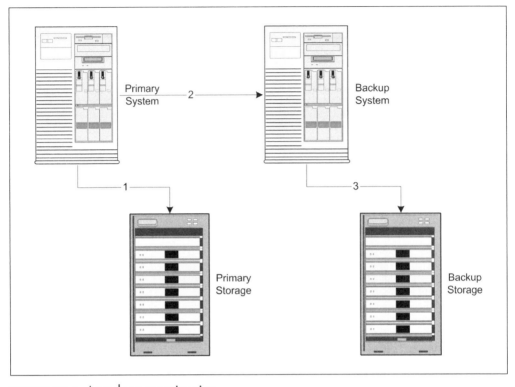

FIGURE 17-6: Asynchronous mirroring.

➤ **Mirroring.** Disk mirroring involves the use of a single RAID controller writing the same data to two separate disks simultaneously. A system using mirroring can survive the failure of either hard disk. Both duplexing and mirroring can slow down system performance because the data is being written twice.

➤ **Striping.** Striping involves breaking up the data into smaller pieces and writing the different pieces to multiple disks. The data may be broken up into bits, bytes, or blocks depending upon the RAID implementation used. Striping is faster than either duplexing or mirroring.

➤ **Parity.** Parity is a way to achieve data redundancy without the disk space overhead of mirroring by storing logical information about the data being written to facilitate recovery. Parity is used with striping and requires at least three disks. The parity information is either stored across multiple disks or on a separate disk.

There are several levels of RAID operation, each with its own balance of redundancy, fault tolerance, cost, and complexity.

➤ **RAID 0.** Disk striping. This implementation of RAID uses disk striping. The data are divided among several disks, which allows for good performance, but with no redundancy. This level offers no protection against data loss if a disk were to fail, and it is not recommended for data recovery purposes.

➤ **RAID 1.** Mirroring and duplexing. This level of RAID involves mirroring or disk duplexing of the data across two or more disks. This provides for redundancy in case of a disk failure. Performance is slower than with RAID 0, especially during data writes. This level is simple and inexpensive to implement, but 50 percent of the storage space is lost because of the data duplication.

➤ **RAID 2.** Bit-by-bit striping. This level stripes data bit by bit across multiple drives and is used with disks without built-in error detection. Since most modern disks have built-in error detection, this level of RAID is rarely used today.

➤ **RAID 3.** Byte-by-byte striping. This level stripes data byte by byte across multiple drives, with the parity information stored on a separate disk. The parity disk can be used to restore data if a failure occurs. The parity information is at risk because it is stored on a single drive.

➤ **RAID 4.** Block-by block striping. This level of RAID stripes data at the block level. Just like RAID 3, the parity information is stored on a separate disk. Performance is greater than with RAID 2 or 3 because the data are handled in block sizes.

➤ **RAID 5.** Striping with distributed parity. This level is similar to RAID 4, except that the parity information is stored among the available disks. RAID 5 is a common implementation of RAID.

➤ **RAID 10.** Mirrored striping. This level of RAID (sometimes called RAID 0+1) is a combination of RAID levels 0 and 1. Data are striped across multiple disks and also mirrored. It provides the best fault tolerance of all the RAID levels but is obviously the most expensive.

Load Balancing

Load balancing is used to distribute network traffic dynamically across a group of servers running a common application to prevent any one server from becoming overwhelmed. Using load balancing, a group of servers appears as a single server to an application on the network. The load balancing process is part of the network operating system; the process monitors each server to determine the best path to route traffic on the network to increase performance and availability. Load balancing also allows the application to continue running even if one of the servers goes down. So long as at least one server is available, the application will continue running. Load balancing can be implemented on different servers at a single location or at different sites. If load balancing is implemented on servers at different sites, it can act as a method to allow access to applications in the event of an incident at one of the locations.

Network Attached Storage

A network attached storage (NAS) environment is a common storage area for multiple servers. NAS environments are useful for storage or file server applications, such as mail and Web services. A NAS server runs a minimal operating system, and is optimized to facilitate the movement and storage of data. Using a NAS environment creates a centrally managed storage pool, which allows new storage devices to be added without requiring network downtime. Storage volumes from a down server can be easily reassigned, or new storage can be easily added if needed. The flexibility provided by a NAS environment increases the availability and reliability of network storage, adding value to your disaster contingency plans.

Storage Area Networks

A storage area network (SAN) is a high-speed, high-performance network that allows computers running multiple operating systems to store data on a single virtual storage device. A SAN is designed to handle backup traffic more efficiently than a NAS environment. The SAN can be local or remote, and usually communicates with the server using a fiber channel. By moving the storage off the LAN, backups can be performed without affecting the performance of the applications on the LAN.

Online Backups

Online data storage is becoming popular as software as a service (SaaS) is being used more and more to provide services to end users. With online data storage, changes to your data are delivered via the Internet to the service provider. This allows your data to be stored at a secure, professionally managed location away from any dangers to your facility. Online data storage provides the following benefits for disaster recovery:

➤ The most obvious benefit is that your data is automatically stored to another location. Backups do not have to be manually started or managed.

➤ Your data can be protected using a single solution that is accessible anywhere there is an Internet connection.

➤ Remote offices and road warriors can back up their data without requiring separate hardware or complex VPN solutions.

➤ There are lower upfront costs to implement an online backup solution—service is normally provided on a subscription basis.

➤ No special in-house technical skills are required as this becomes the backup service provider's responsibility.

As with anything else, there are tradeoffs you must be willing to make to implement an online data storage solution for use in disaster recovery:

➤ Likely higher overall costs since the service is normally provided on a subscription basis—the provider recoups its equipment and software costs over the term of the subscription agreement.

➤ There may be issues with retrieving your data from the provider.

➤ Your provider could experience an outage which prevents you from accessing your data.

➤ Restoring large amounts of data over the Internet is time- and bandwidth-consuming.

➤ What happens to your data if your online data storage vendor goes out of business?

A hybrid option for online backup combines the best of onsite backup storage with the best of traditional online backup services. Some vendors will provide you with an appliance and software that allow you to use the Internet to do online backups, yet still have physical access to the backup device at a location that you control. This protects you against some of the disadvantages of service-only online backup solutions, such as losing your data to bankruptcy of your service provider. It also makes complete restorations easier, as the device can be physically brought onsite and connected directly to the local network for quick restoration.

Figure 17-7 is a comparison of the relative availability value of the different data storage options described here.

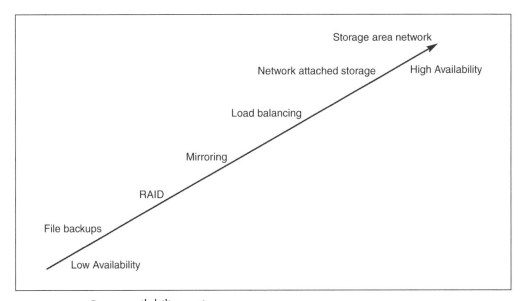

FIGURE 17-7: Data availability options.

VIRTUALIZATION

An increasingly popular technique for managing the explosion of data storage is the use of virtualization. Virtualization as it is most used today essentially uses software to mimic hardware. The typical software application wastes a tremendous amount of storage space. Many applications require that some minimum amount of storage be allocated for their use, and then in many cases only a small fraction is actually used. Storage virtualization allows the physical storage from multiple storage devices to appear to be a single storage device to the operating system or application. The storage can then be allocated as needed for use by users, applications, and servers. Storage virtualization can increase utilization to 75 percent or better. (See Figure 17-8.)

There are three basic approaches for virtualizing storage. The most common (called in-fabric) is the use of storage area network (SAN) devices connected using a high-speed fiber channel network. Software is then installed on a host server or a storage virtualization device is installed as part of the SAN; either provides the layer of abstraction between the hosts performing the I/O and the storage controllers providing the storage capacity. The second method, called host-client, uses software running on file and application servers to detect available storage and to maintain the metadata necessary to manage them. The third method, known as in-array or embedded functionality, uses a special network controller and management software to manage different storage systems as one large resource. All methods provide the advantages of storage virtualization, which from a disaster recovery prospective means:

➤ Data storage becomes more mobile and easier to deploy.

➤ Virtual tape library (VTL) technology can be used to decrease total backup time.

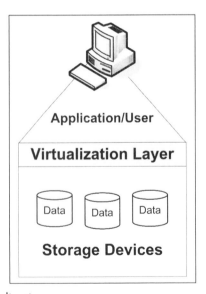

FIGURE 17-8: Storage virtualization.

➤ Production and recovery storage environments no longer need to be strictly homogeneous.

➤ Disaster recovery costs can be lower, as less expensive storage devices can be used at the recovery site. The less expensive devices, while maybe not ideal, might work fine until the production devices have been restored.

➤ Easier administration during recovery as virtualized storage can be managed from a single administrative console.

➤ Greater flexibility in managing changing application storage requirements.

Issues to be aware of when considering storage virtualization include:

➤ If you have heterogeneous storage devices, are they all compatible with the virtualization technology you're considering?

➤ Applications could experience a decrease in performance if the recovery site data storage hardware has a slower response time.

➤ Ensure that the storage metadata is protected and backed up.

➤ Be aware that whichever option you choose, you'll be locked into a particular vendor.

SOMETHING FOR YOUR SUPPORT PLAN

Your plan will need to be tested and updated periodically to keep it effective. Testing allows you to identify any deficiencies in your plan so that they can be corrected. This includes not only equipment and backup issues but personnel issues as well. Each component of your plan must be tested to verify the accuracy and completeness of your recovery procedures and to determine the overall effectiveness of the plan. Some areas to review when testing your plan include:

➤ Ability to restore critical applications from backups.

➤ Performance of recovery personnel.

➤ Performance of backup equipment.

➤ Communications.

To remain effective, your plan must be kept up to date with changes in your production systems. Changes in your IT infrastructure can be caused by business process changes, technology upgrades, regulatory requirements, employee turnover, or new policies. Any of these events should trigger a review of your recovery plan. It is therefore essential that your plan be reviewed and updated frequently to ensure that new processes are documented and that the recovery process is updated to reflect these changes. Items to be monitored for changes include:

➤ Hardware, software, and peripheral equipment.

➤ Business operation requirements.

➤ Security requirements.

➤ Technology changes.

➤ Recovery team contact information.

➤ Vendor information.

➤ Regulatory requirements.

Because your recovery plan contains potentially sensitive personnel information, its distribution must be controlled. Copies should be stored at the home of key recovery personnel, at your production location, and at your off-site recovery location with your backup media. The individual in charge of recovery planning must maintain a list of who has copies of the plan, and a record of when changes were made (use Form 17-1, Recovery Plan Distribution List, and Form 17-2, Recovery Plan Change Record, found on the enclosed CD, as examples).

CONCLUSION

Data are the lifeblood of modern businesses; by having an effective data recovery plan you can help ensure that your business will survive an unexpected emergency. The steps are simple, but must be diligently performed to be effective:

➤ Identify what data are important.

➤ How soon do you need it?

➤ What is it going to cost not to have it?

➤ Test your recovery procedures.

CHAPTER 18

WORKSTATIONS
The Weakest Link

Why is it drug addicts and computer aficionados
are both called users?
— Clifford Stoll

INTRODUCTION

At the user end of our networks are typically workstations (or personal computers). Over the years, workstations have evolved first to supplement mainframe computer terminals (dumb terminals) and then to replace them. Few companies still employ dumb terminals. PC-based workstations have become so inexpensive that they can be found all across companies performing a wide range of functions. And, from a business continuity point of view, this is exactly the problem.

Mainframe computers centralized computing power and also centralized data storage. To view data stored by a mainframe required a password, and data files had various levels of security to protect them. Important data were stored in a central location, making backing up the data relatively easy. But a problem with mainframes was that programmers could never keep up with demands for their services. Personal computers, along with their easy-to-use programs, gradually migrated this capability to the individual's desk (hence the "personal" in Personal Computing). As this occurred, all the environmental, electrical, and physical security protections that are provided for the backroom mainframes were no longer available to the workstations and the data residing in them. You've got a problem!

In discussing critical workstations, keep in mind that servers (specialized systems optimized for storage speed and other services) located outside the protection of the computer room are always considered critical units and must be protected as such.

RISK ASSESSMENT

As always, begin with your risk assessment. Normally workstations are listed in the departmental risk plans. Are there any critical workstations in your department? Before answering, think about what a workstation can be today. It can be a desktop unit. It can be a notebook PC that a manager uses at work and then carries home at night to catch up on urgent projects. It can be the PDA (personal digital assistant) unit carried around by the inventory manager to track shipments. It can even be a Web-enabled cell phone. In a factory, it could be a machine tool controller. In a hospital, it could a testing or monitoring device. Computing power is now everywhere!

So what to do? The first thing to do is an asset inventory. Check to see how many of each type unit you have. Categorize them by what they are (notebook, PDA, desktop) or what they are used for. Every computer has several things in common:

1. At some point, the hardware must be repaired or replaced.
2. It runs a stored program, often from a hard disk. In some cases, the program is stored in a ROM chip and rarely changes.
3. In almost every case, it stores data.
4. They are delicate flowers adrift in a cruel world.

So let's take these one at a time. We said at some point the hardware must be repaired or replaced. Funny thing about workstations is that their usefulness fades away long before they stop working. If your processes depend on the constant availability of a specific machine, then imagine what would happen if some day it stopped working. Often you can replace it, but if the machine used an older operating system, you might have difficulty getting the old software to run on the new machine. In general, if a workstation is used in your business, it should be replaced at least every 4 years. If the workstation is critical, the hardware should be upgraded at least every 2 years. Your concern is maximum availability. If a change in hardware forces a change in the software, then at least it will be a planned event with time to address the issues that arise instead of something patched together in a crisis.

The second function common to every computer is that it is running software. This is true, even if it only runs the same software application over and over again. Like hardware, software has a useful life. If it gets too old, you should reconfigure the workstation to use more contemporary hardware and operating systems. This assumes you have the source code. If you cannot find it, then re-create the same software functionality immediately. Do not wait for the other shoe to drop! If the software was purchased as a "package" from a company, periodically check with the company to ensure the software is still supported. The supplier will provide updated versions of the software that will run on current operating systems. If not, then this must also go on your controlled upgrade list. Without support, the software may not work on replacement hardware in an emergency.

By keeping your software up to date, you reduce the number of spare workstations necessary to keep onsite. If a workstation running a critical application stops working, you can quickly exchange the hardware, reload the data from backup and proceed with your business with a minimum of downtime.

In addition, software sometimes requires upgrading. This both updates the software's function and repairs problems in the code. Unfortunately, it may also introduce new problems. Have you ever installed an operating system upgrade that killed the workstation it was supposed to save? Controlling versions and testing software is a subject for a data processing book. The key here is that you need to be aware of any changes to a critical workstation's software.

Always keep backup copies of critical software. The ability to restore a PC's software from a backup copy is critical to a prompt recovery.

Be sure to include on your asset list all software used in critical units to support critical business functions. When in doubt, list them.

The third function that all computers have in common is that they store data. Most data are not worth retaining or can be lost without damage to the company. Those files are not our concern. Do your workstations hold any critical data? We will delve deeper into this subject a bit later, but as you make your asset inventory, note any critical files or general categories of files these units hold. Your list of data files should indicate:

➤ Size. Determines optimal backup/recovery method.

➤ Format. Is it in Access? Excel? WordPerfect?

➤ Data Origin. Does this workstation create or modify it?

➤ Volatility. How often does it change?

The fourth function that computers have in common is that environmental stresses may weaken the hardware. Always use a properly rated, functioning surge protector for your workstation and notebook PCs. Compared to your workstation, notebook PCs have the advantage of defaulting to battery power if they lose power from the wall plug. This acts as a built-in Uninterruptible Power Supply (UPS). Critical desktop PCs also need the protection of a UPS to ensure they do not suffer a "hard stop" when losing electrical power. This reduces the likelihood of a power outage resulting in a corrupted data file. After installation, ensure your users do not burden the UPS by plugging nonessential devices into it.

In addition to clean power, workstations are designed to exist within specific temperature and humidity ranges, as established by the manufacturer. Stray outside of these and your hardware will weaken and eventually fail. A typical office environment is usually fine. But a hot, dirty factory stresses the equipment. Notebook PCs left overnight in a car during the depths of winter can be damaged by freezing—or baked in the hot sun on a scorching summer day. Problems may not immediately appear but marginal components may begin to fail.

So far, you have identified the risk assessment from data provided from each department about its critical assets and your own asset inventory made walking around and looking at what needs to be supported. Now, the question is, how can you mitigate the risks (or threats) to your equipment, programs, and data? The most basic step involves the physical security of these assets. As you work through these steps, keep in mind your focus is on supporting your vital business functions, but from time to time you will want to extend this to other machines as well.

Physical Security

Physical security protects your unit from unauthorized access, theft, and sabotage. Sabotage can have a temporary effect if, for example, a cable is unplugged, but it can also be more devastating and permanently destroy the unit. Physical security is also important to protect software and backup files. Stolen software, which can be copied and distributed across the company, can create significant legal problems.

To prevent unauthorized access, lock the computer in a room open only to authorized people, such as a computer room or an executive's office. These are secure locations because the computer room is always locked and the executive's office is watched by the secretary or locked when not in use. Locking the room or watching the unit provides a barrier to theft and sabotage.

Other workstations in your company also require protection. One would be the workstation that controls the electronic door locks, such as in a hotel, or to your employee entrances. Someone sneaking in to steal something may also steal or destroy the records of their entry into this unit. Therefore, this workstation is also normally under lock and key.

How about the workstation that records the time attendance for your employees? Some companies use a barcode, magnetic strip, or RFIS chip on their employee badges to indicate when each person arrived at or departed from work (punched in/punched out). This information is recorded in a database for payroll purposes. Such a workstation must be in a place where it cannot be stolen (they contain significant private information about employees) or sabotaged.

However, most workstations are not kept in locked rooms. They are out where workers, visitors, and others have access. In some companies, a lot of people pass by the desks or float through the offices. It is not always possible to be sure who belongs there and who does not. During lunch, when everyone has abandoned the office, it takes but a moment to snap shut a notebook PC, slip it into a briefcase, and go out the door! Desktop units are also fair game, but they are a bit bulky and more likely to disappear overnight or on a weekend. Handheld units, such as PDAs or cell phones, barely make a bulge in the pocket of (stylishly) baggy trousers.

One way to hang on to your equipment is to strap it down to your desk. This is typically a steel cable through a loop in the back of your workstation. You can also buy a similar device for your notebook PC. To remove it, you must have the key to the lock. True, this can be defeated with brute force, but it drastically reduces the number of units stolen. However, it will not stop the deliberate attempt to damage the unit, so do not keep anything critical out in the open when it can be hit, burned, shocked, crushed, etc.

Workstations used in warehouses and on the factory floor should be housed in locked cabinets. Factories are a harsh environment for electronic components. A monitor and keyboard are all that a user requires. Ensure that the cabinets are well ventilated to avoid overheating the components. Locking the cabinet protects the unit against theft and sabotage. It also prevents someone from loading unauthorized software onto it.

Another important physical security issue for personal computers involves safeguarding the workstations' vital records. It is important that all PC software licenses are gathered after purchase and filed for future reference. Some companies create a software "image" of the operating system and all standard programs. This image is then copied into each workstation they own. The serial numbers on the software then all read the same. By holding these licenses in a secure location (often the same off-site storage used for your backup media), you can readily prove how many copies of a program you own.

The other vital workstation records are the backup media. These devices (CD-ROMs, tapes, external hard drives, etc.) all contain confidential company data. They must be correctly labeled and safeguarded as such.

Backing Up Your Workstation Programs and Data

The key to a rapid recovery from a theft, damaged workstation disk, or sabotage is restoration from your last good backup copy. Mainframe computers typically make a full copy of everything they have stored on disk once a week. Every day, they make an incremental copy of whatever has changed that day. In this way, they capture all the data and software necessary for them to function. The storage media (usually magnetic tape) is carefully transported and stored. Over time, some tapes are kept for historical copies and others are rotated back into use.

Workstations are another matter. The data are often scattered about the hard disk mixed in among programs, obsolete data, and pictures of Aunt Meg, and following a naming convention that defies most logic. Although a complete (image) backup of each workstation is desired, it is expensive and most users will not faithfully do it. In addition, there is the cost of the backup hardware, handling the backups, and all the media necessary to copy these disks.

Selecting a Workstation Data Backup Strategy

Hard disk capacities in workstations have grown rapidly over the years, and the smallest available disk sizes are more than most users can fill. Still, your backup tool must be capable of copying everything on the disk on to the media selected.

Before beginning your data backup strategy, *require* users to store all mission-critical files on a computer room file server. Make this a firm rule and, whenever you find such a file, stay after it until it is migrated properly. These files should not be left to chance, and the computer room staff will ensure they are included on the normal backup tapes. This category should include databases, spreadsheets, legal documents, and anything that is truly mission critical, which includes all documents that must be retained for legal or regulatory reasons. For a few individuals, this may mean that all their files will reside on the server. So be it! The end-user's workstation can still access these data as if they were present on their workstation's disk.

That said, your first consideration is, "What do I want to back up?" Workstations hold a lot of programs that may not even be used but could require a considerable amount of space to repeatedly back up. For example, a workstation's operating system may require several gigabytes just to back up the software. Applications software can easily triple this number. Most of these programs rarely change. If a workstation were stolen or otherwise rendered unusable, you should be able to install your standard software image on a new workstation and load any additional authorized programs from your support staff copies. Then the data can be loaded and you are finished. Therefore, for most workstations, it is not necessary to make backup copies of the programs—just the data.

Special-purpose workstations may have specific configuration settings in the software or operating system that are necessary for it to work properly. For these workstations, you may want to make image backup copies (the entire disk).

This is important because the larger the amount of data to back up, the longer it will take. If you are copying unnecessary materials, it will make your backup strategy more expensive to no purpose.

Once you have trimmed the job down to copying only data, consider which data you want to save. If you are keeping copies of old files and correspondence on your workstation for historical purposes, consider moving them to a CD and deleting it from the workstation. Again, why copy something over and over when once will do? The archive CD should have the proper level of security on it. Either store it off-site with your other vital records or in a locked vital records storage onsite. Mark every CD legibly as to the originator, date created, and contents. Do not stuff it in your desk if it contains any sensitive information.

Another valuable space saver is to delete files you no longer need. Some people never clean out their attic and others never delete files from their PCs. If it isn't needed—delete it! If in doubt, copy to a CD and then delete it.

So with only active data files left, containing data that are useful, the last and very important step is to store all your data under one master directory. A common choice is to use C:\Data. Under this are folders by topic and by product, such as Excel. To back up all the data, copy them to a CD-ROM for storage with a drag and drop. Click on the Data directory, drag it over to the CD-RW drive, and drop it. The operating system copies it for you and then waits for you to tell it to burn the CD. You can type away while the copy is made.

CDs are so inexpensive, on average less than 20 cents each, that they are practical for data backup so long as the older, unneeded copies are properly destroyed. For most end-user workstations, this is the easiest way to make their own copies. Be sure they understand and comply with your standards for marking backups (for easy identification when it is needed for a restore). In addition, simplify the collection and filing of backups. From time to time, check off who is handing in backups to identify the people who are forgetting their good data processing practices.

With that said, here are the factors to consider when selecting a backup strategy for your users.

➤ **Storage Volume Requirements.** The backup media used should be capable of handling the anticipated volume.

➤ **The Length of Time to Make the Backup Copy.** Huge amounts of data take huge amounts of time to copy. However, a typical end-user workstation should not require more than a single CD to back up its data, if storage-intensive files such as audio, movies, and pictures are stored separately from the data.

➤ **Interoperability.** The backup media should ideally be compatible with the operating systems and applications in use today and in the future. For example, in 2003, most major PC assemblers announced their intention to drop the 3.5-inch floppy disk from their new PCs.

➤ **Backup Software.** Ensure that users know the process for making backup data copies and that their tools are easy to use. This will improve the chances that backups are regularly made.

Backup Technologies

Many different backup technologies are available for end-user backups. Whatever is used, be sure to mark the backup with the date and the user's name. The most popular include:

➤ **Tape Drives.** These are readily available for desktop computers. Most tape backup software can be set up to run automatically. Tapes provide the greatest amount of storage space, Depending on the technology, a single cartridge can hold several hundred gigabytes. However, to fill such a large tape may require a considerable amount of time. Further, the higher the capacity, the greater the cost per cartridge. Multiply this by the number of workstations that need to be backed up and this can be an expensive proposition. Tape is best suited for server backups.

➤ **Removable Media.** This includes products such as Zip cartridges from Iomega, and are used similarly to floppy disks. They are faster and easier to use than tape drives. The cartridges are comparable in cost to tape media, but they have a lower capacity.

➤ **Compact Disk Read Only Memory (CD-ROM or CD).** CD-RW drives are standard on new PCs and have replaced the old floppy disks as the medium on which to load software and data. CDs are low in cost and have a capacity of approximately 700 MB of data per disk. Most CDs (known as CD-Rs) can only be written to once, but CD-RWs allow you to write to and edit the material on the disk. Given the low cost of CDs, they are the most cost-effective way to back up end-user PCs. If all your data are consolidated under one master directory, you may be able to fit them all onto one disk.

➤ **DVD-Rs (DVD Writers).** These are a step up from CDs in that a DVD holds approximately 4.2 GB per disk. The disk is the same compact size as a CD. These devices are gradually dropping in price. Most PCs now have one drive that formats and reads both CDs and DVDs.

➤ **Internet Backup.** This is normally a commercial service that uses the public Internet to back up data from the end-user workstation to a remote server connected to the Internet. Software is loaded onto the workstation that is used to schedule the backups, select the files to be backed up, and communicate to the backup server. Data are normally encrypted to ensure security during transmission. A major advantage of this method is that the user does not have to deal with backup media, and the backups can be run unattended. One disadvantage to this approach is time, as the speed of your Internet connection affects how fast data can be transferred to the backup system.

  However, this is a very useful tool for "road warriors," as it allows them to back up their data while traveling. Remember, only back up the critical files that have changed. Almost all hotels have installing broadband services for travelers, so this option is becoming more attractive.

➤ **Network Storage.** If the workstation is connected to a network, that unit can back up its data via the network to a server. The network file servers are then backed up daily so your files eventually end up on tape. There are two basic ways to use the network:

  1. **Backup Initiated by the Server.** The server can be configured to read the data from the workstations and store the data either to the server hard disk or to a backup medium.

  2. **Store Data to the Server.** A networked disk can be configured for use by the end users. The end users configure their application software to write to the virtual drive rather than to a local drive. The networked drive is then backed up as part of the normal server backup process.

Backing up to a server can present several problems. The first is space. Most servers limit the amount of space available to an end user. Once the limit is reached, the backup dies. Estimate the size of your typical workstation data directory. Multiply it times the number of users. This approach, while elegant, may not be practical.

The second obstacle is bandwidth. All these workstations can clog the network with massive data transfers. Finally, the server disks can only run so fast.

WORKSTATION VIRTUALIZATION

Another option for making recovery of workstations easier is to use virtualization technology to run an image of the workstation on a protected server. If the workstation is lost in a disaster, the workstation image can be restarted on a new workstation, and the end user does not miss a beat. This also makes the workstations easier to maintain as new software is installed and old applications are removed. A virtualized workstation can provide a managed, stable desktop environment that can be accessed using a standard PC or a less expensive thin client device. The virtualized desktop software (such as VMware Workstation or Microsoft Virtual PC) provides a virtualized full client environment using a server-based hypervisor. This allows the user to have full administrative control over the desktop environment and applications. Some of the advantages of desktop virtualization include:

➤ Easy to deploy desktops to new users.

➤ Desktop machines can be less expensive PCs or thin client devices.

➤ Ability to use your desktop environment from any PC with network or Internet access.

➤ Access to typical desktop features such as multiple monitors, USB devices, etc.

➤ Disaster recovery at the desktop is simplified as a new device can be quickly installed to use the virtualized image on the server. Backups can be managed at the server level.

Virtualization of desktop workstations also creates the opportunity to have desktops provided via the Internet, much like many vendors are doing with applications using the "software as a service" (SaaS) model. For desktops one term being used is "desktop as a service" (DaaS), while others use the term Virtual Desktop Infrastructure as a Service (VDI).

Some issues to be aware of when considering desktop virtualization:

➤ Your "per-seat" cost may be initially higher due to the cost of the servers, virtualization software, and Windows licenses.

➤ The OEM version of Windows that comes with most new PCs cannot be used in a virtual environment; new licenses must be purchased.

➤ User resistance to giving up their full client PCs.

END-USER BACKUP ISSUES

It is important that the data recovery plan emphasize the availability of the data, protect the data's confidentiality, and ensure the data's integrity. Some processes to follow to make restoration of workstations easier include:

➤ Train end users on the importance of backing up data on a regular basis. If the process is simple and easy to follow, they will usually cooperate.

➤ Document vendor and configuration information for all specialty workstations.

➤ Establish a mail slot–type drop-off for backup media in the data center where they can be dropped off securely. Provide labels that may prompt them to fill in essential information. When tapes are recycled (old backups no longer needed), provide them to users at a pick-up point. From time to time, test these backups to ensure they can be read. Sometimes data backups look like they worked but they did not.

Hard Disk Recovery

Sometimes you are just sure that whatever was on your hard disk is lost forever. This could be a workstation that was melted in a fire or submerged for days in a flood. It could have suffered a head crash. Don't be too depressed. There are companies that specialize in recovering data from severely damaged disks. They can also recover data from deleted files (the ones that the usual file recovery software cannot rebuild).

These companies use specially trained engineers to disassemble the hard disk unit in their clean rooms and extract the data. The services can be expensive but the savings to your company can be considerable.

MOBILE DEVICES

Mobile devices are the wave of the future. The ideal is a unit that can accompany you throughout your workday. A unit that is unobtrusive, light, and always ready for use. Today we have notebook PCs, netbooks, e-readers, PDAs, and web-enabled cell phones. Once these devices depart the cozy confines of the office, they introduce a new range of issues to be addressed.

Mobile Security

Unlike desktop workstations, notebook PCs advertise how light and easy they are to carry. This portability also makes them easy to steal. Once a mobile PC is taken out of the office, it loses whatever protection your facility's security force provides. Several steps should be taken to protect this equipment:

1. Keep it out of sight if possible.

2. Do not carry it in a carrying case that is obviously for notebook PCs. Use a standard briefcase or pack it in your luggage.

3. When it is not in use in your hotel room, store it out of sight.

4. When attending seminars or business meetings outside the office, never leave it unattended.

5. While it is in your car, keep it out of sight. Then if you go to a restaurant for lunch, it isn't visible sitting in your car.

6. When passing through airport security, ensure no one is ahead of you before laying it on the scanner's conveyor. This way it should arrive at the other side the same time that you do.

Essentially the same holds true for a PDA. While it is carried on your trip so it could be used, if a thief cannot see it, they cannot target it. Airports are a favorite place to steal notebook PCs, and there are many ways to waylay the unsuspecting. Targeting a company's executives in an airport and stealing their notebook PCs is a very effective tool for industrial espionage. You think it was just a thief, but your competition may now know many hidden details of your operation.

Some managers take their notebook PCs or PDAs home to catch up on work. The problem is that if they have an accident on the way, someone must know to promptly remove the notebook from the vehicle as soon as possible (with the permission of the police). A notebook is an easy theft item that could be removed from a wreck and not be missed for several days. More than the PC itself, it is the data you are safeguarding.

Mobile Data Backup

Mobile devices present their own particular backup issues. This is even more of a problem for other mobile devices, such as PDAs, smart phones, and pagers, which are less likely to be connected to the corporate network. Users are also a problem, as most think that a disaster such as a lost or damaged device will not happen to them. These devices are much more fragile and more easily stolen than desktop PCs.

Always make a full backup or virtual image of your notebook PC before a business trip. This will lessen the impact on your job, because the replacement unit can be restored from the backup. If necessary, a new unit can be loaded and sent out to you.

If your PC has critical data files (such as legal briefs of contracts), they can be burned to a CD and stored in a different piece of luggage. Again, if the PC is lost, the CD can be loaded onto a new unit. Guard the CD carefully—your coat pocket will do!

The average IT-enabled person uses at least three portable devices and spends more than 1 hour per day trying to keep these devices synchronized.

PROTECTING END-USER VITAL RECORDS

Ensure that your department's vital records program includes the handling of your data backups. Workstations tend to be somewhat secure, but if competitors can lay their hands on your data backups, in most cases, you would never know. Further, to break into your workstation they must hack past the password, but no such obstacle confronts someone who wants to read the backup tape. Therefore, always treat backup media as critical data and store it properly.

Another vital record is the paper copies of your workstation software licenses. These are essential to prove the number of licenses you have purchased in the event of a software audit. If your equipment was lost in a fire, the licenses can be used to demonstrate ownership and the software copied onto your new equipment (always consult your company's attorneys if such a situation arises).

Along with the licenses, the original software media must be secured as a vital record. This reduces the likelihood that people will install unlicensed software on multiple workstations. On the one hand, they may believe they are helping fellow employees by providing programs for their use. On the other hand, they may be ready to resign and are setting you up to be turned in for using pirated software! Don't take chances. After installing programs, promptly gather the media and store it with the vital records. Then if you are accused, you can show you have taken prudent steps to control and stop it.

Vital records can turn up in several unwanted places. Before recycling tapes from storage, be sure to erase them because they may not end up with the same user every time. Backups on CDs cannot be recycled and should be rendered unreadable, usually by crushing them or putting them through a paper shredder.

Another set of vital records to protect is found in your surplus workstations. When a PC is ready for donation to charity, remove the fixed disk and destroy it. Some people crush it; others make holes in it with a heavy drill. There is a lot of sophisticated technology in the world that can recover data from your disk no matter how thoroughly you reformat it. The charity receiving the PC will need to find someone to loan it old hard disks. *Never* send one out in your surplus PC.

Additional Resources

www.globalcomputer.com—Devices for securing workstations to a desk, backup hardware, and media.

www.bsa.org—Business Software Alliance. BSA educates consumers on software management and copyright protection, cyber security, trade, e-commerce, and other Internet-related issues.

(From http://www.bsa.org/usa/about/)

CONCLUSION

When supporting workstations, it's not a matter of if it will break, but when. Periodic upgrading of both hardware and software is necessary to ensure that support will be possible if a critical PC fails.

Although the proliferation of personal computers has produced many benefits, it has made life more difficult for those charged with protecting vital corporate assets. Physical security is now more of a problem, as these systems are scattered throughout the organization. Data security is also more difficult, as data are no longer concentrated in a central location. But proper policies and procedures for managing these devices can help you keep these assets safe and sound.

CHAPTER 19

CUSTOMERS
Other People to Worry About

If we don't take care of the customer . . . somebody else will.
— Author Unknown

INTRODUCTION

Successful businesses are built on the basics: supplying customers with the products and services that they want, when they want them, and at a price they are willing to pay. What would they do if you could not supply them with what they needed to run their business? How many times could this happen before their confidence in you as a supplier is eroded or fails altogether? Good customers are hard to find. It is always cheaper to keep the ones you have than to find new ones. Don't wait until it is too late! Action steps must be identified to support your customer in the face of a disaster in your facility. A disaster plan that considers the customer is important!

The most basic step is to develop a customer notification plan. Properly implemented, such a plan builds a valuable image in your customer's mind about your company and its usefulness to them. We have all experienced troublesome suppliers to our own businesses and value the ones that do not create problems for our operations. When a disaster strikes, it is imperative that your company's hard-won reputation not fall victim to the calamity. You must consider the disaster's impact on your customers and act decisively.

Our plan development steps by now should sound familiar. List what you want to protect, what the threats are, and then take mitigation actions to reduce the likelihood of the occurrence or the severity of a disaster. Of course, you then need to test it. A successful customer notification plan will strengthen the relationship between you and your customer. Just as your parents told you,

"When life gives you a lemon, make lemonade," this plan will demonstrate your commitment to top-quality customer service.

Throughout this chapter the term "product" means all manner of goods and services provided to your customer.

Once a catastrophe occurs, crews will be assigned to contain the damage and restore a minimal level of service. How will your customer find out if their orders will be delayed or are not coming at all? Will they learn this on the evening news? Will it be in the trade press? Don't let competitors tell your story in a manner that is out of your control. It is unlikely that members of your sales force will be among the crews repairing your factory walls. Don't leave them idle. They can assist in the long-term recovery by using their experience in dealing with your customers.

From a business continuity perspective, the best you can do at this point is to control the indirect damage this causes to your customers. As the saying goes, "perception equals reality." To control the perception, the sales force staff will inform the most important customers personally. They will also assist the customer to minimize the shock a possible materials shortage will cause to their operations. We do this by notifying them of the situation, explaining to them what is already en route or available from intact warehouses, providing a realistic timeframe for restoring the flow of goods, and, if necessary, assisting them in locating equivalent products elsewhere.

These are the actions of a partner, not an adversary. Your customer still has a crisis, but now there are two of you working on it! Handle this poorly and long after your facility is operational again, the customer will only remember the time you forced them into scrambling for components. Use the tragedy to strengthen your supplier-customer bond by helping keep their business running. The long-term goodwill will be invaluable.

KEY CUSTOMER ASSESSMENT

Our first step is an inventory of who your key customers are (use Form 19-1 on the enclosed CD-ROM). Then, examine their buying habits to see which times of the year make them most sensitive to a problem. Third, add to the list any one-time customers currently under contract.

Who are your customers? If you are like most businesses, the 80/20 rule applies to your revenue stream: 80% of your revenue stream comes from 20% of your customers. All companies would like to be all things to all customers, but your efforts should focus on protecting core customers. This information might be extracted from historical shipping and billing data. Set a timeframe to reach back, perhaps 2 years, perhaps more, and total the amount of business each customer gives you. Place the big customers at the top of the list and sort in descending order, based on the amount billed. Drop the bottom 80% of customers from the list. Now, add back to the list any specific customers whose business you are cultivating or who have other significance to you.

Using this list of names, add contact information, such as contact names, addresses, phone numbers, and e-mail addresses. There may be multiple locations that buy from you or to which you deliver. Next, add the name of the salesperson who covers this account. In tough times, relationships are important. Now the list tells you whom to call, where to call to, and who should do the calling. The salesperson's name is important because he or she may be sitting idle during disaster recovery.

For the customers on your list for the time period you specified, produce a month-by-month report of total orders or total billings (either one should do). Your goal is to dig out the buying patterns for the customer. You want to understand when the customer's busy season is, which is when you need to be most dependable. The salesperson for this account can adjust the report based on experience with that customer. Before submitting that request, add to it a second report to break down the same time period by the specific products the customer buys. If you offer more than one product, in a disaster you may find your warehouse "fat" on some items and lean on others. It is likely that a disaster will affect some customers more than others.

In the case of specific contracts, either for one-time or ongoing purchases, you must check for a clause dealing with *force majeure*. This describes actions beyond your control, also known as "acts of God," that prevent you from fulfilling the terms of your contract. This is especially important for contracts with penalty clauses. Note on the customer inventory sheet, next to the customer's name, any agreements that contain penalty clauses and the products they cover. Invoking a *force majeure* clause means that the event could not have been avoided. A tornado isn't avoidable, but an argument could be made that a warehouse fire was. If the other party demonstrates that you were careless in your fire prevention, penalty clauses in the agreement may be invoked. To do so, it must be established that your nonperformance was avoidable.

Some questions to consider:

1. If you cannot fulfill a contract, will you incur any penalties?
2. What is the financial and operational impact on your key customers?
3. In the event of a prolonged outage, how long can your customer withstand a loss of services or products?
4. Does your customer have alternative suppliers and supply channels?
5. How many days of inventory do your customers normally carry or are normally in the supply chain to them?

A Just-in-Time (JIT) supplier must have a documented and tested business continuity plan. Disasters happen to us all. One supplier's failure can close down a customer's production if products are not delivered on time.

Exceptions may exist, but most customers just want their goods delivered on time. Delivery credibility can be a positive (or negative) selling point for your company. Many materials managers maintain supplier scorecards to weed out unreliable providers.

With your plan in place (and tested), invite your customers to comment on how to keep them supplied in a crisis. It is in their interests as well as yours that you have a good plan. Invite them to observe a test and even allow them to select one of the disaster scenarios from a list you have prepared. They will see chaos, they will see people scrambling around, but more importantly, they will see how quickly order is restored to the situation and action begins.

This is a good time to further cement your relationship with them and ask them about their own recovery plans. This street runs both ways. Just as they want to ensure you are always ready as a supplier, you want to ensure they are always in business as a customer. This dialogue will be useful in developing or modifying your Supplier Notification Plan.

RISK ASSESSMENT

Looking at the other side of the issue, what are you to do if your major customer suffers a disaster? You need their future business. A quick risk assessment of the customer's facility location may uncover those who might be closed by the same problem:

➤ Hurricane (you are both on the coast).

➤ Blizzard (scenically located in the Rocky Mountains).

➤ Earthquake.

➤ Other wide-area disaster.

To prevent nature's destruction from closing your business, make a conscious effort to obtain customers spread over a wide geographic area. Customers are where they are and you handle as many as you can, but your risk will be reduced if they are spread out. Don't let poorly prepared customers drag down your business as well.

DEVELOP A COMMUNICATIONS PLAN

OK! Now that you have an inventory of your customers, determine how you will communicate with them in an emergency. As always, the best way is by telephone, person to person. Face-to-face contact is fine but much too time-consuming. While traveling to the customer's site, you are out of touch with the latest containment and recovery results.

It is much better for the customer's purchasing agents to hear the first news of the calamity from you rather than from a newscast or your competitors. A newscast by nature consists of an attention-grabbing headline and few details. Your call will provide real information.

Before calling anyone, try to obtain a list of open and pending orders. Call those customers first. Lacking a list of orders, it is an executive decision as to which key accounts to call.

Contact your customers three times:

1. As soon as possible after the disaster.

2. Within 24 hours after the disaster with a clear picture of how this problem affects them.

3. When services have been essentially restored. Recoveries take a long time and your customers will be looking elsewhere. Do not wait until the last new nail is driven but when you can provide predictable delivery dates for their goods.

To facilitate the first call, a standard, written statement needs to be developed that can be used to inform customers of the problem. The statement should acknowledge the calamity, provide a few brief details, and promise to call them back within 24 hours with an update. If the disaster struck the factory but left the warehouse intact, don't be afraid to say so. However, for the first message, all callers must use the same approved, guarded text.

An example text might be:

> "This is to notify you that ABC Company has experienced a serious incident. A _____ occurred that has temporarily halted _____ . This may impact your order by _____ . A detailed recovery assessment is now underway. We will contact you again within 24 hours with a full update to the situation and any impact it may have on your open orders. Thank you for standing by us in this moment of adversity. If you have any questions, please contact _____ at _____ ."

For the first call, it helps to know what they usually buy and when. Keep your conversations positive, but honest. You would want nothing less from them. If this is their busy season, they should be the first called. After reading the text, ask them how this will impact their operations. If it will be significant, then consider assisting them to quickly locate alternative suppliers.

The second call, 24 hours later, should provide specific and useful information to your customer. Tell them when you can deliver their products to them.

➤ If the recovery will be long, help them locate another supplier. You may protect your relationship by acting as an intermediary between the customer and another supplier. It is doubtful you can charge a markup for your services but you are protecting a very valuable relationship.

➤ If the recovery will be short, provide a best estimate for the resumption of shipments. If the goods now in shipping are sufficient for several days, this may keep your customer supplied for the short term. Once production resumes, send the next several shipments by express freight until the normal shipping channels are filled again.

This may sound somewhat strange but your competitors may become your supplier or your customer during a crisis. It all depends on whether you have the disaster or they did.

Do you have reciprocal-processing/servicing agreements with your competitors? In the event of a disaster, reciprocal-processing agreements should be available for immediate execution. For instance, a competing bank may clear funds for the customers of a competitor bank if the competitor bank cannot clear funds because a disaster has taken down its network. Or a competing airline may honor air travel tickets from other airlines in the event of a disaster that grounds the competing airline. It is good business and in the best interest of all competitors in the marketplace to make these kinds of reciprocal arrangements with each other, if possible, to minimize the impact of a disaster and be able to fulfill your obligations to your customers.

ACTION STEPS FOR YOUR PLAN

A customer notification plan is not necessary for small or well-contained disasters. It is only executed when your ability to deliver goods and services has been greatly diminished or temporarily halted. It is also used if a disaster is well publicized. The key items to cover in the notification are:

1. Conservatively estimate how long the facility will be out of service and what products are affected.

2. Establish what finished goods are available for shipment and allocate according to those customers who need them the most or as required by contract.

3. Gather the sales force and explain the situation. Provide general details of what may be damaged and what is intact.

4. Provide a copy of the preprinted text and explain any limitations on what should be said.

5. If the sales offices are not available, cover all expenses for them to call from home or from their cell phones.

6. For products affected by the disaster, identify alternative sources of materials.

7. Prepare the follow-up message for customers to set an expectation as to when the facility will be back to normal.

CONCLUSION

Don't allow a disaster to become worse by failing to communicate with your customers. Most customers will work with you to get through the disaster if they are kept informed about the progress of your recovery efforts and status of their orders. Instead of a disaster becoming an opportunity for your competitors, make it into an opportunity for you to show your customers what a reliable business partner you are.

CHAPTER 20

SUPPLIERS
Collateral Damage

Advice is the only commodity on the market
where the supply always exceeds the demand.
—Author Unknown

INTRODUCTION

Every business has suppliers. If you have not been farsighted in dealing with the impact that a disaster may have on your ability to work with them, it may result in financial and operational hardships for your company. Some disasters have the ability to not only shut down your business for a time but could also affect your suppliers' ability to provide the necessary goods for your business. If this happens, your business suffers. For example, if a tornado hits a section of the community where your supplier for raw materials is located, that supplier might not be able to produce the goods you need for your operation. Their building may be damaged, and their employees cannot get to work. Even if they still could operate, their distribution channel may have been affected. They may not be able to get trucks to their building so they can ship their products to you. Either way your business will be in trouble; your supplier cannot deliver the goods required for your business, which results in your not being able to satisfy and ship your customer orders. In turn, your customers won't pay for unshipped orders, and you suffer serious financial problems.

KEY SUPPLIER ASSESSMENT

All companies, large and small, need to address how they will be affected by a disaster experienced by one of their suppliers. Businesses are linked together in the supply chain, each needing the other to complete the business cycle. The adage "you're only as strong as the weakest link" is so true when it comes to the strength of the supply chain. Every business must work out with their trading partners how to deal with disasters that may result in the link breaking between the businesses.

As you conduct a review of your business practices and operations, identify the suppliers critical to your business. These suppliers can be local, national, or even international. Also, don't overlook third-party influences. For example, if you buy products or services from abroad, then don't just look at your supplier's ability to deliver the products or services you need, but also consider the risk of the shipper not being able to operate or a delay or failure in supporting import/export documentation. Your supplier may be healthy, but the transportation method may be affected by the disaster. This was all so apparent when the disaster struck on September 11, 2001. For days after the attack, airline travel and even air cargo transportation was either completely at a halt or severely curtailed. Even though the disaster took place in New York City, Pennsylvania, and Virginia, the whole nation was affected. How prepared were you? Did you have an agreement with your suppliers on an alternative transportation plan or how they would supply their services to you?

Identify all business operations that could be affected if your suppliers are unable to provide the raw materials, supplies, or services required for your company to function. It is all too easy to concentrate on the major suppliers of products and services in your business, such as telephone, electricity, raw materials, etc., but do not forget to examine the role of all the firms you deal with, both large and small. Your smaller suppliers could be equally or even more important than your larger suppliers. For instance, your supplier for raw materials may not be affected by the disaster, but what about your advertising agency or printer? More often than not, a small local firm may be very critical to your recovery efforts. Without additional advertising or collateral, you may not be able to advertise or market your products effectively, even though you can manufacture them. If your ad agency or printer were affected by a disaster, would you have an alternative supplier?

Sometimes, there is no other supplier you could use. In such cases, one option is to store enough of the supplies so that you can function in the event of a disaster until you could get resupplied. For instance, if your business relies on printed material, such as direct mail pieces, to generate revenue, print additional pieces and store them in an off-site facility. In the event that your printer cannot supply these materials, you can use your stored supplies. Storing these supplies may have an additional cost, but not doing so could result in reduced sales and loss of revenues. What if you can manufacture your products, but you can't use a local transportation company to deliver them to a larger shipper? Could these local suppliers be affected by the same disaster that has affected you? What alternatives do you have if you don't have access to your local distribution channel? Can you rent your own vehicles to transport your products to your national shipper? Is there an alternative shipping method that you can use?

> **Several years ago, a regional shipper had a work stoppage because of a union strike. There was no natural disaster but an outage just the same. Those customers who didn't have an alternative shipping method for their products lost millions of dollars in revenue because they couldn't get their products to market.**

Do not take for granted that your smaller and other third-party suppliers are not important in the supply chain; they just may be your "weakest link."

Managing your vendors or suppliers in the aftermath of a disaster is critical. As with your customers, prioritization of your vendors is the key. Focus your business continuity planning on those suppliers that have the largest impact on your recovery efforts and are the most critical to the support of your business. Again, these may not be your largest suppliers! Set priorities for the management process on this priority basis.

Do you know who your supply chain partners are?

➤ Large and small suppliers?

➤ Service providers?

➤ Security alternatives?

➤ Public infrastructure service providers?

➤ Other agencies and business partners?

➤ Regulatory bodies?

➤ The public?

➤ The news media?

RISK ASSESSMENT

Failure of an important vendor can have a devastating impact on your business. Whether the result of a natural disaster or bankruptcy, your plan must include steps to manage the failure of an important vendor. This vendor could be supplying a critical component on a just-in-time basis, or it could be your ISP (Internet Service Provider) that is hosting your online ordering system. Quick action on your part could mean the difference between keeping your customers happy and losing business to your competitor.

The basic steps involved in handling the loss of an important vendor are to quickly assess the situation, mitigate the risks to your business, and develop a plan to keep the business moving while the vendor recovers or is replaced. Put together a small team of three to five people to handle the crisis; a larger team can cause you to waste valuable time arguing things in committee, and this is a time for quick decision making.

The selection of the right team members is important to the success of this effort. The team should have at least one member who understands the technical issues involved. Depending on the vendor, this might require someone familiar with the company databases, Web servers, or network infrastructure. Someone on the team should also have enough authority to cut through any red tape that might be in the team's way. Team members should have experience with legal contracts and should also be able to evaluate new vendors if necessary. The team may also need to be able to negotiate service-level agreements with possible replacement vendors.

If the likelihood of the vendor not surviving is high due to a bankruptcy or major disaster, you may want to consider suspending all payments to the vendor. This is especially important if you have prepaid for some services. This will help to prevent any financial reclamation issues down the road.

The next step is to review carefully all legal contracts between you and the vendor. Make sure you understand your rights and obligations during this time. If a lawyer is not on your team, make sure you get advice from the corporate legal counsel. In many cases you will have a service-level agreement (SLA) that guarantees you a minimum level of performance and should provide for penalties if the vendor cannot meet the minimum service levels. An SLA should cover the following issues:

➤ What is the minimum acceptable level of service?

➤ What is the standard for measuring the service level?

➤ How and when are service statistics calculated?

➤ What is the process for notifying customers if service is affected?

➤ Are there alternative sources of the service?

Once you have a complete understanding of the situation, your next step is to contact the vendor to discuss the problem. Work to help the vendor through the problem. If the vendor is providing technology, make sure you work out what you will need to continue operating. This may include software licenses, source code for custom software applications, architecture documentation for infrastructure providers, etc. Whether you ultimately switch vendors or see this one through the crisis, your first responsibility is to keep your own business functioning.

ACTION STEPS FOR YOUR PLAN

There are five steps to developing your plan to protect against supplier problems affecting your organization. These steps are:

1. Data collection.

2. Investigation.

3. Assessment.

4. Agreement.

5. Mitigation.

Data Collection

The first step is to collect your supplier's vital information and data. Each internal department should appoint a supplier coordinator responsible for ensuring that the critical suppliers for that department or business unit are identified and documented. The department coordinator should document the process and specific approach to identifying the key suppliers. One good source for the initial identification process is to run an accounts payable list of current and past vendors. It's pretty obvious that you need to identify and document the vital information of your current suppliers, but why include past suppliers? Past vendors are important because they may become your alternative vendors in the event that your current vendors cannot fulfill their obligations. Maintaining a dialogue with your past suppliers is extremely important for this reason. Some past suppliers may not want to work with you since you don't buy from them any longer. Make sure you identify and document these as well so that if you need to select an alternative supplier, you don't waste time finding out after a disaster occurs that a certain supplier doesn't want to work with your business any longer.

Other means of identifying your suppliers should also be used because not all suppliers may appear on the accounts payable list. The supplier may not be paid through normal channels or there may be no payment for the service or product. Research "other" suppliers by conducting interviews with key personnel and research product documentation to identify suppliers that are not on the accounts payable listing. For instance, the supplier that packages your product may be a subsidiary of your company and no money changes hands for payment of their services. Their "payment" is only a journal entry in accounting. Missing this supplier as a key vendor may mean that if a disaster occurs, your products cannot be packaged and therefore they cannot be shipped to your customers. After each department has researched and compiled its supplier list, each coordinator should note the product or service that is supplied by the vendor or organization and how critical the product or service is to the organization. Each supplier coordinator should then assign an impact score for each supplier based on the criticality of the supplier's product or service.

Apply the "KISS" (Keep It Simple Stupid) principle for developing your scoring system. Don't overly complicate your decision process by dreaming up an intricate scoring process that requires a Ph.D. in mathematics to figure out and to maintain. A simple 1 to 10 scoring system is adequate, where 1 is very little impact and 10 is very high impact. The supplier impact score should relate to the impact on the organization based on the risk assessment for your entire organization, ranked by type of disaster and how critical the product or service is to the organization. Don't give suppliers high-impact scores simply on the basis that they are your largest suppliers. As we saw earlier, your smallest supplier may just be the supplier that has the largest impact on your organization if they cannot supply you with their product or service in the event of a disaster. Use Form 20-1 on the CD-ROM to organize the data on your suppliers.

Investigation

The next step is to communicate with suppliers to determine how you will operate together in the event of a disaster. After you have collected and analyzed the data and completed your master supplier list, get in touch with them to investigate their capabilities and to achieve agreement on how to operate in the event either of you experiences a disaster. Don't forget it's to their advantage to work with you during this process. If you find a certain supplier is not cooperating and finds this process unimportant, then it may be time to find an alternative supplier. This supplier may be your weakest link in your supply chain; you must take measures to strengthen it!

The first step in forming a dialogue with your suppliers is to compose a letter that lays out the process that you are using for all suppliers and how each supplier fits into your supply chain. Let them know how important they are to your success in the event of a disaster. In the letter, ask a series of questions concerning their own ability to recover from a disaster. Some questions that you might ask them are:

➤ Do you currently have a disaster plan?

➤ Does your plan provide for supplying products to my business?

➤ How important is my business to your supply chain?

➤ Do you maintain safety stock for my products?

Form a dialogue with your suppliers to make them aware that you are formulating a business continuity plan and that their input into the plan is important and necessary in the event of a disaster. The next step is to mail out the letter to each supplier. Make sure you indicate when you want the questionnaire returned to you. Once you have received all the questionnaires back, arrange to discuss in person any concerns you may have in regard to their ability to keep you supplied with products or services. With each supplier, perform the appropriate level of investigation according to the priority and critical nature of the product or service. Determine if the supplier has completed a business continuity plan and to what extent that plan considers your operation. Determine if the plan adequately protects you, its customer, in the event that your supplier has to implement the plan in a disaster. If the supplier does not have a plan, offer to help develop one. You may even be able to charge for this service.

Discuss with your vendors the role they would play in the event that you experience a disaster. Discuss alternative processes in the event that suppliers could not deliver on their contracts to you. You might also want to explore changing your purchasing policy for certain products and services. Historically, your business might have purchased single orders from the lowest cost supplier. This may not be the best approach to help you through a disaster, as you might not be confident that the cheapest supplier on any one day will be able to supply you after a disaster occurs. An alternative policy could be to form a longer term relationship with a smaller number of trusted suppliers so that you can work with them to ensure continued supply in the event that you have to declare a disaster.

This might cost slightly more money than a completely open approach to purchasing but it might pay off in the long run.

Assessment

Some questions that can be asked about a supplier to assess the impact criticality should include:

➤ What happens if the supplier is struck by a disaster?

➤ Will the supplier's failure have an immediate financial or operational effect on your business?

➤ Will the failure result in total or partial loss of support levels from your supplier?

➤ Can you insulate your operations from this supplier?

➤ Is there a workaround for this supplier?

➤ Is this supplier a sole, primary, or secondary supplier?

➤ What is your exposure based on alternative suppliers?

➤ How long can your company function without the services or products from this supplier?

➤ How does the supplier affect your operational processes?

➤ Does your supplier have a business continuity plan in place?

Once each department has completed its individual supplier list and has scored the suppliers, compile one company supplier list that will now become the Master Supplier List. Once the Master Supplier List is completed, categorize each supplier by type of service or product. For instance, combine suppliers by raw material for production of your product; combine suppliers who supply communication services; and combine distribution suppliers that are used for delivery of products. The category type of suppliers will depend on your particular business and also on the number of your suppliers. If you have a large number of suppliers, you may want to break them down into very narrow categories; on the other hand, if you have a small number of suppliers, you may only have three or four categories. It all depends on your business.

Categorizing your suppliers is extremely important because it will allow you to see relationships of which you may not have been aware. It may point out that you may be able to consolidate suppliers to a smaller number. This will enable you to decrease your costs for certain supplies and streamline your supply channel, thus strengthening your supply chain. It may also point out alternative suppliers for the same products or services that you can use in the event that one of your suppliers has been affected by an outage. You may also find that any one supplier may be the only supplier in a particular category. This would indicate a potential weakness, or a single point of failure in your supply chain. Make sure that you address this issue immediately and determine if there is a quick fix for this potential risk. If there is not a quick fix then develop a separate plan to rectify this situation in the near future as soon as you are able. Once rectified, make the solution a permanent part of your business continuity plan.

Agreement

Agree with your critical suppliers on how you will deal with problems that surface as a result of a disaster. For instance, how will the supplier communicate with you if your communications lines are down? Do you operate with your supplier via EDI or another electronic means of communications? In today's environment, look for ways to utilize the Internet to facilitate communications with your suppliers. Look for Web-enabled software that allows you to communicate orders, invoices, and other documents and information. Get your suppliers to agree to utilize these same communications methods in dealing with you. Document these agreements, develop operating policies, and document how these policies will be enforced if necessary. Investigate workarounds, such as producing paper copies for use rather than relying on computer-generated documents; this solution may not be elegant but it might just save your business. After a disaster occurs, communications lines or electronic means to communicate with your suppliers may be offline. The main point to remember is that during a disaster a reliable process is one that is repeatable and standardized, and where terminology and techniques are clearly defined. The process doesn't have to be elegant to work; it just has to work until you are able to bring up your standard operating procedures.

One very important point is to agree with your suppliers on the framework for resolving any disputes that may arise during a disaster, theirs or yours. For instance, it may be pointless sticking to the letter of your supply contract in the event of a disaster. While you and expensive attorneys are arguing over the point in court, you still might not be getting the products, parts, or services you need for your business. Your business would not only suffer severe financial problems from not getting the products you need, but you will also spend valuable resources, time, money, and personnel on legal issues that could have been worked out in advance. You must avoid litigation during a disaster. You have leverage with your suppliers during this planning process to work out the details of how you will operate, utilize workarounds, and deal with problems. If you wait until the disaster strikes, your bargaining power is greatly diminished. It is always in your suppliers' best interest to work with you during the planning stages of putting together a plan to determine how you will work outside the contract if the need arises. This planning process will also help you in future negotiations with other suppliers, as you can then include these agreements in a contract before you and they commit.

Depending on how important any particular supplier is to your business, you might want to investigate alternative sources. If you adopt this means, do not forget that merely identifying another vendor is not sufficient. You must ensure that the alternate supplier is in a position to supply you with your product or service as soon as possible after a disaster. The same assessment should be taken with any alternative suppliers as you did with your current suppliers.

Mitigation

As with any associated risk, events and factors that cause or even contribute to supply chain disruptions cannot always be stopped or even predicted. Any associated risk to your supply chain should be viewed as a possibility, and plans should be put into place to mitigate those threats or you should document why the risk is not worth mitigating.

Mitigation of these disruptions can be accomplished in several ways. One of the best methods is to establish a technology-based framework that will allow the prompt exchange of data and information about your supply chain activities. This framework allows the integration of data and information between your supply chain partners; it monitors your supply chain partners' activities to detect irregularities and disruptions in the "chain." It also provides for rapid resolution of disruptions as they are detected and provides a framework to manage the entire process to ensure continuity of resolutions as they occur. Some other mitigation factors to consider are these:

➤ **Current Inventory Information.** Know what products you have in stock, where your products are being stored, who is shipping your products, and if any are in transit. Knowing when your products are arriving or the scheduled arrival of products can be crucial to determine how you will respond to a disaster and how you might deploy products to your customers in the event of a disaster.

➤ **Knowing How to Communicate with Your Suppliers.** As stated, good communications with your suppliers in the event of a disaster is crucial! If your suppliers don't know what is going on, how will they be able to respond to your requests? Knowing how to and whom to communicate that you have had a disaster may mean the difference in getting products or not.

➤ **Test/Test/Test.** Documenting your disaster plans is essential, but that alone is not nearly enough. Exercising or testing your plan is crucial to the success of your recovery and the health of your company. Don't just let the plan sit on your bookshelf and collect dust. Make sure it becomes a living breathing document within your organization. The way you will interact with your suppliers in the event of a disaster will depend on how accurate and up to date your plan is and if you have actually tested your plan. Like any procedure you have in your organization, if you have never tested it, how will you know if it will work?

CONCLUSION

In summary, the five elements in supply chain management continuity are these.

1. **Data Collection.** Identify every supplier to your organization, the products they supply, and how they supply them, as well as the product supply schedules and how you will operate with vendors in the event of a disaster. Collect data

on your products or services, including how they are manufactured or delivered to your customers. Who are your alternative suppliers? Be certain that you collect all the data concerning your supply chain.

2. **Investigation.** Investigate alternative strategies with your supply chain. Can current vendors ensure product delivery if you or they have a disaster? Do they have a disaster recovery plan in place and are you an important element in their plan? Can the product be drop shipped directly to customers? Can existing inventory meet the demands of high-priority customers? Who are your weakest supply chain links? Can you strengthen these weak links through better communications or alternative processes or suppliers? Recoveries have a much greater likelihood of success when a company has already investigated their supply chain and has means in place to quickly react to a disaster with appropriate and tested procedure and policies.

3. **Assessment.** Once all your data have been collected and a thorough investigation of possible weaknesses and appropriate responses has been conducted, assess the risk associated with each supplier if a disaster or an event occurs. Identify by supplier the associated risk and the impact that may occur if the supplier is not able to fulfill its obligation to supply you with products or services. This assessment will determine the correct course of action to be taken if a disaster would occur and any additional cost that may be associated with the recovery.

4. **Agreement.** Form agreements with your suppliers on how they and you will react to a disaster should it occur. Don't wait until a disaster to determine if there are any associated additional costs if your supplier has to use alternative shipping methods to supply you. Get agreement from your suppliers on how to deal with contract points. Don't try to negotiate new contract terms while you are in a recovery process—and for sure don't try to litigate a solution while you are trying to recover from a disaster!

5. **Mitigation.** As a company, you want a supplier that is a strong and viable partner, one that has planned for business interruption and has your interests as well as its own in mind. To ensure this, you should put into place a vendor management program while creating your disaster recovery plans. A vendor management program is a partnership between your company and your suppliers. Ensure that you have communicated to your suppliers the development of your disaster recovery plan and how they are important to its success. Work out any concerns they or you might have if they are not able to fulfill their commitment due to a disaster. If they do not have a disaster recovery plan in place, help them to develop one. The effort you take in helping them will be well worth the time if it clarifies everyone's role in the event of a disaster.

Remember, business continuity planning in your supply chain is your responsibility; it is not your vendors' or suppliers' responsibility to manage the impact on your business.

CHAPTER 21

FIRE
Burning Down the House

Books have the same enemies as people:
fire, humidity, animals, weather, and their own content.
—Paul Valéry

INTRODUCTION

A fire can severely damage a business in many ways. The extent of the damage is determined by the fire's location, timing, and size. Fires damage a business's property through heat, smoke damage, and damage caused when putting it out. (Did you ever see the gusto with which a volunteer firefighter swings a fire ax?) Stolen objects can be recovered and returned. Water-damaged objects can be cleaned and restored. But burnt objects and documents are destroyed forever.

A fire can have far-reaching impact on a company's profitability. Depending on the size and location of the fire, the damage may include:

➤ **Structural Damage.** A fire can destroy or weaken walls, floors, ceiling/roof assemblies, and structural supports. Smoldering fires often make a home within walls, which must be opened so the fire can be suppressed.

➤ **Loss of Valuable Documents and Information.** Financial records, personnel files, and a wide range of vital company records can disappear in a fire. Some of these documents can be reconstructed from other information sources; some of this information can never be recovered.

➤ **Injury or Death.** Fire threatens the lives of your employees. Some of the physical injuries will take a long time to heal, and the mental injuries can take even longer.

➤ **Customer Relations.** Your customers are expecting that the goods they have ordered will be delivered on time. A delay due to a fire will lessen their confidence in your reliability and may cost them lost profits.

➤ **Vendor Relations.** Vendors deliver their goods on credit (terms often delay payment for 60 days or more). A fire that temporarily disables your business may delay your payments to them, thereby damaging your credit—or they may demand immediate return of goods already delivered!

➤ **Building Security.** A fire is a major security threat to your business. Massive volumes of smoke pouring through your facility will sow panic among the employees. This makes an ideal opportunity for theft. Intentional fires are also set to cover up crimes.

THE ANATOMY OF A FIRE

A fire is a chemical reaction in which a fuel mixes with oxygen and is heated to a point where flammable vapors are created. A typical workplace contains numerous items that can become fuel for a fire, including furnishings, business records, interior finishes, display cabinets, office equipment, laboratory chemicals, and machining lubricants. Look around your office or workplace. Anything that contains wood, plastic, paper, fabric, or combustible liquids can fuel a fire.

The key ingredients of a fire are:

1. **Fuel.** Any combustible material.

2. **Oxygen.** The air we breathe is approximately 20 percent oxygen, more than enough to nurture a fire.

3. **Heat.** Something to raise the fuel's temperature until it combusts.

Remove any of these elements and a fire will cease to burn.

A typical fire begins as a slow-growth, smoldering process. The smoldering stage may last from a few minutes to several hours, depending on the fuel type, arrangement of the fuel, and available oxygen. During this stage, heat will increase, and the fuel will begin producing smoke. A smell of smoke is usually the first indication that a fire is under way. Early detection (either human or mechanical) at this early stage can trigger fire suppression efforts before significant loss occurs.

As the fire reaches the end of the smoldering phase, flames will become visible. Once flames have appeared, the fire will begin to spread. The temperature of the burning object will quickly exceed 1800 degrees Fahrenheit. At this point, a room's contents will ignite, structural fatigue becomes possible, and occupant lives become seriously threatened. Within 5 minutes, the room temperature will be high enough to ignite all combustibles within the room. At this point, most contents will be destroyed, and human survival becomes impossible.

As a fire progresses into open flames, some chemical interactions occur. Let's use a piece of wood as an example. Wood contains all sorts of stuff, such as water, minerals, and volatile organic compounds. As the heat source applied to the wood exceeds 300 degrees Fahrenheit, the volatile organic compounds begin evaporating. This is typical of a smoky fire. Eventually, the fire gets so hot that these vapors begin to burn, which is typical of a fire with a lot of flame and not a lot of smoke.

Fires are classified according to their fuel, and the method used to attack a fire is generally based on the type of fuel that is burning. Each class of fire has some basic concepts that can be used to reduce the likelihood of an occurrence. The classes of fire are:

➤ **Class A** fires are made up of ordinary combustibles, such as paper. Class A fires can be prevented through good housekeeping practices, such as keeping all areas free of trash and the proper disposal of greasy rags.

➤ **Class B** fires are based on gases or flammable liquids. These fires can be prevented by never refueling a running or hot engine, storing flammables away from spark-producing sources, and always handling flammable liquids in well-ventilated areas.

➤ **Class C** fires are ignited by electricity, such as an overloaded wall outlet. Sometimes, the electricity is still running when you move in on the fire. Class C fires can be prevented by inspecting for worn or frayed electrical wires and promptly replacing them. Never install a fuse with a higher rating than called for by the manufacturer. Keep electrical motors clean and monitor them for overheating. Always have a wire guard over hot utility lights to prevent accidental contact with combustibles.

➤ **Class D** fires feed on flammable metals, such as magnesium. These fires are very difficult to extinguish and must be suppressed by use of a special firefighting agent.

RISK ASSESSMENT

Given the seriousness of a fire, what can you do to prevent one? The easiest and cheapest thing is to identify and eliminate potential fire hazards, and educate employees about these risks.

Begin by identifying what you are trying to protect. Offices move around, interiors get redecorated, and vital records repositories spring up in new executive offices. Rarely are a company's fire protection plans updated to protect this ebb and flow of equipment and documents around an office. Begin by making a list of your facility's critical areas and ensure they are adequately protected.

Next examine your building's layout. Minimal fire safety is governed by local building codes and fire safety regulations. Violating these codes can shut your business as quickly as any fire! Hire a fire safety engineer consultant to evaluate the adequacy of your existing fire alarm and suppression systems. If money is an issue, invite the local fire inspector to perform this task. Inspectors will provide free evaluations of a structure's fire risk, indicating both recommended and required changes.

An added benefit to using the local fire inspector is that the inspector can explain something about the fire potential of other occupants in the building or surrounding buildings, such as a facility that stores or uses combustible liquids, etc. Inspectors can also provide a wide-area picture of your fire threat and the ability of local services to contain it. Is there something in your facility that will require special fire suppression equipment to control a fire? For example, how quickly should you expect the first fire truck to arrive on scene? (This indicates the volume of fire suppression you should provide yourself.) Is your facility in the country or in the city? If your facility is in a rural location, do you have a pond nearby to refill the fire trucks?

Evaluate your facility's fire program. If it isn't written and available to employees, then it isn't worth much. Ensure that the fire safety plan is incorporated with your other emergency plans as well. Things to look for include:

➤ Automatic fire suppression systems to contain a fire. The most common approaches are gas fire suppression systems or sprinkler systems.

➤ Internal barriers to a fire in the form of fire doors and firewalls to hinder the spread of a fire. Place special fire barrier emphasis on expensive computer and telecommunications rooms.

➤ Well-marked emergency exits that are kept free from clutter.

➤ Automatic fire detection to alert occupants and the local fire department. Automatic fire detection systems are especially important in areas that are not normally occupied, such as closets, attics, and empty rooms.

➤ Manual fire alarms as a means to quickly alert all occupants to evacuate.

➤ A system of fire extinguishers and fire hoses that can be used to contain small fires. Both types of equipment require trained operators.

Many fire hazards in the workplace are employee-related items, such as space heaters and coffee pots. Review any existing policies concerning the use of these items. Consider including these issues the next time that your company safety policies are reviewed:

➤ **Personal Space Heaters.** These are popular in colder climates in the winter time. As companies economize by lowering workplace temperatures, some people compensate by purchasing personal heaters to place under their desks. The danger is that the heaters can start a fire. Heaters provide the elevated temperature necessary to start a fire, and fuel is all around it. Heaters may be overturned, left on after hours, or have something pressed against them that could catch fire. If possible, heaters should be banned. If that is not practical, then an acceptably safe heater must be identified by the company for all who need one.

➤ **Coffee Pots.** Banning coffee pots is a fast way to make enemies all across the company! However, like all electrical appliances, the issue is that they may be of low quality or left on with no one to attend them. The best strategy is to select a high-quality coffee maker that is as safe as you need it to be in your environment (office, factory, warehouse, etc.). Require that someone occasionally checks to ensure that the appliance is turned off when not in use. A timed electrical outlet set to normal business hours can be used to ensure the pot is turned off at night.

➤ **Overloaded Outlets.** Sometimes the tendency is to add more and more extension cords and surge protectors to a single outlet to feed the ever-growing flood of office electronics. This should not be allowed. A periodic safety inspection should be made of all work areas, and overloaded outlets should be immediately addressed with either the addition of more outlets or the removal of the extension cords.

➤ **General Housekeeping.** Simple housekeeping can be a major source of fire prevention. Some people seem to want to keep their offices and workspaces as simple and uncluttered as possible. Others seem to be following them around and stuffing their papers into the recently cleaned-out areas. Excess papers and other materials are potential fuels to a fire. If you have valuable documents that you must retain, then treat them as such and store them properly. Utility closets and rarely used facility areas must be inspected regularly to ensure no one has started an unauthorized storage depot.

Another easy housekeeping issue is to ensure that nothing is blocking emergency exits or the paths to them. Sometimes boxes and factory components find their way into aisleways and around exit routes. These must be moved immediately. If they are truly needed, then an adequate storage place will be found. Otherwise, they need to go! Use Form 21-1, Sample Fire Poster, on the enclosed CD to help get the message out about fire safety.

BUILDING A FIRE SUPPRESSION STRATEGY

Once you have controlled the possible sources of fire, the next step is to look at how you will suppress a fire if one occurs despite all your efforts. Handheld fire extinguishers and automatic detection and sprinkler systems are the most common means of fire suppression.

A thorough understanding of fire safety systems can help you to evaluate your company's existing safeguards to ensure they are current, adequate, and focused on employee safety. Before tackling a section in your plan for fire safety, be sure to inspect your existing company plans. This area may already be adequately covered.

Fire Extinguishers

Fire extinguishers can be used to contain very small fires, but they lack the capacity to attack large fires. The contents of a fire extinguisher determine the type of fire for which it is best suited. For example, using a water-filled fire extinguisher to fight an electrical fire would be a dangerous thing to do. Electricity from the source that started the fire may still be active and could travel up the stream of water and injure the extinguisher's operator. The "class" of the extinguisher corresponds to the previously described class of fire. The types of extinguishers include:

➤ **Class A** uses pressurized water to cool the material below its ignition temperature. This deprives the fire of its fuel. Never use a class A extinguisher on an electrical fire!

➤ **Class B** uses foam, carbon dioxide, or a dry chemical to smother grease or flammable liquid fires. This deprives the fire of its oxygen.

➤ **Class C** uses carbon dioxide, a dry chemical, or halon to smother the fire.

➤ **Class D** uses a dry powder specifically for the metal fire being extinguished. In most cases, the powder dissipates the heat from the burning materials so it will cool below its combustion level.

➤ **An ABC-rated** extinguisher is a multipurpose dry chemical extinguisher that is good for class A, B, or C fires. However, the extinguishing agent may leave a residue that is mildly corrosive and potentially damaging to electronic equipment.

➤ **A BC-rated** extinguisher is a dry chemical extinguisher that is good for flammable fluids and electrical fires, but not suited to containing class A fires.

Fire extinguishers have conspicuous labels that identify the class of fire for which they are suitable:

➤ ABC-rated extinguishers are almost always red and have either a spray nozzle or a short hose. Halon extinguishers look identical to ABC-rated units. These units are lightweight.

➤ Water-based extinguishers are generally chrome colored and are quite large.

➤ Carbon dioxide (CO_2) extinguishers are usually red with a large tapered nozzle and are quite heavy. Care must be taken when handling these units because the contents are under very high pressure. CO_2 extinguishers must be weighed to evaluate the volume of their contents.

After any use, fire extinguishers must be inspected and recharged. You cannot "test" a unit and then return it to its rack. It may not be ready for you when it is needed most! Most organizations have an ongoing maintenance program to inspect fire extinguishers monthly and to promptly recharge and repair leaky or discharged units.

Fire extinguishers are useless if no one knows how to use them. Include basic fire safety and the proper use of fire extinguishers in your company's annual safety briefing. Rules for using fire extinguishers are:

1. Always fight a fire with your back to your escape route. If the escape route is threatened, leave immediately.

2. Remember the acronym PASS:

Pull the pin.

Aim at the base of the flames.

Squeeze the trigger.

Sweep from side to side.

In summary, know the location and type of fire extinguishers in your work areas—and in your home. Ensure they match the types of fires that are most likely to occur in these areas.

Detection Systems

Fire detection systems are required in most states to alert you to the presence of a fire and to protect human life. These systems enable you to contain a fire with minimal damage. The earlier that an alarm detects a fire, the more expensive the alarm will be and the greater maintenance it will require. However, in some areas of your facility, the extra expense will be well worth the cost.

Detection systems provide early warning to allow for evacuation and fire containment. Fires do not always occur when people are standing nearby. They can occur at night, in vacant rooms, in back closets, or even behind cabinets. Be sure that you have the proper detection system in all these places—and a way for someone to react to it. A fire alarm system that sounds at night when no one is there does you little good. It must be connected to a remote alarm monitoring facility (usually the same company that monitors your burglar alarms).

There are two signs of a fire that can be detected: heat and smoke. Both of these can damage your facility without flames ever touching an object. We already briefly discussed the characteristics of both a smoky fire and a fire that was more flame than smoke. As we cannot be sure if a fire will be a slow starter (smoky) or fast and furious (little smoke), you should install both types of alarms in sensitive areas.

There are three basic types of fire detection alarms.

1. Photoelectric detectors detect smoke from smoldering fires. These are fires that generate a lot more smoke than heat because of the type of fuel that is burning and the temperature of the fire. This is the most common type of detector.

2. Ionization detectors are better at detecting fires that have more flame than smoke. Flash fires can be ignited based on the fuel and heat source combination, such as in some industrial applications.

3. Temperature detectors detect excessive temperatures from fires or other heat sources.

A fire alarm system must do more than just ring a bell. It should:

➤ Trigger the closing of fire doors.

➤ Activate the early fire suppression system (usually CO_2 or halon) if the fire is in that room.

➤ Release electronic locks so that people can get out and rescue crews can get in.

➤ Notify the people within the facility to evacuate. This should at least include both audible and visible (strobe lights) alarms.

➤ Notify the fire department of the emergency.

➤ In some cases, shut down automatic factory equipment.

Sprinkler Systems

Fire protection experts believe that automatic sprinklers are the most important feature of a fire management program. Properly designed, installed, and maintained, sprinklers are your first line of defense against a fire.

Fire sprinklers are the cheapest method of containing a fire while people evacuate a facility. They are most effective during the fire's initial flame growth stage and will contain a fire's growth within a few minutes of their activation. More than half of all fires are contained by one or two sprinklers. A typical sprinkler system will deliver 25 gallons of water per minute. Sprinkler systems offer several benefits to building owners, operators, and occupants.

Television dramas give sprinkler systems a bad name. It is highly dramatic to see a matrix of sprinklers begin spewing water across a large open office. Life, however, is a bit more mundane. Sprinkler systems only spit water from activated sprinkler heads. They do not waste water on a place where there isn't enough of a fire to activate a sprinkler head.

These benefits include:

➤ Sounding the alarm. Most sprinkler systems are connected to an alarm system that sounds when the sprinkler head is activated. Sometimes this is by detecting the flow of water in the pipe.

➤ Sprinklers are always on duty. Even if no one is present when a fire starts, the sprinkler will activate.

➤ Early detection reduces the amount of heat and smoke damage and allows for a more orderly evacuation of the facility.

➤ Sprinkler control of fires minimizes intrusion opportunities because the fire is contained and detected early.

➤ Insurance companies normally offer reduced premiums for buildings with sprinkler systems as compared with buildings without them.

When selecting a sprinkler, consider:

➤ Desired response time. How fast do you want the sprinkler to kick on?

➤ Criticality of what you are protecting. The value or importance of what the sprinkler protects can move you to a more expensive quick-reacting sprinkler system.

➤ The volatility of what you are protecting.

➤ Aesthetics.

➤ Normal room temperature.

For most fires, water is the ideal extinguishing agent. Fire sprinklers apply water directly onto flames and heat. Water cools the combustion process and inhibits ignition of adjacent combustibles. Basic sprinkler systems are a relatively simple concept that consist of three primary elements:

1. A dependable water supply. Water must be available even if electrical service is lost.

2. Connecting the sprinkler heads to the water supply through a network of water pipes. Rusted, weak, clogged, or too-narrow pipes will reduce the effectiveness of a sprinkler system.

3. The sprinkler head. At intervals along these pipes are independent, heat-activated valves known as sprinkler heads. The sprinkler head distributes water onto the fire.

The sprinkler head is a valve attached to the pipe that is "plugged" by a fusible link. This link might be plastic, solder, or anything that melts at the desired temperature. While a fire is in the smoldering stage, the heat output is too low to activate a sprinkler. As the heat increases, the sprinkler's thermal linkage begins to deform. If the temperature remains high, as it would in a growing fire, the sprinkler's thermal linkage will fail within 30 seconds to 4 minutes. This releases the sprinkler's seals and allows water to flow.

A sprinkler head has five major components: a frame, a thermally operated linkage, a cap, an orifice, and a deflector. Sprinkler heads vary among manufacturers but all use the same basic components.

➤ **Frame.** The frame provides a structure that holds the sprinkler components together. Frame styles can be low profile, flush, standard, or concealed mounts. Selection of a frame type depends on the area to be covered, the type of hazard to protect, and the visual effect desired.

➤ **Thermal Linkage.** The thermal linkage controls the water release. In normal use, the linkage holds the cap in place and keeps water from flowing out of the pipe. When the link is heated and gives way, the cap is released allowing water to flow. Common linkage types include soldered metal levers, frangible glass bulbs, and solder pellets.

➤ **Cap.** The cap provides the watertight seal over the sprinkler orifice, held in place by the thermal link. When the thermal link fails, the cap is released and water flows out of the orifice. Caps are always made of metal.

➤ **Orifice.** The opening in the water pipe at the base of the sprinkler valve is called the orifice. As its name implies, this is the opening in the water pipe where the water comes from. Orifices are about 1/2 inch in diameter. The orifice size may vary from larger for hazardous areas to smaller in home sprinkler systems.

➤ **Deflector.** The deflector splatters the water stream shooting out of the orifice into a pattern that is more efficient for fire suppression. The deflector styles vary: mounted above the pipe, mounted below the pipe, and sideways in a wall mount. Deflectors mounted above the pipe are found in ceiling plenums. Below-the-pipe deflectors are commonly found in office ceilings—just look up!

A key element in your sprinkler system is a reliable water source. This can be from public water systems, rural lakes, or water cisterns. Wherever your water comes from, it must be ready when the sprinkler cap pops off or it has all been a waste of time.

If your water source is not reliable, then water must be provided from more than one source. The supply of water must be sustained until the fire is extinguished. Along with the sprinklers, the water supply may be called upon to support the fire department's fire attack hoses. If so, then both requirements must be met. Things to consider when evaluating your water supply:

➤ It must be resistant to drought. Dry conditions outside increase your fire chances. If drought dries up your water supply, sprinklers may not work to full capability.

➤ Pipe failure can keep water from where it is needed. If your pipes cannot support the water flow, then again the sprinklers will not work to full potential.

➤ In conjunction with the need for water flow is a need for water pressure. The water supply must be able to maintain a steady water pressure or a pressure tank system must be added.

Sprinkler water pipes are the way to ensure a steady water flow to the sprinkler head. Steel is the traditional material used. There are many other features available for sprinkler systems:

➤ **Alarms.** The most basic fire alarms that are built into a sprinkler system are based on gongs that sound as water begins flowing in the sprinkler pipes. There may also be pressure switches and detectors at the sprinkler head to identify where the water is flowing to.

➤ **Control Valves.** A control valve allows you to shut off the flow of water to sprinkler heads. If the fire is out, the sprinkler cannot stop by itself. Remember, that open sprinkler head is spewing about 25 gallons of water per minute over your carpets, desk, and down the hall. Once the fire is extinguished, the sprinkler's water source must be shut off promptly. Shutting off the water to the sprinkler system is also useful for allowing periodic maintenance on the pipes and sprinkler heads. There is also a drain valve to allow the water in the pipes to drain out for easier maintenance. The control valve is kept locked to prevent an arsonist from disabling your sprinklers, so ensure a key is available when needed.

There are four basic types of sprinkler systems: wet pipe, dry pipe, preaction, and water mist. Wet pipe is by far the simplest and most common type of sprinkler system. In a wet pipe configuration, water pressure is constantly maintained in the sprinkler pipe. The advantage is that the only delay in action is however long it takes for the link to fatigue. The disadvantage is that the pipe may leak or the sprinkler head may become damaged and accidentally discharge.

Wet pipe systems have the fewest components and are the easiest to install. They are the easiest to maintain or modify. After a fire, they are the easiest configuration to restore to service. The major disadvantage to a wet pipe system is that the pipes must not be allowed to freeze. Frozen pipes may burst or weaken joints. Therefore the temperature of the building spaces with these pipes must be maintained above freezing at all times. This can be particularly troublesome if the pipes are run along exterior walls or in high ceilings in buildings located in very cold climates.

A dry pipe system uses a valve to hold the water out of the pipe. Instead of water, the pipe holds pressurized gas or air. When the thermal link is melted by the fire, the cap is released and the air in the pipe escapes. The water pressure pushing against the valve overcomes the declining air pressure and water flows to the sprinkler head.

Dry pipes are useful in unheated areas in cold climates. This prevents freezing of pipes, especially for exterior applications. Some people believe that a dry pipe is superior to a wet pipe because, if the sprinkler head is damaged, the surrounding areas will not be hurt by unneeded water. This is not the case. A dry pipe system would also leak and just deliver the water a bit later.

There are several disadvantages to using dry pipe systems. First, they are more complex to install and maintain. Second, the maximum size is limited, which makes it difficult to add on to an existing system later. Finally, there may be a delay of up to 60 seconds in the water flowing to a fire.

The most sophisticated approach is through the use of a "preaction" configuration. A preaction system uses a dry pipe approach, but the valve controlling the water is activated by a fire detection system. The preaction system uses a two-step process to fire suppression. The first step is when a fire detection system detects a fire. This releases the valve and allows water to enter the pipe. The second action is when the sprinkler head's thermal link fatigues and allows water to flow onto the fire.

Disadvantages of the preaction system include higher initial costs and higher maintenance costs. There is also a short delay while the air in the pipe is displaced by water.

A variation of the preaction configuration is the deluge system. A deluge system is triggered by a fire detector and releases water through all the sprinkler heads over a given area. Deluge systems are used wherever high-velocity suppression is required, such as a paint booth and in chemical storage areas.

An emerging technology is a sprinkler system that uses a water mist to suppress fire. Micro mists discharge fine water droplets at a very high pressure, which has been shown to control fires with very little water. This technology minimizes secondary water damage to your property.

An automatic sprinkler system is your best first line of defense against fires. A properly designed and installed system is very reliable. If your sprinkler water pipes will be subject to freezing temperatures, use a dry pipe or preaction system. Remember, most system failures are due to poor maintenance. Always consult a sprinkler system professional before selecting or modifying a sprinkler system.

ACTION STEPS FOR YOUR PLAN

Two areas that should be included in your plan are storage that can resist the fire for your important documents and the evacuation of personnel safely from the building.

Fire-Resistant Storage

One defense against the damage caused by fire is the use of fire-resistant storage, which can be anything from a small cabinet to a large room. Fire-resistant storage is based on preventing combustion by removing oxygen from a fire (remember the three key ingredients of a fire?).

"Fireproof" containers consist of thick walls and a tight-sealing door. These containers are called fireproof because their thick insulated walls will protect documents and other valuables against a small, short-duration fire. The containers themselves are fireproof and will not burn, but the contents are what you really want to protect.

In a large or long-duration fire, the benefit of these containers is less complete. As the heat outside the container rises, the thick insulation walls slow the flow of heat into the container. If the container remains in the midst of a hot fire, eventually the interior temperature can rise high enough to begin a smoldering fire. This incipient fire will quickly die as soon as the oxygen within the container is consumed.

Depending on the amount of heat applied to the container, the contents can still be seriously damaged. At high interior temperatures, flammable materials will still char (until the oxygen runs out). Magnetic media will deform at temperatures above 125 degrees Fahrenheit and 80 percent humidity, much less than the heat required to burn paper.

Underwriters Laboratories has a standard for evaluating the protection value of a storage container. A "one hour fire rating" interior will not exceed 350 degrees Fahrenheit when exposed to an external temperature of 1700 degrees Fahrenheit. A "two-hour-rated" container would withstand this temperature for 2 hours and withstand a drop of 30 feet (since a fire of this magnitude would probably also cause structural failure).

After the fire has passed, you must allow adequate time for the interior to cool below the fuel's flash point. Remember, the container starved the fire for oxygen. The interior still has fuel (your valuable documents). If high heat is still present and you open it, then you get to see your documents flash into smoke before your eyes! Always allow plenty of time (at least a day) before opening a fireproof container after a fire.

What does a typical business need to store in a fireproof container? Begin with:

➤ Cash, checks, and securities.

➤ Software licenses.

➤ Magnetic backup media (use a container specifically rated for this).

➤ Engineering documents, including work in progress.

➤ Any legal papers difficult or impossible to replace, such as tax documents.

➤ Works of art.

➤ Precious materials.

Other steps to take include:

➤ Make copies of critical documents and magnetic media and store them in a different building.

➤ Place fireproof storage containers in your facility where they won't fall through a floor weakened by a fire (such as in the basement or on a ground floor) and where there is minimal material overhead to fall on it and crush the container. Ruptured containers will let the fire in to burn your documents!

Evacuation Planning

An essential part of any emergency plan is to provide a way to safely evacuate the building. A well thought out evacuation plan will ensure that everyone has left the building and that no one was left behind. This helps the fire and rescue squads to focus their efforts on locating people known to still be in the building. Without an accounting of who may be still inside the structure, the fire department may needlessly risk their lives searching the entire structure, wasting time they could be using to contain the fire damage.

Evacuation plans come in many forms.

1. **Evacuate the Building.** Everybody out, due to perhaps a fire or earthquake.

2. **Evacuate the Area.** Everyone must leave to avoid a natural disaster such as a hurricane or a forest fire.

3. **Evacuate into a Shelter.** Leave your offices for the storm shelter for safety against a tornado, etc.

Normally, evacuation involves getting everyone out of the facility as quickly as is safely possible. Evacuation planning is an 11-step process.

1. Determine the conditions that would trigger an evacuation.

2. Establish "evacuation supervisors" to ensure areas are clear, to assist others, and to account for everyone at the rendezvous site.

3. Pull together a system for accounting that everyone is out of the building or in the storm shelter.

4. Assign someone to assist anyone with disabilities and those who may not speak English. This is important in your customer areas, reception room, delivery driver lounge, or any other area where outsiders may be in your facility. They need someone to show them what to do and where to go.

5. Post evacuation procedures around the facility. Also, post maps showing the nearest building exits. Identify primary and alternate evacuation routes. Ensure they are clearly marked.

6. Designate key people to shut down critical or dangerous operations during the evacuation. This might be transferring toxic chemicals, halting automated paint spraying operations, or disconnecting power to high-voltage equipment.

7. Designate someone to quickly secure the petty cash box, close the safe, and lock all cash registers before evacuating the area.

8. Ensure evacuation routes are always kept clear and unobstructed by material. They should be wide enough to handle the volume of people that may need to use them. The route should not take anyone near other hazardous areas in case the disaster spreads rapidly.

9. Install emergency lighting in case electricity fails during the evacuation. Some companies also install "knee-high" exit signs near the floor so that anyone crawling under the smoke can still find a building exit.

10. Designate outside assembly areas for each section of the building. Assembly areas should be well clear of the structure and clearly marked so they are easy to find. Some companies use signs on their parking lot light poles. Assembly areas should be located away from the roads required by the emergency crews so they do not interfere with incoming fire trucks.

11. Actions in the assembly areas should be clearly understood by the evacuation supervisors. To facilitate the headcount, department rosters should be kept adjacent to the evacuation exits so they can be picked up on the way out. These rosters list the name of every employee and long-term contract worker by department.

    a. Keeping rosters up to the minute is an impossible task. Instead, use the roster to see if the normal staff is accounted for. Ask if the missing are out sick that day or known to be working elsewhere in the facility.

    b. Ask if any other contract employees were working in the area that day.

    c. Ask if any visitors were in the area that day.

d. Forward the completed roll call results to the Evacuation Command Center as soon as possible. Note the names and last known locations of any missing people. DO NOT reenter the building as these people may be at a different rendezvous point.

In some emergencies, you will evacuate your workspaces and head to the storm shelter. This might be as protection from a tornado. Evacuation supervisors will ensure the orderly entry and exit from the shelter and ensure that space is fairly allocated.

Employee training is essential if plans are to be executed as written. Training should be a part of initial employee (and long-term contract worker) orientation. An annual refresher class along with an evacuation drill will improve employee understanding and reduce some of the panic and chaos of an actual emergency.

FACTS ON FIRE

Fire in the United States:

➤ The United States has one of the highest fire death rates in the industrialized world. For 2006, the U.S. fire death rate was 13.2 deaths per million population.

➤ In 2006, 3,320 Americans lost their lives and another 16,705 were injured as the result of fire.

➤ Approximately 100 U.S. firefighters are killed each year in duty-related incidents.

➤ Each year, fire kills more Americans than all natural disasters combined.

➤ Fire is the third leading cause of accidental death in the home; at least 80 percent of all fire deaths occur in residences.

➤ Direct property loss due to fires is estimated at $8.6 billion annually.

➤ There were approximately 1.5 million fires in the United States in 2006.

➤ Residential fires represent 22 percent of all fires and 74 percent of structure fires.

➤ Eighty percent of all fatalities occur in the home. Of those, approximately 85 percent occur in single-family homes and duplexes.

➤ Causes of fires and fire deaths:

◆ Careless smoking is the leading cause of fire deaths. Smoke alarms and smolder-resistant bedding and upholstered furniture are significant fire deterrents.

◆ Heating is the second leading cause of residential fires and the second leading cause of fire deaths. However, heating fires are a larger problem in single-family homes than in apartments. Unlike apartments, the heating systems in single-family homes are often not professionally maintained.

◆ Arson is the third leading cause of both residential fires and residential fire deaths. In commercial properties, arson is the major cause of deaths, injuries, and dollar loss.

Source: U.S. Fire Administration - www.usfa.dhs.gov

CONCLUSION

Fire is one "natural" disaster that knows no geographic boundaries. Where there is fuel, oxygen, and heat, you can have a fire. The key elements to avoiding a disaster caused by fire are:

1. Assess the risk to your business.

2. Have policies in place to reduce the risk from fire.

3. Have appropriate detection mechanisms in place.

4. Know how to extinguish a fire as quickly as possible.

CHAPTER 22

HUMAN RESOURCES
Your Most Valuable Asset

You win with people.
—Woody Hayes

INTRODUCTION

Your Human Resources department has an important role to play in business continuity planning. Major business emergencies are very stressful events. From a business perspective, stress reduces the productivity of the work force. The Human Resources department ensures that the "people side" of an emergency is addressed for the best long-term benefit of the company. The staff can also take steps to ensure that the essential human needs of the work force are addressed so that they are ready to resume work as soon as the problems at hand are addressed. In manufacturing jargon, the Human Resources specialists are the "human machinists" who maintain the "people" machines.

Employees spend a great deal of their life at work. Their workplace becomes a separate community for them, paralleling the one at home. They make friends, celebrate life's milestones, and develop an identity with those around them. When this is properly cultivated by the company, the employees become more productive. If this aspect is ignored by the company, then this can turn negative and become a drag on employee efforts. Business continuity planning for Human Resources works to address the employee concerns during a crisis to minimize the negative impacts and position the work force for a successful recovery.

Most Human Resources departments already have in place approved procedures to handle some of the things addressed here. These processes should be incorporated into the plan insofar as they touch on business continuity planning.

HUMAN RESOURCES ISSUES

Stress

Probably the biggest issue with employees in the aftermath of a major disaster is stress. The mental injuries caused by serious incidents have long been recognized. Like a physical injury, if it is properly treated, it will heal—if ignored, it may fester and grow worse over time. Different people react in different ways to the traumatic incidents around them. Everyone has their own way of coping with the sights and sounds of a disaster, which is shaped by their personal environment, faith, family, and many other factors.

Any major emergency can bring on a great deal of stress to your employees. It could be a coworker who was injured or killed in a fire, witnessing serious workplace violence, or even working in a building when a major earthquake strikes. Stress-related reactions are normal in people and can be addressed with prompt action.

"Combat stress is a natural result of heavy mental/emotional work, when facing danger in tough conditions. Like physical fatigue and stress, handling combat stress depends on the level of your fitness/training. It can come on quickly or slowly, and it gets better with rest and replenishment."

Source: U.S. Army Office of the Surgeon General

Pertinent to business continuity planning is how stress relates to your work force. Critical incidents are traumatic events that create overwhelming stress in some people. The reaction may not appear for many days. Employees may have known someone who was seriously injured or even witnessed the accident. Symptoms include heightened tension, anxiety, disturbed sleep, and impaired concentration. If the employee's reaction interferes with his or her ability to work, professional assistance may be needed.

Even after the emergency has passed, stress-related damage may linger for months. It is essential that confidential follow-up counseling be available to employees for up to 1 year after an event.

A good place to begin is to include a mental health counseling program along with your other company medical benefits. These programs assist employees in coping with the stresses of everyday living. Mental health counselors assist employees with a wide range of issues from divorce to handling teenagers to moral dilemmas. Mental wellness programs address the essential human concerns: social, emotional, occupational, physical, intellectual, and spiritual.

Another proactive step is to include stress management techniques in routine employee training. Helping employees cope with their daily stresses will reduce recovery time after injury or illness. It also strengthens their ability to cope with problems, reduces depression, and even increases energy levels. Some companies operate in a high-pressure environment. For these companies, routine mental health counseling can include stress management and stress relief training. This should also include training in ways to recognize stress in others and steps they could take to help them.

When drafting the services contract for stress and mental counseling, include a clause for onsite support in the event of a disaster. By adding this on-demand service, you have someone to call on short notice to assist in an emergency. Be sure you understand how that company reacts in wide-area disasters and where you are on the overall priority in the event that all the clients call at once.

In an emergency, three basic intervention techniques can be used with your employees. The first is "defusing," which allows workers to release their pent-up feelings much like relaxing immediately after strenuous exercise. In this approach, employees meet at the end of the day in informal discussion groups. Topics in these groups range from what has occurred to stress management techniques. These meetings are short and last about an hour. This is best done no later than the day after the tragic event.

A more formal and focused discussion called a "debriefing" is a common way to address stress accumulated from a major event. This meeting may run for hours and allows people to explain their feelings and interpretation of the events. For many, this meeting will release the emotions that have been shoved aside in the rush to complete the recovery. It may also clear up misconceptions of what happened in the emergency or its immediate aftermath.

Person-to-person "crisis counseling" is the most time-consuming action for those most affected by the event. This should be made available to anyone who wants it but, based on how the debriefing or defusing sessions went, you may identify some people to refer to this program.

After the disaster strikes, everyone is focused on containing the damage, and so should you. However, the damage you are containing has nothing to do with the facility. After calling in your mental health service, walk around the disaster area and talk to the workers. Your containment action is to identify overstressed people whose judgment may be too impaired to safely assist with the immediate recovery. Dazed people are a potential danger to everyone, so gently escort them to emergency medical authorities. If this stress is not promptly addressed, the symptoms may linger for months. This will affect their ability to make critical decisions, rendering them of much less use as workers.

Employee coordination is a significant part of Human Resources contingency planning. As the recovery continues, the Human Resources specialist can refer to the employee skills matrix to suggest substitutes for recovery workers, allowing them to rest. Workers assigned to a rest period must not be allowed to continue working but must rest. This implies accommodations for a rest site.

Symbols and sensitivity are extremely vital to the surviving employees. Expressions of support for the families, organizing and attending memorials for the victims, and supporting trusts for the families are positive outlets for grief. Someone must organize these activities. Often the Human Resources department will help find sponsors within the departments and represent the company at all functions.

Labor Management Issues

A disaster will disrupt your employees' normal routine. While there will be plenty of work to do to get the business back on track, it will not be the same work done during normal times. What type of work employees will be expected to do and how they will be paid needs to be thought out before a disaster occurs.

What is the company policy for paying employees after a major disaster that prevents them from working? This is a very sensitive issue. On one hand, you have some hourly workers who need every paycheck on time to keep food on the table, and you have others with the financial resources to carry their family for several weeks until the paychecks begin flowing again. Continuity of income is a key family concern. Is it fair for a company to pay someone to sit at home? If you discharge your employees because recovery will take several months, then how much will it cost to hire and train new ones?

Some companies use an outside payroll service and some handle their paycheck generation internally. However you do it, consider cutting regular paychecks for all employees during the emergency. If using an outside concern, quickly arrange for regular paychecks. Hold all overtime claims until after the emergency is passed. If this will be too difficult, in the interim, consider paying everyone the same amount and reconcile the differences later.

Decisions like this are often complicated by legal requirements surrounding employment law. There is also the moral issue of abruptly discontinuing a family's potentially sole source of income. Things to consider are:

➤ Depending on your local laws, when you tell your employees that due to a disaster they have no work until the damage has been repaired, did you just incur unemployment insurance liability? Is there a minimum notification period that must first be met?

➤ If people are not being paid, have their medical benefits, etc., just stopped? What are the local employment law issues involved with this?

➤ If people are not being paid, can they take vacation or sick leave to keep the money flowing? How will you handle the ones who immediately call in sick?

➤ Your best or highly technical employees may be the first ones to jump ship if they think their family's cash flow is in jeopardy. How much does it cost to attract new talent to your company?

➤ What is fair?

   a. How much should you pay the people whom you do not need for the containment and recovery effort and who are sitting at home?

   b. How much should you pay the people working long hours on the disaster site assisting on the containment and recovery effort?

➤ What should you do if you are paying the people to sit at home, and when you call them to come in and help with the cleanup, they refuse? What if they claim illness?

➤ Is it easier to provide some sort of reward (bonus, extra vacation, promotions, etc.) for the people on the recovery site than to take away something from the employees temporarily sitting at home?

Containment and cleanup efforts can be very manpower-intensive. As order returns to the emergency scene, general labor may be needed to help the emergency teams. Rather than automatically call in temporary outside help, you can tap the people on your payroll who are sitting at home. Some additional issues to consider include:

➤ How will you select people to come in to help with the cleanup and "extra hands" effort? (We will address building an employee skills matrix later in this chapter.)

➤ How will you track ("clock in and clock out") people to the work site to fairly account for their hours? This could be a clipboard, an honor system, or delegated to the supervisors to report daily.

➤ If someone's house is swimming in 2 feet of swirling muddy water, is it fair to demand that they come in to work? What if this is a key person?

➤ What if someone is physically able to help but refuses as the assigned job is beneath their dignity? (This is where your leadership skills will be tested!)

Outside Help

In an emergency, it can be very difficult to obtain high-quality technical help. Wide-area disasters can strain local technical talent pools. Usually, the first company to call for help will soak up everyone who is available. For example, in the event of a major hurricane, such as when Hurricane Andrew struck south Florida in 1992, the area of devastation was so broad that all the available local technicians were fully occupied both with helping their companies and with saving their own homes. Even with the help of outside electrical line repair crews, it took more than a month to fully restore electrical power.

Bringing in outside help is also fraught with perils. There is no time to obtain background checks, to carefully select the best people, and to weed out the highly paid incompetents. These well-meaning people may have technical knowledge, but how much do they know specifically about your processes, equipment, and software systems? If you have used specific technical consultants in the past, they may be suitable—if they are available! Remember, you are in an all-out struggle to restore a minimal level of service to your facility. Every day your facility is hindered or inoperable, your competitors are becoming ever closer to your customers!

If you are a branch in a large company, you should be able to borrow the technical staff members from sister companies to begin emergency repairs. This avoids the problems of background checks and the high cost of consultants (since they are already employees). They may also be familiar with the company's terminology, priorities, and methods of approaching a problem. To tap this pool, you will need a telephone number at which they can be reached at any time.

To prepare for this, establish a mechanism to borrow personnel from other departments/divisions or branches/facilities within the company. Arrangements can be on a mutual exchange basis, depending on who needs what when. This will require additional funds for transportation, housing, and meals, but overall is much cheaper than hiring consultants.

Family Assistance

In a wide-area disaster, you have the additional problem of people worrying about their families and their property. This can be a major distraction to people working on the disaster site. Wide-area disasters might be earthquakes, hurricanes, or severe winter storms. Time spent helping your employees' families in a wide-area emergency can pay off with key workers staying focused on their jobs.

It is not unusual to have single parents among your key employees. In a wide-area disaster, their normal childcare arrangements may unravel and unless you assist in finding some arrangement, this key person may not be available. Another potential issue is if the disaster glances off of your facility but severely damages your employees' homes. What can be done?

To address these issues, temporary Human Resources policies can be implemented. These would include such things as:

➤ Flexible or reduced work hours so that childcare issues can be addressed.

➤ The establishment of a temporary day care facility for the children of recovery workers.

➤ Providing emergency shelter for employees' families, to include food and essential comfort items.

➤ Assisting employees with requesting help from relief services, such as the American Red Cross, Salvation Army, or government agencies.

➤ Stress counseling for families who may have lost their home or whose family members may have been injured during the disaster.

➤ Soliciting donations of goods or money from other company sites for the relief of the workers' families.

RISK ASSESSMENT

While we like to think that our employees are an asset, there are times when they can be a threat to the business. Stress can cause some individuals to act out violently, labor unions can go on strike, and key employees can be called away by government agencies in times of national emergencies.

Workplace Stress

Routine workplace stress affects different people in different ways. Some people take it in stride and leave it at the door when they go home. Others internalize their frustrations and slowly build a wall of resentment and distrust. Routine stress can be created by many things such as:

➤ An abusive management climate.

➤ An unstable employment environment where people are (apparently) discharged for minor offenses.

➤ Peer pressure that focuses on singling out coworkers for abuse.

➤ In-fighting among managers.

In extreme cases, workplace stress may manifest itself as a violent outburst by the employee against coworkers, critical machinery, or even themselves. Personnel managers must be on watch for stressful situations and implement stress abatement actions whenever the tension level rises too high. Personnel managers can casually monitor for excessive daily stress levels by regular employee meetings, walking around the facility chatting with workers, or even attending departmental staff meetings. All can serve to raise awareness of a problem area or person.

Some companies provide an outlet for overstressed workers with free and anonymous counseling services as an ongoing part of their workplace violence abatement programs.

Labor Stoppage

Few business situations evoke such strong emotions as a labor strike. Even the existence of a contingency plan for addressing such a thing makes people uneasy and fearful that the company is planning some vague negative action toward the workers. Given this perception, such plans are normally not kept in the master binders with the rest of the business continuity plans. However, they must exist somewhere close at hand, be tested, and kept up to date.

Whatever the reasons for a strike, your employees will experience a wide range of emotions and reactions toward it. Always remember that when the dispute is settled, the strikers will again become your coworkers. Efforts must be made to eliminate the likelihood of long-lasting animosity by staying on top of the situation and not permitting events to escalate out of control. In this sense, the Human Resources department is "in the middle," watching both the strikers and the people crossing the picket line and dealing firmly with anyone who violates the rules.

The primary goal of a strike is to stop production as an economic lever to force a favorable agreement with the company's owners or managers. The Human Resources department will be deeply involved with those negotiations, which are beyond the scope of this chapter. What is included in this chapter are those Human Resources actions useful for maintaining the flow of labor into the facility during a strike. From a business continuity standpoint, the goal is to maintain a flow of goods to your customers to meet their business needs. This outflow of finished goods also provides some cash flowing in to lessen the financial impact of the strike.

Depending on your local labor laws and agreements, a strike usually does not include management personnel. Employees classified as "management" or supervisory can enter or leave the facility and either continue production at a reduced level, finish uncompleted goods in the facility, or ensure that production equipment is properly maintained. They should be prepared for long hours and very few days off.

However you use your management workers, you must be sure that prudent measures are taken to safeguard them whenever they come into contact with the strikers—usually when crossing the picket lines. Courts are inclined to grant large damage awards to victims of strike violence, but the party that pays this cash depends on how well the company has documented its mitigation steps. Will you be paying the damages, or will it be the strikers?

To begin with, every person who enters the facility needs to be informed about the security situation before coming in contact with the picket line. This includes suppliers, contract employees, and management employees—everyone who will cross the picket line at your request. They should be fully aware of the security procedures and any special circumstances, such as threats of violence.

In all dealings with strikers, frequently refer to your legal counsel to ensure that your actions are in accordance with your company's legal rights. At the first instance of strikers engaging in disruptive behavior, obtain a court injunction against the union to restrain them from any illegal activity. This will put everyone on notice that their behavior is being monitored. By firmly addressing any violations of your company's rights, the potential for violence is decreased.

BEFORE THE STRIKE Before the strike begins, or immediately after the beginning of a wildcat strike, all management personnel should be thoroughly trained on the company's security policies, procedures, and activities that will be used during the strike. Do not assume that management will know your current policies or procedures. This is one of the mitigation actions to prevent problems before they occur. Document when this training occurred, an outline of the topics discussed, and who attended.

In preparing for a strike:

➤ Ensure that all exterior lights are in good working order. Stockpile spare bulbs in the building in case existing lights are put out.

➤ Do not allow any hourly workers into the facility without specific company permission. Some workers may disagree with the strikers or may be essential to maintaining the facility's equipment.

➤ When a strike is imminent, gather supervisors and security personnel together to explain the importance of documenting any strike-related incidents.

Provide preprinted forms to everyone to help ensure all the essential elements are captured. Everyone must have copies of these forms readily available.

➤ Remind your management team that they too will be held accountable for their conduct when crossing the picket line.

➤ Explain to everyone who may come in contact with a picket line as to their rights and the rights of the picketing workers.

➤ Change all external locks immediately before the strike.

➤ Establish a hotline to immediately report any incidents so prompt legal action can be taken.

➤ Establish an information telephone number where management personnel can call in to find out when and where they are needed.

➤ Establish a series of sites, usually shopping center parking lots, where anyone needing to cross the picket lines can meet and carpool into the facility.

➤ Verify that all company employee ID cards are current.

To reduce the chances of an incident, there should be as few vehicles as possible crossing the picket line. A Human Resources specialist should take the lead and form management employee carpools. When it is time to cross the picket line, assemble all the workers at a parking lot and pool them into as few company-owned vehicles as possible. Then all the vehicles can cross the picket line at once, both coming in and going out. Coordinate the crossing with security before it occurs.

Contractors must be informed and briefed as to the proper crossing of the picket line. Their company may not permit crossing the line, so you must check with each critical contractor before the onset of a strike. Truck drivers belonging to a union may refuse to cross a picket line. When using these companies, they must be notified to send out a supervisor or independent truck driver to move the truck across the line. Otherwise, you may see sorely needed incoming shipments turn away from your gate.

When negotiating service contracts, determine company guidelines for crossing a picket line. Often, they only require that the company send a vehicle to pick up their technicians and carry them across the line. Spell out your expectations as a clause in all your service contracts. At the first whiff of trouble, do not expect any further contractor support. It is considered your fight—not theirs.

RECORD KEEPING It is important that security guards maintain an ongoing record of illegal activities by strikers. This record will be invaluable if the company attempts to recover damages from the union at a later time. These records must include the time of the incident, the events leading up to it, and the incident itself. Review and collect these records daily.

One of the best ways to do this is by videotaping the entry gate any time that someone crosses a picket line. In this way, you can prove to the authorities who did what, and when. Although its primary intent is to deter violence by the picketing workers, it can also identify anyone crossing the picket line in a manner that may further inflame the situation.

Assign a photographer to all entrances with a videocamera. Anonymity is a critical element of picket line violence. If you can strip that away, then most people will be reluctant to participate in an incident. A company employee who can identify incoming workers should accompany the security guard along with a trained photographer with a videocamera (at each gate). Keep close tabs on who is manning the picket line, their attitude, and what they are doing (chatting, drinking alcohol, shouting, fighting, sleeping, etc.). Like anyone else, they will pass their time on the picket line in their own fashion. Immediately report problems noticed on the picket line (such as alcohol) as a written protest directly to the union president, who likely will not want a problem on the picket line either.

Establish a hotline to report any incidents so prompt legal action can be taken. The Human Resources department should assign someone to take these calls around the clock and to address them accordingly.

Collect all records daily and guard them closely. Things to record:

➤ The exact wording of picket signs must be recorded every hour, along with the number of picketers present and, if known, their names. Incidents can happen in an instant. After a violent incident, many of the people involved or witnesses may quickly disperse, making it difficult to determine who was present.

➤ Anytime anyone crosses the picket line. This can be people entering or exiting the facility as well as deliveries into the facility and finished goods leaving the facility.

➤ Any tampering with security arrangements around the company perimeter, such as cut fences, attempts to force open locks, and other signs of attempted sabotage.

FACILITY SECURITY During the time that labor negotiations are under way, the facility and all workers must be safeguarded against violence or sabotage. The key component of this is a reliable security force to enforce the integrity of the facility's perimeter and ensure that anyone crossing the picket line can do so in safety. Success requires extensive planning and actively seeking to eliminate the opportunities for mischief by the strikers.

As the strike approaches, be on guard for major sabotage by outgoing employees. There are normally choke points about your facility where very expensive damage can be done with little effort. Post someone to watch over them as the strike deadline approaches and the workers file out. This minimizes the chance of a casual attack.

Anyone crossing a picket line for the benefit of your company becomes your responsibility to safeguard. They should call ahead and notify you when they will cross the picket line. Pass this on to your security staff, which should be present and monitoring the situation. They should park far enough away from the fence that objects cannot be tossed over onto their vehicles.

Everyone must be told of any violent incidents or threats. Employees, contract workers, and other personnel should make their own determination as to the safety of the situation. In addition, inform the police and fire departments of every threat and incident. Remember, some companies will not allow their employees to cross a picket line out of fear of violence. Others will enter your facility if you will transport them both ways across the picket line.

Ensure that the local law enforcement authorities are informed about the strike as soon as it begins. It is important that they are aware that this is a potential flashpoint. Be sure to call them in whenever a confrontation is brewing. If they do not respond in a timely manner, then you must escalate the matter immediately to higher governmental authorities (county and then state).

All employees must show their employee ID card to security personnel when entering the facility. In this way, you can track who is entering and leaving the facility. In a labor dispute, there is often additional security staff hired. These individuals do not know even the top executives by sight. Ensure that all employees and contractors invited in during the dispute know they must show their company identity cards to gain entry.

On the other hand, these people are not required to show identification to anyone on the picket line. This is a tactic by strikers to slow down picket line crossing, which may increase the likelihood of an incident. Management employees should avoid speaking to or provoking strikers on the picket line. Vehicles should proceed very slowly but resolutely across picket lines without touching any strikers. They have a right to picket, and you have a right to cross the picket line.

National Guard and Military Reserves

As illustrated during the second Persian Gulf War and the ongoing wars in Iraq and Afghanistan, members of the National Guard and Reserves may be called upon for national service for extended periods of time. Their civilian jobs are protected by federal law during their absence. The Human Resources Manager should ensure that someone is cross-trained in their critical job skills (because deployments come on short notice). Your list should include their name and their unit (sometimes the news services announce a call-up before the individuals are notified).

Every year, National Guard and Reserve units perform at least 2 weeks of annual training. Although this is often done during the summer months, it can occur any time during the year. From time to time, Guard personnel may attend a formal training school for the 2 weeks in lieu of the unit's training. In either event, the individual will be absent for this time and cannot be forced to take vacation for this time period. Continuity plans should include cross-training someone to cover these absences.

A similar issue involves volunteer emergency services such as EMTs and firefighters. In a wide-area emergency, they may be called away for several days. An example might be a flood or an earthquake. Although they are volunteers, it may be negatively viewed by the employees and the community at large if you blocked their departure.

ACTION STEPS FOR YOUR PLAN

The two most important activities to cover in your plan are developing an employee skills matrix and communications. The skills matrix will track skills such as who knows CPR, who might be trained EMTs, etc. The employee skills matrix will allow you to apply the proper human resource at a particular problem at the right time. A well-designed communications plan will ensure that the right information is given to the right people at the right time.

Employee Skills Matrix

An employee skills matrix is a tool that compares the skill levels employees have attained for specific tasks or processes. From a business continuity perspective, this matrix can quickly identify whom we can call on to stand in for a key person who is not available during an emergency. As a movie so succinctly put it a number of years ago, "Who ya gonna call?" Much of this information is buried in the Human Resources department's personnel files and may have been included in resumes when the workers were hired. In a crisis, you need it at your fingertips.

An employee skills matrix can also be used to identify people from other departments who have an understanding of a business process or function. These people become excellent departmental plan testers as they know enough about an area to help test it but are somewhat distant from the plan's authors. Use Form 22-1, Skill Matrix by Job Process (on the enclosed CD), to help you build a skills matrix for your organization.

Skills matrices are another area where business continuity planning can overlap with other business areas for mutual advantage. The matrix developed for your business continuity planning can be used to drive company training plans, management succession plans, identifying people for staffing new business initiatives, and a wide range of other uses. It is not unusual to uncover valuable employee skills not previously realized by company management.

When you are staffing your disaster containment and recovery teams, the matrix is a handy tool for identifying a specific individual to the proper group. Each team requires knowledgeable people but slightly different skill sets. The matrix can also identify people to write or review specific subplans.

BUILDING A MATRIX Skill matrices tend to be unique to an enterprise. They can also become quite long. To gauge the level of detail you want to use, model a matrix on a single department. This should reduce the likelihood that it will be too large (time consuming to complete) or too small (causing you to revisit people to fill in the gaps). Another caveat is when employees with skills in one department work in a different area of the company. This is common in departments such as Data Processing where an understanding of accounting makes it easier to support their programs. These cross-department skills are very important to note, but what was once a clean department by department report becomes somewhat entangled.

Assembling an employee skills matrix is a multistep job. The first step starts with a department's job descriptions. The department manager must ensure that there is a published job description for each position in the area and that these descriptions are up to date. The job description should generally describe the routine tasks that this person is expected to perform along with any specific (usually unique) duties required. As a side benefit, current job descriptions can provide the text when posting or drafting new job openings.

You can use the example skills matrix provided in Form 22-1 (on the CD) or follow along and build your own. It is recommended that you use a spreadsheet program such as Microsoft Excel to build the matrix as it easily organizes information into rows and columns. The first step is to skip down a few lines (or "rows" in spreadsheet jargon) and begin entering the names of all employees in a department, from the manager at the top to the part-time clerk at the bottom. It is easier to build the matrix if the names are sequenced according to their work teams.

On the row above the names, enter column headings for the skills each of the people may have. The first headings should be for common skills expected of all employees, which may include safety issues, company process knowledge, or product knowledge. Each person will be assigned a score based on these skills. Each skill listed should encompass a process within the department. This is where you must determine how much is included in each category. As the matrix begins to fill in, expect that additional categories will be required. Categories are usually grouped by related subject matter. In an accounting department, you might group all the processes associated with accounts receivable with general ledger or accounts payable. Under these, subcategories might be collections, credit, reconciling purchase orders to materials receipt, etc.

After you have created a column heading, write a brief narrative of what you mean by that skill and any important subtasks it must include. Most people may claim mastery of a subject but, in reality, they mainly understand a subset of it. Few people know a process or subject completely from edge to edge. This narrative will be useful when debating what is included in a particular process. See Form 22-2, Skill Matrix by Technical Skill (on the enclosed CD), for another example you can use.

RATING EMPLOYEES Consistently rating all employees can be a major challenge. Each evaluator will see things through the filter of their preferences and biases. Some people are by nature more modest about skills; some are overly boastful. If the workers feel this will be a tool for identifying future career advancement, then they will have an incentive to overstate their accomplishments.

The first step is to show the matrix to employees and ask them to rate themselves in each category. They should have a copy of the narrative that each skill is supposed to encompass so they can make their determination. They should understand that these ratings will not be used in a negative manner.

The second step is for the supervisor to rate the employees according to the same matrix while the employees are filling it in. The supervisor should not see the worker self-evaluation before filling in their opinion. They should make notes as to why someone was assigned a specific rating. This information will be very useful later. The scores entered by the employee and by the supervisor should be noted side by side on the matrix, maybe using a different color.

A meeting between each employee and his or her supervisor should provide individualized discussions to determine a final rating. This should not be a confrontational event since the supervisor may not always be aware of the extent of a team member's experience. Be sure to quiz each person for any outside hobbies, community services, or other skills that would be helpful to the business continuity effort. An example is someone who is a paramedic with the local volunteer fire department. Another example is someone serving in the Armed Forces Reserves or National Guard. Their military training may be pertinent.

Based on the final scores in each area, the manager can identify specific persons to provide backup support during an emergency or even when the primary person is ill. If there are few people skilled in a specific area, the matrix can be used to identify training opportunities. See Form 22-3 on the enclosed CD-ROM for a sample of Skill Matrix by Job Function.

ADDITIONAL SKILLS MATRIX BENEFITS A manager can use this completed matrix in many ways. One is to develop a disaster management succession plan for filling key roles in a crisis. This plan identifies who will temporarily stand in for a key manager who has been killed or disabled. Succession plans are essential for business continuity but should not be used to identify "predetermined" promotions. That removes the incentive for people within that organization to work hard because the next promotion is already locked in. Succession plans are also used to identify executives who should not travel together in the event of a transportation tragedy.

When conducting periodic performance reviews with your employees, include a review of the job descriptions. Any changes in responsibilities or expertise can be noted on the employee skills matrix and passed on to the training plan. Fairly applied, such recognition of skill improvement can become a powerful performance motivator.

Many managers have ambitions of advancing their careers. A completed and current employee skills matrix is a powerful tool to a new manager. It provides a quick snapshot of the competencies of the team as determined by the employees themselves. Company executives should insist on current matrices to aid them in moving around managers with a minimum of production impact.

A new matrix should be developed every year to identify improving skills. If the employee skills are not improving, then you must question if the manager is developing the talent in the department or babysitting a bunch of losers. Compare the matrix from year to year to ensure employee expertise is improving.

In most companies, the Human Resources department provides all non–job-specific training. The Human Resources manager ensures essential training is conducted for incoming employees and ongoing training in departments. This should include safety training for the facility in general as well as a department-specific explanation.

EMPLOYEE SKILLS MATRIX AND YOUR TRAINING PLAN A current employee skills matrix can turn a passive training program (tell me what you want) into a proactive asset (I see what you might need). It highlights areas where there are too few people trained to support a business function. Depending on its depth, it can also show which general training subjects should be offered, such as Microsoft Excel training, in-house developed classes on writing ad hoc SQL queries to the AS/400, etc. A close look at the matrix may even identify some in-house instructors among your ranks!

Communications

Some companies have a designated spokesperson who will handle official communications or at least communications with the news media. If your company has one, then use this section to verify that all the essential tasks are covered by them. Branch offices will normally refer any important news media inquiries to their corporate headquarters spokesperson. Use this section to ensure that your company's spokesperson is ready in case a disaster arises.

If you are a small company, and these tasks are not covered, then they need to be included in the Human Resources plan. Consider carefully how you will address this. It is recommended that a few stock answers be written in advance as news releases for persistent reporters. These stock answers may buy you some time to gather your thoughts for a more comprehensive news release later.

WITH THE EMPLOYEES Sometimes in the heat of the emergency, executives are so focused on the problem at hand that they forget about the other people in the company. The Human Resources department can step forward and ensure that the other employees know the degree of the problem and the status of the recovery. After all, the health of the facility is the health of their job, so they are very much interested parties. Decisive actions here will minimize the rumors, which invariably are negative.

Communicating the same message to every person can be difficult. Often in a crisis the employees are dispersed around the facility and some of them may be at home (such as the off-shift teams). Communication can be one-way (announcements) or interactive (face-to-face). One-way communications is the fastest way to communicate. Unfortunately, the message received is open to interpretation.

Interactive communication provides for questions and comments by the recipients. This tells you if the message was well received, misunderstood, or not addressing their most pressing concerns. Interactive communications methods include:

➤ Addressing people directly in groups.

➤ Using a voice mailbox.

➤ Online chat.

➤ Intranet Web site.

Addressing people directly in groups is always the most personal way to communicate. It is also a good way to gauge the mood and temperament of the people by their response to your announcements and their questions. In this approach, your immediate answers to one person may alleviate the anxiety of many in the group.

A personal address moves the communications from the distant front office to a face-to-face meeting. This approach allows you to tailor the message to the audience so that participants hear what is most pertinent to them, as well as the overall situation. The problem with face-to-face meetings is that it may be hard for a large crowd to hear you and, as you address different groups, your message may vary enough for each group to perceive it differently. The questions asked by later groups may include information that would have been helpful to earlier groups. Be sure to have someone recording every question raised and the answers provided. The entire list can be reviewed after the meetings and then republished to everyone.

Using a voice mailbox that everyone can dial into ensures that everyone hears the same message in the same way. Of course, you can quickly see that voice mail does not provide a forum for questions or requests for clarifications. It is useful to provide a second telephone line with someone to answer questions or where they can leave a message. The answers to the most pertinent questions can be included in the next voice mail announcement. Also, if you have a lot of employees, the line may become jammed and very annoying to use.

In a wide-area disaster where the telephone service is disrupted or limited, employees should be encouraged to call between 10:00 PM and 6:00 AM to avoid peak telephone network traffic. Even in disasters where telephone lines are saturated, they are generally available in the late night hours.

If a majority of your employees have access to the Internet, using an online chat system or an Intranet Web site to announce disaster recovery updates can be effective. The server that supports either of these options should be at a separate location to reduce the chance that would be affected by the same disaster you're currently recovering from.

WITH EMPLOYEES' FAMILIES People work to earn the wages needed to support their families. Therefore, it is understandable that their families may be anxious that a disaster at their place of work could have a serious impact on them. A negative or worrisome attitude by the employees' families may have a negative impact on your work force. This will increase the overall stress level of the workers.

Similar to the choices of how to communicate with the employees, you must consider how to best talk to the families. Always remember your audience.

Meeting with the families in a mass venue will require a facility to shelter them during the presentation. Avoid use of industry jargon because some families may not completely understand your message.

One approach is to establish a family information line that is normally used to pass on company information. Using a voice mailbox allows for a single message to everyone. When an emergency arises, everyone knows where to dial in to. Be aware that the news media may tap into these messages if they are not kept fully apprised of the situation. Web-based communications should be restricted to employees only via a secured login process.

WITH SURROUNDING RESIDENCES AND BUSINESSES When an emergency occurs, make a quick assessment of whether this event will impact anyone who works or resides near your facility. They must be immediately informed of anything that will harm them, such as a fire in a toxic chemical area that may spread fumes outside of the facility. If public safety officials are on the scene, consult with them first.

When in doubt, caution and assist your neighbors in their evacuation. Provide some place where they can go, such as a nearby hotel or public facility. You should also provide basic shelter for their pets, which may accompany them.

Your goals here are to avoid the likelihood of a lawsuit for exposing an innocent person to danger by neglecting to tell them. It will also help to build goodwill with the local government and your facility's neighbors. The people may not be pleased with the forced move at the time, but they will appreciate your consideration later.

WITH THE GENERAL PUBLIC The range of people interested in your disaster may be quite wide. If the emergency involved something newsworthy (as defined by the news media—not by you), then they may show up quite suddenly on your doorstep. What you say is always open to interpretation whether you like it or not, so it is best to provide them with a written statement concerning the incident. This statement should acknowledge the incident, state that the extent of damage is still being determined, and that as further information becomes available, it will be issued as a news release. Never express an opinion about the problem's causes or the extent of the damage. It is possible that your opinions stated to the news media will resurface later labeled as an official company announcement in some sort of legal proceedings.

Caution your employees working on the containment and recovery to not speculate to anyone as to the cause of the emergency or extent of the damage. Of course, they can speak freely with properly identified law enforcement personnel but should never take for granted the true identity of the person asking questions. If you cannot guide the news media away from your employees at the disaster site, then provide an escort knowledgeable in the problem and the recovery efforts so you at least know what was said by whom. The escort can quickly clear up any misunderstandings and guide the reporter to knowledgeable people.

On the other hand, the news media's coverage of your emergency is an opportunity to showcase your company's highly competent response. All emergencies have a large element of chaos. How well the chaos is handled will directly impact the perception of interested observers. Skillful handling of the media may lead to favorable stories on this event and issues in the future. If possible, keep the news media regularly informed of the progress made and consider making key executives available for interviews.

CONCLUSION

Mitigating the physical and emotional damage to your employees is just as important as protecting your physical assets. By demonstrating concern for your employees and their families, your recovery time can be dramatically shortened. Know how your employees can help you in an emergency, and how you can help them, as it is to everyone's benefit that the business recovers and gets back to normal as quickly as possible.

CHAPTER 23

HEALTH AND SAFETY
Keeping Everyone Healthy

Our health always seems much more valuable after we lose it.
— Author Unknown

INTRODUCTION

A step-by-step approach to analyzing your business situation and developing written procedures for avoiding problems or reducing their damage should they occur includes consideration of environmental, health, and safety issues. Issues that affect the health and safety of your employees and the surrounding community are becoming much more high profile, as the investment community evaluates corporate sustainability reports with the same level of scrutiny as the financial reports. Environmental and safety disasters have the potential to cost much more than the immediate damages; these disasters can tarnish brand names, force closure of operations in a community because of distrust, or become the subject of every anti-industry blogger on the Internet. This chapter will help you identify the plans you may need to protect your employees and the public from hazards in the workplace.

PLANS ADDRESSING HEALTH, SAFETY, AND ENVIRONMENTAL ISSUES

The emergency action plan is the most basic plan that should be developed for any workplace. Health, safety, and environmental issues are the focus of many emergency plans. Multiple federal agencies require emergency plans. This plan should address fires, evacuations, and sheltering during natural disasters. It may also include plans for responding to workplace violence. The Occupational Safety and Health Administration (OSHA) has an especially helpful eTool on its Web site to assist in the development of evacuation plans. Other OSHA emergency plans are needed when employees are exposed to certain chemical hazards, work in confined spaces or trenches, etc. The Environmental Protection Agency (EPA) also requires the development of plans to prevent damage to the environment or harm to the public resulting from business activities. Its focus is primarily on the impact that chemicals will have once they escape the workplace and enter the environment. A nationwide response system is in place to respond to these disasters.

The plans required by these two agencies follow a common approach. The risk assessment phase focuses on identifying hazards that pose a risk. Some plans are required to have a formal evaluation of hazard rankings; in others, the ranking is implied by what you choose to include or exclude. Either way, a judgment is made regarding the potential of occurrence and the severity of the hazard. The severity of the hazard may be limited to estimations of physical damage or expanded to include public relations impacts. After risks are assessed, the plan will present measures taken to prevent or mitigate the hazard. A hierarchy of controls is employed; eliminate the hazard, construct engineering controls to contain or reduce the hazard, implement administrative procedures to prevent or contain the hazard, and lastly, provide personnel protective equipment to protect individuals from the hazard. In addition, the plan may also include the recovery stages—how to get the business back to normal.

Since the attacks on 9/11, the Department of Homeland Security (DHS) was created and issued additional regulations that are designed to prevent chemical emergencies resulting from terrorist attacks. The rules require plans when companies store, use, or transport listed chemicals. Some chemicals on the list have no minimum threshold before a threat assessment report is required. After submitting a screen level assessment, a full-blown security plan that details how you would prevent the intentional release or theft of your chemicals can be required by the DHS. While other plans may contain confidential business information, the DHS reports are developed with national security in mind. The contents, even the existence of the reports, is to be kept secret from anyone who has not received DHS and corporate approval.

Figure 23-1 lists some of the more common emergency plans required by OSHA and the EPA that apply to many companies. This list is not complete for all federal, state, and local requirements. Furthermore, if protecting the business from disasters is important, don't wait for the government to require it.

A first step will be a review of the threshold requirements to each of these rules to see which ones are already required and start with these. (OSHA rules are cited for general industry; comparable Department of Labor rules may exist for construction, longshoring, mining, etc.) To do this, you need to make an inventory of your chemicals, wastes, processes, and confined spaces.

RISK ASSESSMENT

Risks that are assessed in various safety, health, and environmental plans include fire, natural disaster, workplace violence, and chemicals. The assessment must

	Agency	Plan	Subject	Threshold	Citation
1	EPA	RCRA Contingency	Hazardous waste releases	> 1000 kg of hazardous waste per month	40 CFR.262.34
2	EPA	Spill Prevention Control and Countermeasures	Oil spills to water	> Gallons of petroleum products stored above ground or . . . complicated	40 CFR.112
3	EPA	Emergency Planning and Community Right to Know Act	Reporting of environmental releases and coordination with Local Emergency Planning Commission	> Reportable Quantities (RQs) for chemicals	40 CFR.301 - 303
4	EPA and OSHA	Risk Management Plan and Process Safety Mgt.	Certain listed chemicals that have potentially large off-site impacts	> RQ for listed chemicals; see rules	40 CFR.68 and 29 CFR 1910.119
5	OSHA	Hazardous Waste Operations and Emergency Response (Hazwopper)	Emergency response – safety of response team	If have a Hazwopper team	29 CFR 1910.120
6	OSHA	Emergency Action and Fire Prevention Plan	Fires, emergency notifications and evacuations	If > 10 employees	29 CFR 1910.38
7	OSHA	Confined space rescue	Rescue employees in a confined space	If > 10 employees and if have confined spaces entered by your employees	29 CFR.1910.146
8	OSHA	Vertical standards for specific chemicals	Emergency plans involving the specific chemical	See individual rules	29 CFR 1910 various chapters

FIGURE 23-1: Federal emergency planning regulations.

include a thorough examination of the business activities with respect to the specific plan. For example, a plan addressing chemical releases will inventory chemicals, quantities, containers, locations, and users. A natural disaster plan will identify structurally sound areas and areas to avoid. A workplace violence plan will describe potential means of entry by an assailant and probable target locations.

Some risk assessments may only include the identification of the risks without any formal evaluation or comparison of the probability or severity of the disaster. Simple emergency action plans may fall into this category; the responses are limited to evacuation or sheltering. However, many plans continue the assessment with a comparison of the potential results from the disaster. The probability of occurrence is one factor evaluated. The plan developer will consider the specific history of the site, the history of similar sites, and site-specific factors that are deemed important. The purpose is not to calculate a precise probability but rather to recognize the difference between almost certain events from occasional events to extremely rare events.

The inventory is followed by the evaluation of the resulting harm. Harm, like probability, should be categorized into relative categories from lethal or catastrophic loss of property to serious, moderate, and mild levels. Various approaches may also take into consideration the ability or speed of detecting the problem, the public relations impacts, etc. Usually these are combined in some form of a mathematical equation to yield a score for comparing each of the cataloged items. You can use the risk assessment forms from Chapter 3 to help prioritize these risks.

Chemical Hazards

OSHA, EPA, DHS, and other agencies require emergency plans for various chemical activities. If you are already filing a Tier II report to the EPA, you may have most of the information at your fingertips. If not, use the Material Safety Data Sheets (MSDS) for each chemical to determine if the product contains any of the specific chemicals listed in items 1–4 in Figure 23-1. You should develop a data table that includes the product name or part number, chemical ingredients of concern, quantity used annually, quantity stored at one time, and the locations stored. From this list you will be able to determine if certain prevention or response plans may need to be developed.

One of the most fundamental questions you need to ask yourself is, "Why do I have all these chemicals anyway?" The best control plan is to plan not to have the chemicals. If this isn't feasible, then consider substituting it with a less dangerous chemical or reducing the quantities stored onsite. Property protection insurers look to the size of the container as a measure of risk. Bigger containers mean bigger risks even if the same quantity of chemical is stored.

As an example, a chemical inventory conducted at your facility shows that you have a 1000-gallon gasoline tank and a 5000-gallon diesel fuel tank for your fleet of vehicles, a paint booth that uses 3800 gallons per month of paints containing no EPA-listed solvents, and seven drums per month of methyl ethyl ketone (MEK), which is used as a paint thinner and cleanup solvent. The cleanup solvent and scrap paint yield six drums per month (about 2500 lb) of liquid waste.

Based upon this information, you determine that EPA requires an SPCC (Spill Prevention Control and Countermeasures) plan and a Hazardous Waste Contingency Plan. In addition, you realize that an accidental release of 5000 pounds of MEK would need reporting to various local, state, and federal agencies.

Another kind of chemical release is one that you have control over: operational releases. Say you have a catastrophic failure to an air pollution control device that is required by your operating permits. Due to a lightning strike or fire, the only damage at the facility is this piece of equipment. Your ability to operate the business is unhindered except that you would be out of compliance with your environmental permits. Is this a disaster? You bet! Many air pollution control devices are built to order. Lead times may be months. Many permits are federally enforceable so that even the state does not have the authority to grant waivers. Your only course of action may be to shut down the process for several weeks until you shift production elsewhere or to operate in violation of the law unless you have a plan. What's worse is that activist environmental groups mine data at the EPA looking for facilities that have operated during malfunctions and bring citizens' lawsuits against them. The laws do not preclude criminal prosecution of a plant manager for operating outside of permitted limits of an air pollution or wastewater discharge permit. It is critical to know the details of your permit; some things to think about when getting your permit include:

➤ Try to get flexible terms.

➤ Know the malfunction laws.

➤ Know the political landscape.

➤ Know to whom you need to talk if there's a problem.

➤ Know to whom you can switch production in an emergency, and have contracts ready.

➤ Know what it takes to replace critical equipment.

➤ Have business interruption insurance that specifically addresses the issue.

Employee Fatalities or Multiple Hospitalizations

In addition to the chemical plans, OSHA requires plans that protect people from hazards in the workplace. These include the response to fires, to chemical emergencies (Hazwopper), and to emergencies in confined spaces. All of these plans require the same basic elements of identifying the hazards and developing plans to prevent or to mitigate the unwanted outcomes.

Whether or not you identified regulatory requirements for emergency planning, you need to notify OSHA immediately when there has been an occupational or workplace violence fatality or multiple hospitalizations in the workplace (29 CFR

1910.39). An investigation may begin within a few hours and may continue for weeks. Some manufacturing operations or pieces of machinery may be shut down until the investigation is completed.

A plan to protect employees and the business starts with the identification of these hazards. This includes the labeling of all electrical disconnects, storage tanks, and pipes, etc., and making sure that documentation of processes is available in an emergency. Next is the development of engineering controls, administrative procedures, and employee/contractor training. Confined spaces, sources of energy that require energy control, protection, and lockout, fall hazards, machine guarding around presses, robots, shears, and gears, etc., all result in numerous occupational hazards. Several of these hazard categories are required to have specific written control plans. A carefully developed plan may be just the tool to identify a hazard that must be identified and abated which otherwise may have killed a valued employee and shut down your business.

For example, you begin the development of a confined spaces entry plan. You inventory spaces that meet the OSHA definition for confined spaces and realize that pits under your presses, chemical storage tanks, a boiler, and the wastewater sewer line all meet the definition of a hazard. The most likely entry scenarios are identified as well as any unusual ones. Perhaps the normal entry in the chemical storage tank is cleaning with water during which no hazardous vapors are generated. However, once every 10 years the tanks are lined with an epoxy coating that is applied by hand spraying. This liberates large quantities of potentially dangerous vapors. An employee is overcome. The attendant outside the tank rushes in to help and immediately succumbs to the same vapors. Two are now dead.

Many rescuers have died in confined spaces because they did not have a plan or failed to follow it. The unidentified, invisible, or odorless hazards that placed the first entrant in danger will do the same to the rescue team that is unprepared. For this reason, OSHA requires a written plan and training to the plan. OSHA prefers rescue from outside the space via a retractable lifeline. Whenever this option is feasible, it should be used. It requires identifying the spaces where it can be used, making equipment available, training employees how to use the equipment, etc.

Workplace violence and acts of terrorism are an increasingly common form of disaster. Multiple shootings, letters containing anthrax, bomb threats, and more are occurring with greater frequency. The two most important elements of a security program are the creation of a physical barrier to unauthorized entry and a procedure to identify people as they enter the premises. After these two steps are achieved, then higher levels of security can be developed as specific risks are identified.

Off-Site Hazards

One result of the Risk Management Plan (RMP) regulation mentioned in item 4 of Figure 23-1 is that off-site consequences must be considered and some of this information is publicly available. As a result, you can assess some chemical hazards that could occur off your property that may have disastrous effects on your business. Although the federal government elected not to put detailed information on the Internet, you can quickly find out if an address of interest to you could be affected by a chemical accident at another facility. The most common scenarios are clouds of toxic chemicals or explosions with the ability to cause damage over a great distance. The EPA Web site has a Vulnerable Zone Indicator System (VZIS) which can be used to determine whether your address may be in the vulnerable zone of a facility that submitted a Risk Management Plan. Major transportation arteries should be considered a risk for hazardous material incidents with the potential of large-scale evacuations. Whether it is a tanker overturned on an icy interstate or a train derailment, when large quantities of chemicals are involved the emergency management authorities will not hesitate to order an evacuation of all downwind and at-risk areas. Other off-site hazards that can invade your property include flood waters (which can easily bring in contamination from outside sources), wildfires, and various chemical releases by air, surface or subsurface.

For these off-site–initiated incidents, you need to develop plans for a safe and orderly shutdown of the business in the event an evacuation is ordered. This plan may be the same one you would use for a hurricane or any other incident requiring evacuation. The primary considerations during an evacuation are to protect the people evacuating, to protect anyone reentering the building by shutting down potentially dangerous equipment, and to protect your investments as time permits.

Another off-site incident can be the loss of potable water due to accidental or deliberate contamination of public water supplies or other problems that shut down a municipal water treatment works. How is water used in your facility? How much is used? What quality is required? The answers to these questions may cause you to consider placing contracts for water to be trucked in from another municipality in the event of an emergency. If the neighboring communities all receive water from the same body of water, you may consider having a contract with a company that can get their water from another source, such as a private well or a different lake or river.

Indoor Air Quality Problems

Because indoor air quality problems have become more prevalent in recent years, a programmed response to these complaints may contain many of the same elements of your emergency plans. The scenarios are different but the results are similar. Something has invaded the building that makes it uninhabitable for people. People begin to complain of respiratory illnesses. They compare notes on everyone they know who has worked here and has cancer or emphysema or asthma. Pretty soon an attorney is involved. Sometimes the sources can be found and controls installed in the heating and ventilation system to eliminate the problem—radon gas, formaldehyde from carpets and pressed wood, volatile chemicals from copier machines, office chemicals, industrial chemicals, and vehicle exhausts, etc.

The newest problems are biological in nature and, therefore, are more difficult to control because these tiny organisms may remain hidden and reproduce only to strike again. "Toxic mold" is the name given to many assorted molds and mildews and bacteria that grow on or in building structures. Biological attacks such as the anthrax spores in the Capitol offices are another example. Both can require extensive decontamination and may result in the abandonment of a building.

Indoor air quality concerns may be the result of outside factors such as the anthrax letters, pollution from a neighboring business, or the contractor who is patching the asphalt roof of your building where you didn't turn off the fresh air intake. Or, indoor air quality concerns may be the result of your building design, housekeeping, or processes. Although the causes are many, the symptoms and therefore the plans share many similarities. Generally people are worried about being exposed to something in the air they breathe. Address these issues as they occur quickly and with concern. Prevent. Investigate. Mitigate. Control it before it controls you.

EVACUATION

According to OSHA, people should be evacuated to a safe area of public access. Local fire codes will dictate how many exits are required from rooms and buildings based on the occupancy, construction, and other hazards present. Exit routes need to be well marked, even in the event of a power outage. This can be accomplished with battery-powered backups on exit lighting, emergency standby generators, or glow-in-the-dark signage. Some of the problems encountered by OSHA or fire code inspectors are unmarked exits, exits blocked inside or outside, aisleways blocked, and evacuation routes not up to date with changes to building layouts. Equipment is only useable if it is maintained. Alarms, emergency lights, battery backups, smoke detectors, and exit lights all need to be tested regularly and verified that they still perform. Failure to maintain emergency equipment places lives at risk.

A roll call to account for people may be one of the more difficult tasks, especially for large facilities or those where people frequently come and go. However, as soon as possible after disasters that may have the potential for loss of human life (e.g., fire, tornado, and explosion), you need to get a headcount. If Joe isn't there, is it because he wasn't at work, he left for a doctor's appointment before the explosion, he is on the rescue team and stayed behind as directed, or he is among the casualties? The quicker this can be determined, the quicker the emergency scene will be brought under control and potential danger to other rescuers reduced. Employees need to know they should not leave the property after a disaster until they have been accounted for and dismissed. Employees who left or called in sick might be asked to call in to an emergency number. There have been cases where the missing were presumed casualties and rescue workers continued to search for them, only to find out the person was safe at home. Other less obvious disasters that require employees to check in include company travelers after a disaster, man-made or natural.

There can be many ways to conduct a head count. The most basic requires all people to go to a standard location or muster area, much like school children practice. At this location someone takes a roll and compares it to a list of those known to be present at that time. Communication between muster areas is needed at larger locations. At least two means of communication should be identified because the emergency may render one of the systems unusable. For example, following large-scale disasters like 9/11, cell phone systems were overloaded. A key element of the accountability procedures is that every employee knows they need to keep trying until contact has been made, even if it takes hours or days.

MITIGATION

Dealing with environmental emergencies often means that some chemical has escaped its desired container or location. You must quickly determine how to stop the ongoing release, assuming some remains, and how to prevent the release from spreading and causing harm. If you have developed a good working relationship with local police, fire and emergency response agencies, they will be better prepared to respond to emergencies at your location and limit the final impact. One best practice is to invite them in once per year for a tour or luncheon.

The health and safety of the people responding is always the greatest concern of professional emergency responders. You should consider the health and safety of your response team in the development of your plans. Proper qualifications, initial and refresher training, development of procedures and identification of tools and personal protective equipment need to be addressed. Ancillary hazards such as electrocution when the floor is wet, inhalation of smoldering smoke or contact with toxic chemical residues such as asbestos or mold may also need to be considered.

The EPA may require engineering controls for certain situations; for example, containment dikes that hold 110 percent of the capacity of the largest tank. However, many chemicals are legally stored outside of containment dikes. Other engineering controls include designating storage locations that are not susceptible to damage by forklifts and are placed away from floor drains.

Spill response equipment must be purchased and placed in strategic locations to effectively contain a chemical spill. Determine the types of response equipment required, and whether you need to stop leaks in drums or tanks, slow the flow of chemicals across the floor, in a sewer, or down a creek, etc. Ensure that the spill control materials you select are appropriate for the chemicals you need to control. Some supplies are selective to petroleum products, others to aqueous products. Non-sparking brass tools are needed when responding to spills of materials that may ignite or explode. Acids or bases may react adversely with some metals or rubber.

Contracts should be in place or a ready list of contractors for services ranging from removing water from carpets to patching a hole in the roof to moving your critical equipment. Remember that in a large natural or man-made disaster, the demand for local services will exceed the supply of contractors available. Have contracts in place with local companies and national companies that can bring in the help you need.

Notifications to government agencies are required by various rules. Determine which rules require you to notify whom. Notification should be done as soon as it is practical. Notifications definitely should be within minutes if a spill is reaching a public waterway or is off the property or has the potential to harm the environment or people. In all cases, notifications should be made within the work shift when it occurred. The order of notification should be local, then state, then federal. This corresponds with their ability to mobilize in response to the incident.

Not all personal protective equipment (PPE) is created equal. Some may be effective in responding to one chemical or hazard and totally ineffective for another. Check the manufacturers' data for respirators, gloves, chemical-resistant clothing, etc., to determine the exact requirements for the potential hazards you might encounter.

DEVELOPING A PLAN

As you review those categories required by the EPA and OSHA, you may discover the focus by the EPA is on off-site environmental impacts and the focus of OSHA is on employee impacts. You must decide for your operation where the business impacts intersect these regulatory categories. In some cases, the regulatory threshold will be sufficiently protective; if you do what is required by the rules, you may deem nothing else is required. Other times, you realize that the regulatory minimum is not enough and that the plan should include more than EPA or OSHA would require.

What can happen here? Tanks leak, containers rupture, incompatible chemicals are mixed, valves are left open, alarms fail, and containment systems leak. Or is the problem people-related? The new worker, a new procedure, or something changed and somebody was not informed. The contractor's employees couldn't read the warning signs or instructions, either because they could not read or were not fluent in English. These are some of the common scenarios you must consider when developing the plans identified above. What happens once a chemical release begins? Which way will it go? Will it cause an explosion, kill the fish in the creek, or upset the city wastewater treatment plant? Do the neighbors need to be evacuated? Who needs to be evacuated? Let's take a few of these in more detail.

Releases of chemicals can be in the form of solids, liquids, or gases. Gases will disperse the fastest so plans must take this into account. There will be no time to make decisions on the spot if the potential releases could cause explosions or if they are toxic. Evaluate the most likely fault scenarios and make the changes now that will reduce their likelihood. Develop engineering controls such as protective barriers. Create administrative procedures such as using only trained employees and sign-offs. Provide readily available leak detection equipment. Prominently display on the cover of the plan whom to call immediately. Two special notes for gases: some gases are heavier than air and seek the lowest levels and may travel long distances at floor level unnoticed until finding a pit, basement, or other lower space. Those gases that are lighter than air rise and disperse. These require different placement for leak detection.

Releases of liquids are the next priority. Again, the characteristics of the specific materials will dictate the response actions. Liquids flow downhill: this means sumps, dikes, etc., can be an effective means to prevent the spread of a release and leak detection equipment can be placed in fewer places. Depending on the liquid, it may or may not evaporate quickly and result in both a gaseous and a liquid release.

Solids may not be thought of as a particularly hazardous physical state. Consider, however, that fine dusts created from grain, grinding operations, etc., can create explosive atmospheres. In addition, spills of solid materials may wash into a drain during a rain event and be quickly transported off the property.

ACTION STEPS FOR YOUR PLAN

Here are things you will need to write your plan. They are in no special order and, of course, you can tailor these items to meet the needs of your site.

➤ Begin with your standard plan format. Keep in mind that regulatory requirements may drive the development of your plan to include many things beyond your standard format. Your audience includes the late-shift security staff but may also designate specific persons under the law who act as emergency coordinators or incident commanders who have the full support of management to do whatever it takes to bring the emergency under control. This person may be onsite or on-call depending upon the specific regulatory requirements and your individual circumstances.

➤ You need the names of your primary and secondary support people who work at this site, plus the primary and secondary support people whom you can call on from another company site. You may make an arrangement with a professional emergency response team to send people during a disaster. In many cases, their arrival will be hours away so you may need some onsite ability to keep the problem from getting worse before they arrive.

➤ Include the chemical maps previously discussed. Use a floor plan generated using computer-assisted drafting (CAD) to indicate all the main chemical storage, use, and waste locations on the property and storm and floor drains. Indicate the direction of flow in drains and for the surface around major chemical storage locations. Note the presence of lower levels where liquids or vapors could migrate.

➤ Add in the emergency response equipment inventory list with the description for each item. Prepare a checklist of your monitoring, testing, and alarm equipment that includes their location and how to test them. You may need to preplace some supplies and equipment for use on short notice. Also, in your checklist, include detailed instructions on how to check the devices for use on the spot. Validate the checklist by using someone unfamiliar with it.

➤ Identify the personal protective equipment (PPE) required to respond to emergencies. Determine the sizes required for your response team, the quantities required, and the location(s) where they will be stored. Include PPE inventory status on a scheduled inspection. Some equipment may have a limited shelf life. Make sure to rotate supplies so they are effective when needed most.

➤ Communication with media, employees, and especially government contacts is critical. If the emergency generated activity on police and fire scanners, then the local news crews can be expected to know of the situation and a phone call or visit onsite will likely come soon. Establish who will be the primary and secondary media contact. This should NOT be your emergency coordinator. You do not want your coordinator pulled away from other duties to answer questions to the media. It is best to have someone who is not a technical expert but rather someone who can handle themselves well in front of a camera or with a reporter. To that end, a response of "I don't know but I can find out" is better than a technical person speaking from the top of their head without preparation and providing information that is played up negatively by the media.

Be careful what you ask for from local governments. Some businesses have called local fire departments or other emergency agencies for nonemergency assistance, such as the use of large fans to exhaust smoke or vapors from a building, only to have that department "take control" of the emergency once its personnel are on the scene. Remember that their primary job is to protect the safety of people, the environment, and properties, not to reestablish your operations as fast as possible. What you thought was going to be 30 minutes of interruption while you cleared vapors from the building may turn into a 2- or 3-hour ordeal. Having your own equipment or obtaining a source other than the fire department to borrow equipment is the best way to avoid this problem.

After a Disaster

There are several things you should do after the disaster to make sure you have covered all the bases and are better prepared for the next disaster.

➤ Follow up with an incident debriefing. Ask yourself many questions. What were the lessons learned? Could the incident have been prevented? Did the emergency detection and notification systems work? Did the company follow the plan? Were the supplies available? Was anyone hurt? Did the company have trouble finding out the properties of the chemicals involved? Ask the local emergency responders who were involved for their input as well. Maintain a copy of this report with the incident report. Regulatory agencies want to see that you have learned from the past and are taking precautions to make sure it doesn't happen again. If you fail to learn, history may repeat itself—and it may even be worse the next time.

➤ Follow up the reports to the regulatory agencies as required. Some of the federal and state laws require a written followup once a release has been reported.

➤ Update the written emergency plans. Again, some of the federal regulations require plans to be updated following an event where the plan was determined to be inadequate. Usually the updates are expected within 6 months. Even if nobody requires an update of the plan, the value gained is being better prepared for the next time. It is hard to imagine any plan that was perfect or perfectly executed.

Testing

Will the plan be executed in the manner you wrote it? Will people remember what is in the plan or even remember there is a plan? These are some of the reasons plans need to be tested. Testing a plan provides the opportunity to learn what might go wrong or what might be done more efficiently. Many professionals who have worked hard to develop the plan are often disheartened to find out how many people never open the plan in a drill; they attempt to do everything by memory and experience. A good plan will be an indispensible reference during an emergency, not just a training guide before the emergency. Drills are also useful in identifying changes that have not been documented since the last plan update.

Drills can take several different forms. All tests don't have to be live; they can also be simulated. A Table-Top drill can be developed with "what if" scenarios that are scripted but require those responding to make decisions and consider their consequences. These drills compress time so that an 8-hour exercise may be reduced to just 2 or 3 hours and do not require mobilization of people or equipment. Table-Top drills are often used as a first-time drill to familiarize key leaders with a plan or with seasoned professionals who have experienced many live action emergencies just to keep them fresh. Live drills can be as simple as a fire or tornado drill or may include a multiagency drill with lots of equipment and manpower. The key to a successful drill is determining what learning outcomes are desired and planning the exercise to meet those outcomes. Surprise drills are like the real thing except that they are scripted but do include physically going through the motions required in the plan.

Where possible, include your emergency service providers—the local HazMat response team, fire department, or contract service providers. Having someone play the role of the "Live at 6:00" TV news reporter is also valuable since the greatest damage may be to the corporate image. What is said, how it is said and whom it is said by during the first interviews after an emergency begins will create a public opinion for the good or the bad of your organization.

Debrief and incorporate the suggestions into the plan where appropriate. If the drill ends with the drill, then the most important opportunity to improve has been lost. A debriefing after the drill will identify what was done well and what could be improved. Some of the opportunities will require portions of the plan to be changed; others will require more education or just more practice.

CONCLUSION

As safety and environmental issues become a greater part of the public con-science, protecting the health and safety of your employees and the surrounding community has become mainstream in many organizations. It is more than just "the right thing to do." Preparing your organization for disasters in safety and environmental issues will be a competitive advantage when disaster strikes. Failure to plan may lead to bankruptcy, or worse.

CHAPTER 24

TERRORISM
The Wrath of Man

Terrorism: the systematic use of violence as a means
to intimidate or coerce societies or governments.
—WordNet® 1.6, © 1997 Princeton University

INTRODUCTION

Terrorism has many definitions. In its simplest form, it is a violent action intended to inflict harm on some person or object with the intention of coercing someone in the future to act in a specific way. Terrorists function similarly to a publicity-hungry cinema actress. They will create any spectacle or perform any action to gain attention for their organization or cause.

The other chapters of this book assumed you had some personal knowledge of the nature of the risks your company faced, such as a fire, a power outage, or severe weather. The issues surrounding terrorism are somewhat foreign to many businesspeople, so a brief history is provided. This may help you to better prepare a risk assessment and initiate mitigation actions to protect your employees and your company.

Some governments use terror as a coercive tool to manipulate their own populations. The French Revolution's "Reign of Terror" and Stalin's suppression of the Ukrainian farmers are classic examples. Other masters of this evil action include Hitler and Cambodia's Pol Pot. This is known as state terrorism. Recent exposure of mass graves in Iraq vividly demonstrates that the practice continues in some parts of the world. This type of terrorism generally remains within its own borders. You must be aware of such activities when exporting goods or traveling internationally to such places.

Terrorism can be against property as well as people. Some animal lovers have splashed blood on people wearing fur coats. Although somewhat violent, this action is intended to dramatize the killing of animals for their fur and not to permanently harm the fur wearer.

Terrorists seek to magnify their power through the news media. They strive to obtain maximum publicity from the meager means at their disposal. An attack on a "mom-and-pop" grocery store doesn't have the same impact as attacking the corporate headquarters of a multinational company. In fact, an attack on the store will swing public opinion against the attackers. Many people are apathetic if large companies are attacked, so terrorists focus efforts on them (and also this is where the money is).

Some terrorists look for visible targets where they can avoid detection before and after an attack, such as international airports, large cities, major international events, resorts, and high-profile landmarks. Some terrorists are suicidal and committed to die during their attack, such as a suicide bomber. Others mix with the crowds before and after the attack.

The form of a terror attack depends on several factors: the means available, the political issues involved, and the weaknesses of the target. The means available refers to the weapons the terror organization has at its disposal. Not everyone is familiar with handling explosives or is an accurate marksman. The political issues refer to what is bothering the person. If they personalize their issue by identifying it in a single individual, then the attack may be sharply focused on that person. Weakness in targets can be from how available they are to how easy it is to commit the crime. A clean getaway is not always a requirement, and an arrest may be one of the goals to further publicize the issue.

Terrorism can be broken down into two primary categories: "domestic" and "international." This distinction refers to the origin of the individuals or groups responsible for it.

Domestic terrorism involves groups or individuals whose terrorist activities are directed at the people of a specific country or its government. Domestic terrorists are organized and exist within this country and do not receive any foreign direction or support.

International terrorism involves groups or individuals whose terrorist activities are foreign-based. These groups exist outside a country or are directed or supported by someone outside.

Counterterrorism actions are proactive steps to deter a terrorist attack and to respond quickly. Counterterrorism actions include increased police patrols and fighter aircraft patrolling key cities. Other counterterrorism actions involve police monitoring of suspected terror groups to prevent or protect against an attack.

Antiterrorism steps are defensive in nature and reduce the vulnerability of people and property to terrorist acts. Antiterrorism involves mitigation action to reduce the likelihood of an attack or its damage.

A BRIEF HISTORY

Most terrorist organizations espouse some sort of social or political agenda as a justification for their actions. Terrorism is defined in the Code of Federal

Regulations as "the unlawful use of force and violence against persons or property to intimidate or coerce a government, the civilian population, or any segment thereof, in furtherance of political or social objectives." The key elements to remember are violence, intimidation, and coercion.

In 1605, England was in the midst of sectarian strife between Protestants and Catholics. To further their cause, a group of Catholic supporters plotted to blow up the English Parliament as it sat in session. A coconspirator, Guy Fawkes, managed to stockpile 36 barrels of gunpowder in the cellar of the Parliament building. When authorities were tipped off to the plot, the conspiracy was foiled. Using violence to advance or defend a religion? Bombing of government buildings? Does this sound familiar?

Assassination had long been a method of terrorism. The Guy Fawkes bomb plot against the English Parliament would easily meet our current definition of terrorism. Terrorist groups as now known began to emerge in the late 19th century in Europe. One of the reasons was changes in technology that created powerful explosives and weapons that are small and easy to handle. Modern communications ensures new visibility for terrorist groups out of proportion to their actual size.

Some terrorist acts are just a cover for old-fashioned criminal activities, such as kidnapping, bank robberies, etc. Jesse James, whose criminal career spanned 20 years, always tried to cast himself as the defender of the common man, all the while robbing and murdering.

The concept of terrorism is more acceptable in some cultures than it is in others. Depending on your point of view, one person's terrorist is another person's patriot. Western culture seems to favor the underdog. Hollywood movies love to show one person (the "common man") overcoming all odds to defeat the undefeatable. Depending on your political point of view, Robin Hood was a protector of the people or a common thief. The same goes for terrorists. Are they heroes or murderers?

To magnify the effect of their attack, terrorists depend on widespread public notice of their actions. World leaders are normally as well protected as they want to be. A nation's citizens see themselves as vulnerable to a terrorist action and could potentially apply pressure on their leaders to accommodate them. Playing to this public sentiment is the reason terrorists espouse some form of social or political platform.

One common goal of terrorism is to establish a fear in the population while showing the authorities as incapable of protecting everyone, everywhere, all of the time. The terrorists seek to goad law enforcement authorities into actions that may be viewed as repressive by the population to gain sympathizers or overt supporters for their cause. Their violent actions are combined with political announcements espousing selfless actions (food for the poor, freedom for jailed comrades, or any number of things). Terrorism always tries to cloak itself in some "just" cause, whether true or not. Terrorism sometimes attempts to excuse its indiscriminate violence as attacking those who benefit from whatever evil they are attacking. Fulfilling any demand leads to others because the demand is only a cover for the violence.

Terrorist attacks range from a single impulsive person to a large group and carefully planned actions. A common element is that they are all calculated to gain the greatest impact with minimal resources. They are found throughout history. Some countries have used terrorist threats to extort "protection" money (Barbary pirates), to sell their services (Ninja assassins), or even to intimidate their own population.

Terrorism is different from guerilla warfare. Terrorists attack the opponent's population because they lack the strength to attack their armed forces. Guerilla warfare includes some terrorist actions but is focused on military targets. The main difference between the two is the number of casualties among the general population. Terrorists work for maximum damage, and the guerillas seek to establish a "moral" status by minimizing them.

Whether you feel that terrorists are patriots or murderers, in terms of business continuity planning, it does not matter. They represent a threat to the ongoing profitability of the business. The risk of a terrorist attack occurring must be assessed and a mitigation plan implemented.

RISK ASSESSMENT

Like any other part of your plan, you must make a risk assessment of the threat to your facilities and employees from terrorism. Based on this risk assessment, a mitigation plan can be assembled to protect your property and improve the safety of your employees. Unfortunately, the nature of terrorism is surprise and, in some instances, the attackers are more than a little mentally unbalanced, so even if you believe you have nothing to fear you should still perform a risk analysis.

On February 29, 1993, a bomb exploded in the parking garage of the World Trade Center in New York City, resulting in the death of five people and thousands of injuries. The crater was 200 by 100 feet and five stories deep.

The first thing to assess is the location of your facility. Begin your risk analysis with an examination of your location. Stand outside and look around. Are you near:

➤ A government building (some people have a grudge against the IRS, for example)?

➤ A landmark whose destruction might have symbolic significance, such as a war memorial, a natural feature, a major bridge, or a famous building?

➤ A defense supplier? An attack on them may close the roads surrounding them and therefore you!

The definition of what is "too near" is up to you. If one of these nearby facilities was attacked, how disruptive would it be to your business? At a minimum, the streets around the target would be blocked for rescue teams and then, later, investigations. If you are several city blocks away and there are many avenues of approach, you should be all right. If the potential target is next door, then there is a risk.

Your mitigation plan for your location is to:

➤ Identify ways to keep your business open if a nearby attack occurs. You may need to provide information on alternate access routes to suppliers or customers. In general, it would be difficult to move your location, but you can pay close attention to who your neighbors are and who may be considering relocating to your vicinity.

➤ Provide some separation or barrier between your building and a close neighbor that may be a target. Concrete walls may slow down a fire or the blast of an explosion. Ensure vulnerable spaces within your facility (such as your computer room) are not located on the side of the building toward the potential target.

➤ Relocate to another site if your building also houses potential targets. If you cannot relocate, can you move out your most sensitive operations?

What goods or services does your company provide? Sometimes seemingly innocent lines of business can attract violent protest. Sometimes peaceful protest can turn violent if demands go unfulfilled and the people involved feel threatened by something. What is the risk that the products or services provided by your company will make it a target?

"On September 9, 1980, the 'Plowshares Eight' carried out the first of what have come to be known as plowshares actions. Eight peacemakers entered the General Electric plant in King of Prussia, PA, where the nose cones from the Mark 12-A nuclear warheads were manufactured. With hammers and blood they enacted the biblical prophecies of Isaiah (2:4) and Micah (4:3) to 'beat swords into plowshares' by hammering on two of the nose cones and pouring blood on documents."

(Source: From a Web site maintained by the organization "Swords into Plowshares," http://www.craftech.com/~dcpledge/brandywine/plow/webpages/plow8.htm)

Organizations or places that may be in danger include the following:

➤ **Police or Military Suppliers.** Some people feel that suppliers of military goods are contributing to the violence between nations, while others are thankful for a strong defense industry. If you directly or indirectly supply goods to the military or even police departments, this may place you in the sights of a terrorist. As related in the box above, a supplier of components for nuclear weapons could attract antiwar as well as environmental issues protesters.

➤ **Controversial Businesses.** Some businesses can raise the emotions of people by the mention of their name. One of these controversial businesses is women's health clinics that perform abortions. Whatever your opinion of this service, these facilities have over the years been the target of violent attacks. Is such a facility near you?

Animal rights groups have targeted fur coats as unethical and have publicly attacked people wearing them by splashing blood on the coat and the person wearing it. Other animal rights groups include those people who believe that dolphins are killed and discarded during tuna fishing, those in opposition to some livestock farming practices, and on and on. Unless you are the first target, you can gain some insight into how controversial your business is to some groups by regularly monitoring news broadcasts and your industry-specific media.

➤ **Government Buildings.** The infamous attack on the Murrah Federal Building in Oklahoma City in 1995 was a violent protest against U.S. government policies. Whatever the reason, government offices will remain a target of violent protest in the future. Sometimes these buildings rent excess space to other companies. If you are in such a building, consider what the risks may be and how they might be mitigated.

Another potential source of terrorism is your employees. Some things to consider when evaluating the potential for terrorism include:

➤ **Who Are Your Employees?** Even with a proper screening, employees can be a source of risk of domestic terrorism. Sometimes, crime can be an act of opportunity. It is important that all employees are screened before hiring and monitored for unusual behavior.

➤ **Security for Your Employees.** An important counterterrorism function is your facility's security. But all life (for most of us) is not within your company's four walls. People drive to and from work and around their community. Train your employees, and specifically your executives, to watch for suspicious behavior. Kidnapping is a high-profile crime that a terrorist can use for daily publicity.

An easy action is to vary your travel times. When traveling away from the facility, keep your itinerary vague, including departure and arrival times, flight number, etc. In smaller airports this may be more difficult.

When traveling away from your facility, there are some simple steps to take that will lessen the likelihood that you will be caught up in a terrorist attack.

➤ **Avoid Crowds.** Crowds are easy to find; just look at an airport's luggage carrousel. People crowd around waiting for their bags. Instead of joining the crowd, select a point off to the side or where the crowd is the thinnest to watch for your bags. Crowds are easy to find at public venues, such as sports events and other gatherings. In 1996, a bomb was placed near a sound stage during the Olympic Games in Atlanta. Keep on the lookout for people acting suspiciously. Other crowded places that have previously attracted terrorists include nightclubs and theaters.

➤ **Dress to Blend in.** Do you look as if you belong there or are you obviously a traveler? Try to look unimportant and focused on where you are going.

➤ **Avoid Unattended Parcels or Baggage.** The 1996 Atlanta bomb was in a knapsack. Although people sometimes carelessly discard parcels or even forget things, if you see a package and no one is around, alert the police. Never accept packages from strangers.

➤ **Hire a Driver.** If you are driving in a strange city, consider hiring a local driver or security company to move you around.

➤ **Always Be Alert and Aware of Your Surroundings.** The nature of terrorism suggests there will be little or no warning. Take a few moments to see where the emergency exits and staircases are and consider how you might exit a congested area quickly.

A terrorist attack can take several forms, depending on the technology available to the attacker, the nature of the political issue motivating the attack, and the points of weakness of the target. Therefore the goal is to identify and eliminate the points of weakness to protect your facility. Some items to consider include:

➤ **Enforce Your Security Plan.** Most companies use security guards to ensure that only employees can enter. Sometimes this is as basic as a receptionist with a remote switch for opening the entrance door. Ensure that only properly identified personnel can enter the facility. Even if the front door is locked and well protected, often the receiving dock in the rear of the building is wide open! A chain is only as strong as its weakest link.

➤ **Ensure Everyone Understands the Evacuation Procedures.** Depending on the circumstances, you may want to take shelter within the building (storm shelter) or evacuate outward. If there was a problem outside your building, it would not be a good idea for everyone to exit according to the normal evacuation plan. It might be better to move them away from the walls in question or to direct everyone out a specific side of the building.

➤ **Bomb Threats.** Your security plan should contain detailed instructions on what to do when a bomb threat is received. Try to get as much information from the caller as you can *and write it all down* as it is said. Notify the police and the facility management immediately.

Information on what to do when a threat is received should be placed at all "public" inbound numbers such as switchboard, receptionist, help desk, or 800 numbers. Time should be set aside to train everyone how to fill out incident report forms and the best way to react to a threat.

In most cases, the building should be promptly evacuated using your evacuation procedures.

➤ Ensure the people standing outside do not block access routes for emergency vehicles. Avoid standing in front of windows in case the bomb blows glass shards out onto the people.

➤ Avoid suspicious packages and keep everyone else away from them.

Sometimes, the use of bombs is a matter of how convenient your building is. Permitting parking immediately adjacent to your building could set the scene for a vehicle-transported bomb, as in the case of the 1995 Oklahoma City bomb. In the 1993 vehicle-transported bomb attack against the World Trade Center, the vehicle was parked in the lower-level parking garage.

To reduce the likelihood of an explosive-filled vehicle destroying your facility, do not allow anyone to park near the building. In the case of under-the-building parking garages, place strong steel bars across the door opening so that only passenger vehicles can enter (no trucks). Install large obstacles around the main entrance (often large cement planters holding trees) to reduce the likelihood that someone could drive straight into the building.

Install heavy curtains with weighted bottoms to cover windows. This will reduce the amount of inward flying glass from an explosion outside your building.

Some facilities and public buildings have removed trash cans from outside their structure. Trash cans are an easy place to dump a bomb disguised as a discarded box.

Your employees are an important line of defense in detecting terrorist activity. Educate your employees by doing the following:

➤ **Explain the Importance of Your Facility's Security Program and Ask for Their Help.** You can't be everywhere but your employees are. Teach them what to look for. How would you describe a person acting suspiciously? What should they do if they see an unattended parcel? Do they keep their packages with them or properly stowed away? How much of this training your employees should have is based on your risk assessment of an attack. If you are a high-risk target, then they should be very involved. If the employees understand how the security process benefits them, they will be more inclined to actively support it.

➤ **Report Suspicious Activity to Police.** Explain how to file a police report of suspicious activity. The police need the traditional facts of who, what, where, when, why, and how. Your security policies should provide guidelines on who should file police reports. The policy might require all observations to be confirmed by a second person before reporting. Your security policy might require that a security supervisor investigate before calling in law enforcement. Perhaps an incident report form would be helpful to gather the details.

➤ **Report All Threats to Police.** The old saying is that barking dogs don't bite. However, a threat is not a time to gamble whether it was real or not. All threats should be reported immediately to the police. The police will also want to know how the threat was transmitted to you, when you received it, etc. You might add these fields to your incident report form.

The next step is to determine what the Homeland Security Threat Levels mean to you. Based on its intelligence sources, the Department of Homeland Security issues changes to its threat level (see the end of this chapter). Given your assessment of the risks to your facility, what will this mean to your company? You may establish contingency plans based on elevated threat levels if your situation is risky. These might be to increase security patrols, temporarily close some operations, or to confine all freight pickups and deliveries to a few hours of the day.

You should also check your insurance coverage. Just exactly what sort of threats does your insurance cover? Are you covered against a terrorist attack? In the aftermath of the attack on September 11, 2001, some insurance companies invoked the war clause, which states that no losses are covered due to war. This statement was inadvertently supported by the government when they declared a "War on Terrorism."

Check with your insurance company to determine what is and what is not covered. In general, domestic terrorism is covered as a criminal action. However, international terrorism may not be covered. Now is the time to find out.

HOMELAND SECURITY ADVISORY SYSTEM

1. **Low Condition (Green).** This condition is declared when there is a low risk of terrorist attacks. Federal departments and agencies should consider the following general measures in addition to the agency-specific Protective Measures that they develop and implement:

   ➤ Refining and exercising, as appropriate, preplanned Protective Measures.

   ➤ Ensuring personnel receive proper training on the Homeland Security Advisory System and specific preplanned department or agency Protective Measures.

   ➤ Institutionalizing a process to ensure that all facilities and regulated sectors are regularly assessed for vulnerabilities to terrorist attacks and that all reasonable measures are taken to mitigate these vulnerabilities.

2. **Guarded Condition (Blue).** This condition is declared when there is a general risk of terrorist attacks. In addition to the Protective Measures taken in the previous Threat Condition, federal departments and agencies should consider the following general measures in addition to the agency-specific Protective Measures that they develop and implement:

   ➤ Checking communications with designated emergency response or command locations.

➤ Reviewing and updating emergency response procedures.

➤ Providing the public with any information that would strengthen its ability to act appropriately.

3. **Elevated Condition (Yellow).** An Elevated Condition is declared when there is a significant risk of terrorist attacks. In addition to the Protective Measures taken in the previous Threat Conditions, federal departments and agencies should consider the following general measures in addition to the Protective Measures that they develop and implement:

➤ Increasing surveillance of critical locations.

➤ Coordinating emergency plans as appropriate with nearby jurisdictions.

➤ Assessing whether the precise characteristics of the threat require the further refinement of preplanned protective measures.

➤ Implementing, as appropriate, contingency and emergency response plans.

4. **High Condition (Orange).** A High Condition is declared when there is a high risk of terrorist attacks.

➤ Coordinating necessary security efforts with federal, state, and local law enforcement agencies or any National Guard or other appropriate armed forces organizations.

➤ Taking additional precautions at public events and possibly considering alternative venues or even cancellation.

➤ Preparing to execute contingency procedures, such as moving to an alternate site or dispersing their work force.

➤ Restricting threatened facility access to essential personnel only.

5. **Severe Condition (Red).** A Severe Condition reflects a severe risk of terrorist attacks. Under most circumstances, the Protective Measures for a Severe Condition are not intended to be sustained for substantial periods of time.

➤ Increasing or redirecting personnel to address critical emergency needs.

➤ Assigning emergency response personnel and prepositioning and mobilizing specially trained teams or resources.

➤ Monitoring, redirecting, or constraining transportation systems.

➤ Closing public and government facilities.

Source: Department of Homeland Security www.dhs.gov.

CONCLUSION

While terrorism is not a new threat, until recently the threat of terrorism was miniscule in the United States. Recent political events have made this a threat that you need to consider when developing your disaster recovery plan. Even if you are unlikely to be a target, your neighbors might be. The world has become a scarier place, and you must be aware of your surroundings to keep safe.

INDEX

Note: *f* following the page number indicates a figure.

A

ABC-rated fire extinguishers, 370
abortion clinics, 418
access
    to facility, 88–91
    to people, 87–88
accidents, 67
    involving chemical spills, 407–408
    and networks, 278
ACD (Automated Call Director), 173
acts of God, 351
additional personnel, acquiring, 144
administrative functions, of Emergency
    Operations Center, 207–208
administrative plan(s), 115–132
    assumptions of, 118–119
    and business continuity plan, 116, 117
    distribution/updating of, 130–131
    document repository for, 125
    executive/departmental support for, 117
    and IT systems, 130
    and program awareness, 128–129
    purpose of, 116
    recovery strategies in, 122–123
    reference section of, 131
    risk assessment in, 123
    role players in, 119–122
    scope of, 117–118
    table of contents for, 117
    three-year program strategy for, 124–125
    and training, 125–128
    writing, 123–124
Afghanistan War, 391
after-action reports/reviews, 244–245
air, as component of fire, 366
air conditioning, 53
air-drying (of paper records), 311–312
airports, 345
air-quality problems, indoor, 405–406
alarms
    fire, 368, 371–372, 374
    and telecommunications equipment room
      mitigation plan, 287
    and vital records storage, 301–304
alternate shifts, as part of pandemic plan, 194
alternating current, 250, 255
AM/FM radios (in Emergency Operations
    Center), 211
animal rights groups, 418
annual tests, 226
anthrax, 406

antiterrorism, 414
application failures, data risk from, 316
application requirements, in technical
recovery plan, 154
Application Service Providers (ASPs), 75, 77
assassinations, 415
assembly points, in crisis management plan,
135–136
assessment of key suppliers, 361–362
asset inventory, as component of interim
plan, 95–96
asynchronous mirroring, 328*f*
Asynchronous Transfer Mode (ATM), 274
Atlanta, Georgia, Olympic Games, 419
AT&T, 271
attendance policy, 193
Automated Call Director (ACD), 173
automatic dialers (autodialers), 138, 139
automatic fire suppression systems, 368
automatic number identification, 271

B
backhoes, 280
backup media
interoperability of, 341
recovering, 161–162
safeguarding of, 339
backup(s), 58, 324–326, 330–331
of critical software, 337
Internet, 342
online, 330–331
tape, 285, 324, 341
workstation, 339–344
backup software, 341
barriers
internal fire, 368
protective, 409, 417
batteries
for Emergency Operations Center, 209
UPS, 256–258
BCPs, *see* business continuity plans
BC-rated fire extinguishers, 370
benefits, employee, 384
biological attacks, 49
bit-by-bit striping, 329
blackouts, electrical, 251–252
blending in, 419
blizzards, 45, 277
block-by-block striping, 329
bomb threats, 55, 419, 420
brownouts, 250–251
brush fires, 47
building codes, 367

building evacuations, *see* evacuation(s)
building power system, 252
building security, and fire, 366
buried lines, breaks in, 278
business case, building a, 23–24, *see also*
Business Impact Analysis (BIA)
business climate, 187
Business Continuity Manager, 2–5
and administrative plan, 119–121
and funding, 8
and ongoing support, 9
and project team, 10, 12
and risk assessment, 16
and testing team, 226, 228
business continuity plans (BCPs), 2–3, 116, 117
business continuity strategy, 82–83
business critical data, 323
business departments, 196
Business Impact Analysis (BIA), 24–34, 124
benefits of, 25–26
data collection for, 27, 31–33
definition of, 24
identifying respondents for, 28
managing a, 26–27
and pandemic plan, 182–183
questionnaire for, 28–31
reporting results of, 33–34
and technical recovery, 150
and testing strategy, 224
byte-by-byte striping, 329

C
cabinets, workstation, 339
cable mitigation plan, 286
cable modem, 274
cabling (networks), 279–282
external, 280
internal, 279–280
maps of, 282
and route separation, 281–282
CAD (computer-assisted drafting), 409
calendar, testing, 226, 227*f,* 228
call accounting, 271
call lists, in crisis management plan, 138–139
call management systems, 271
call monitoring, 271
call trees, 138
cap (sprinkler heads), 373
carbon dioxide (CO2) fire extinguishers, 370
categorization
data, 323
of suppliers, 361–362
CD-ROM, 342

CDs
  backups on, 341
  water-damaged, 314
cell phones, 287, 288
chemical hazards, 402–403
chemical spills, 407–408
chemical users, as manufactured risk, 48
civil risks, 49
clamping voltage (surge suppressors), 254
Class A fires, 367, 370
Class B fires, 367, 370
Class C fires, 367, 370
Class D fires, 367, 370
cleanup efforts, 385
climate control, as facility-wide risk, 53
coffee pots, as fire hazard, 368
"cold seats," 168
cold sites, 321
combat stress, 382
command and control, by Emergency
    Operations Center, 201, 206–207
Command Center, 147
communicating
  with customers, 352–354
  with employees, 395–396
  with news media, 410
  with suppliers, 360–361, 363
  as term, 137
communication(s)
  by Emergency Operations Center, 220
  interactive, 395–396
  in pandemic plan, 188, 189*f*, 190–192
  as pandemic technique, 185
  in technical recovery plan, 160–161
  see also telecommunications
communications function, of Emergency
    Operations Center, 207, 210–214, 220
communications plan, 17–19, 137–138
community relations personnel, as team
    members, 11
company information, and work area
    recovery, 166
compromised information, 318
computer-assisted drafting (CAD), 409
computer hardware
  and electrical problems, 251–252
  standardizing, 285
computer networks, *see* networks
computer peripherals, standardizing, 285
computer viruses, 60, 316
confidential information, 56
confined spaces, 404
connectivity requirements, in technical

recovery plan, 154
contacted hot sites, 169, 171
containers, fireproof, 302
containment, damage, 146
containment team, and Emergency
    Operations Center, 205–206
continuity of leadership, 111
contractual obligations, and pandemic
    plan, 183
control function, of Emergency Operations
    Center, 207
control valves (sprinkler systems), 374–375
controversial businesses, as terrorist
    targets, 418
corporate communications, 147
corporate communications manager, 135,
    141–142
costs, downtime, 39–40
counseling
  crisis, 373
  posttraumatic, 145
counterterrorism, 414, 418
crisis counseling, 373
crisis management plan(s), 133–148
  essential elements of, 135–139
  executive staff responsibilities in, 139–142
  Human Resources function in, 143–145
  problem identification in, 134
  Purchasing function in, 145
  role players in, 134–135
  Sales function in, 145
  sections of, 145–148
  solution identification in, 134
critical business function, identification of, 97
critical data, identification of, 322–323
crowds, avoiding, 419
customer notification plan, 349
customers, 349–354
  data loss and, 318, 319
  and fire, 365
  key, 350–352
  in pandemic plan, 183, 184
  pandemic strategy with, 81
  plan for communicating with, 352–354
  risk assessment with, 352
  and work area recovery, 166
customer support, data loss and inability to
    provide, 319

D
DaaS (desktop as a service), 343
damage
  fire, 365–366

water, 313, 314
damage containment, 146, 219–220
dams, as manufactured risk, 48
data, 315–334
    backups of, 324–326, 330–331
    identifying critical, 322–323
    and IT infrastructure, 316, 317*f*
    nonessential, 323
    planning for recovery of, 320–322
    policies and procedures involving, 323–324
    process of recovering, 324–325
    risk assessment with, 316–319
    steps in recovering, 319–320
    storage of, 325–331
    testing of support plan for, 333–334
    virtualization of, 332–333
    see also vital records
data backup(s)
    mobile, 345
    and telecommunications equipment room
      mitigation plan, 287
    for workstations, 339–344
database requirements, in technical recovery
    plan, 154
data collection
    for Business Impact Analysis, 27, 31–33
    and suppliers, 359
data communications, for Emergency
    Operations Center, 211
data network, as facility-wide risk, 53–54
data processing support manager, for
    Emergency Operations Center, 218
data systems
    departmental, 64
    in work area recovery plan, 175–176
data systems risk(s), 57–62
    communications network as, 59
    hackers as, 61
    shared computers as, 60
    telecommunications system as, 59–60
    theft as, 61
    viruses as, 60–61
day of the week, 66
DDoS (Distributed Denial of Service)
    attacks, 278
deaths, *see* fatalities
"debriefing," 373
deflector (sprinkler heads), 374
"defusing," 373
deluge sprinkler systems, 375
Denial of Service attacks, 278
departmental recovery plans, writing,
    105–110

departmental risks, 62–64
departmental support, for administrative
    plan, 117
Department of Homeland Security (DHS),
    400, 402
Department of Labor, 400
desktop as a service (DaaS), 343
dialup connection, 273
Disaster Containment Manager, 215–216
disaster declaration, 147
disaster recovery project(s), 1–21
    closing, 20–21
    executing and controlling, 16–20
    funding for, 8–9
    initiating, 3–4
    planning, 13–16
    and role of Business Continuity Manager,
      4–5
    scope of, 5–8
    selecting a team for, 9–13
Disaster Simulations, 229, 240–243
disk mirroring, 326–329, 327*f*, 328*f*
disk space requirements, in technical recovery
    plan, 154
disk striping, 328–329
distance, between primary and backup
    recovery sites, 73
Distributed Denial of Service (DDoS)
    attacks, 278
distribution, of administrative plan, 130–131
documentation, of computer networks, 285
document formatting guidelines, 104–105
document repository
    for administrative plan, 125
    creation of a, 112
domestic terrorism, 414
downtime costs, 39–40
dry pipe sprinkler systems, 375
duplexing, 327, 329
DVD-Rs, 342

E
earthquakes, 44, 44*f*, 66*f*
8 to 5 service contracts, 92
80/20 rule, 350
electrical blackouts, 251–252
electrical equipment, and vital records storage,
    302–303
electrical service, 249–265
    and actions steps for outages, 259–261
    and building's power system, 252
    Hurricane Andrew and loss of, 385
    and line conditioning, 255

loss of (example), 201–203
and power generators, 259–261
risk assessment for, 250–252
and strategy for power protection, 252–253
and surge protection, 253–255
and uninterruptible power supplies, 255–259
electricity
for Emergency Operations Center, 209
as facility-wide risk, 51–52
fires ignited by, 367
electronic keys, 90–91
electronic locks, 160
electronic vault storage, 324
e-mail updates, in pandemic plan, 190
emergency action plans
and health/safety/environmental issues, 399–400, 401*f,* 408–409
and vital records, 307–310
emergency equipment list, 98
emergency exits, 368
emergency lighting, 262, 378
Emergency Medical Technicians (EMTs), 56, 209, 391
Emergency Operations Center(s), 199–220
administrative functions of, 207–208
command function of, 206–207
communications function of, 207, 210–214, 220
containment team and, 205–206
control function of, 207
defined, 201
essential functions of, 201
example of absence of, 201–203
location of, 203–204
materials for, 209–210
mobile, 204–205
priorities of, 218–220
recovery team and, 206
security for, 214
staffing of, 214–218
types of, 200
emergency recall list, 137
employee downtime, data loss and, 318
employee fatalities, 403–404
employee ID cards, 391
employees, 381–398
communicating with, 395–396
family assistance for, 386
labor management issues with, 384–385, 387–391
military service issues with, 391
notification of, in work area recovery plan,

171–172
and outside help, 385–386
in pandemic plan, 183
pandemic strategy with, 81
plan action steps with, 392–398
rating of, 393–394
risk assessment with, 386–391
and stress, 382–384, 387
as terrorism risk, 418
employee skills matrices, 392–395
EMTs, *see* Emergency Medical Technicians
end-user backups, 344
end-user vital records, protecting, 346
environmental issues, *see* health, safety, and environmental issues
Environmental Protection Agency (EPA), 400–403, 405, 407, 408
equipment room
mitigation plan for, 286–287
telecommunications, 278–279
errors, testing to reveal, 222
evacuation(s), 406–407
in crisis management plan, 136
due to release of hazardous materials, 405, 406
by Emergency Operations Center, 219
for fire, 377–379
and terrorist attacks, 419
exchange service contracts, 92
executive staff
in crisis management plan, 139–142
and work area recovery, 166
executive support, for administrative plan, 117
exercise participants, 228
exercise recorder, 228
exercises, tests vs., 223
exercise scenarios, 229–231
exits, emergency, 368
expressions of support, 373–374
extension cords, 303
external cabling, 280
external risk(s), 41–50
civil risks as, 49
manufactured risks as, 47–48
natural disasters as, 43–47
supplier risks as, 49–50
extreme temperatures, 45

F
Facilities Director
in crisis management plan, 139–141
damage containment by, 146
facilities engineer, for Emergency Operations

Center, 218
facilities manager, 10
Facility Engineering Manager, 217
facility manager, 135
facility security, during labor unrest, 390–391
facility-wide risk(s), 50–57
    climate control as, 53
    data network as, 53–54
    electricity as, 51–52
    fire as, 54
    medical concerns as, 56
    security as, 55–56
    structural problems as, 54, 55
    telephones as, 52
    water as, 52–53
families, communicating with employees',
    396–397
family assistance, 386
fatalities, 67
    in crisis management plan, 143
    employee, 403–404
    from fire, 365
Fawkes, Guy, 415
Federal Emergency Management Agency
    (FEMA), 45, 66, 201
files, deleting unneeded, 340
finance personnel, as team members, 11
fire alarms, 368, 371–372, 374
fire control system, 301–302
fire damage, of paper records, 313
fire departments, 410
fire detection systems, 371–372
fire drills, 302
fire extinguishers, 302, 368–369
fire hoses, 368
fire inspectors, 367–368
fireproof containers, 302, 376–377
fire ratings, 376
fire(s), 365–380
    anatomy of, 366–367
    as facility-wide risk, 54
    forest, 47
    and media storage, 299
    plan action steps for, 376–379
    risk assessment for, 367–369
    statistics on, 379–380
    suppression strategy for, 369–376
    and telecommunications equipment
      room, 279
    and telecommunications equipment room
      mitigation plan, 286
    types of damage caused by, 365–366
    and vital records storage, 300–301

first point of contact (crisis management
    plan), 135
first responders, as component of interim
    plan, 98–99
flashlights, for Emergency Operations
    Center, 209
floods, 45, 46, 47*f*, 278
floppy disks, water-damaged, 314
flu, seasonal vs. pandemic, 181*f*
force majeure clauses, 351
forensic experts, data loss and need for, 319
forest fires, 47
formatting guidelines, 104–105
frame (sprinkler heads), 373
frame relay, 274
freeze-drying (of paper records), 312–313
freezing (of water-damaged documents), 310
fuel, as component of fire, 366
funding, for disaster recovery projects, 8–9

G
gas fire suppression, 302
general public, communicating with the,
    397–398
generators, *see* power generators
GFS backup scheme, 325–326
goal, testing, 224
government buildings, as terrorist targets, 418
governments, and pandemics, 185
government-sponsored terror, 413
Grandfather-Father-Son (GFS) backup
    scheme, 325–326
ground eliminators, 255
guerilla warfare, 416

H
H1N1 (swine flu) pandemic, 186, 196
hackers, as data system risk, 60
hail, 45
ham radio operators, 288
hand sanitizer, 190
hard disk recovery, 344
hard drive crashes, 316, 318*f*
hardware, workstation, 336
head counts, 406–407
health, safety, and environmental issues,
    399–412
    action steps with, 409–412
    and chemical hazards, 402–403
    and emergency action plan, 399–400, 401*f*,
      408–409
    and employee injuries/fatalities, 403–404
    and evacuation, 406–407

and indoor air-quality problems, 405–406
mitigation of, 407–408
and off-site hazards, 404–405
with power generators, 261
risk assessment with, 400, 402–406
and vital records storage, 303
heat, as component of fire, 366
help desk support, data loss and, 318
highways, as manufactured risk, 48
HIV/AIDS, 180
Homeland Security advisory system, 421–422
hospitalizations, multiple, 403–404
hotlines, in pandemic plan, 190
"hot seats," 168
hot sites, 169, 171, 321
housekeeping
    and fire prevention, 369
    and telecommunications equipment room
        mitigation plan, 287
    and vital records storage, 302
human-created outages, 316
Human Resources function, 143–145, 147,
    381, *see also* employees
human resources manager, 135
    for Emergency Operations Center, 217
    and pandemic plan, 192–194
human resources personnel, as team
    members, 11
humidity
    and media storage, 297–299
    and telecommunications equipment
        room, 278
    and telecommunications equipment room
        mitigation plan, 287
    and vital records storage, 301, 303
Hurricane Andrew, 385
Hurricane Hugo, 286
hurricanes, 45, 278
hygrometer, 298

I
ice storms, and networks, 277
ID cards, employee, 391
Illinois Bell, 281
immunizations, 191
inbound communications, for Emergency
    Operations Center, 213
indoor air-quality problems, 405–406
industrial sites, as manufactured risk, 48
influenza pandemics, 186
information, compromised, 318
information technology (IT)
    infrastructure of, 317*f*

recovery strategy for, 122
    see also IT systems; Technical
        recovery plan(s)
injects, 231
injuries, 403–404
    in crisis management plan, 143
    from fire, 365
insects, 301, 303, 305
instructional videos, in pandemic plan, 190
insurance, 111
    and sprinkler systems, 372
    unemployment, 384
insurance companies
    in crisis management plan, 141
    and Emergency Operations Center, 212
integration testing (integrated system testing),
    223, 233–235
intellectual property, 56
intelligent port selectors, 271
interactive communication, 395–396
interactive teams, in work area recovery plan,
    174–175
Interactive Voice Response (IVR), 270
Interexchange Carriers (IXCs), 271–272
interim plan(s), 85–99
    access to facility as component of, 88–91
    access to people as component of, 87–88
    asset inventory as component of, 95–96
    critical business function identification as
        component of, 97
    emergency equipment list as component
        of, 98
    operations restoration as component of,
        97–98
    service contracts as component of, 91–94
    software asset list as component of, 96–97
    toxic material storage as component of, 98
    trained first responders as component of,
        98–99
    vendor list as component of, 94–95
internal cabling, 279–280
internal fire barriers, 368
internal investigations, and data loss, 319
international terrorism, 414
Internet backup, 342
Internet Service Providers (ISPs), 276, 278
interoperability, of backup media, 341
inventory
    and suppliers, 363
    of workstations, 336
inventorying, of vital records, 293–295
ionization fire detectors, 371
Iraq War, 391

ISDN connection, 274
ISPs (Internet Service Providers), 276, 278
IT, *see* information technology
IT Business Continuity Manager, 120–121
IT infrastructure, and data, 316, 317*f*
IT systems
    and administrative plan, 130
    identification of critical, 130
    recovery strategy for, 74–78
IVR (Interactive Voice Response), 270
IXCs (Interexchange Carriers), 271–272

J
James, Jesse, 415
janitorial service, 162
Just-in-Time (JIT) suppliers, 351

K
key customers, 350–352
key operating equipment, 63–64
keys
    electronic, 90–91
    and network security, 284
    physical, 88–89
key suppliers, 355–357
KISS principle, 359

L
labor disputes
    as civil risk, 49
    security during, 390–391
    and suppliers, 357
labor management issues, 384–385, 387–391
labor stoppages, 387–389
labor union representatives, as team
        members, 11
landslides, 47
LANs, *see* local area networks
laptops, and data risk, 316
leadership, continuity of, 111
legally required data, 324
legal staff
    in crisis management plan, 141
    as team members, 11
legal team, and crisis management plan, 135
licensing requirements, in technical recovery
        plan, 154
life, protection of, 219
life insurance, 143
lighting
    emergency, 262, 378
    for Emergency Operations Center, 209
lightning, 45, 55, 277

light sticks, 209
line conditioning (electrical service), 253, 255
line interactive UPS, 256
line managers, as team members, 11
litigation expenses, from data loss, 319
load balancing, 329
local area networks (LANs), 60, 273–275,
        274*f*, 330
local governments, 410
location of risk, 66
location(s)
    of Emergency Operations Center, 203–204
    UPS, 258
    see also site, recovery
locks, electronic, 160
logical network security, 284–285

M
magnetic fields, and vital records storage,
        301, 303
magnetic media
    storage of, 299–300
    transport of, 296
    water-damaged, 313–314
maintenance
    preventive, 95
    of recovery site, 177
    and vital records storage, 306
manufactured risks, 47–48
MAO (maximum acceptable outage), 25
maps, of network cabling, 282
marketing personnel, as team members, 11
materials, for Emergency Operations Center,
        209–210
Material Safety Data Sheets (MSDS), 402
materials manager, for Emergency
        Operations Center, 218
maximum acceptable outage (MAO), 25
media relations, in crisis management plan,
        141–142
media storage, of vital records, 292, 297–300
medical benefits, 384
medical concerns, as facility-wide risk, 56
medical director, for Emergency Operations
        Center, 218
medical insurance, 143
medical kits, for Emergency Operations
        Center, 209
meetings
    for standalone testing, 232
    virtual, 195
MEK (methyl ethyl ketone), 403
mental health counseling, 145, 382–383

messengers, for Emergency Operations Center, 211
metals, flammable, 367
methyl ethyl ketone (MEK), 403
microfilm
    storage of, 298–299
    water-damaged, 313
Microsoft Virtual PC, 343
microwave communications, 288
military personnel, as trained first responders, 98
military reserves, 391
military service issues, 391
military suppliers, as terrorist targets, 417–418
mirrored sites, 321
mirrored striping, 329
mirroring, disk, 326–329, 327*f,* 328*f*
missing steps, testing to reveal, 222
mitigation
    of health/safety/environmental issues, 407–408
    of suppliers, 363
    telecommunications, 285–288
    of vital records, 301–305
mobile data backup, 345
mobile devices, and workstations, 344–345
mobile Emergency Operations Centers, 200, 204–205
mobile recovery equipment, 171
mobile security, 344–345
mobile sites, 321
moisture sensors, 303
mold, toxic, 406
MSDS (Material Safety Data Sheets), 402
mudslides, 47

N
NAS (network attached storage), 330
National Guard, 391
natural disaster(s), 43–47
    and data risk, 316
    earthquakes as, 44, 44*f*
    extreme temperatures as, 45
    floods as, 45, 46, 47*f*
    hurricanes as, 45
    pandemics as, 44
    snow as, 45, 46*f*
    thunderstorms as, 44, 45
    tornadoes as, 43
natural hazards, with networks, 277–278
neighboring residences and businesses, communicating with, 397

network attached storage (NAS), 330
networks, 272–276
    as data system risk, 60
    and plan development, 284–285
    risk assessment with, 276–282
network storage, 342–343
newsletters, company, 128–129
news media, 141–142, 147, 410
    and Emergency Operations Center, 212
    and terrorism, 414
noise, electrical, 251
noncompliance issues, data loss and, 319
noncritical data, 324
nonessential data, 323
notebook computers (notebook PCs)
    for Emergency Operations Center, 210
    security for, 345
    surge protectors for, 254
notification
    of customers, 349
    employee, in work area recovery plan, 171–172
    of incidents, 146, 408

O
Occupational Health and Safety Administration (OSHA), 399–404, 406, 408
office supplies, for Emergency Operations Center, 209–210
off-site duplication, of key vital records, 303
off-site hazards, 404–405
Oklahoma City bombing, 418, 420
online backups, 330–331
online UPS, 256
operational control, by Emergency Operations Center, 201
operational efficiency, data loss and decreased, 319
operations restoration, as component of interim plan, 97–98
opportunities
    lost, 40, 319
    unplanned, for testing, 244–245
orifice (sprinkler heads), 374
OSHA, *see* Occupational Health and Safety Administration
outbound communications, for Emergency Operations Center, 213–214
outlets, electrical, 302, 369
outside help, getting, 385–386

P
page layout guidelines, 104

Pandemic Emergency Manager, 122
Pandemic Plan Administrator, 182, 188
pandemic plan(s), 179–179
   and business climate, 187
   and business departments, 196
   and communications, 188, 189*f,* 190–192
   risk assessment for, 183–185, 184*f*
   and role of human resources manager,
     192–194
   and sanitizing, 190, 195–196
   sources of information for, 187
   and technology, 194–195
   testing, 197
   triggering of, 186–187
   writing, 182–183
pandemic(s), 44, 179–181
   definition of, 179, 180
   recovery strategy for, 81–82, 122–123
paper documents
   storage of, 298
   water damage to, 310–313
parity, 328, 329
passwords
   system, 91
   in technical recovery plan, 151–152
Payroll function, 147
payroll issues, following a disaster, 384–385
payroll policy, 144–145
PBXs, *see* Private Branch Exchanges
PCs, *see* personal computers
PDAs (personal digital assistants), 336, 345
peer pressure, 387
performance reviews, 394
Persian Gulf War, second, 391
personal computers (PCs)
   for Emergency Operations Center, 210
   risks associated with, 65
   in work area recovery plan, 172–173
   see also networks; workstations
personal digital assistants (PDAs), 336, 345
personal protective equipment (PPE), 408, 410
personnel
   acquiring additional, 144
   borrowing, 386
   tracking of, in technical recovery plan, 157
   see also employees
photoelectric smoke detectors, 371
physical keys, 88–89
physical security
   of property, 55
   of workstations, 338–339
   see also security
picket signs, 390

pipelines, as manufactured risk, 48
pipes, 55
   overhead water, 278–279
   for sprinkler systems, 374
planning disaster recovery projects, 13–16
Plowshares Eight, 417
point of presence (POP), 271–272
police
   reporting suspicious activity to, 420
   reporting threats to, 421
   as terrorist targets, 417–418
policies and procedures, data, 323–324
POP (point of presence), 271–272
posttraumatic counseling, 145
power generators, 259–261
   environmental/regulatory issues with, 261
   sizing of, 259–260
   switching time of, 260
   testing of, 260–261
   and working with your public utility, 261
power loss (power outages)
   action steps for, 261–265
   and telecommunications equipment
     room, 278
power shedding, 264–265
PPE (personal protective equipment), 408, 410
preaction sprinkler systems, 375
preventive maintenance, 95
printers, in work area recovery plan, 173–174
Private Branch Exchanges (PBXs), 59, 269–271
problem, identification of, in crisis
     management plan, 134
productivity, lost, 39, 40, 318
professional storage facilities, 292
program backups, for workstations, 339–344
progressive testing, 225
proofreading, of technical recovery plan, 155
property, physical security of, 55
protective barriers, 409, 417
PSTN (Public Switched Telephone Network),
   268–269
public information officer, as team member, 11
public relations coordinator, for Emergency
   Operations Center, 217
Public Switched Telephone Network (PSTN),
   268–269
public utility, working with your, 261
punch blocks, 275–276
purchasing agent, for Emergency Operations
   Center, 217
Purchasing function, in crisis management
   plan, 145, 147
purchasing manager, 135

purchasing personnel, as team members, 11

Q
quarterly tests, 226
questionnaire, for Business Impact Analysis, 28–31

R
radio communications, for Emergency Operations Center, 211
RAID (redundant array of inexpensive/ independent disks), 327–329
rain, and networks, 277
ratings, employee, 393–394
reassignments, 143–144
recall rosters, 159
recall tables, 152, 152*f*
record keeping, and strikes, 389–390
recovery, of vital records, 310–314
Recovery Activity Log, 157–158
Recovery Gantt Chart, 158–159
recovery planning, 110–112, 201
recovery point objective (RPO), 26, 73, 324
Recovery Site Manager, 156–157
recovery strategy, 71–83
    in administrative plan, 122–123
    business continuity, 82–83
    definition of, 71
    IT, 74–78
    pandemic, 81–82
    selection of, 72–74
    work area, 78–80
recovery teams, 146–148, 206
recovery time objective (RTO), 25–26, 72, 158
    in data recovery plan, 324
    and testing, 223, 246
    in work area recovery plan, 167
redundant array of inexpensive/independent disks (RAID), 327–329
reference materials (reference section)
    in administrative plan, 131
    in work area recovery plan, 174
regulatory issues, with power generators, 261
reporting
    of Business Impact Analysis results, 33–34
    in technical recovery plan, 160–161
    using communications plan, 18–19
reports, after-action, 244–245
reputation, damaged, 40, 319
respiratory illnesses, 405
response time (surge suppressors), 254
restoration policy, 168
rest plans, 162

retention, of vital records, 296–297
reviews, performance, 394
riots, 49
risk analysis
    building a, 37–39
    definition of, 37
risk assessment, 15–16, 35, 37
    in administrative plan, 123
    creation of, 68–69
    with customers, 352
    with data, 316–319
    for electrical service, 250–252
    with employees, 386–391
    for fire, 367–369
    with health/safety/environmental issues, 400, 402–406
    with networks, 276–282
    for pandemic plan, 183–185, 184*f*
    sources of information on, 66
    with suppliers, 357–358
    with telecommunications, 276–282
    with terrorism, 416–421
    with vital records, 300–301
    with workstations, 336–338
Risk Management Plan (RMP), 404–405
risk(s)
    attributes of, 37*f*
    data systems, 57–62
    definition of, 35, 36
    departmental, 62–64
    external, 41–50
    facility-wide, 50–57
    layers of, 41
    scope of, 39–40
    severity of, 65–66
    types of, 36
    your desk's, 64–65
RMP (Risk Management Plan), 404–405
rodents, 301, 305
role players
    in administrative plan, 119–122
    in crisis management plan, 134–135
roll calls, 406–407
route separation (network cabling), 281–282
RPO, *see* recovery point objective
RTO, *see* recovery time objective

S
SaaS (software as a service), 330, 343
sabotage, 55–56, 301, 304–305
safety issues, *see* health, safety, and environmental issues
safety person, for Emergency Operations

Center, 217
safety personnel, 11
Sago, West Virginia, coal mine disaster, 142
sags, voltage, 250–251
sales, lost, 39–40
Sales function, in crisis management plan, 145
sales manager, 135, 218
sales personnel, as team members, 11
sandstorms, 47
sanitary facilities, for Emergency Operations
    Center, 209
sanitation
    as pandemic technique, 185
    and water risk, 53
sanitizing, and pandemic plan, 190, 195–196
SANs (storage area networks), 330, 332
SARS (severe acute respiratory syndrome), 81
satellite communications, 288
scenarios, exercise, 229–231
scope
    of administrative plan, 117–118
    of technical recovery plan, 153
scope statements, 6–7
scoring, of risk assessment, 68
seasonal flu, 181*f*
security
    for computer networks, 284–285
    in crisis management plan, 139
    for electrical support equipment, 253
    for Emergency Operations Center, 214
    for employees, 418
    as facility-wide risk, 55–56
    during labor unrest, 390–391
    mobile, 344–345
    in technical recovery plan, 160
    for telecommunications equipment room,
        279, 286–287
    and vital records storage, 303
    for vital records transport, 296
    in work area recovery plan, 176
    of workstations, 338–339
security guards, 419
security manager, for Emergency Operations
    Center, 217
security personnel, 11
sensitive data, 324
September 11, 2001 terrorist attacks, 74, 204,
    288, 356, 421
sequencing, 15
servers
    backup to, 342–343
    in technical recovery plan, 154
service contracts

as component of interim plan, 91–94
    in technical recovery plan, 154
severe acute respiratory syndrome (SARS), 81
shifts, alternate, 194
sick leave, 384
sickness, 67
simulations, 223, 229, 237–238, 240–243
sinkholes, 47
site, recovery, 167–171, 177
skilled labor, finding, 144
smartphones, 316
smoke, and vital records storage, 300
smoke alarms, 301–302
smoke detectors, 371
snow, 45, 46*f,* 54
social distancing (pandemic technique), 185
software
    backup, 341
    and data risk, 316
    off-site storage of, 285
    standardization of, 285
    updates to, 319
    workstation, 336–337
software as a service (SaaS), 330, 343
software asset list, as component of interim
    plan, 96–97
solution, identification of, in crisis
    management plan, 134
space heaters, 368
Spanish Influenza pandemic, 180
spikes, voltage, 251
Spill Prevention Control and
    Countermeasures (SPCC), 403
spills, chemical, 407–408
sponsor
    of business continuity program, 119–120
    project, 2–4, 9
    and testing team, 228
sprinkler systems, 302, 372–376
staffing, of Emergency Operations Center,
    214–218
staff reassignments, 143–144
stakeholders, project, 10
standalone testing, 223, 231–233
state terrorism, 413
status boards, for Emergency Operations
    Center, 212–213
status reports
    in pandemic plan, 190
    in technical recovery plan, 160–161
stock price, data loss and decreases in, 319
storage
    of data, 325–331

fire-resistant, 376–377
network, 342–343
recovering backup media from, 161–162
storage area networks (SANs), 330, 332
storage facilities, professional, 292
storm shelters, 419
strategy
for power protection, 252–253
for recovery, *see* recovery strategy
stress, employees and, 382–384, 387
stress management techniques, 382–383
strikes, 387–389
striping, 328–329
structural damage, from fire, 365
structural problems
as facility-wide risk, 54, 55
and vital records storage, 300
subpoenas, data loss and resulting, 319
substitutes, trained, 193
success, criteria for, 7–8
suicide terror attacks, 414
supplier risks, 49–50
suppliers, 355–364
agreement with, 362
assessment of, 361–362
and data collection, 359
dialogue with, 360–361
and Emergency Operations Center, 212
Just-in-Time (JIT), 351
key, 355–357
mitigation of, 363
in pandemic plan, 184–185
and plan action steps, 358
risk assessment with, 357–358
see also vendors
support, expressions of, 373–374
support software, in technical recovery
plan, 154
surge protection, 253–255, 337
surges, voltage, 251
surge suppressors (surge protectors), 253–255
suspicious activity, reporting, 420
switching time (power generators), 260
synchronous mirroring, 327f
system costs, data loss and increased, 319
system passwords, 91
"Systems Requirements" (technical recovery
plan), 154
system support charts, 152
system users, 153

T
T-1 connection, 274

T-3 connection, 274
table of contents
for administrative plan, 117
for technical recovery plan, 153
Table-Top drills, 411
table-top testing, 223, 238–240
tape backup, 325–326, 341
tape drives, 341
tapes
backup, 285, 324
water-damaged, 313
team(s)
at assembly points, 136
collocating interactive, 174–175
for disaster recovery projects, 9–13
for handling vendor loss, 357
in pandemic plan, 182, 190
recovery, 146–148
technical recovery, 121
in technical recovery plan, 160
testing by, 222, 226, 228
technical recovery plan(s), 149–163
determining focus of, 149–150
and recovery team leader, 156–162
steps to creation of, 150–152
template for creating, 152–156
technical recovery team, 121
technical support charts, 159
Technician Tracking Log, 157
technology, in pandemic plan, 194–195
tech support, 153
telecommunications, 267–272
and Interexchange Carriers, 271–272
and plan actions steps, 288–289
and plan development, 282–288
and Private Branch Exchanges, 269–271
and Public Switched Telephone Network,
268–269
risk assessment with, 276–282
and testing, 289
in work area recovery plan, 175–176
see also networks
telecommunications equipment room,
278–279
telecommunications mitigation plan,
285–288
telephone circuits, identifying critical,
283–284
telephone company
central office of, 271
working with the, 287
telephone line support (surge
suppressors), 254

telephone lists, maintaining, 137
telephones
  for Emergency Operations Center, 210–211
  as facility-wide risk, 52
  and Public Switched Telephone Network (PSTN), 268–269
  in work area recovery plan, 173
telephone service, disrupted/limited, 396
televisions, in Emergency Operations Center, 211
temperature fire detectors, 371
temperature(s)
  extreme, 45
  and media storage, 297–299
  and telecommunications equipment room, 278
  and telecommunications equipment room mitigation plan, 287
  for transport of magnetic recordings, 296
  and vital records storage, 301, 303
template training, for technical recovery plan, 155
terrorism, 404, 413–422
  as civil risk, 49
  definition of, 413
  history of, 414–416
  and Homeland Security advisory system, 421–422
  risk assessment with, 416–421
  types of, 413–414
testing, 221–247
  benefits of, 221–222
  of data support plan, 333–334
  developing a strategy for, 224–227
  of disaster recovery plan, 19–20
  and Disaster Simulation, 240–243
  and exercise scenarios, 229–231
  of health and safety plan, 411–412
  integration, 233–235
  of pandemic plan, 197
  of power generators, 260
  progressive, 225
  and recovery time objective, 223
  and RTO capability, 246
  and simulations, 237–238, 240–243
  standalone, 231–233
  and suppliers, 363
  table-top, 238–240
  as team effort, 226, 228
  of technical recovery plan, 162–163
  of telecommunications, 289
  types of, 222–223
  unplanned opportunities for, 244–245
  of UPS, 258–259
  walk-through, 235–236
  of work area recovery plan, 176–177
testing calendar, 226, 227*f*, 228
tests, exercises vs., 223
theft
  of computers, 338–339
  and data risk, 316
  as data system risk, 60
  and vital records storage, 301, 304
thermal linkage (sprinkler heads), 373
thermograph, 298
threats
  analyzing, *see* risk assessment
  reporting, 421
thunderstorms, 44, 45, 277
time and materials service contracts, 92
time goals, for recovery strategy, 73
time of the day, 65–66
"time to data," 322
timing, as pandemic technique, 185
TJX, 318
tornadoes, 43, 277
toxic materials, storage of, 98
toxic mold, 406
trailers, mobile recovery equipment on, 171
trained first responders, as component of interim plan, 98–99
training
  and administrative plan, 125–128
  and employee skills matrix, 395
transport (transportation)
  as manufactured risk, 48
  of vital records, 295–296
travel
  and notebook PC theft, 345
  in pandemic plan, 183, 193
  and terrorism, 418–419
trespassing, 55
triggering, of pandemic plan, 186–187
24/7 service contracts, 92

U
Underwriters Laboratory (UL), 376
unemployment insurance, 384
Uninterruptible Power Supply (UPS), 202–203, 253, 255–259
  and telecommunications equipment room mitigation plan, 286
  for workstations, 337
updates, administrative plan, 130
upgrades, software, 337
UPS, *see* Uninterruptible Power Supply

U.S. Centers for Disease Control and
   Prevention, 186
utility services, in crisis management plan, 140

V
VA (volt-amps), 257
vacation, 384
vaccines, 191
VDI (Virtual Desktop Infrastructure), 343
vendor lists, 94–95, 159
vendors
   computer-network-related, 285
   and data risk, 317
   and fire, 366
   pandemic strategy with, 81
   see also suppliers
videotaped reports, in pandemic plan, 190
videotaping, of entry gate, during strikes,
   389–390
violence, workplace, 55, 404
Virtual Desktop Infrastructure (VDI), 343
virtualization
   data, 332–333
   of workstations, 343
virtual meetings, 195
Virtual Private Networks (VPNs), 79, 275
   and pandemic plan, 194–195
   and work area recovery plan, 167
virtual tape library (VTL) technology, 332
virtual workers, 192
viruses, computer, 60, 316
vital records, 291–314
   definition of, 292
   emergency actions with, 307–310
   fire and loss of, 365, 376–377
   inventorying, 293–295
   media for storage of, 292
   and media storage, 297–300
   mitigation of, 301–305
   and plan action steps, 305–307
   recovery techniques with, 310–314
   retention of, 296–297
   risk assessment with, 300–301
   transporting, 295–296
   and workstations, 339, 346
vital records manager, in Emergency
   Operations Center, 218
VMware Workstation, 343
voice mailboxes, 396
voltage sags, 250–251
voltage spikes, 251
voltage surges, 251
volt-amps (VA), 257

VPNs, *see* Virtual Private Networks
VTL technology, 332
Vulnerable Zone Indicator System (VZIS), 405

W
walk-through testing, 223, 235–236
WANs, *see* wide-area networks
"warm seats," 168
warm sites, 321
water
   as facility-wide risk, 52–53
   for sprinkler systems, 373–374
   and vital records storage, 300, 310–313
water-based fire extinguishers, 370
water mains, 52
water mist sprinkler systems, 376
water pipes
   for sprinkler systems, 374
   in telecommunications equipment room,
      278–279
Web site(s)
   for Emergency Operations Center, 211
   in pandemic plan, 190
wet pipe sprinkler systems, 375
whiteboards, in Emergency Operations
   Center, 212
WHO (World Health Organization), 81, 186
wide-area networks (WANs), 273, 275, 275*f*
winds, high, 45
wireless connections, 275
wiring closet, 275, 279–280
wood, combustion of, 366
word processing guidelines, 104–105
Work Area Recovery Manager, 121–122
work area recovery plan(s), 165–178
   and employee notification, 171–172
   and maintaining the recovery site, 177
   options in, 170*f*
   security issues in, 176
   and selection of recovery site, 167–171
   telecommunications issues in, 175–176
   testing, 176–177
   tools for, 172–174
   using interactive teams in, 174–175
   writing, 166–176
work areas, recovery strategy for, 78–80, 122
workplace stress, 387
workplace violence, 55, 404
workspace, minimum, 167–168
workstations, 335–347
   end-user backup issues with, 344
   and end-user vital records, 346
   and mobile devices, 344–345

physical security of, 338–339
and program/data backups, 339–344
risk assessment with, 336–338
special-purpose, 340
virtualization of, 343
work surfaces, minimum, 168
World Health Organization (WHO), 81, 186
World Trade Center bombing (1993), 416, 420
writing the plan, 101–113
    and administrative plan, 123–124
    and choosing a standard format, 102–103

and creation of document repository, 112
for departmental recovery, 105–110
and including recovery considerations, 110–112
and pandemic plan, 182–183
and use of plan, 103–104
word processing guidelines for, 104–105
and work area recovery plan, 166–176

Z
Zip cartridges, 342

ABOUT THE AUTHORS

MICHAEL WALLACE has more than 25 years of experience in the information systems field. He began his career as a mainframe operator for Super Food Services and then moved to a programming position at Reynolds & Reynolds, where he developed financial applications for automotive dealers.

He became a consultant after graduating magna cum laude from Wright State University (Dayton, Ohio) with a Bachelor of Science degree in Management Science. For eight years he was president of Q Consulting, a custom application development firm. Mr. Wallace has been an application developer, a business analyst, and a technical and business consultant assisting companies in using information technology to solve business problems.

Mr. Wallace has served on the board of directors of various information technology user organizations and is active in the local technical community. He is currently President of the Columbus Chapter of the International Association of Microsoft Certified Partners (IAMCP), is a Competent Toastmaster and Competent Leader with Toastmasters International, and graduated from the Executive MBA program at the Fisher College of Business at The Ohio State University.

After working as a practice manager and director for the last few years, Mr. Wallace is now Vice President of Consulting Services at Result Data, which provides clients with guidance on IT strategy, application development, business intelligence, disaster recovery planning, and policies and procedures. He has also taught in the graduate programs at The Ohio State University and DeVry University Keller

Graduate School of Management and has published several articles and books on business and technology topics.

Mr. Wallace can be reached by e-mail at michaelw@columbus.rr.com.

LAWRENCE WEBBER has more than 25 years of experience in the information services field. He began his career in the U.S. Marine Corps as a digital network repairman and then moved to a position as a COBOL programmer supporting the Marines' Logistics traffic management systems.

After his release from active service, he worked as a COBOL programmer on an IBM mainframe for Waddell & Reed in Kansas City before moving on to program factory support systems on a UNIVAC system at Temperature Industries. During his tenure at United Telecommunications in Kansas City, he rose to the position of Manager of the Information Centers, providing mainframe and personal computer support to four mainframe data centers and nine subsidiary telephone companies.

His next position was as Applications Manager at the law offices of Shook, Hardy & Bacon where he migrated a Data General professional services accounting system to a DEC cluster. He also migrated the 600+ person office from standalone IBM magnetic card machines to a PC LAN-based word processing network.

For the next 12 years, Mr. Webber held various systems engineering and data processing management positions with Navistar International Truck and Bus in Springfield, OH, where, among other achievements, he authored an extensive data systems Disaster Recovery plan for the 2-million-square-foot manufacturing facility. He is currently a Project Manager and Six Sigma Black Belt consultant.

Mr. Webber has an Associate in Science degree from Darton College in Albany, GA, in Data Processing, a Bachelor of Science degree in Business Administration and an MBA, both from Rockhurst University in Kansas City, MO, and an Associate in Science degree in Industrial Engineering from Sinclair Community College in Dayton, OH. He recently completed a Master of Project Management degree from West Carolina University.

Mr. Webber is a former Marine and retired from the U.S. Army Reserve as a First Sergeant in the Infantry. He is a certified Project Management Professional by the Project Management Institute, Certified in Production and Inventory Management by APICS, and is a Microsoft Certified Professional.

Mr. Webber can be reached by e-mail at ljwljw@hotmail.com.